REAL ESTATE BROKERAGE

Sixth Edition

President: Roy Lipner
Publisher: Evan Butterfield
Managing Editor, Print Products: Louise Benzer
Development Editor: Christopher Oler
Production Coordinator: Daniel Frey
Typesetter: Todd Bowman
Quality Assurance Editor: David Shaw
Creative Director: Lucy Jenkins

Published by Dearborn™ Real Estate Education
a division of Dearborn Financial Publishing, Inc.®
30 South Wacker Drive
Chicago, IL 60606-7481
312-836-4400
http://www.dearbornRE.com

Library of Congress Cataloging-in-Publication Data

Cyr, John E.
     Real estate brokerage : a management guide / John E. Cyr, Joan M.
Sobeck, Laurel D. McAdams.—6th ed.
          p. cm.
Includes bibliographical references and index.
     ISBN 0-7931-6785-X
     1. Real estate agents—United States. 2. Real estate business—United
  States. I. Sobeck, Joan m. II. McAdams, Laurel D. III. Title.

HD278.C95 2003
333.33'068--dc22   2003021424

CONTENTS

PREFACE

Managers in today's real estate companies are thrust into a multitude of exhilarating and challenging roles simply because of the way the industry is evolving. Technology, which has touched virtually every aspect of the business, and economic, geopolitical, social, and legal climates that create as many threats as opportunities challenge the creativity and enterprising skills of today's managers. Running a business in this environment most likely means an attitudinal shift, thinking outside-the-box of traditional practices so as not to hamper an organization in the contemporary environment.

Management roles appeal to people's desires to be creative and be in a position to influence, to lead and inspire others. The reward is that the company, department, or office for which they are responsible does more than simply exist, but rather thrives or perhaps becomes a trendsetter under their direction. Most of all is the satisfaction of seeing the people they supervise grow in their professional accomplishments.

As exhilarating as management is, it can also be an intimidating and humbling experience. Managers have awesome responsibilities, as everything that happens in an organization rises or falls on their decisions. Today's companies are complex sets of systems, processes, and people that function in a fluid or changing business environment, which requires entrepreneurial leadership for a company to succeed. Even with well-laid plans for the company's future, a manager's ability to act and react in responsible ways is tested daily.

The humbling part of the experience is that managers are not always right. Although any seat of power is a conspicuous place to be, the mark of a good leader is the grace with which one handles a step of misjudgment. Management is not an exact science, but the artful application of certain principles that management scientists have discovered are fundamental to the inner workings of a successful business enterprise. The art of management arises from the character, knowledge, and skill of the manager and the lessons he or she learns from past experiences and from others, including subordinates.

Lest being manager sound like a rather overwhelming job, consider that thousands of people in our nation's workforce find themselves in some kind of supervisory position. Although not every supervisor has the same scope of responsibility or the same degree of influence in an organization, everyone who crosses the threshold into management needs some tools of the management trade. An enormous number of contemporary resources are available to help assemble those business management tools; *Real Estate Brokerage: A Management Guide* is one of those resources.

Perhaps the most significant feature of the title is that it is a *guide*. Today's real estate companies don't fit into one model or mold, and, certainly, managers don't fit into a single mold either. Each company is unique, and each manager is an individual. There are, however, certain basic principles for running a business enterprise and supervising people that are the foundation of a well-run company. The purpose of this book is to help managers understand the science of management and develop the art of applying those principles in ways that suit their individual circumstances.

Real Estate Brokerage: A Management Guide is directed to anyone who is a *manager*, the person who supervises or directs the conduct of business. You may be the broker/owner, an administrative or departmental manager, or a sales or office manager. The principal difference in any of these jobs is the degree of authority in the organization. The commonality is that each manager has some amount of responsibility for directing the company's financial and human resources in cost-efficient and effective ways so that the organization functions as a profitable enterprise.

A Guide to Using This Book

Many fine management theorists have studied how business enterprises operate, how managers function, and how people become effective leaders. *Real Estate Brokerage: A Management Guide* strives to apply their theories to the operation of a real estate brokerage company. Although there are numerous ways to present these theories, one of the generally accepted approaches is to group various management activities by functions—*Plan-*

ning, *Organizing*, *Staffing*, *Directing*, and Controlling. This POSDC model is a useful way for exploring the activities in a logical, methodical fashion.

The book is divided into five units, with each being introduced in an overview that explains how the chapters within the unit fit into the grand scheme of an organization and the job of a manager. Each chapter is introduced with several questions to ponder and concludes with discussion exercises to aid the learning experience. The units conclude with scenarios and analyses that are relevant to the unit chapters and typical of the situations that managers may encounter. A guide to the role a manager has in each function, depending on his or her level in the organization, is also provided.

The most important place to begin is with the manager, which is the first unit. The personal attributes and skills of the manager affect every administrative management function in an organization. The purpose of the first unit is to explore effective leadership, management styles, communications, and decision making, the personal tools of the management trade that are critical for successful administrators.

The subsequent four units explore the administrative functions in the POSDC model. Regardless of the role a manager has in the organization, the planning, organizing, staffing, directing, and controlling functions are relevant to understanding how organizations work cost-efficiently and effectively. Today's real estate company is more likely to be an institution of more complex systems and processes, staffed with more employees in addition to independent contractors, and subject to a greater number of workplace as well as industry laws than in the past. The result is that today's managers must be more knowledgeable and skillful.

Users of previous editions of *Real Estate Brokerage: A Management Guide* have observed that one of its greatest strengths is its futuristic yet timeless value in a wide range of applications. While the fundamental management functions don't change, the environment certainly does. Each marketplace is also governed by its own laws, adopts its own customs, and at any time can evolve in new, perhaps unpredictable, ways. This book provides a framework within which to manage in any environment. Whether first used for classroom study or a private read in a quiet corner, the book is an indispensable resource in a personal library. A bibliography of selected publications is also provided for further inspiration.

You may be embarking on a new career or be a novice or have experience as a broker/owner or the manager of a sales office. Or you may be a salesperson, not yet involved in management but seeking an inside look into the operation of a brokerage company. In any case, *Real Estate Brokerage: A Management Guide* is useful for gathering the tools of today's management trade and seizing new opportunities that are on the horizon. We wish you much success!

ACKNOWLEDGMENTS

Real Estate Brokerage: A Management Guide is now in its sixth edition, having been transformed three editions ago into solely a business management guide. While there are many fine general business management and real estate sales books, this publication intends to fill a void by providing a practical manual for managing a real estate company. The authors are grateful to a number of people who provided valuable input to this sixth edition.

Special thanks is owed to Jim Skindzier, DREI, nationally recognized as an outstanding real estate educator and an officer of the Real Estate Educators Association, who among his many activities has 25 years of experience in organizational and management development. His insight into the knowledge base and skill sets that are needed to successfully lead today's real estate company was invaluable in the enhancement of this sixth edition.

Reviewers who participated include:

Jack R. Bennett, Gold Coast School of Real Estate, Florida
Paul S. Black, University of Miami, Florida
William J. Cahaney, Jefferson Community College, Kentucky
Laurie S. MacDougal, Chicago Association of REALTORS®, Illinois

We all wish you a rewarding and successful career in the leadership of your real estate brokerage company in the new millennium.

CHAPTER ONE

1

THE CHALLENGE
OF CHANGE

How have the economy, geopolitics, and the behavior of consumers affected the real estate industry in recent years?

What do you think will change about the way real estate companies do business in the coming years?

————————

There are no magic answers, guarantees are few, but change is certain. An unexpected opening for a book, you say?

More than anything, this says that we are not afraid to be candid at the outset. No one has all the answers when the barometer on current events changes daily. We are living in unusual times and, in many respects, an economic and geopolitical climate that today's younger generations have not previously experienced.

The best way to begin the journey into business management is by looking at the big picture. Think about what were, what are, and what will be the

1

events framed in that picture that create opportunities and challenges for business owners and their companies' managers.

■ THE CHANGING CLIMATE

As we write this, our nation and the international community are trying to find ways to secure safety in our lives and at least peaceful coexistence among differing cultures. Before 9/11, which as of this writing is history of over two years ago, modern day geopolitical conflicts have been fought on battlegrounds far removed from our mainland's shores. On that September day, however, the assault of conflict and the unspeakable trauma it inflicts on families touched homeland residents in ways that were previously unimaginable.

This is a time when the bubble has burst in other ways as well. While the stock market has always cycled on the feet of bulls and bears, investors came face to face with the harsh reality that the bulls do eventually run out of steam. The whys and wherefores of their treks are too complex for most of us to completely understand, and even the most respected analysts have difficulty predicting, much less agreeing on, the bull's and the bear's next moves. Certainly, investors are far more content when the market is vigorously striding in positive territory, and that has clearly been the exception, rather than the rule, recently.

To add to their woes, investors learned that all was not totally as represented on Wall Street. The fundamental integrity of the institution was called into question when officials of some heretofore respected corporations were forced to explain how they deceived investors and employees, or could be deceived by partners or other organizations with whom they had associations. By some estimates, the average investor lost $60,000 (and many, considerably more) as the market lost ground and struggled to restore investor confidence.

The important point in all of this is that any business, a real estate company included, is at the mercy of a number of forces over which it has little control. What separates those that succeed from those who don't is a keen awareness of the environment and the ability to adapt as it changes.

Homeland Security

Our nation's businesses have learned what companies in parts of the world where terrorism has been commonplace have known for years: It's more costly to run a business when attentiveness to security is necessary. Businesses in Israel, for instance, spend an estimated 5 percent of their revenue on security. The editor-in-chief of CSO *Magazine*, a trade journal for security executives, observes that before 9/11, many U.S. companies didn't have security budgets. (Who would have thought about hiring a security executive, either?) But that's simply the world we live in now, one where security will become a permanent cost of doing business.

Virtually every industry, from the nation's airlines to food manufacturers and importers of produce, and every company, regardless of size, has been affected. Real estate companies managing large office buildings have found that the bill to install badge-reading systems (which can start at $250,000) and hiring extra security personnel can be quite sizable. Even the smallest companies have been willing to spend $3,000 for security cameras or security software for their computer systems, all in an effort to provide a safer place for workers and customers and to secure their company's operations. Often, this means postponing other expenditures in favor of security.

The cost of vigilance doesn't end with the initial expenditure. In addition to the cost of maintaining personnel and equipment and upgrading systems as needed, there is the cost in productive time, and perhaps missed business opportunities, that are the result of new security procedures. Certainly, more detailed paperwork procedures (perhaps necessitated by the Patriot Act anti-money-laundering programs) impact real estate transactions.

Despite the cost and hassle, business owners are willing to pay the price, recognizing that much of that cost must be absorbed rather than passed along to the consumer. Companies are also becoming proactive in assessing risk, a posture that is necessitated in many respects because of the effect of 9/11 on casualty insurers. Not only have premiums skyrocketed for many types of policies but insurance companies have also drawn lines around locations, buildings, and circumstances related to terrorism that are now deemed high risk and even uninsurable.

Only time will tell how resilient our nation's economy and its businesses will be while the Middle East is at the center of the geopolitical agenda. The ripple effect of conflict in Iraq can have possibly long-term consequences if the world economy suffers or sizable financial resources and manpower are required to secure lasting peace in that region and safety on homeland shores. Fewer resources will be available for revitalizing cities, enhancing transportation and infrastructure, and aiding homebuyers, all of which would affect the real estate industry.

The Marketplace

After nearly a decade of steady growth (with only minor setbacks) and unprecedented highs posted by leading economic indicators, we learn that the stock market can lose value and corporate profits do diminish. We also see that, once lost, restoring investor confidence is a major challenge.

The result is that displaced workers are left scrambling to reengineer careers. Older workers are forced to rethink retirement strategies and plans for their golden years. Endowment-dependent institutions, like the cultural arts, have become strapped by diminished values of investment portfolios.

Those who have lived through cycles of growth and deceleration are more likely to have a circumspect view. This, too, shall pass, and we'll adjust in the meantime. For those who have known only the good times, the adjustment seems far too cruel. There may be more adjustments yet to come as the Federal Reserve maneuvers interest rates or consumers try to figure out whether it's wise to spend.

As you are reading this, if you can see opportunities for your business, then that's very good news. If you can think of ways to readjust your priorities or reset your expectations, that's also a step in the right direction. Look at some possible ways to make the changing environment work for you.

- When equity investments (stocks) and even bonds fall out of favor, investors look for other places to put their money. Real estate, not just the typical types of investment property but the second and third home as well, becomes an attractive haven. Recently, low mortgage interest rates, while unappealing to bond holders, have made second homes (using the equity in the first home) the investment option of choice for many baby boomers. According to the National Association of REALTORS®, demand has also pushed up prices 27 percent between 1999 and 2001. The real estate company that is attuned to the investment market can position itself to serve the changing priorities of investors.

■ As lifestyles change, people seek different ways to house themselves. The real estate company that is attuned to growth in families (whether by birth or the addition of an elderly parent to the household), diminishing family size (the near-retirement or retired empty nester), and changing economic circumstances of workers or retirees can tailor services to respond.

■ As interest rates change, mortgage loans are either more or less attractive. It's easy for companies to flourish during periods of low interest rates and get lulled into a false sense of security. Because interest rates have cycled throughout history, the company that watches the horizon and has a solid plan for enhancing revenue and/or economizing on expenditures is the one that prospers during periods of high interest rates.

■ As consumer confidence peaks and wanes, spending patterns change. Here again, it's easy for companies to do business when consumers are freely spending. But the company that has developed market niches that are less impacted by fluctuating consumer behavior or the company that is positioned to help consumers alter their housing arrangements if need be can withstand the times when consumers reign in their spending.

One last issue to address before moving on is the credibility of business institutions. Certainly, nothing has rocked corporate integrity as badly as recent stock-manipulation scandals, leaving people with a jaded view of what goes on in corporate boardrooms or backrooms. Unfortunately, that perception paints the upstanding leaders (who are most likely the majority) with the same brush as the few individuals who mis-stepped.

The outcome is a general climate that is more watchful, less tolerant of self-serving dealings, and more demanding for accountability in the business community. The real estate industry has had its critics over the years. Ethical issues are an old-news story, given that surveys consistently rank the ethics of real estate salespeople in the bottom third of selected professions.

This state of affairs may be the good news for the real estate industry. While its failings may be more readily identified or criticized, that scrutiny can help the industry move forward in institutionalizing ethical business practices that critics within as well as outside the industry have long maintained need to be improved.

■ CHANGING ORGANIZATIONS

In past editions, the point has been made that the real estate industry has progressed from a land or brick-and-mortar business to a service and information business. Putting this in perspective, think about the fact that many of today's 21st century real estate practitioners and consumers don't see the business any other way.

How do real estate companies serve today's consumers? And perhaps just as important, if not more so, is how do companies do this in the prevailing business climate?

Changing Business Models

The landscape of the industry has changed considerably in recent years, the result being that, very simply, there is no *one* model for a real estate company today. A company may be a single office, small-staff operation that offers just a few services or as sizable as a multiple-office organization staffed by hundreds of personnel, offering a wide range of services and affiliations with allied service groups. And there are variations in between, all because today's companies must devise operations to serve the diverse needs of today's consumers and do so under enormous financial pressures.

Real estate companies merge, divest themselves of previous affiliations, or forge new alliances with other real estate enterprises or with enterprises offering complementary products and services. Some are drawn under a single corporate umbrella along with a number of diverse or even non-real estate-related corporate units. Real estate companies change their organizations in the same ways our nation's major corporations restructure theirs, and they do so for the same reason: They are striving to achieve more profitable operations.

Salespeople often think that the broker is reaping a bundle of money from a 60/40 or 50/50 commission split. The truth of the matter is that the bottom line is very lean, often about 2 percent of earnings (or even less) after expenses and before taxes.

A recent white paper distributed by industry consultants John Tuccillo and Stefan Swanepoel suggests that companies only made between $47 and $132 pretax profit per transaction in 2002, curiously, a year when more homes sold, at higher prices, than ever before. Certainly, sobering statistics that speak to the financial burdens that drive companies to reevaluate their internal operations, their services, and their methods of doing business.

Large brokerage companies keep getting bigger, assimilating smaller ones into their operations. Often, mid-sized companies are targeted because they command an appealing market share. Megabrokers have merged with other megabrokers to strengthen their position in the marketplace or to capture a larger geographic market. Megabrokers have also formed brainstorming groups, such as the Realty Alliance, to enhance their competitive advantage as independent companies. Outsiders have entered the real estate business, becoming parent companies of organizations such as Coldwell Banker and franchises such as Century 21 and ERA.

The banking industry, which has flirted with real estate for a number of years, continues to push for regulatory permission to enter the real estate business. Companies commonly forge alliances with other organizations that offer complementary products or services to better serve consumers. Typically, such alliances are a win-win for each of the business units. Opponents of these alliances, as in the case with the banking industry's overtures, fear that the collective unit will gain undue power in the marketplace or will favor business from their aligned units over business from outsiders.

Regardless of how the bankers, real estate brokers, and lawmakers settle their issues, real estate companies continue to pursue alliances with complementary service providers to gain a competitive edge.

Does this mean that bigger is better? No, not necessarily. The majority of our nation's businesses are small enterprises. This is also true in the real estate industry, one that was originally founded by independent brokers who ran loosely formed organizations with relatively unsophisticated business methods. There is still a place for small companies, their appeal often being their smallness and the ability to offer more personalized or specialized services.

Regardless of size, organizations must find successful ways to do business, though their strategies may differ. The common thread is their willingness to shed "traditional" ways of doing business. When once successful strategies no longer reap the same benefits, companies must change. The external environment plays a significant role in driving those changes.

Changing Services

Traditionally, businesses employed a supplier model, meaning that the supplier controls the selection of products or services offered in the marketplace. The defect in this model, however, is the assumption that consumers will take what is offered. Instead, *companies must aggressively investigate demand and then create services or products that match demand.*

Today's consumers are discriminating shoppers. They want products and services that are tailored to meet *their* needs rather than tailoring their wants and desires to match that which is available. Furthermore, today's consumers are far more independent and self-sufficient than in the past. They want to and can do more for themselves, especially with the help of the Internet. They can not only access volumes of information but can also complete a wide range of purchases on line.

Today's consumers are convenience-driven. They want "one-stop shopping." That stop is either in front of their computers or at vendors who can link them with the wide range of services needed to carry them seamlessly through a transaction. Those services may include mortgage financing and settlement. They may also include job placement for a spouse; daycare for a child or elderly parent; or moving, housecleaning, yardcare, or handyman repair services.

Today's consumers are also price-and-value conscious, hence the appeal of cross purchasing or affinity programs. Consumers are offered enticements like coupons or discounts through shoppers' clubs and point programs elsewhere in the marketplace. Real estate companies have responded by building alliances (e.g., HOMELINK®) so they can offer similar enticements.

Affinity programs have their critics, however. Salespeople who must relinquish part of their commissions to participate in these programs often question their cost versus value benefit. In addition, because most states' licensing laws prohibit commission rebates, regulators have had to wrestle with deciding whether these rebates adversely affect the consumer. Proponents maintain that the controversy is largely due to misconceptions about the way affinity programs work. Nonetheless, regulators in some states have banned these programs.

As much as today's consumers like the convenience of one-stop shopping and the cost efficiencies that bundling services and products offers, they have also become very discriminating about exactly which of those services they want to buy. The one-size-fits-all service package that real estate companies have customarily provided no longer suits today's independent, self-sufficient consumer. Furthermore, because of the growing popularity of buyer agency, real estate companies are hard pressed to justify charging the seller or landlord a transaction-based commission for all of the services provided to both sides of the transaction.

The result is that real estate companies are being increasingly challenged by consumers to shed transaction-based fee structures in favor of alternative pricing models. That is, unbundle services and offer a menu of options from which consumers can choose and then pay only for the services they use. While the majority of real estate companies did not offer these options several years ago, today's companies are far more likely to offer pricing alternatives to suit the desires of today's consumers.

Changing Delivery

Today's companies must find ways to connect themselves with a large, geographically diverse, and independent population of consumers. This means not only tailoring products and services to satisfy today's consumers but also delivering them in ways that suit today's purchasing patterns. Because the electronic platform has become the forum of choice for many consumers, this means, very simply, that companies must have an Internet presence.

The *cyber economy*, as it is known, has opened many doors for vendors and consumers alike. Today's consumer can purchase, trade, or auction on the Internet virtually any commodity that is available in the marketplace. Although there are two sides of the debate about the practicality or desirability of electronic real estate purchases, the fact remains that each year an increasing number of consumers turn to the Internet for some type of information or service.

■ **CASE IN POINT . . .**   Internet commerce even in 1998 was a $102 billion revenue producer, derived from online products, fee and subscription-based companies, online advertising, and online travel providers, according to NAR's Real Estate and Technology Report. In 2001, 41 percent of homebuyers used the Internet for information (according to NAR's 2002 profile of buyers and sellers), and those numbers are growing yearly. Interestingly, homebuyers were more focused on property listings, rather than using the Internet to locate firms or salespeople.

One of the real estate industry's greatest challenges has been finding ways to assert a presence on the Internet and provide the information today's consumers thirst for, when that very information has been viewed as the industry's primary and proprietary asset. For the most part, this means property listings. But because virtually every part of a real estate transaction can be linked electronically, the industry also must find ways to stay in the information loop throughout the transaction.

The burgeoning amount of information that is available electronically has moved the industry into a new arena of service—to help sift, sort, and interpret all the information that consumers access. Perhaps more significant, however, is the kind of information real estate companies themselves are now providing on the Internet.

Internet Data Exchange.   The traditional management and distribution of multiple listing service (MLS) data have undergone dramatic changes because of technology. Previously, only a real estate company's own listings could be posted on the company Web site. Today, with Internet Data Exchange (IDX), the central MLS database can be accessed through any MLS member's Web site that participates in the IDX program. Essentially, the technology gives a visitor to your site access to not only your listings but to the listings of your cooperating MLS competitors as well.

The evolution of IDX has raised a host of business and policy issues. How much information about an individual property or owner should be displayed? Can a broker opt out of IDX, thus preventing that company's listings from being displayed on another broker's site? Can an individual property owner prevent his or her listing from being displayed? Can salespeople or only their brokers link their sites to IDX? The answers are decisions that state regulators and local MLS members must make.

Virtual Office Web Sites. IDX has spawned another development, that being a version of e-commerce. While the debate continues over the viability or feasibility of negotiating an entire real estate transaction electronically, the real estate industry has begun to link consumers more formally with its companies through Virtual Office Websites (VOWs). These are essentially online or electronic models of a real estate office.

There is an IDX component in VOWs, but the distinguishing characteristic is that VOWs require that visitors establish a client-broker relationship before they can access postings of property listings. Proponents of VOWs suggest that by requiring visitors to register and provide pertinent qualifying information, listing searches can be tailored to their needs in much the same way salespeople qualify buyers face-to-face.

Furthermore, registration provides contact information that real estate salespeople can use to establish interactive relationships with consumers. Proponents suggest that consumers who are willing to register are more serious prospects than those who visit more public Web sites.

VOWs, like IDX, raise a number of policy issues. One involves access to property listings. Because VOWs typically connect registered visitors to the MLS's entire database, this means that visitors also have access to the listings of brokers who have opted out of IDX participation. This essentially defeats the purpose of a broker preventing his or her listings from being displayed on another broker's site.

Another issue involves the relationship created between a registered visitor and the broker. On one hand, the registration and an acknowledgment process satisfy a host of agency disclosure actions commonly required by state licensing laws. The result is that listing data can be accessed by only those with whom a business relationship has been established. On the other hand, visitors must enter into a client relationship so they can access listing data, which may not necessarily be a relationship they want, intend, or fully understand. The process may chase a visitor to a site where registration is not required.

Although some of these issues may be resolved soon, the fact remains that the real estate industry is moving forward and attempting to seize opportunities afforded by today's technology. The crux of the matter is that the electronic platform provides a crucial link for information. A two-way street, if you will: One way disseminates information; the other captures contacts that can be nurtured into closed transactions.

■ CHANGING OPERATIONS

As organizations change to meet the challenges in the environment and seize opportunities to better serve consumers, this means that organizations must also alter their internal operating structures. In other words, align the organization to function in the prevailing climate.

Downsizing and *reengineering* are terms commonly heard in corporate boardrooms. Often, companies suffer from misaligned structures and bloated workforces as a result of mergers or acquisitions or a change in the way goods are manufactured or products and services are delivered. Frequently, those changes come about because of technology. As costs of operation increase, businesses must learn to work smarter, with more cost-efficient structures, smaller workforces, and better technology, to be profitable.

Real estate brokerage companies are confronted with similar challenges and are reengineering in similar ways. Because real estate companies already function on narrow profit margins, costs of operations must be managed very carefully. This is a two-edged sword because the costs that diminish bottom lines, such as technology and support for the sales staff, are the very expenditures that help the organization work smarter and enhance efficiency and productivity. Bottom line is that costs can be cut only to a certain level.

Staffing

One of the ways today's organizations become more cost-efficient is by making more effective personnel expenditures.

Some real estate companies do this by downsizing the sales staff, hiring a smaller number of people but ones who are highly productive. Companies can then justify the cost of support personnel and technology. Even companies that still subscribe to the practice of hiring large sales staffs (with the expectation that larger staffs will produce comparably larger revenue) are more closely scrutinizing production per person in this strategy. It's becoming too costly to provide the workplace enhancements needed to attract and retain the top producers while carrying a large staff of marginally productive salespeople.

Another way companies can work smarter is by hiring salespeople as employees rather than as independent contractors. The appeal is that companies can exercise greater control over sales activities, and, ultimately, revenue production. While employee costs are higher, the expectation is that those expenditures can be offset with higher revenue. Although this strategy has not yet been widely embraced by residential sales companies, it has become more prevalent and could become a widespread practice in the coming years.

Certainly, the number of available licensees plays a role in staffing decisions. After a decade of decline, statistics from the National Association of REALTORS® indicate that the number of licensees nationally has started to grow again, to approximately 2.3 million licensees in 2002, with 892,000 of them being NAR members. This growth trend, however, may not prevail in all parts of the country, depending on the local economy and home sales activity. Technology, which was once feared to be a deterrent to recruitment or retention, especially of the older salesperson, does not appear to have had any significant effect.

One other issue to consider regarding the pool of available sales talent is portability of licenses. The industry has customarily functioned within geographic boundaries that correspond to the jurisdictions of state licensing authorities. Today's real estate market, though, is not limited by boundaries, be they interstate or even international. While a number of states have had some version of license reciprocity with their contiguous counterparts, there has not been an efficient or nationwide process that permits licensees to cross jurisdictions. This is changing rapidly, and before long a company's doors will be open to licensees from far and wide.

Salesperson Efficiency.   Salespeople in today's companies are also striving to work more efficiently. They are turning to *personal assistants*, employed either by the broker or the salesperson, and *transaction coordinators* to perform nonsales and administrative functions so they can focus on direct, revenue-producing activities. Salespeople are also forming *sales teams*. By working in collaborative efforts with other salespeople and perhaps nonselling personnel (like a personal assistant), they can capitalize on one another's strengths and perhaps diverse expertise, work smarter rather than longer hours, and ultimately, provide better service to the consumer.

The real estate company that endorses these activities gains a recruiting edge and also potentially higher revenue. However, the cost of providing nonselling staff creates financial pressures, which the company then often shifts to the salespeople. This is another two-edged sword because the support services that attract salespeople are also the services they wind up paying for out of their commissions. As the salespeople's costs of doing business increases, the less attractive a real estate career becomes, the result being an additional recruitment and retention challenge.

Supervising

Today's workforce in a real estate company bears little resemblance to that of a decade ago. Salespeople are far more mobile than they once were, and some rarely cross the doorstep of the real estate office more than several days each month. In addition, today's office staff often comprises more employees, certainly more than a secretary. Today's manager must learn new ways to supervise personnel in today's workplace environment.

■ *Home officing:* An increasing number of salespeople work primarily from home and use the brokerage office only for conferences with customers. Home officing enables salespeople to work more efficiently, on their own timetables, and without commuting to an office to do things that can easily be done off site. The manager who is accustomed to keeping tabs on salespeople in an office now has to find a better way to monitor activities. Fostering camaraderie among the sales staff and planning group functions, such as sales meetings and training sessions, is also more challenging.

■ *Employees versus independent contractors:* As more nonselling staff and perhaps salespeople are hired as employees, brokers and managers have to set aside their independent contractor, commission-oriented mindsets and learn how to manage employees. People must be fairly compensated for the work they do, which is often difficult for brokers to determine for those who are not directly engaged in revenue-producing activities. The day-to-day supervision of employees is also different, though some managers consider the control they can assert over employees (as opposed to independent contractors) very desirable.

■ *Sales teams:* Supervising sales teams means that the manager is supervising the individual salespeople as well as the collective unit. The manager needs to know how team members intend to share compensation and work tasks. This is especially important for knowing which team member is accountable when a transaction problem arises. A team should be assembled for efficiency and productivity, not to function as an independent company. Effective supervision of sales teams is critical because the broker is ultimately responsible for the activities of all licensees and is also accountable if unlicensed people perform activities for which they should be licensed.

■ *Professional growth:* A company's human resources are its most valuable asset. Companies protect this resource by providing opportunities for professional growth and job enrichment. Often, they do this by providing education and training. Job enrichment also takes the form of a less dictatorial and more supportive and energized work environment. Frequently, this means that salespeople are involved in collaborative efforts for the company, such as problem solving and brainstorming projects, and may even have an ownership stake in the company.

Enhancing Revenue

Service businesses, like real estate, have fewer direct means of increasing revenue than manufacturing businesses have. Manufacturers can manipulate production and distribution of tangible goods and thereby enhance revenue. Service businesses, on the other hand, market intangible commodities whose cost, price, and value are difficult to measure, let alone maneuver. Often, service providers and their consumers have disparate views of cost, price, and value as well, especially when consumers expect to receive more services for the price than the provider intends to deliver.

The real estate industry is on the brink of a revolution over fee structures as companies wrestle with financial pressures and the consumers' perception of value. Obviously, many of the organizational changes discussed suit the purposes of increasing revenue and enhancing service. Linking with ancillary services generates direct revenue for the business units and indirectly through referral fees. Unbundling services and the resulting fee structures intend to capture business that traditional transaction-based commission fees would not. So far, this is a win-win for company revenue and consumer service.

The value part of the equation, at least in the minds of consumers, gets muddled with a practice that has become more prevalent, even customary, in many parts of the country—the practice of real estate companies charging *transaction fees*. While these fees are rather nominal in some areas, they amount to several hundred dollars per transaction in others. Transaction fees intend to offset a company's clerical and administrative costs for processing transactions. Consumers, on the other hand, have difficulty justifying the additional fees, in light of the services they thought they would receive, anyway.

Certainly, there is no point in running a for-profit enterprise that isn't profitable. But companies have to consider at what point their revenue enhancing efforts can backfire and wind up costing them business. "Nickel and diming" the consumer for each task that is performed, while also charging the customary commissions, will eventually raise the ire of consumers. At what point will they then revolt and eliminate the real estate licensee from the transaction?

The challenge for the real estate industry at the moment is to keep licensees at the center of a transaction, particularly when they are no longer the gatekeepers of information. Unless a consumer perceives value in a company's services, he or she will then turn to the competition. Or to a company that has entered the real estate business as a way to also capture customers for that company's customary products or services.

■ A FINAL THOUGHT

Some observers say that fundamentally nothing has changed about the real estate industry. In a sense, there is an element of truth in that notion, considering that the industry is still real estate based, serving a wide range of buyers, sellers, landlords, and tenants. The change, be it a tweak or a dramatic development, relates to the *way* the industry has learned to serve real estate over the years. In this regard, the industry has definitely changed.

All business organizations face similar challenges for similar reasons. Bottom line pressures, economic downturns, abundant regulations, and aggressive competition are but a few of the realities of life. The latest challenge is the competitive forces brought about by the Internet. The real estate business isn't any different in these respects. What separates the survivors from the victims is the way organizations meet these challenges. Ignoring and hoping they will go away only makes victims.

Many valuable lessons can be learned from the corporate world. But this means stepping outside the real estate industry and learning how business organizations, in general, function. The processes that are explored in later chapters are similar to those that any business organization goes through. That is, business management. The challenges mentioned in this first chapter are just typical examples of the external and internal forces that companies must recognize and prepare to meet head on.

■ CONCLUSION

The fitting conclusion to this chapter is really a beginning. Having opened some lines of thinking from a national perspective, now you can take the next step. Look at your local business environment and your own organization. Some situations may be similar or you may identify other forces that impact your business. The point to remember is that change is inescapable. Astute businesspeople see change as an opportunity. Be open-minded and innovative. No old way is so good that it can't be improved on. Keep this in mind as you work through the management functions explored in this book.

■ DISCUSSION EXERCISES

Discuss changes in the real estate industry, especially in your local market, that you envision during the next three years.

What do you think your real estate consumers want from the Internet? How do you think the real estate industry and a company should be utilizing the Internet?

Considering the financial pressures on today's organizations and the consumers' attitudes about the cost of real estate services, how do you think fees for real estate services and costs for transactions should be structured?

THE MANAGER

The logical place to begin a business management discussion is with the manager. While a company is an organization of systems and processes, the driving force that combines or coordinates these is the manager. In fact, many contemporary business writers take readers through organizational functions solely through the viewpoint of a manager. Regardless of how the subject is discussed, however, the fact remains that organizations are administered by virtue of the interpersonal, decision-making, and informational actions of their managers.

Consider for a moment that a business organization is nothing more than an aggregation of people. All the other systems are simply ways to organize the collected people so they can work effectively and efficiently and make money for the organization. Someone needs to lead the group through an orderly progression of processes, and that someone is the manager. In a real estate company, a manager can have such titles as broker/owner, sales manager, or department manager.

Whether or not the manager is successful in leading the assembled group depends on a number of factors that have less to do with the formal organization and much more to do with the person. Because there is a human element in everything a manager does, a manager's effectiveness is directly related to his or her people skills.

Developing these skills begins with a critical assessment of self and understanding how one's basic nature affects a person's ability to command a leadership position in an organization and manage the interdependent relationships of its people. With that understanding, a person can then identify ways to grow as an individual. This is really a self-improvement process that also enhances a person's effectiveness as a manager.

The emphasis on interpersonal skills arises from an evolution of management thinking that began in the 1930s when theorists began studying human relationships in an organization. The recognition that people are an organization's most valuable resource led to studies about the psychology of work and workplace motivations; in essence, why people work.

Theorists learned that organizations benefited when they invested in the workers' professional growth and engaged them in the organization's processes. The outgrowth of these discoveries is the job enrichment and participatory environments that are common in the workplace today.

Having set this stage, the first unit is a journey through some discussions that are intended to help develop effective management skills. Unlike the one-two-three-step formulas commonly learned in sales, management development is a process that begins with understanding how one's personal traits, strengths, and weaknesses affect (positively or negatively) the human dynamics of an organization. With that understanding, a person is better able to successfully assume the role of manager. To help meet the personal challenges of management, we explore

- leadership and the characteristics in leaders that inspire people to follow,

- management of people and understanding human behavior in the workplace, and

- communications and effective ways to gather and disseminate information and make quality decisions.

Entire publications (see the Bibliography) by notable authors are devoted exclusively to various aspects of the personal skills managers need to be successful. These are useful whether you are the broker/owner of the company or hold another management position in the organization.

CHAPTER TWO

LEADERSHIP

Whom do you admire as an effective leader? Why?

What do you know about yourself that would help—or hinder—you,
as a leader?

The reputation of an organization as an institution of integrity, as a compassionate workplace, as a fair and honest competitor is a direct reflection of its leadership. The leaders of the institution set the tone for the way the organization and the people who work for it do business. Admirable character traits and leadership qualities foster admirable institutions. The opposite is also true.

The reputation of an organization as a trendsetter is also a reflection of leadership. Organizations successfully navigate changing environments under the leadership of those who have vision for the future and see change as an opportunity to be creative. With creativity, though, also comes risk. The risk is that some things people try don't work. But growth rarely comes without a little daring.

Some of our nation's most successful corporations are led by people who have established reputations as innovators. In many cases, the outgrowth of their efforts become models that others now follow.

So, why do we hold some people out as exemplary leaders? And why do we follow them or duplicate what they do?

The answers revolve around the essence of leadership. That is, the ability to influence other people. People are inspired to be supportive or cooperative when the leader earns their respect and when it's obvious that the leader has a clearly defined purpose or mission. Because of the strength of their convictions, their passion, and their determination to embrace certain principles or ideals, it's clear where they are headed. This strength engenders faith in others that following such a person is the right thing to do.

■ LEADERSHIP VERSUS MANAGEMENT

Not all managers are leaders. The distinction relates to the ability to influence others and the contrasting ways leaders and managers approach their jobs in an organization. Our premise is that managers can be more successful when they understand the differences and are then inspired to develop as leaders.

Beginning with group dynamics, consider that we spend much of our lives as members of groups—at work, in the community, in the family, in the classroom. In the group hierarchy, someone becomes the leader. That person may be formally appointed, as in the chairman, manager, or teacher. Or that person may informally rise to the position.

Herein lies the first lesson. Just because a person has the title of *boss* in whatever context doesn't necessarily make that person the leader. People embrace a person as their leader because of his or her personal qualities, not because of the title.

Now comes the newly appointed manager, armed with a title and the notion that if he or she does wise and wonderful things, the troops will follow. That can be the case if the manager possesses the qualities that people respect and value in a leader and demonstrates behavior that is consistent with those qualities. Otherwise, people will follow someone else or stride off under their own direction.

The next lesson is that just because an organization has a formal structure and an established hierarchy doesn't necessarily mean that people will support their superiors. This assumes that the organization has a great deal of control over people. That simply isn't the case, especially in today's organizations, which are less autocratic or dictatorial.

Even in organizations with highly structured ranks (like the military) and serious negative consequences for failing to acquiesce to superiors, there are always the subordinates that don't fall into line. In fact, a person may choose the negative consequences rather than abide a superior who is not deemed worthy of attention. The point is that no one can actually force another person to do anything, but a person can inspire or influence people to move in the desired direction.

Finally, we turn our attention to the organization as a whole. This is where we discover that management and leadership are related, but also different. Managers function within established systems and seek orderly formulas. They see themselves as caretakers, focused on monitoring the organization and correcting deviations to protect the bottom-line dollars-and-cents and keep the organization on course.

Leaders, on the other hand, are the entrepreneurs, the people who "think outside the box" rather than within the parameters of established systems. They are the long-range, independent thinkers who look for creative, more inspired ways to do things. To leaders, innovation (and the extra costs that may be involved) is the way to achieve bottom-line success.

Organizations benefit from both management and leadership. Certainly, organizations need management to keep them on course. But the course set by leadership is more likely to lead to success. Leaders inspire organizations to be proactive and quickly reactive in the changing environment, to test limits and grow by blazing new trails.

■ UNDERSTANDING YOURSELF

How can a person become not only a manager, but a leader? This is really a self-development process that begins with understanding the essence of leadership and the character and qualities that cause people to view a person as a leader. There are many excellent publications devoted exclusively to these subjects that are very worthwhile (see the Bibliography). The purpose of the discussion in this chapter is to introduce some thoughts to start you on your way.

Contemporary writers such as Warren Bennis and Stephen Covey stress the importance of self-awareness in the leadership development process. This involves evaluating personal strengths, weaknesses, and values and then, most importantly, using the knowledge gained from that process to grow. Much can be learned through introspection. Pay attention to several leadership characteristics that seem to be particularly noteworthy.

Are you willing to learn? The strength of conviction, passion, and vision that leaders possess comes from learning. Not just that which is gained from a book (reading or taking courses) but from the continual process of evaluating one's experiences, probing and asking questions, listening and observing. Leaders have great intellectual and emotional curiosity and are energized by what they learn. Energy fosters conviction, passion, and the evolution of thought that manifests itself in vision for the future.

Are you willing to take care of others? Leaders distinguish themselves because of their *selflessness* rather than self-centeredness. They value people (over systems and procedures) and have a capacity for nurturing and contributing to the lives of others. Leaders rejoice in the accomplishments of others. The process of caring for others also contributes to self-growth.

Do you have a positive attitude? Leaders focus on the positive rather than negative aspects of life, other people, and themselves. This does not mean an artificial rah-rah, all's grand kind of posture (which can be annoying and in many cases, simply implausible), but a genuine spirit of optimism that allows them to cherish the good and pleasurable. In so doing, they can take the negative in stride and grow beyond their weaknesses. It is also an infectious spirit that brings out the best in others, which doesn't

happen when people are subjected to the "if only" mentality of the belea-
guered, the fault-finders, or the cynics of the world.

How compassionate are you? So, perfection doesn't exist, either in one's
self or in others. Compassion means having a healthy appreciation for
being human. This is not to say that being human is an excuse, but rather
an acknowledgment of what is. People need to feel acceptance, for their
flaws as well as their strengths. Then they can grow, and if not correct
their weaknesses, certainly develop compensating enhancements. Compassionate leaders create an environment in which this can happen and don't
use the weaknesses in others to build up themselves.

How open-minded are you? Being able to see all sides of a story or entertain
a variety of viewpoints certainly inspires creativity, but it also helps build
consensus, which is important for harmony and helping an organization
to function. Little in life is "black/white" or "either/or." People who insist
on absolutes are not only unable to see all dimensions of a situation and
stifle the thinking of others but invariably offend someone with their
absolute or possibly extremist views. Open-minded people are typically
more tolerant or respectful of divergent viewpoints, easier to get along
with, and better listeners.

What about ego and empathy? Webster characterizes *self-esteem* as being
synonymous with *ego*, that is, confidence and self-respect. In other words,
these are attitudes people have about themselves. *Empathy* is the ability to
be sensitive to the thoughts, feelings, and experiences of others. In pon-
dering the previous questions, note the correlation between those and the
elements of ego and empathy. Confidence and self-respect contribute to
the ability to be compassionate and tolerant and to nurture others. Greater
confidence is gained as one learns and grows from experiences.

How do you rate? On a scale of one to five (five being highest), score
yourself on each of these characteristics. With an honest assessment, one
can learn where the strengths and the areas of improvement are.

■ CHARACTER OF A LEADER

One of the ways people judge the worthiness of a leader is based on what they see in a person's character and the congruity between that person's value systems and their own. Character is formed by values, morals, and ethics and is revealed by such things as integrity, honesty, and trustworthiness, or the lack thereof, all of which speak volumes about the essence of a person.

Leadership comes from the ability of a person to engender the faith of others that the person deserves their following. There is great personal risk in aligning with someone who is in the position to profoundly affect a person's life. People need to feel that their leader is incorruptible and can be trusted to use the position responsibly. Several of the most notable character traits that foster confidence that this risk is worth taking include the following:

- **Integrity:** Webster's dictionary says integrity is *a firm adherence to a code of especially moral or artistic values, implying trustworthiness and incorruptibility.*

- **Honesty:** Back to Webster, and honesty is found to imply *a refusal to lie, steal, or in any way deceive, an unswerving fidelity to the truth.*

- **Trustworthiness:** The essential element is *confidence that a person can be trusted, the faith others have that a person will use the position of trust responsibly and no harm will come to them.*

- **Loyalty:** Webster, again, says loyalty implies a *faithfulness that is steadfast in the face of any temptation to betray.*

- **Respect:** This is the *high regard for the welfare and rights of others* and when mutual, others highly regard that person.

The fundamental trait, which also plays a role in all the others, is *integrity*. Integrity comes from a person's intrinsic sense of values or moral order, which are influenced by the value systems and moral codes formed in a family, society, culture, or organization. Hence, one universal set does not exist. This is why character flaws under one system may be acceptable in another.

People commonly use their own value systems and moral codes, or their perceptions of those that are generally accepted in their society, to measure other people. In their leaders, people tend to expect the highest standards.

The integrity of the institution, as in the organization, is a reflection of the integrity of its leaders. When there is a lack of congruity between one person's values and another's or those of the institution, a moral dilemma results. One of the best examples involves money. Is money valued at all cost, regardless of how it is gotten? Or is money valued only when gotten honorably?

When value systems are not aligned, the fundamental integrity of one of them is challenged. For instance, when the worker functions with the money-at-all-cost notion while the organization functions on the honorable notion (or vice versa), the holder of the honorable notion feels that integrity has been violated. Eventually, the moral compromise can become intolerable.

Honesty and integrity are frequently associated because with integrity also comes the expectation that one does not lie, cheat, steal, or deceive. This is revealed in the way a person uses knowledge. It can be used for truthful and honorable purposes or, in the hands of a dishonest or deceitful person, can be used for manipulation or self-serving gain. Once the latter happens, people no longer feel that a person can be trusted.

Trust arises from the confidence that a person will use knowledge and position responsibly. Trusting one another is risky, but it is a risk people are willing to take when they feel that no harm will come to them. Once harm occurs, be it from dishonesty or self-serving actions, trust is violated.

Do you see the correlation between this discussion so far and the challenges discussed in the first chapter as today's corporations try to restore confidence in their institutions?

Some leaders are so successful at engendering people's trust that they are able to persuade people to believe in them despite their gross failings—Adolf Hitler, for example. This is certainly not to suggest that he is a model to emulate, but it does make the point that leaders have an enormous influence. This also says that leaders have a responsibility to use their positions wisely so as not to abuse people's trust.

Loyalty arises from the trust that pledging allegiance to an individual or a cause is beneficial. People will be faithful when they feel their personal needs are being satisfied. Once their devotion no longer reaps those benefits or they discover that their allegiance was misplaced, people are no longer inclined to be loyal.

Respect is essentially the culmination of all one learns about a person's character. People may not necessarily love, like, or even feel any particular kinship with another. Yet, a person gains their respect because he or she is worthy of the regard.

Power of a Leader

The very nature of a leadership position confers power. Power is exercised by making decisions and, in so doing, can dramatically affect other people's lives. The effect could be very positive or beneficial or it could be deleterious. The responsible or irresponsible use of power reflects character. The way others react to that power reflects their perceived worthiness of a person to hold the position.

When power is used to coerce people, obedience comes from fear rather than respect and, eventually, can breed resentment. Coercion no longer works when people feel that they've surrendered too much control to someone else or become suspicious of a person's motives. We often hear that power corrupts. Power in the hands of a corruptible person does.

A leader is constantly being scrutinized and will have influence only as long as people feel that power is being used fairly and justly. If a salesperson, for example, feels that the manager does not respect that salesperson's needs, expects the salesperson to compromise his or her ethics, or is willing to compromise the principles or ethics of the company, the manager can be judged unworthy of the power. The most enduring influence a leader has is when both the leader and the followers share similar values.

■ LEADERSHIP QUALITIES

Leaders emerge not just because of who they are as persons but because they also have certain skills that enable them to effectively influence or inspire others. In some respects, these skills can be viewed as natural attributes, but they are also personal qualities than can be developed or enhanced.

Accountability

With leadership comes enormous responsibility, both responsibility for the institution (the group or organization) and responsibility for the individuals within it. Virtually everything a person in a leadership position does involves decision making, including deciding a personal course of action. While some are more significant than others, all decisions have consequences. Accountability means that a person is willing to take responsibility for the outcomes of his or her decisions.

A decision may produce the desired outcomes or even exceed expectations. Or a decision could turn out to be a fiasco. Of course, accountability is easy to handle when a decision turns out to be right. But that won't always be the case. Surrendering or resigning from the responsibilities of the position out of fear of being wrong simply doesn't work. The institution and the people within it look to the leader for guidance. Better the person who takes charge, learns to be up front and say "oops" if necessary, and then take corrective action.

Accountability also means not shifting blame. Certainly, there's less personal risk when someone else is responsible for an errant development. Children learn early that there are fewer undesirable consequences (until the parent learns the truth of the matter) when they let the other kid take the blame. Leadership, however, can ill afford to fault an inept sales staff, a broker's unrealistic policy, or flawed laws or procedures for failing production or wayward behavior. The "buck stops here"—that is, with the leader.

A leadership position holds a person accountable for all that happens under his or her domain. In a real estate company, accountability is further explained by licensing laws, which hold brokers responsible for the activities of the licensees who work for them. Regulators do not excuse a salesperson's ineptitude or a broker's inability to know all that the licensees are doing as a defense for violations of their laws.

Decisiveness

People in a leadership position are expected to provide direction. Otherwise, the organization is akin to a rudderless ship. That is, the institution has no direction. Ambiguity or indecisiveness not only muddles perceptions about who is in charge but also thwarts the organization's ability to achieve its goals. Lacking direction from elsewhere, people will chart their own courses, which may or may not be to the organization's benefit.

Someone has to guide the assembled group and provide order, but stepping up as the leader is a conspicuous and vulnerable place to be. It takes some courage to assume the role and, most importantly, provide clear and decisive direction. Back to the earlier point about the fact that sometimes leadership makes mistakes. It's far better to make a decision and risk being wrong than to do nothing and thereby fail to provide the direction the group needs.

Some people are naturally inclined to be decisive, while others have to learn how to form definitive direction for themselves and for others. Still others habitually snap out orders before thinking about what they are doing. (Granted, we said do something, even if it's wrong, but that doesn't mean that one should not be prudent.) While legitimate decision-making processes can vary, the important point is that someone must provide decisive direction, which includes clearly communicating that which has been decided.

Team Building

Just as the organized group needs decisive direction, it also needs to learn to work together as a unified force. Leadership's responsibility is to draw everyone together in common pursuits on behalf of the organization.

Team building is the name given in the contemporary business world to the way organizations go about mobilizing the group's efforts (though sometimes, formal teams are appointed for specific purposes). The notion is that people must work together, even though the organization has a designated hierarchy, for the organization to accomplish its mission.

If leadership does nothing to corral the group, people will "do their own thing." That thing can be a variety of activities that satisfy the individuals, which may have very little to do with satisfying the organization. People have very personal and sometimes very different reasons for working:

- Some want to be busy and will be perfectly content eking out whatever living they can make doing busywork.

- Some are building their résumés, and a job is but one of a number of entries that will be made.

- Others use the job as a means to an end, the most common being money.

- Some are looking for the satisfaction of contributing to the lives of others and see the organization or its consumers as a means to this end.

There are many more reasons people work. The point is that people work to satisfy personal needs. The organization, on the other hand, has goals (needs) that have to be satisfied as well. The charge for leadership is to muster the individuals into a unit that then works for the benefit of the organization.

Team building is grounded in the notion that by creating an environment that respects the worth of individuals and encourages their contributions, both the organization and the individual workers will benefit. Even if the motives are different, all can work toward similar ends and still gain satisfaction along the way.

Collective efforts, or teams, are evident in a number of places in the group. Peers within the group hierarchy, such as members of senior management, first-line supervisors, or members of the sales staff, often work together among themselves. Cross-hierarchy (boss and subordinate) partnerships form between supervisors and the people being supervised. In addition, representatives from all levels within the organization may be involved in projects for the institution's benefit.

When leadership engages people in (rather than isolating them from) the organization, this fosters commitment and thereby helps the collective unit work toward the goals of the organization. Working together also stimulates ideas, creativity, and initiative, another benefit for both the individual and the organization. In a real estate company comprised of an army of independent contractors, this is one of the best ways to elicit the cooperation of independent salespeople.

Delegation

With leadership also comes the responsibility of delegation. This is often one of the most difficult things to do because it involves trusting someone else to get a job done. Just as people must be able to trust the person in a leadership position, that person must be able to trust others as well.

The most important part of delegation is conferring *authority,* or the power, to command all aspects of the task that is to be performed. Authority includes the right to make certain commitments, use resources, and take other steps that are necessary to accomplish the work. Leadership must be able to trust the person to use that authority responsibly.

Delegation also tests the confidence level of the person in a leadership role. Confidence can be threatened by fear that prestige or importance in the organization will be diminished when others do a job or do it better. Delegation means stepping aside and letting others do the job and, often, then sharing credit for the accomplishment with those others.

Delegation is not a sign of weakness, but rather a way to get an enormous amount of work done in an efficient manner and help people feel good about themselves in the process. The tasks that are delegated have to be meaningful, though, or people will feel insulted. Delegation works when

- the right people are identified for the specific tasks. They must have the experience, knowledge, or skill to carry out the assigned task. They also must be willing to accept the responsibility and be accountable for the task's performance.

- the delegator lets go. People must be given the authority to perform a task without interference. Once the task is delegated, the person to whom it is assigned must be given the opportunity to decide how to do it and to get it done.

Often, experience is the best teacher for learning how to pick the right people and how to stay out of the way. But few mistakes are fatal. Leadership can also learn from others. Each person may approach a job differently; one way isn't necessarily the only right way. The point is that the assignment gets completed. Stepping into the process uninvited only diminishes the authority conferred on the person who was given the assignment.

■ SOCIAL AWARENESS

Leadership doesn't end with the responsibilities to one's own group or institution. Interestingly, the people who hold leadership positions in one organization also often have similar roles in others. Leadership becomes a lifestyle, in a sense. The qualities we respect in leaders are those that also foster passion and concern for the world beyond an organization.

Organizations themselves are part of a larger collective group, and each organization can affect another. Often, the organizations are dependent on one another for survival. The influence a leader can exert outside the organization benefits the community at large and also the environment in which his or her organization functions.

The term *environment* has several connotations. There are legal, political, and economic environments that affect an organization. A good example is the effect of government regulations on the real estate business and the rights of private property owners. Leadership involves becoming part of the solution, lending technical expertise to municipal and state governing bodies, zoning and planning commissions, and community development groups, rather than standing by while problems develop.

Environment also has ecological, biological, or natural resource connotations. Certainly, environmental regulations affect a company's internal operations (not the least of which is the way property managers must accommodate waste recycling regulations). But business organizations are also under pressure to become role models as protectors of the environment for the greater good as well.

Social awareness in the workplace has become one of the business community's top priorities in recent years. This comes about because of changing demographics in the workplace and heightened awareness of individual lifestyles. The outgrowth is flextime and childcare to accommodate working parents and adult caregivers, gay-friendly and femininity-friendly environments, zero tolerance for sexual harassment, and recognizing multicultural and multireligious systems to accommodate (and certainly not offend) the broad spectrum of today's population. Some companies have become role models in these regards.

Finally, leadership that is personally involved in the community guides an organization to act in similar fashion, that is, by giving back to the community with volunteer and/or financial support of community activities and social service projects. Image and reputation of the company are often measured by the organization's willingness to reach out for the public good. This is particularly important if the public perceives that an industry as a whole is self-serving.

■ CONCLUSION

Leaders have a powerful influence over a group or organization and its individual members. The responsible or irresponsible use of that power is a direct reflection of the character of the person who holds the position. People expect their leaders to meet the highest standards of integrity and trustworthiness and to use power fairly and justly. Those who do so are deemed worthy leaders. They succeed in their command when they take charge with decisive direction, draw people into collective efforts, delegate appropriately, and are willing to be accountable for their actions. As leaders inspire a following, they become role models. From this, new leaders emerge.

■ DISCUSSION EXERCISES

What have you learned about yourself as a potential leader? What do you think your greatest challenges will be?

Discuss past experiences in which you felt that your trust in another person was violated—in which you questioned another person's integrity.

How do you assess your ability to build a team? To delegate responsibility? To be decisive? Use a scale of one to five (five being highest) to rate yourself.

CHAPTER THREE

3

MANAGEMENT SKILLS

Think about people you've worked for . . . What do you admire most about the way they handled the job? What do you admire the least?

What are your strengths as a manager?

Using what you've learned about leadership in the previous chapter, now look more closely at the interpersonal role of a manager. This is really an exercise in managing the dynamics of human behavior. In order for leaders to influence that behavior in ways that benefit the organization, they need certain skills.

Managing human behavior cannot usually be done successfully based solely on gut instinct. Yet this is the way many people attempt to do it. Their models are parents, teachers, or previous managers, even if they don't particularly like the way these people treated them, because they know no other way. (This is one of the reasons why stifled workers tend to become dominating and controlling managers.) The purpose of this chapter's discussion is to show you the way.

■ MANAGEMENT STYLES

Management styles are essentially the various ways leadership provides direction and uses authority and the ways workers are expected to respond. There are significant philosophical differences about the role of management and workers in the various styles. At one extreme, workers are to be seen and not heard; at the other, workers are seen as a valued force in molding outcomes for an organization. The atmosphere in the workplace is also considerably different, depending on the style of management.

Although management styles are discussed below under tidy headings, the reality is that organizations typically embrace a philosophy that is either some individualized version of one style or a blend of styles, sometimes with one being predominant and others being used in selected situations. A manager of a department or an office could also have his or her own style, which may or may not be similar to the culture established by the organization's senior management.

By exploring the following, you can decide which philosophy best suits your view of the role of a manager and people in the workplace.

Dictatorial Style

This is the "I say, you do," Theory X style of management. Don't ask questions; don't offer suggestions. Toe the line or get out. The dictatorial manager has absolute and total control, no authority is delegated, and only orders are issued. Often, the dictatorial manager also micromanages the details of every task, thinking that people wouldn't know how to do it if left to their own devices.

In a dictatorial environment, the "dictator" speaks and people are expected to respond promptly and enthusiastically, without questioning the directives. Any inclination to offer suggestions or opinions or exercise initiative is viewed as an act of defiance. Faithful obedience is expected or undesirable consequences, or punishment, will result.

Obviously, this style of management creates an oppressive atmosphere and certainly is not the compassionate environment that contemporary management theorists espouse. While it may still exist in some workplaces, the dictatorial style of management was more prevalent before people realized that they could effectively influence others without trying to control them (back to the comment in the previous chapter's leadership discussion). A dictatorial environment, today, is more likely to prompt a "Who needs this?" reaction and chase people elsewhere to work.

Autocratic Style

Autocratic management is a more humanistic or benevolent approach than dictatorial management. The autocratic manager still dominates the scene, but in a less intimidating way. While the dictatorial manager gives orders, the autocratic manager gives direction, and by so doing, relieves people of the responsibility for self-direction so they can concentrate their efforts on their tasks. Workers acquiesce: "Just tell me what to do."

An autocratic organization is more respectful and a less threatening or adversarial environment than a dictatorial organization. Tasks are assigned with an eye for individual capabilities (the dictatorial manager does so without regard for a person's skill or limitations) so people feel more secure in their jobs, that they haven't been set up to fail.

Decision making in the autocratic environment clearly rests with management. As in the dictatorial environment, others are not invited to participate in the process, nor is any input solicited. The assumption in an autocratic environment is that management will make quality decisions because of its superior expertise and access to all the pertinent information. Furthermore, people's attention shouldn't be diverted from their jobs to think about things that management is responsible for.

Many people respond to autocratic management because it most closely resembles that which they as children, as students, or as workers in other organizations have known.

Participatory Style

Participatory management is the most democratic, humanistic style. This creates the job-rich environment that contemporary theorists favor. Management is still in charge, but in a more subtle way. The participatory manager prescribes the work outcomes and then people are expected to self-direct the way they will accomplish that work. The participatory manager delegates some amount of authority to the person responsible for doing a job.

A participatory environment values people and their individual skills and abilities. In other words, the individual is seen as a whole person, not just a worker or employee. Encouraging people to take initiative demonstrates respect for their talents and also provides an opportunity for them to learn and grow. The benefactor of all of this is the organization. The environment creates a sense of belonging, which also enhances commitment, and inspires (rather than controls) people to work toward the goals of the organization.

Decision making in a participatory environment is also different from that in the others. While managers still have ultimate authority, they encourage and even formally invite participation in problem solving or brainstorming sessions rather than making all decisions unilaterally. The assumption is that leadership can make better quality decisions by gathering input and creative ideas from a variety of sources. By giving people an opportunity to influence decision making, it is also assumed that they will cooperate in implementing the final decision.

The benefits of participatory decision making will be overshadowed, however, if people feel that leadership is not providing clear guidance or is unwilling to take responsibility for making decisions. People also will feel deceived if their input is invited and then later ignored. There ends their willingness to cooperate in implementing a decision or to participate in future decision-making processes. Participatory decision making (as opposed to unilateral) also takes more time. All of these issues need to be considered when formulating participatory processes so that they have beneficial outcomes for the organization.

Laissez-Faire Style

Laissez-faire management is really a contradiction in terms because it is essentially *non*management. Its predominant characteristic is nonintervention. The people who are the organization's designated leaders provide little, if any, guidance and exercise little of the decision-making authority that is customary in the position.

A laissez-faire environment is the epitome of a self-directed workplace. Either people will individually direct their own work or an unofficial leader will emerge to direct the group. While permitting this degree of initiative may be desirable for work groups that are involved in very specialized, technical, or innovative projects, as a general rule, the majority of organizations do not formally adopt a laissez-faire style of management.

More commonly, a laissez-faire environment evolves out of leadership's failure to do its job. Managers may succumb to this style of management when they have too many, or perhaps conflicting, roles (as in sales managers who also sell) or after they've lost control and see little hope of reestablishing their positions. (The independent contractors got too independent, so there's no hope of corralling them again.) Managers may also fear that they will make the wrong decisions or no longer be popular, so they leave people to their own devices, with the result being a chaotic environment and a department or an organization that is incapable of staying on course or meeting its goals.

A laissez-faire environment can also breed indifference. People tend to feel that if the manager doesn't care about what does or doesn't happen, why should anyone else? So they proceed to do their own thing, if they work at all, and being part of the team organization is no longer important. Eventually, the organization can languish into nonexistence.

■ MANAGING PEOPLE

A workplace is a collection of people who behave in various ways for various reasons. While management style reflects the official roles of management and the people being supervised and sets the tone for the workplace environment, an organization still must find ways to effectively manage human behavior so that the collective efforts of the group produce desired results.

Managing Behavior

Some suggest that management's primary job is managing human behavior. That as management does this job, all the other systems, procedures, and processes that institutions hold dear will fall into place.

Some noted behavioral scientists, among them Thomas Maslow, Douglas MacGregor, and Fredrick Herzberg, devoted considerable study to human behavior and motivation in the workplace. (Many writings about their findings are readily available in the marketplace.) The crux of their work is that as organizations gain greater understanding of human behavior, they can better manage their human resources. The outgrowth of this is a more humanistic, participatory environment that is prevalent in today's organizations.

The science of human behavior is a study all of its own, and is not the kind of professional background that the typical manager brings to the job. Trying to understand "what makes people tick" and then eliciting the desired behavior by appealing to their inner psyches isn't something an untrained person can do with any degree of certainty. The result is often faulty assumptions that result in unjust or inappropriate actions by a manager.

Managers are typically promoted to their positions because of their technical (as in real estate) or business expertise or their leadership ability. Few have the sophisticated backgrounds of people like Denis Waitly and Clifford Baird. What people need to successfully manage their offices, departments, or organizations is a practical way to manage human behavior.

A popular human resource management approach today, which is well described by Ferdinand Fournies in his book *Coaching for Improved Work Performance* (see the Bibliography), focuses solely on behavior, rather than trying to figure out the reasons people behave the way they do. Very simply, the process involves learning to observe behavior, learning to describe the behavior that is observed, and then doing things to elicit behavior that management considers desirable.

Assessing Behavior

A very basic, but somewhat profound, lesson about human behavior is this: *Behavior is a function of the alternatives one sees at the time.* It's really a very simple concept. A person sizes up a situation, comes up with alternatives about how to act, and then picks one, which is the behavior. The entire process could take only a second or two or it could take several minutes, hours, days, or weeks. Sometimes, it is a conscious and deliberate exercise; other times, it's an unconscious or reflex action.

If there's any fault in the behavior, it lies in the alternative gathering process. Emotions, motivations, and sundry other human elements play a role. It's a very rare mindset that consciously says "I want to look stupid today, so I'll do something stupid." It's far more likely that people don't take the time or don't have the wherewithal to properly assess a situation so that they can come up with suitable alternatives. Or they don't have the intellectual, emotional, or psychiatric facility to identify appropriate alternatives on which to act.

A bystander may see alternatives that would have resulted in a more desirable course of action. Even the person making the decision may have second thoughts about the choice after the heat of the moment has passed. Behavior is simply a matter of making choices.

From a manager's point of view, behavior falls into two categories: acceptable and unacceptable. Acceptable behavior is often taken for granted because that's what people are supposed to be doing anyway. So, managers look for the undesirable behavior, thinking that they aren't doing their jobs unless they take people to task for behaving in unacceptable ways. Yet, it's important to manage both the acceptable and unacceptable behavior.

Praising Behavior.   Certainly, the most desirable and pleasurable workplace is one in which people are doing the things they are supposed to be doing and not causing problems. The best way to keep people on that track is to reinforce desirable behavior. Behavior that is reinforced is behavior that is repeated. Reinforcement can be a kind word, a pat on the back, or some more formal kind of praise such as an award.

A manager who is long on criticism and short on praise falls into the same trap many parents do, that is, the assumption that acceptable behavior will endure simply out of a sense of "right." But people need to be told they're "doing right." People who feel starved for attention have learned, even as children, that the way to be noticed is to act out. Then more undesirable behavior gets more attention.

It's far better to set up a positive cycle that reaps more desirable behavior. Everyone does something worthy that merits attention. In real estate companies, the tendency is to place a lot of emphasis on production outcomes (sales and listings). But there are many other ways people contribute to the organization, the industry, and their own professional development that are worthy of recognition.

Two simple rules to keep in mind about praise: One is it must be *genuine*. Spouting words of praise for every move people make (especially if the manager has never been particularly effusive) sounds insincere. More harm than good is done unless genuinely praiseworthy behavior is acknowledged.

The other rule is to praise the *performance*, not the performer. In other words, look at the behavior separately from the person. The only job of a manager is to evaluate behavior that affects a person's work, not to judge the person and all the accompanying motivational, emotional, and character baggage. Even the person with most unpleasant baggage can do acceptable or desirable things.

Skeptics may say that this all sounds like mollycoddling, that work isn't supposed to be pleasurable or that management isn't supposed to help people feel good. This line of thinking says a lot about how people have been conditioned to approach the workplace. The fact is there's a whole lot of benefit and very little risk when managers make the effort to recognize the good people do, especially when the organization's interests are at stake.

Modifying Behavior. This is the part of behavior management that focuses attention on undesirable or unacceptable behavior. Certainly, managers would like it to stop or at least point out the errors of the ways lest they be repeated. While a manager would like to think that he or she could "correct" behavior, the fact is that the manager is not the one who can change it. Change has to come from within the person who demonstrated the unacceptable behavior.

The instinctive things people do when they are displeased won't alter someone else's behavior. Some people are just plain good at harping, criticizing every little move people make. Some have yelling, screaming, and shouting down pat, believing that the greater the emotion expressed, the more seriously people will be inclined to behave differently. Others expect that issuing orders will cause people to fall into line. Any of these actions is more likely to anger or frustrate people and cause them to turn a deaf ear, rather than to modify their behavior.

One rule to remember is to "pick your battles," so to speak. Not every missed step deserves attention. Eventually, people feel that it's an exercise in futility trying to please when they work in an environment of constant criticism. Some people are just easier to find fault with, often because of personality clashes.

The wiser course of action is to decide whether the consequences of the undesirable behavior are serious enough to warrant attention. If the achievements of the organization, the professional individual or other workers are in jeopardy, or there is significant legal or public relations risk, then intervention is in order.

Next, the manager needs to do things that cause the unacceptable behavior to change. This is a methodical process that begins with the manager clearly describing the behavior that is unacceptable (not attacking the person) and explaining the reasons why. The offender may not be aware of the manager's displeasure because a course of action seemed perfectly acceptable to the person. In other words, the person chose an alternative to act on; the manager saw a preferable one.

Once the unacceptable behavior is identified, then the two must agree on a plan of action that the person will undertake to change behavior or prevent such a transgression from occurring again. Finally, they must also have a plan to follow up to ensure that the corrective action takes place.

As described here, this is the schematic version of the process that will be demonstrated in greater detail in a later chapter. The purpose at the moment is to say that a deliberate rather than an instinctive approach on the part of the manager is a more effective way to manage behavior. Certainly, anyone can fly off the handle in the heat of the moment. But that flare does more for letting off steam than it does for changing behavior, at least for any longer than it takes to lash out.

Managing the Manager

While discussing human behavior, it's important not to overlook how a manager's behavior adds to the dynamics in the workplace.

Simply Being the Manager.   The official position of manager creates a class distinction, even if a subtle one, between the supervisor and the people being supervised. The very nature of this boss-and-subordinate hierarchy sets up group dynamics.

The class distinction becomes very apparent when the manager is supervising those who were once his or her peers, especially in the same organization. The salespeople, who previously saw the manager as "one of us," may feel that the person is worthy of the position and deserves their allegiance. Or they may feel that their peer has betrayed them by becoming "one of them," the management corps.

Gaining the cooperation of subordinates (and acceptance by the management corps as well) depends to a large degree on the way the manager approaches the position. Being boss is not a popularity contest, hence the manager cannot be apologetic about being in the position or the decisions that he or she makes. But the relationship does not have to be an adversarial one either. The person who is consumed by an exalted sense of self-importance or an inflated ego is less likely to command respect than the person who is modest and demonstrates a genuine respect for the position and the people being supervised.

Labeling. It's not uncommon for people to use a kind of shorthand to describe other people. This shorthand becomes a label, which typically identifies a dominant feature or characteristic of a person. Labels simply reflect the perceptions of the people assigning the labels.

Some people pride themselves on being able to "size people up," feeling that they have an innate ability to apply this shorthand accurately. That is not necessarily the case. A label may be an inaccurate characterization or it may not be the same label everyone would give a certain person. Nonetheless, a label becomes a moniker or "handle" that follows an individual everywhere he or she goes, including into the workplace.

Labeling is part of human nature, though that doesn't necessarily mean it does people any favors. Once labels are assigned, people tend to behave in ways that are consistent with the label. A "successful" label generally enhances self-esteem and causes a person to strive to live up to the reputation. A "loser" label typically causes a person to lose confidence or disengage, to feel that if no one thinks he or she is capable of anything better, then there's no point in trying. In effect, the poor soul has been labeled into failure.

For managers, the effect of a label is that they tend to manage the label rather than the person. The "successful" label can cause the manager to surrender responsibility for supervising, thinking that "successful" suggests that no oversight is necessary, or to overlook undesirable behavior that would not be tolerated in others. The "loser" label can cause the manager to give up on a person, regardless of that person's admirable qualities or abilities that could be nurtured. Or the manager may be more critical of behavior, even if the criticism isn't justified.

The managing-the-manager part of this discussion says that managers can ill afford to slight a person in favor of a label. No one person can be so neatly or accurately categorized as a label suggests. People expect leadership to respect their individual talents and to treat them fairly and justly. As in the examples above, inconsistent oversight or intolerance of behavior or an appearance of favoritism adds to the dynamics in the workplace that only make management's job more difficult.

Diversity and Prejudice.   Everyone has different personalities, talents, styles, and physical and cultural characteristics. The diversity of all of this is what makes people interesting and adds a useful dimension to the workplace.

Today's workplace is reflective of today's population. The white population declined from 76 percent in 1980 to 69 percent in 2000, and Latinos now equal or exceed the number of African Americans in this country. An increasing number of people are multiracial, blends of race and ethnicity, and more people with disabilities are able to be active, productive workers. The workforce is also aging, a large number of whom will be retiring from full-time employment within the next ten years.

The managing-the-manager part of this discussion comes quickly by saying two things. One is that the manager is very likely to be supervising a person whose profile is different from his or her own. This requires learning appropriate behaviors from both a cultural and a legal perspective to properly supervise persons of differing age, race, color, ethnicity, or gender. Simply the difference in age between the manager and the person being supervised can create a culture clash, particularly if the two are several generations apart.

The second point is that the manager supervises a workplace group that is its own melting pot, in a sense. This diversity can cause people's underlying stereotypes and prejudices to surface or personalities to clash. While it's unlikely that the assembled collection of personalities will be so simpatico that everyone will become best friends, people certainly deserve an accepting and respectful environment in which to work.

The responsibility for creating that environment falls squarely in the hands of the manager. The job begins with the manager's becoming aware of and then setting aside his or her personal stereotypes or prejudices. Just as a manager must guard against labels, the manager needs to see people as something other than tall or short, fat or skinny, male or female, white or black, Hispanic or Asian, Christian, Jewish, or Muslim, physically challenged . . . any of the characteristics that may have influenced preconceived notions about people.

Dissension in the workplace can easily arise if the manager is perceived as being more concerned about or less attentive to, or more tolerant or more critical of, some people than others because of their physical, cultural, religious, or ethnic characteristics. Not only is this unfair but in many cases it also is illegal. Everyone deserves the manager's management in ways that are solely related to job performance. As the manager embraces diversity, others in the group have a model to follow as well.

Life's Unpleasant Little Tricks.   People are rarely able to put things that are happening in their lives into separate compartments. Personal lives spill over into the workplace and vice versa. When all is going well in one sector of a person's life, that often carries over into others. The not-so-well can be dragged along too.

In addition to all the other aspects of human behavior and personalities that are part of the assembled group, the workplace is a collection of differing degrees of pleasure, disappointment, stress, anger, sadness, even grief and major trauma. This is not to say that management has to become the group's therapist or psychologist. But management does need to be empathic to the dynamics that life's little tricks add to the workplace.

The managing-the-manager part of this scene says that the manager has to guard against allowing developments in his or her own life to complicate the group dynamics. Managers are always on stage, so to speak. Because they wield a lot of power over the lives of others, people are ever watchful of a manager's words and actions, the indications of acceptance or rejection, approval or disapproval.

People tend to associate the manager's behavior toward them with something *they've* done rather than with something that may be going on in the manager's life. The grumbled, quick "hello" as the manager heads back to his or her office can easily be interpreted as criticism or rejection rather than what it really means, that the manager is having a disastrous morning. A simple explanation can prevent erroneous conclusions, the "don't take it personally" kind of words that keep the air clear.

Stress.   A number of studies cite real estate sales as one of the most stressful occupations. It's no wonder that real estate offices are charged with high energy, high emotion, and perhaps short fuses. Certainly, the financial pressures that drive today's companies to work harder to stay afloat cannot be ignored. But companies can reach a point of diminishing returns when the health and well-being of the workforce is jeopardized.

There's more to life than work. People must make time for play and time for solitude, the battery-charging time that helps us be better people in all sectors of our lives. Unfortunately, there are those who feel that unless people are working at breakneck speed, they are somehow less devoted to their careers or the company.

It's no small task playing all the roles that are expected of a manager. Being thrust into a position of authority, being accountable to the organization and superiors, and supervising subordinates only makes the job that much more stressful. Carrying this load with calm good humor and personally benefiting from the experience, while not making the job more difficult, requires some self-discipline.

The manager can become a role model (and protect his or her own well-being in the process) by setting realistic expectations about that which is humanly possible to accomplish, establishing priorities, and adopting good time-management skills. The end result is minimized stress. Interestingly, one of the hottest topics in workplace training today is stress management.

By helping people to reprogram attitudes and develop healthy lifestyles, everyone, including the company, benefits.

■ ASSUMING THE POSITION

Throughout the discussions about the environment and behavior in the workplace, the constant theme is the pivotal role the manager plays in the dynamics of the workplace. The fitting final discussion is to look at how a person steps into that role. Even those who have already taken this step can learn more about being a manager as we look at some of the challenges people face when assuming management positions.

The common strategy of promoting the best technicians into managerial roles is also prevalent in the real estate industry. The good salespeople are often elevated to management. Some may have long aspired to manage an office or own a brokerage company, and being a salesperson was just the first step in a carefully developed career plan. Others may have fallen into the role because a new opportunity suddenly presented itself.

Few people arrive in these positions with the necessary management skills or even realistic expectations about the job that needs to be done. When a person becomes part of the management corps within the same organization where he or she has been a salesperson, this adds to the transition challenges.

Technical Role

In addition to the interpersonal role of a manager, which has been the focus of the chapter's discussion, a manager has a technical role. For this role, a manager needs the specific knowledge and skill that relates to the product or service that is the organization's business. Proficient real estate salespeople come into management presumably already equipped with good transaction-based (technical) skills.

Credibility as a worthy manager is threatened if the salespeople know more about the technical aspects of real estate than the manager does. While this is not an incurable condition, it says two things: One is that in order for a manager to be the technical resource that people can rely on, the manager needs to be on top of the latest industry developments and legal issues. The other is that the salespeople may, indeed, have more knowledge and better transaction skills than the manager (that's their daily job). A manager can preserve credibility by demonstrating respect for that superior talent and can also learn from it.

Perhaps one of the most challenging parts about having been a proficient salesperson who then winds up in management is changing hats from being the "doer" to being the supervisor. Sometimes, it seems easier and quicker to just take over a transaction rather than trying to tell someone else what to do and then waiting on the sidelines until that happens. Yet, being the doer is not the manager's job. Everything discussed about creating a favorable workplace environment is undone if a manager is unable to trust people to do the jobs for which they have been hired.

Business Management Role

It's not uncommon for people to speculate about ways their superiors should be running the company differently. The newly appointed manager or new business owner can be in for a rude awakening, though, because as workers in the trenches they rarely see (nor is it their job to be concerned with) the inner workings of an organization and the multitude of issues that affect its profitability.

The collective efforts of the members of the organization must be guided in ways that achieve profitability for the company. This is the essence of the business management role of a newly appointed manager or business owner. The manner in which the manager influences human behavior to this end is the interpersonal role of a manager. The bottom-line purpose of this role, however, is the bottom line.

Business management involves planning and setting goals for the organization, its departments and sales units or offices; developing structures and systems that help the organization function effectively and efficiently; and monitoring and coaching the personnel and systems within the organization so that the goals are achieved. Depending on the culture of an organization, these efforts are to some greater or lesser degree focused on dollars and cents.

The harsh reality for a newly appointed manager or new business owner is the real world of those dollars and cents. Today's cost of doing business, especially the sizable investment in technology that is needed to be competitive, creates enormous financial pressures. Small businesses are most likely to fail in their first three years of operation, primarily because of lack of planning, undercapitalization, unrealistic expectations of a company's success in its early years, or the owner's lack of experience in running a business. Established companies face similar challenges from time to time as well.

Successfully transitioning into management or ownership requires not only good business management skill but also some realistic expectations about the personal implications of the move. Being the owner is not necessarily more lucrative than sharing sales commissions with a broker, considering the above discussion. Buying or starting up a business is most successful when done by those who are sincerely committed to becoming astute, entrepreneurial business owners.

Sales Management Role

The business management function of a sales manager is smaller in scope than it is for individuals in senior management or company ownership positions. Customarily, sales managers are responsible for the activities of their sales units or offices, functioning as first-line supervisors or middle managers in the organizational structure.

The transition from salesperson to sales manager presents new financial and perhaps time-management challenges. Compensation for sales managers has been a bone of contention within a number of organizations for years. In some cases, the sales manager takes a pay cut (earns less than he or she could as a salesperson) for the benefit of gaining added responsibility and a position of influence within the organization. To offset the financial hit, sales managers may also have to sell or be engaged in other income-producing activities so they can maintain the lifestyle to which they have become accustomed.

The purists would say that the only way for a manager to be effective is to devote 100 percent of his or her time to management responsibilities. Others argue, often when the sales staff is small, that it *is* possible to both manage and sell (or provide other professional services). The amount of time devoted to either activity can vary considerably, and in some cases, management runs a distant second to sales activities. In some companies, managers who do not, as a routine, also sell are encouraged to do so once in a while just to stay in touch with the marketplace.

Being a full-time manager has its advantages. The job responsibilities are very clear: supervise the activities of the salespeople, coach them through their problems, and help them reach their production goals. Because the manager is not also trying to sell, he or she can devote full attention to these responsibilities. Furthermore, the manager is not viewed as a competitor with the salespeople.

Blending management and real estate activities successfully is more challenging. In addition to criticism that managers are too busy with personal sales activities to devote time to their salespeople and the possible resentment that managers grab the best leads to fuel their own business, managers can find themselves in an untenable time-management tug-of-war. Managing and selling are separate and very demanding jobs in their own rights. The manager must learn to do both well and also preserve his or her sanity and personal life in the process.

- *Prioritize responsibilities.* The manager's sales and management priorities are typically defined by the organization, that is, whether one job is primary and the other is a secondary assignment or whether each has equal priority. Unless the priorities have been clearly stated and the manager and his or her broker or supervisor are on the same page, conflicting expectations and ultimately disappointing performance outcomes will result.

- *Determine the amount of time and effort that must be devoted to each role.* While it might seem like a statement of the obvious, that time and effort should be aligned with priorities, there's more to the time-management challenge than first appears. Administrative, supervisory, and problem-solving tasks can take up considerable time, even if those responsibilities are supposed to be secondary to the sales job. With experience, these responsibilities can be discharged efficiently and effectively. For new managers, however, unfamiliar tasks may seem overwhelming and often may be left to slide in favor of the more familiar (sales) activities. The caveat here is that the manager's ultimate effectiveness can be threatened if the management role is not firmly established at the outset.

■ *Prepare contingency plans.* Issues will likely arise that demand the manager's attention on both the management and sales fronts simultaneously. Salespeople count on the manager being available to help when the brushfires flare in their transactions, but that can't happen if the manager is out stroking his or her own sale. For the benefit of all concerned, a backup plan is in order so that someone is available to help either the salespeople's or the manager's transactions move forward.

■ *Protect harmony in the office.* Perhaps the most challenging issue to manage is the competition between selling managers and the salespeople. One way managers can minimize this is by restricting their sales activities to previous customers and personal referrals rather than taking leads from the office. In some companies, managers avoid sales entirely and engage in other real estate activities, such as leasing or property management.

■ *Maximize the use of technology.* One of a manager's biggest allies is technology. The mobility of today's workforce because of pagers, e-mail, cell phones, and portable computer networks can also work to the manager's benefit. Multiple tasks can be performed far more efficiently from any location and with less stress, thanks to technology.

Professional Credentials

The ability of a newly appointed manager to establish credibility and successfully perform all of the roles that are expected of a manager is directly related to the professional credentials the person brings to the job. It's difficult to feel confident in the position without the necessary tools, and it's difficult to establish credibility when people are unsure of their leader's competency.

The manager's technical role can be supported by the expertise and training gained as a licensed salesperson. Because most state license laws require that brokers, and in some cases sales managers, satisfy advanced real estate licensing requirements, this is typically the case. However, the manager cannot rely solely on the knowledge and skill gained as a salesperson. A manager can quickly look like a dinosaur (and lose credibility in the process) in today's rapidly changing environment unless he or she continues to pursue technical education.

For state licensing and continuing education information, consult the *Digest of Real Estate License Laws—United States and Canada* published by the Association of Real Estate License Law Officials (ARELLO).

Unless the newly appointed manager has collegiate training in management or corporate experience, the business management role is one that he or she is typically least prepared to handle. The fact that you are sitting with this book in hand suggests that you're engaged in a brokerage management course of study. A general business management course of study, one that does not focus exclusively on the real estate industry, also provides valuable insight into running a business. In addition, many seminars and training programs are available in the marketplace to help develop management skills.

Personal growth and development and leadership training can be gained from seminars and the many fine publications written by today's noted authors, some of which are listed in the Bibliography. In short, a wide variety of resources are available for exploring visionary ideas in the general business world and the real estate industry.

■ CONCLUSION

With a keen understanding of the human dynamics in the workplace and sharp interpersonal and business management skills, a manager can successfully direct the company's human resources. The style of management, be it dictatorial, autocratic, participatory, or laissez-faire, or a variation on any of those themes, sets the tone for the environment in which people work. That environment is also a melting pot of individuals and behaviors, including the manager's, that need to be guided in constructive ways so that the workplace supports desirable outcomes for the organization. Management is really a people business, and the way a manager conducts this business reflects the individual's personality.

■ DISCUSSION EXERCISES

Discuss the management style that most closely approximates your instinctive style. What is most constructive about your approach? What is most destructive? How would you revise your style based on what you've learned?

What tendencies do you have that work for or against you as a manager?

What have you learned about approaching the behavior of your salespeople? Consider typical scenarios or problems in an office and ways to handle them.

CHAPTER FOUR

COMMUNICATIONS AND DECISION MAKING

What is the best way for people to get your attention and give you information? Talk to you? Send you an e-mail? Write you a memo or a report? Give you a Web site address?

And what do you do with all the information that is swirling around you?

Among the many roles a manager plays are the informational and decision-making roles. The interpersonal role that has been explored in the previous two chapters is interrelated with these roles, in that effective interpersonal skills aid in the processes of gathering and disseminating information effectively, which is the essence of communications.

Managers are vital information links with others in the organization, acting as gatherers and distributors with both superiors and subordinates. Some say that through the manager flows all information that is crucial to the existence of the organization. Because one of management's functions is to monitor performance and correct deviations as necessary, information is necessary to identify what, if any, action is needed to maintain, enhance, or alter the organization's activities.

Action comes in the form of decisions. Sometimes the decision is essentially an informed conclusion that all is well and that no demonstrative action is needed. Other times, the decision is indeed a specific response on the part of management. Some decisions are more monumental or more deliberately made than others, but once made, any decision must be communicated in ways that provide clear and decisive direction.

■ THE INFORMATIONAL WORKPLACE

Today's workplace is consumed, some would say overburdened, with information and paper. While some people suggested that computers would give us paperless offices, there seems to be no limit to the number of words, facts and figures, and glorious documents that abound, often committing to paper that which also resides on hard drives and disks.

E-mail, alone, has cost hundreds of manpower hours, while people sort through the endless words, comical thoughts, and advertisements that would otherwise have been delegated to someone else to handle or quickly tossed in the wastebasket. Processing e-mail is often reported as taking twice (or more) the amount of time that workers previously devoted to postal mail.

Perhaps this observation about e-mail tells the first lesson about today's workplace. Important information can easily get lost in the shuffle. This impedes both the process of gathering information that is necessary to do one's job and the process of distributing information that is critical to others. Another dimension to this is the fact that a piece of information doesn't have the same relevance or importance to everyone. A thought or fact that one person feels is especially significant or urgent may not be received in the same spirit by another, if it's noticed at all.

Volumes of information cycle through the spoken and written word and body language, the nonverbal expressions and mannerisms that people use. Separating that which is inconsequential or faulty from information that is crucial or accurate is the challenge of good communications. Sometimes the communications accurately reflect the intended message, and other times they set up a cycle of misunderstanding. All of this depends on the substance, the forum or atmosphere, and the method by which information is exchanged.

Gathering Information

Effective managers actively seek information, be it a fact, a feeling, or an idea. They are also receptive to the input or insight of others, even if it was unsolicited. Sometimes the most valuable information is that which the manager overlooked, including that offered by subordinates.

The challenge is to learn to gather as much information as possible and then process it efficiently so that the truly relevant rises to the top quickly. Subordinates are not the only ones in the organization who fail to notice the critical or monumental messages in the mass of words and paper. The reports, statistics, or personnel and transaction problems that are uppermost in the manager's mind get noticed, but there may be concerns subordinates have that management really needs to notice.

First, let's concentrate on the gathering process, beginning with the manager's powers of observation. Simply watching the people in the workplace provides clues about whether the organization's systems are functioning well or problems are brewing that deserve attention. Not just people's activities but their body language, especially in one-on-one conversations or group meetings, often tell far more about what they are thinking than their words do.

Learning to truly listen to what people are saying provides information that often goes unnoticed. Everyone's had the "I told you" experience at some time. Whether the fault is the ineptness of the sender of the message, the unwillingness of the receiver, or the distractions that surround the exchange, the fact is that somewhere along the line what one person thought was said didn't reach the ear or mind of the other person.

This syndrome isn't limited to the spoken word. Written words get lost, whether by virtue of a lost piece of paper or one that got buried or discarded because it appeared to be unimportant or low priority. This is the "I sent you that" experience that everyone has also had. Valuable ideas, critical requests, and time-sensitive data fail to reach the desired recipient, often because a piece of paper didn't catch the person's eye.

The more subtle messages are those that are communicated between the lines. People may intentionally nibble around a point with circuitous words to soften the blow. Or they might unintentionally impart a message, simply because of carelessly or hastily chosen words. Not to pick on e-mail again, but because it is an easy and expedient way to communicate, people often click-and-send without polishing the words. Any message, regardless of import, can set up a firestorm of unexpected reaction if it is carelessly worded or fails to clearly express the intended message.

The point of all this is that a manager needs to take responsibility for gathering accurate, timely, and relevant information. By sharpening observation and listening skills and making judicious requests for reports (meaningful quality rather than unnecessary quantity), managers can gain the facts, figures, and feelings that are necessary to properly monitor activities and make decisions.

Disseminating Information

Managers distribute copious amounts of information to their superiors and subordinates and do so in the same ways they gather it, that being through nonverbal and verbal communications. Whether they succeed in disseminating information that is accurate, timely, and relevant depends on their ability to overcome the same communications problems that cause the gathering process to go astray.

Several of those conditions are particularly relevant in the context of the dissemination exercise. One is just that: relevance. Managers are often inclined to issue endless, sometimes repetitious, directives and requests for status reports or feedback. While all these words may seem important to the manager, they can seem like little more than annoying clutter to others. People are far more likely to pay attention when they don't feel like this is a story they've heard before or when the story has an urgent or important meaning.

Just as managers need to gather accurate information, they need to distribute information accurately. In other words, tell people what they need to know or to do in ways that leave no question about what is meant.

Particularly in the case of a potentially unpopular or inflammatory piece of information, the tendency is to sugarcoat or bury the point to avoid unpleasantness. The result is confusion and perhaps more controversy than would otherwise have occurred with a clearer, more precise message.

One of the reasons organizations stray is because management doesn't react or respond effectively, and often that occurs because managers fail to share information or to share it in a timely manner. A manager can be a conduit, a filter, or a dam for information. Certainly, the conduit is preferable to the filter that shares only bits or pieces or the dam that shares nothing of the bad news. Problems aren't likely to go away, so best to share the tale before a small problem becomes a major one. Not only does this demonstrate that the manager is a diligent supervisor but the organization can avert potential disasters with timely intervention.

■ PICK YOUR FORUM

Most likely, everyone has sat through a meeting that seemed pointless or a waste of time, when the substance of the meeting could have easily been handled in a memo. Also likely are the memos in which management dropped some bombs that should have been explained face-to-face, rather than hiding behind a piece of paper. As the gatherer or disseminator of information, the manager is responsible for deciding on the forum that best suits the occasion.

Say It Face to Face   Personal matters need to be handled personally, one on one. Individual goal-setting exercises and performance reviews deserve the exclusive attention of the manager with the person involved. Performance problems or disciplinary issues should also be handled privately, rather than subjecting an individual to the manager's displeasure in front of others. While it takes more time to meet with people individually, far better quality and quantity of information can be exchanged in a singularly focused, distraction-free setting.

One-on-one conversations are also useful for unveiling certain management decisions. While group forums are usually preferable for this purpose, there are times when the manager may take a selected person aside to test reaction or gain insight about a considered decision before it is formalized. One-on-one discussions also provide opportunity to achieve buy-in (cooperation) or resolve objections to a management directive.

There are also times when a management decision affects only certain people. They need to be told individually rather than blindsided in a group meeting.

Put It in Writing

The printed word is an expedient way to distribute industry and company news, updates, reports, and housekeeping-type announcements and makes a stronger and longer-lasting impression than the spoken word. A meeting date is more likely to be remembered from a printed announcement, and lengthy or detailed information is more useful when people have a document to study. A printed document is also available for future reference.

Internal memos, newsletters, reports, or e-mails are one-sided communications. That is, they serve the purpose of simply sending information. When no immediate feedback is required, there is no need to waste one-on-one or group meeting time with facts, figures, and announcements that people can read on their own. People also do not appreciate being "read to," hence the meeting (or classroom, for that matter) in which someone reads page after page of script serves little purpose, other than to bore people.

Even though a printed document is a one-sided communication on the part of the person who prepares it, that is no excuse to merely send words. The reader needs to see the importance of or purpose for the words. People tend to ignore memos, letters, and the like because of past experiences with useless ones. People have also become very discriminating, essentially prioritizing their information gathering on a must, need-to, and would-be-nice-to know basis to insulate themselves from information overload. If a writing intends to prompt a response or provide study material for an upcoming meeting, the writer needs to get that document to the top of a reader's priority list.

A written communication must catch the eye with a distinctive look and an attention-getting headline. To hook the mind, consider, "If someone only skims my writing, will they get the point of my message?" Most people today won't bother wading through a lot of background or historical information. Letters and memos, the most common forms of business writings, must be compelling and to the point. There are many fine publications available in the marketplace to help develop well-organized and effective business writings.

Because the printed word memorializes information, it's best to think about how deleterious it might be if someone other than the intended recipient sees the words. Once sent, the writer can't control how and to whom a memo, report, or announcement will circulate, especially with today's e-mail and fax technology. Ill-chosen words can also come back to haunt the writer. Hence a caveat about making flip, comical, critical, or discriminatory remarks, even in the most informal e-mails.

Hold a Meeting

Aside from the obvious benefit of being able to share information with a number of people at the same time, meetings give the manager control over the way the substance is delivered and provide the opportunity for feedback and discussion. Feedback comes not only in words but also in the nonverbal signals that provide clues about people's reactions to the subject at hand. All of this is missing when information is distributed in writing. Meetings can easily fail to deliver these benefits, however.

First of all, the manager needs to successfully assemble the group. This may be easier said than done, especially after the manager's meetings gain the reputation as being time-wasting exercises. A meeting must have a clearly defined purpose. Just because it's a weekly or monthly ritual, *don't* hold a meeting if there's no meaningful reason for it. Some managers say that there's always something useful that can be accomplished, even if it's social camaraderie. But the people who are expected to attend need to be sold on the benefits (like risk reduction) or there's still no reason to meet from their point of view.

There's more to the relevance of the meeting than simply defining a worthwhile objective. The meeting needs to be held with the proper audience. (If the subject at hand applies to only a few people, then others should not have to attend.) Audiences also need to feel that there has been ample opportunity for them to express their viewpoints or get answers to their questions. An atmosphere that stifles this exchange does little to help people relate to the subject matter.

Holding a meeting is somewhat like getting people to read a memo. Once the manager gets people to the meeting (like getting people to notice the memo), then it's a matter of holding their attention (like getting them to read through the memo). The manager needs to take charge, begin the meeting at the stated time, get to the subject matter quickly, and proceed through an orderly, well-thought-out agenda. Meetings can easily fall flat when they haven't been planned well ahead of time, including interesting presentation materials and handouts.

When the manager gets the reputation for starting late, people learn that there's little reason to arrive on time. There's even less point in being present for opening remarks if the manager typically backs up and repeats the comments for the benefit of late arrivals. And no one needs to listen to a sermon about attendance and punctuality, especially when the people who should hear the sermon aren't there to listen to it, anyway.

A fairly common practice is to publicize an agenda ahead of time and perhaps distribute materials that participants are expected to review for the meeting. Advance notice intends to inspire attendance (the benefit-selling exercise) and help people get into the proper mindset for the planned discussions so that the meeting can proceed efficiently. This also forces the manager to do the necessary advance planning. However, advance notice also gives people an opportunity to decide on the relative merits of attending or to arm themselves with ammunition, some of which will help the agenda.

However, the manager may not be the only one who has an agenda. A disgruntled person (or a clique of them) may seize the opportunity to air a complaint, feeling it's safer to do so in front of a group rather than one-on-one with the manager, especially if there's support from others who have similar views. Meetings can also be disrupted by attention-seeking egos or someone who decides to lead a band of resistance to an issue that is the subject of the meeting.

A meeting is the manager's platform. By anticipating objections and preparing to politely, but firmly, handle problem personalities, the manager can keep control and minimize the possibility of alienating people in the process. Even when the meeting is intended to be a free-flowing exchange of ideas (a minimally structured agenda), the manager needs to keep the conversation on track. And when time is up, it's time to end the meeting. Future attendance depends on a timely ending as much as it does on a timely beginning.

Speaking in Public

Several comments about public speaking are suitable at this point because there are a lot of similarities between successfully handling public speaking engagements and conducting good business meetings. Furthermore, simply being in a management position often means there will be invitations to address groups outside the organization.

Regardless of where the manager is on stage, be it a weekly sales meeting, a training program, or a local REALTOR® or Rotary luncheon, the platform is easier for some people to step onto than for others. Some may even feel the butterflies circling in the pit of the stomach at the mere suggestion of speaking before a group. Nevertheless, the platform comes with the job, and there are ways people can learn to become effective on that platform. In addition to the following suggestions, there are some fine organizations, like Toastmasters International, to help sharpen public speaking skills.

The key to effectiveness in front of a group is good planning. Even sales meetings deserve more preparation than a panicked hour before the scheduled 9 A.M. meeting, trying to decide what to do. Just as the purpose of a meeting must be clearly defined, so, too, must the message be defined, organized, and even rehearsed in some respect so that the speaker can deliver the substance and handle the group dynamics with confidence.

Picking the right topic, especially when speaking to a general audience, isn't always easy because people have a variety of different interests and motivations for attending an event. One of the major pitfalls is thinking that a topic is something people need to hear, but what the speaker and the audience think are necessary may be two distinctly different things. It's best to consider the profile and interests of the audience when planning a presentation.

While everyone who addresses a group would like to feel accepted, that doesn't mean that thought-provoking or possibly controversial messages have to be avoided. The point of the exercise is to make a difference in some way in the lives of those who came to listen. Sometimes, challenging their thinking or comfort levels is a good thing.

The message, regardless of whether it's a 15-minute speech or a three-hour business or training session, generally flows by:

1. Telling people what you're going to say;

2. Telling them your tale; and then,

3. Telling them what you told them.

The first step is the introduction, the "hook" that captures people's attention and provides the objective of and rationale for the program. This also helps to focus everyone's minds (including the speaker's) on the agenda and minimizes the tendency to consume time with idle chatter and announcements. The second step is to get on with the substantive content, which is about 80 percent of the time allotted. The last step is a conclusion or summary, the "close" that, depending on the nature of the program, may be a brief statement or a more detailed wrap-up of the major issues that were discussed.

A carefully developed message deserves a thoughtful delivery plan. Simple things, like where the speaker will stand, how the room will be arranged, and what media will be used (overhead projectors, PowerPoint presentations, and sound systems) are items that can make or break a program and should be prescreened ahead of time. The importance of technology cannot be understated. That said, there's nothing so unnerving as to show up with an entirely media-dependent presentation that won't work, so a "Plan B" for this eventuality isn't a bad idea, either.

Certainly, the delivery plan will be different, depending on the occasion. A classroom or training session or small office meeting can be less formal and easier to foster group interaction than a more formal luncheon speech or a keynote address, especially when the speaker is confined to a stage or behind a podium. But regardless of the setting, good public speakers learn to use their personality and eye contact to communicate over and around the barriers of podiums and overhead projectors.

The notion of rehearsing a presentation may sound foolish. But even 15 minutes in the limelight deserve a run-through; if not a thorough rehearsal (in front of a mirror with attention to gestures, inflection, eye contact, and the like), then at least a few quiet moments of mental preparation. The point is to test drive the presentation so the speaker can deliver a powerful, interesting message. Boring or haphazard presentations don't help the cause or the speaker's reputation. No wonder people leave after lunch is served, before the speaker begins, or don't look forward to the next business meeting.

It's also advisable to consider ahead of time how audience questions and comments will be handled. Some speakers are able to control the presentation while dealing with these along the way; others prefer to handle audience input at the conclusion. To avoid the feeling of being "talked at," the audience must be given the opportunity to interact with the speaker in some fashion. It's also important to ensure that the message has been interpreted correctly, so it's important to resolve any confusion before people leave.

Because the speaker is in charge of the program, no one else knows whether it's going according to plan. With experience, speakers learn to "go with the flow," think on their feet, and, if they make a mistake, acknowledge it in good humor and move on without damaging their credibility. Sometimes, the best programs evolve as the speaker reads the audience and tailors the planned presentation to suit the moment, though inexperienced presenters are not likely (nor is it recommended) to attempt this.

Speaking of humor, it's best to choose humor wisely. It must fit the speaker's style, personality, and, certainly, the nature of the subject matter. Some people are good at telling jokes while others are better at telling light-hearted tales or using humorous examples to make a point. The caveat, however, is that humor can easily be misinterpreted, so that which seems appropriate to the speaker may be offensive to others.

■ DECISION MAKING

Once information is gathered and shared with the appropriate people, management needs to decide what to do with it. The decisions that management makes fall into four general categories.

1. *Entrepreneurial or institutional decisions:* These involve significant strategic directions, policies, or fundamental systems within the organization.

2. *Corrective decisions:* These resolve problems, dilemmas, or crises that require solutions to keep the organization on track or to maintain order in its systems and processes.

3. *Resource decisions:* These involve the allocation of personnel or money.

4. *Mediation decisions:* These are essentially negotiated solutions, primarily involving personnel issues and customer service.

Decision-making processes vary. One process is very deliberate and methodical, analyzing situations and evaluating a wide range of options before deciding on a course of action. Another is equally analytical but goes through this process more quickly. Some focus on the long-range implications when making short-range decisions; others focus on the immediacy and are less concerned about the long-term entanglements.

Different modes of decision making are appropriate in different situations. Therein lies another aspect of decisions: deciding when a quick versus more deliberate process is appropriate or even when *not* to interfere (back to management picking its battles).

Sometimes, people get frustrated with management, a case of violated expectations, in a sense. People expect direction, yet none is forthcoming or is too slow in coming. Or people expect a more studied course of action, yet they get what appears to be a quick fix. People who are inclined to be quick decision makers are put off when others have chosen a more deliberate approach and vice versa. When leadership has made a conscious decision to do nothing, others may feel that leadership has abdicated its responsibility.

The communications part of the decision-making process involves telling people what management has decided in ways that leave no doubt or ambiguity about what is meant. While some may suggest that leadership does not owe explanations, the fact is that a thoughtful rationale goes a long way in gaining cooperation. Even if management has decided that no action is warranted, people deserve an explanation to that effect.

Cooperation is key, since no decision is worth the time and effort if it is not implemented. Therein lies one of the major failings in organizations: the lack of follow-through to ensure that the organization's policies, procedures, and systems are suitably aligned to support implementation of the new directives.

Classic Decision Making

Classic decision making is a deliberate, methodical process. It is somewhat like a scientific model, involving a set of very rational or logical steps:

1. *Define the situation*—clearly describe the problem or circumstance and the cause or causes.

2. *Develop alternatives*—list all the possible courses of action to solve the problem or address the situation.

3. *Evaluate alternatives*—consider the pluses and minuses, feasibility, short- and/or long-term ramifications, and the perceived acceptance of each option.

4. *Select the appropriate alternative*—decide on the most desirable course of action, which then becomes the decision.

5. *Implement the decision*—inform the appropriate people about the decision and institute any necessary changes in policies, procedures, or systems that are affected by the decision.

6. *Follow through*—monitor the implementation of the decision to ensure that the new directive has been institutionalized.

7. *Evaluate the outcome*—decide whether the decision produced the desired results. Did it do what it was supposed to do? Address the situation or correct the problem? If the wrong alternative was chosen or the implementation was faulty, take corrective action.

Used in its purest form, classic decision making is a formal process that is undertaken by an individual manager, a team of managers, or even a cross section of individuals from the organization when the defined situation significantly affects major policies, procedures, and systems within the organization. Deliberating through each of the steps is a thorough exercise that intends to produce the most carefully considered decision, with all possible implications being contemplated so that the decision has the greatest chance of addressing the situation and being implemented successfully.

The classic model is also the mode of decision making that is inherently customary for some managers, even to the extent that they can mentally run through the same series of steps and come up with a viable decision in a relatively short time frame. Some variation on the theme of the model may be constructed to accommodate the nature of the situation, available response time, importance of short-term versus long-term implications of the alternatives, and the like.

Variables in Decision Making

Regardless of whether the classic model is used or the manager must make a spur-of-the-moment decision, the quality of the decision is tied to several variables.

First is the information. A decision is only as good as the quality of the information on which it is based. A situation or an alternative may not be what it appears to be if the information comes from an emotional or biased observation, cooked books, or months-old production reports. The classic model presumes the information is complete, accurate, and timely and that there is sufficient time to gather information and to do so from a variety of sources so that diverse viewpoints, analyses, and even data sources can be considered. While quick decisions don't necessarily fail on the information front, they certainly can be more vulnerable.

Another variable is the business or technical expertise of the decision makers. The classic model presumes they have sufficient skill and professional insight to properly define the situation and generate and evaluate alternatives. This is not to say that they need to come up with perfect solutions, but the quality of decisions is related to the knowledge, skill, and business sophistication of the people who make them. While one person may be totally capable, often a group provides a breadth of perspective and expertise that is desirable.

There is also the human element involved. Personal agenda, bias, or a quest to protect one's turf or authority in the organization can color the view of the situation, the alternatives, and even the final decision. And regardless of the process, there is some amount of gut instinct or intuition that may factor into the equation, sometimes for good reasons and with good outcomes.

When a group of people is engaged in the process, the human dynamics can be even more interesting. Sometimes coalitions form in favor of a certain alternative for a variety of reasons that have little to do with the business merits of a course of action and more to do with organizational or personnel dynamics. A decision could wind up being the alternative that got the majority vote rather than necessarily being the best conclusion.

Announcing Decisions

Decision making is little more than an academic exercise if only the people who were involved know what was decided. This may seem like another statement of the obvious, but many people in organizations can tell "I didn't know that" tales about changes in policy or procedures, all as a result of management's failure to communicate to the people who needed to know or to communicate in ways that were sufficiently explanatory or made an impression. The communications failure also creates more situations for the manager to manage.

The objective of an announcement is to not only clearly communicate a decision but also enhance the likelihood that it will be implemented. The unknown variable is the degree of acceptance a decision will receive. The decision may be welcomed, as when management does something that the workers think is especially helpful or that needed to be resolved. Or the decision may change policies or procedures that people were comfortable with or didn't think needed to be changed in the first place.

A decision that makes sense to the people who made it must be communicated so that it makes sense to all the people who are affected by it. A new process that enhances operations in the marketing or accounting department may seem cumbersome or ill-advised to others. But people are more willing to implement a decision they understand. This is not to say that management has to justify or defend a decision, but rather it needs to provide a rationale, the logic behind the thinking, especially because the entire staff generally does not have a companywide perspective.

Any decision must be presented and supported with a unified voice by everyone in all levels of management. Not all decisions will be popular, but if senior management has decided that certain procedures are to be adopted in the sales offices, then that's what the sales managers are responsible for implementing. If people sense dissension surrounding a decision, they are less likely to cooperate with its implementation or may even sabotage it.

When major changes in the organization are contemplated, management must guard the confidentiality of a decision until it can be properly announced and explained. Otherwise, the company grapevine can start an undertow of rumors and half-truths that can undermine the decision even before people hear the official announcement. Typically, organizations launch major new programs with great fanfare, but the advance teasers or internal public relations hype need to create positive excitement, while minimizing negative anxiety.

■ CONCLUSION

The flow of information in an organization serves many purposes for managers, the people they supervise, and the people the managers report to. Funneling the volume of information in ways that reach the intended recipients in a timely, accurate, and efficient manner is the challenge of good communications. Organizations depend on the fluid exchange of information to function efficiently so that management can make quality decisions and its directives can be implemented.

■ DISCUSSION EXERCISES

What do you see as the strengths and weaknesses of the ways management in your organization communicates? How well informed do you feel about what is going on in your company? How does that aid or hamper your ability to do your job?

How worthwhile are the meetings that are typically conducted in your company? If you have been responsible for meetings, what has been successful and what has been problematic about your meetings?

Think about a business decision that you or senior management has recently made. How do you assess the decision-making process and the way the announcement was handled?

IN CONCLUSION
OF UNIT ONE

Armed with an understanding of the interpersonal, informational, and decision-making roles of a manager, the manager can assume a leadership position, make the decisions that are essential in the job, and command a following of the people on whom the organization depends for its very existence. This is a tall order, but with well-developed skills, the manager can successfully assume the position and the responsibilities that it confers, and find fulfillment and enjoyment in the journey.

■ THE SCENARIO

Having read this unit, what is your analysis of the following scenario?

The broker was sitting alone in her office, having retreated to its solitude after a disturbing meeting that afternoon with the "Chairman's Circle." This is a group of salespeople who are chosen by their offices' sales staffs to be their representatives at periodic meetings with the broker. The Circle acts like the "eyes and ears" within the organization, sharing insight and providing feedback, to help the broker stay in touch with what's going on in her multimillion-dollar, multidepartmental company.

The original topic of conversation that was intended to be the subject for that afternoon's meeting is not nearly as important as the issue that eventually surfaced.

It all began when someone mentioned the company's relocation program. The comment was a passing reference to a procedure that this salesperson's manager had explained at a recent office meeting. But that comment opened the floodgates and turned the Circle's meeting into a full-blown discussion about relocation referrals. The more conversation she heard, the more the broker realized that the program that she thought was carefully laid out to be fair, equitable, and efficient wasn't working that way at all. She learned that several of the office managers, for whatever reason, had neglected to discuss the company's relocation procedures with their sales staffs. Moreover, it appeared that some of the managers had totally disregarded the company program and implemented their own procedures for distributing relocation referrals, and in at least one case, the salesperson suspected that the manager was keeping the best referrals for himself.

The crowning blow was the revelation that the company's relocation director, who outwardly said all the right words at the senior management team meetings, seemed to be playing favorites with certain offices, and in some cases with selected salespeople, without regard to published procedures. And these were procedures that the relocation director had designed, that the senior management team had approved, and that the sales office managers had been fully briefed on.

During the disquieting hour the broker spent in her office after the meeting, she became increasingly disheartened. Recognizing that the distribution of relocation referrals is one of the most thorny issues to manage in any brokerage company, it's conceivable that the spirited discussion simply vented some typically competitive viewpoints. But the more she thought about it, the more convinced she was that what she'd heard said much more about the sales office managers and the relocation director who worked for the company, or at least the way they were perceived. All of which reflected on the broker as well.

■ THE ANALYSIS

After the discussions in this first unit, the situations that the broker faced should be fairly clear. Her Chairman's Circle is characteristic of the participatory culture that is prevalent in today's organizations, and certainly it did what she'd hoped it would do, that is, be a way for her to gather information. Wisely, she decided to let the conversation flow rather than reining it back to her preplanned agenda. The time seemed to be right just to let people talk, and the more they did, the more they revealed.

One breakdown centered on the way decisions about the referral policy had been implemented. Clearly, there was not a unified voice or support within the managerial ranks because the policy had not been discussed, and in some cases had been circumvented entirely, by some of the office managers.

The unknown variables are whether some of the managers just had more pressing matters to discuss with their sales staffs, whether the policy was basically flawed, or whether some of the managers had overstepped the bounds of their authority by instituting their own procedures. In one case, the selling manager's priority appeared to be his or her personal business over that of the sales staff. All of this needs further investigation by the broker.

The breakdown at the senior management level is particularly disturbing because the person in a position of authority is exercising that authority in irresponsible ways. The unknowns in this situation, which the broker needs to explore, are whether the broker misjudged the person she put in that position, or whether there are other dynamics surrounding the policies or the people who interface with the relocation department that are causing the system to unravel.

In the final analysis, trust has been violated: faith that people in the organization had in the trustworthiness of their leaders and the trust the broker had placed in the office managers and the relocation director to do the jobs she expected of them. While none of this is absolutely fatal, as long as the broker takes some steps to "right the ship," it's disheartening to make these discoveries, especially because it takes more time to reengender trust than it does to lose it. If you were the broker, what would you do now?

II

PLANNING THE ORGANIZATION

As introduced in the Preface, the mass of activities that organizations commonly engage in is grouped under functions. The first of those is planning. This is the step that sets all of the wheels in motion and guides virtually everything an organization does and all the decisions that are made.

Planning, however, is the function that is often given the least attention. Typically, people are more focused on "doing," rather than planning what to do. Peter Drucker, a popular management theorist, has observed that most people spend more time working at doing things right, rather than working at doing the right things. Planning charts the course for doing the right things.

Certainly, any new business needs to be armed with a plan. But that's not the end of planning. Organizations need to revisit the process periodically to ensure that they're still doing the right things and to set new courses as needed. Sometimes, organizations also develop auxiliary plans so they have ready courses of action in case the business environment changes dramatically.

Planning involves more that simply writing down some goals. In fact, developing goals or objectives and the supporting activities is one of the last steps in the process. The process begins with several steps that revolve around information and proceeds as follows:

- Analyze the external business environment.

- Analyze the external marketplace and the internal company environment.

- Develop the plan and supporting activities.

- Implement the plan by assigning responsibilities and allocating resources.

Planning begins with what is known as a *situational* or *environmental analysis*. This is the informational part of the process that assesses the prevailing external and internal climate, identifies opportunities and barriers that confront the organization, and does some forecasting for the future. As in most things management does, the informational part of the process is most critical. Without this, there's no assurance that the organization will be doing the right things or that the things it plans to do are feasible. The situational analysis provides the information for making the right decisions.

Many resources are available from which to gather information about local and general trends and conditions, including census data, general business, and real estate–specific research that can be accessed on the Internet. *The Future of Real Estate Brokerage: Challenges and Opportunities for* REALTORS®, a report prepared by NAR's research division, is one such resource.

The chapters in this unit lead you through the planning process. The broker/owner (and senior management in a large organization) is typically involved in all aspects of planning to develop the strategic or general plan for the company. Department managers or managers of sales offices are usually involved in certain aspects of planning, especially those that relate to their specific areas of responsibility. A familiarity with the entire process, however, is necessary to understand how a plan fits together.

CHAPTER FIVE

ANALYZING THE BUSINESS ENVIRONMENT

What factors currently have the most effect on the general business climate in your area? And on real estate companies?

What role will these factors, or others, play in the future?

In earlier, simpler days a property owner merely set out a for-sale sign, found a purchaser, and sold the property with a minimum of fuss. Today, real estate consumers are confronted with a maze of legal, financial, and tax issues for which they need professional advice and assistance. While it may be reassuring to think that a real estate company provides necessary services, the mere fact that the company exists does not guarantee that it will succeed as a profitable entity.

Today's organizations must successfully navigate a complex maze of circumstances in the external environment in which they do business. As demonstrated in the first chapter, that environment consists of a variety of economic and geopolitical factors over which they have little control.

There are also technological, regulatory, and demographic factors that, in a sense, can take control of a business as well.

In order for organizations to seize control, managers need to be vigilant and analytical observers so that they can strategically place the organization in a position to take advantage of opportunities, and also withstand any negative consequences in the external environment. The purpose of this chapter is to shed some light on economic, political, and sociological factors that planners need to consider.

Planning also means doing some forecasting. The unknown variable, of course, is that the future can't be measured in quantified or guaranteed terms. This leaves forecasts to be based on well-studied lessons from the past and the entrepreneurial instincts of an organization's leaders for the future.

■ ECONOMIC FACTORS

A number of key economic indicators provide clues about the climate in which a business functions. One of the indicators that experts seem to agree is a relatively sound gauge of the strength of the economy is the housing market. The number of new housing starts and home sales reflects consumer and investor demand and also indicates demand for other household and consumer goods. These trends are closely monitored by a number of analysts, with some of the most complete research being available from the National Association of REALTORS®.

Keep in mind, though, that economic indicators are just that, indicators. Often, there are divergent interpretations of those indicators. And in times such as those described in the first chapter, even the best predictors of the future can't anticipate such things as a 9/11 event or the corporate scandals that rocked Wall Street and subsequently trickled down through the rest of the economy.

Nevertheless, management still has to get a grasp of the economic environment and learn to make reasonably well-educated guesses. Those predictions also need to be revisited periodically to ensure that assumptions remain valid. Otherwise, the company could be preparing for an economic environment that doesn't materialize.

Gross Domestic Product

The gross domestic product (GDP) is the broadest indicator of the strength of the economy, showing the economic output and growth. Healthy industrialized economies have an average annual increase of 3 percent. A higher percentage indicates that the economy is overheating. In the United States, a sharp decline has historically resulted in stagnant growth. Watching the GDP that is released by the government each quarter indicates how the economy is faring as the year progresses.

Inflationary Cycles

A healthy economy should generate a low, stable rate of inflation. During the 1990s the United States enjoyed slow, steady economic growth, with inflation hovering around 3 percent per year, and even lower toward the end of the decade. That trend, along with optimism in the stock market, continued until 2001 when inflation began to accelerate, the stock market started to lose ground and unemployment, especially in the manufacturing sector, began to climb.

All of this proves that, as trite as it sounds, what goes up eventually comes down, and vice versa. For an indicator of where we are in inflationary cycles, look at the spread between short-term interest rates set by the Federal Reserve and the interest rates on long-term bonds.

- If the spread is large or getting larger—the government is trying to fuel the economy by loosening its monetary policy. This encourages people to spend and grow the economy.

- If the spread is small or shrinking—the government is attempting to cool the economy by tightening the money supply. This discourages people from spending to guard against another inflationary spiral.

In recent years the Federal Reserve has managed inflation with gentle, though sufficient, adjustments in interest rates to keep inflation in check. As a result, inflation during the 1990s did not hit the extreme peaks and valleys of previous decades. The Federal Reserve has continued its vigilant management of inflation, and when economic stimulus was needed, particularly during 2002, continued to lower interest rates.

Of the several lessons learned during 2001 and 2002, one is that the Federal Reserve, alone, does not wield a magic wand over the economy. Cutting interest rates does not necessarily stimulate corporate growth in an environment of uncertain world affairs, a weak global economy, or suspect corporate integrity. The housing market, fueled by the lowest mortgage interest rates in 41 years and investors seeking alternatives to the stock market, has been one of the bright rays in an otherwise gray time.

All is not doom and gloom, however. While it's difficult to predict precisely when and how dramatically inflationary cycles will change, the economy will turn the recessionary corner and start the upside of the cycle all over again. (The Federal Reserve Survey seems to have a fairly good record of forecasting these cycles.) It's also fairly certain that recent corporate cost-cutting measures, as wrenching as they've been, will leave organizations with leaner, more efficient operations that can begin to grow again. As corporate profits grow, unemployment drops, people feel more secure in their work life, investors feel more positive, and the general outlook improves.

During periods of stable inflation, with relatively predictable indicators to rely on, it's easier to plan and make the most of opportunities. But the caveat for any business planner is that it's also easy to get lulled into a false sense of security. Overly aggressive optimism can leave a company vulnerable unless it can pull in the reins quickly when the economy begins to slow. The virtue of vigilance, perhaps by revisiting the economic analysis every six months during volatile times, can help organizations make timely adjustments.

Consumer Confidence

Two-thirds of our nation's income comes from consumer spending. The willingness of buyers and sellers to enter the marketplace (and spend) is tied to their general attitude about the economy and their sense of financial security. This is especially significant when big-ticket purchases, like houses, are involved.

Financial security means a variety of things to different people. For many, it means job security. For others, it means wage scales, wages that stretch far enough to support their costs of living. A recent Center for Housing Policy study indicates that 67 percent of low- and moderate-income households spent 50 percent or more of their income on housing alone. For anyone living on a fixed income, including the elderly, security is a function of the cost of living. For people who rely primarily on investment income, the low interest rates that are a positive for the housing market can have the opposite effect on them.

Consumer confidence and cost-of-living indexes, unemployment rates, and investor behavior are all factors to consider when projecting company activity and revenue. They are also useful for identifying market segments or services where opportunities or vulnerabilities exist. NAR statistics about housing purchases versus trends in remodeling and adding on to existing homes are also helpful. So, too, are statistics about investment in discretionary types of real estate, such as vacation or resort properties or second and third homes.

The job-growth rate, which the government publishes each month, is a particularly useful gauge of the housing market and consumer confidence. The ability of a locale to generate new jobs has a direct bearing on the ability of the housing market to grow. A community's economic growth and development efforts contribute to this as well. Watching the job-growth rate for several months as businesses expand, downsize, or move into or out of an area will help identify the available pool of potential housing buyers and sellers.

■ POLITICAL FACTORS

Depending on prevailing political ideologies, sympathies, and priorities, the effect that public policymakers have on the business environment can vary. Republicans and Democrats see the role of government, especially as it affects the business community, differently. The parties and individual politicians also have differing views about budget matters, tax cuts, entitlement programs, and a host of other issues that directly or indirectly, but nevertheless ultimately, affect consumers and the corporate community.

Swinging with changes in the political landscape is not easy, and most business planners avoid devising plans that align with the political ideology that is currently in power. Nothing's as fickle as politics, and power shifts can occur unexpectedly due to a variety of circumstances that are not readily predictable. There is a role, however, for political vigilance in the planning process. The agenda of federal, state, and local policymakers can certainly affect corporate operations, community development, and the housing industry, all of which have a direct bearing on a real estate company.

Corporate Development

All of a company's best efforts to grow revenue can be quickly neutralized by government regulations and tax obligations. When businesses (as opposed to people) are targets in the government's quest for needed revenue, corporate and business privilege taxes in one form or another can have a significant effect on a company's cost of doing business. The bottom line is also affected by the administrative costs of complying with numerous regulations relating to tax filings and employee benefit and retirement plans.

Some locales are more business-friendly than others. Some states' incorporation and accompanying tax laws make attractive seats for corporations. Companies can also be affected by the role of business development in the overall economic development plan of a state or local political division. In areas where incentives are offered to attract businesses and stimulate accompanying job growth, a company may be inspired to take advantage of these opportunities. A more favorable business climate is also an incentive for established businesses to remain in these areas.

Without venturing into the appropriateness of a particular ideology, the fact remains that the treatment of businesses is subject to political forces. Unless business planners are conscious of strategies being contemplated in the political agenda at all levels of government, companies can be in for a rude and, possibly, costly awakening.

Economic Growth and Development

The economic growth and development policies in an area can affect a real estate company in a variety of ways, in addition to the possible incentives for business development.

The fundamental challenge in economic growth and development efforts is balancing benefits with costs, not only in terms of money but also in the amount of regulatory intervention that may be involved. Preserving the quality of life for a community's residents, revitalizing aging neighborhoods or enhancing the utility of the land, and strengthening a community's economic base serve desirable and often critically necessary purposes.

The price, however, is that residents sometimes fight growth, or any change in their neighborhoods for that matter, simply out of a desire to preserve the community as they've known it. Growth also stresses existing infrastructures (sewer, water, and road systems) and community resources such as schools, libraries, and public safety services. While residents desire the elimination of deteriorating or blighted neighborhoods and the social problems that often accompany them, people frequently grow impatient with the amount of time and money that is required to upright these neighborhoods.

The resolution of the cost-versus-benefit equation comes in different forms, again depending on political persuasions. Some policymakers see government's role as highly engaged, with significant regulatory intervention and financial commitment in the form of hard dollars for brick and mortar and funding for entitlement programs and economic stimulus packages. Others desire greater engagement by the private sector, the thought being that opportunities abound for the private sector's benefit, and government intervention is needed only to the extent that it encourages free enterprise to function.

In either case, the real estate industry has always sat firmly in support of private property rights. Not only can overly aggressive restrictions impede the fundamental rights of ownership but aggressive controls, be they land-use plans, zoning ordinances, or building codes, can discourage development and exacerbate the very problems they intend to solve.

All of this means that sound economic growth and development policies ultimately benefit real estate. Regardless of whether the policies' priorities are job growth, enhanced educational opportunities, improved transportation, or land-use enhancement, the outcome is a community that is more attractive to more people, all of whom represent potential real estate business. Opportunities abound for a real estate company that can readily identify these openings in the marketplace. The participation by a company's leaders in the economic development dialogue is also a worthwhile endeavor.

Environment Issues

As policymakers seek ways to protect public health and safety and the environment, both the property owner and the real estate industry have been saddled with volumes of regulations. In essence, environmental issues have become real estate issues.

While serving the environmental interests, which in many cases also have health-related components, is a noble and necessary cause, the solutions often tangle with private property rights and the checkbooks of sellers, purchasers, and developers of real estate. Enforcement of the solutions often brings an additional price in the legal liability for all parties involved, including real estate practitioners.

Although many environmental issues are universally important, the issues that could have the most noticeable effect on a real estate company can vary by geographic area. In some areas, development is more severely impacted by forestry, water, or wildlife concerns than in others. The age of the housing and the construction materials and methods that have been used over time make issues like lead-based paint, asbestos, and the recent recognition of molds particularly significant. There are also health and safety issues in the workplace that cannot be overlooked.

Because of the ever-expanding list of regulations on the federal, state, and local levels; health-related studies; and civil cases that have been adjudicated, business planners cannot overlook environmental issues. They impact the amount and nature of potential business, the costs of complying with regulations, and perhaps most importantly, can significantly affect the company's liability exposure and insurance needs. Attention to all of these is also important for forecasting future impacts.

Regulating the Industry

While many public policies regulate the real estate industry in some fashion, the industry also lives with a host of laws and regulations that are specific to its business. Some observers suggest that it is one of the most highly regulated industries in our country. When you consider state licensing laws; federal and state antitrust laws; consumer laws; the Real Estate Settlement Procedures Act (RESPA); the Foreign Investment in Real Property Act (FIRPTA); federal, state, and local fair housing laws; the Americans with Disabilities Act; and the Truth-in-Lending Act, the number is considerable.

The challenge is to monitor all the developments as laws are amended and new ones are passed. And little is forgiven for ignorance. Several recent trends have had a particular hand in shaping the way real estate companies do business, driven in part by a heightened emphasis on consumer rights. In a word, *disclosure:* disclosure of agency relationships, disclosure of property conditions, disclosure of environmental substances, disclosure of financing terms, and disclosure of the way that various service providers participate with one another in real estate transactions.

Additional responsibilities mean additional paperwork—and additional liability for the broker, especially if the salespeople are careless about complying with these requirements.

While the industry's laws may not necessarily have a major impact on the volume of business that a company can forecast, they certainly affect the way a company does business. Laws that foster universal licensure of salespeople will also have a bearing on the business. Because of the intricacy of the volume of laws, smart business planners engage the company's legal counsel in the planning process as well.

■ SOCIOLOGICAL FACTORS

As important as the economic and political environment is to the business community, the social or demographic environment has particular significance to business planners. This is the people factor that affects virtually every aspect of a company, from its workforce to its clientele. While the number of people is useful information, the profile of those people (age, education level, cultural origin, and the like) is particularly helpful for tailoring plans that suit the available pool of potential hires and consumers. Figure 5.1 provides an interesting profile of the population.

Companies that manufacture consumer goods and deliver consumer services (that's where real estate fits in) devote considerable resources to studying population demographics. Decisions ranging from what to manufacture or deliver to how to market or advertise are all influenced by what companies learn about the consuming population.

FIGURE 5.1

Age of General Population and Various Types of Citizenry

	25–34 Years Old		35–44 Years Old		45–64 Years Old		65+ Years Old		
	No.[†]	% of Total	No.[†]	% of Total	No.[†]	% of Total	No.[†]	% of Total	Total
General Population*									
1995	42	16	42	16	15.5	20	33.5	13	263
2000	38	14	45	16	60.0	22	35.0	13	276
2005	37	13	43	15	70.0	24	37.0	13	288
2010	38	13	40	13	79.0	26	40.0	13	300
White (Not Hispanic)									
1995	29.50	11.0	31.50	12.0	41.0	15.5	28.75	11.0	
2000	25.75	9.3	32.75	11.9	46.5	16.8	29.50	10.7	
2005	24.00	8.3	30.00	10.4	53.5	18.6	30.25	10.1	
2010	24.50	8.2	26.25	8.8	58.5	19.5	32.25	10.8	
African American									
1995	5.50	2.0	5.00	2.0	5.25	2.0	2.75	1.1	
2000	5.25	1.9	5.50	2.0	6.25	2.2	3.00	1.0	
2005	5.25	1.8	5.50	1.9	7.75	2.7	3.00	1.0	
2010	5.50	1.8	5.25	1.7	9.00	3.0	3.50	1.2	
Hispanics									
1995	5.00	2.0	4.0	1.5	3.75	1.5	1.5	0.5	
2000	5.25	1.9	5.0	1.8	4.75	1.7	2.0	0.7	
2005	5.25	1.8	5.5	1.9	6.25	2.2	2.5	0.9	
2010	5.75	1.9	5.5	1.8	7.75	2.6	3.0	1.0	

* These numbers do not consider people who are younger than 25 years old. Because people under 25 years of age are not included, the numbers do not add up to 100 percent. They are U.S. Census Bureau data estimates.
[†] Numbers are in millions of people.

Baby Boomers and Their Offspring

The Baby Boomer generation (those born between 1946 and 1964) has been a driving force in the marketplace, simply because of its sheer size. This population has affected virtually every system it has touched, from the public schools to the business community and the housing industry, in its advance through life. Boomers are a force to be reckoned with, especially now, as they reach their maximum wage earning years. As the leading edge of the Boomers approaches their late 50s, the demand for goods and services reflects their maturing, though still active, lifestyles.

"Gen X" or *generation* X, as the offspring of the Boomers are known, is the first true technology generation. Many Gen-Xers have never known life without microwave ovens, cable television, or portable phones (let alone cell phones). Born between 1966 and 1980, Gen-Xers are now fully educated and have entered the workforce. The eldest of that generation have achieved financial independence, started their own families, and are parenting their own baby boom, "Generation Y."

Certainly, all of these developments affect demand for housing. Not just in the number of units but also in style, size, and amenities. While Boomers downsize (at least those whose adult children have not moved back home to save money), their children are in the market for their first (some, their second) homes. Generally, the young-family home Gen X prefers is better technologically and environmentally appointed than their parents', and the design reflects today's more active and casual lifestyles.

In recent years, consumer-driven companies have shifted their focus from the Boomers to the 25-to-35-year-old age group (some even to the 18-to-24-year-olds), feeling that by capturing the younger population, they can establish a clientele that will endure in later years. Essentially, they are building a market base for the future. For business planners, this means developing products and services to suit the needs of this age group, product or service placement to coincide with their shopping preferences, and advertising strategies that capture this audience's attention.

Consumers who are older than these age groups, however, may really feel the generation gap. Goods or services they prefer, or are accustomed to, are less available, if available at all. The generation gap may be even more noticeable in advertising, with an "I didn't get the point" feeling about some ads.

Interestingly, older consumers, especially the 50- and 60-somethings, have more spending capacity than younger consumers and are also more technologically sophisticated than some gave them credit for even five years ago. Companies are beginning to recognize the significance of this consumer market and are pursuing a more diversified strategy to capitalize on the older consumers' buying power.

All of this is a lesson for the planning process in a real estate company, not only as it affects the kind of services the company provides but in the way it delivers, markets, and advertises those services as well.

Maturing Adults

The parents of Baby Boomers and the oldest Boomers themselves are a sizable population that is also getting older, or, more kindly put, maturing. Projections by the U.S. Census Bureau suggest that approximately 64,499,000 of the nation's population will be age 55 or older in 2004, about 22.6 percent of the total population. That number increases to approximately 75,145,000 million by 2010, or 25 percent.

It's no wonder that many industries, real estate included, have made the over-55 population a priority target market. However, this is a diverse group, not a stereotypical senior population, that falls into three general categories: the pre–65-year-olds, the 65-to-75-year-olds and the over–75-year-olds. Each group has different needs that are associated with their stages of life and the physical changes that are a natural part of the aging process. This means that one size doesn't fit all in lifestyles or housing preferences.

Many of the Boomers' parents have been retired for some time (a function of corporations encouraging early exits as they streamlined operations) and have found engaging ways to enjoy active retirement. Many Boomers, some of whom have been looking forward to early retirement themselves, may find that financial circumstances will dictate more working years than they originally contemplated. But they will want to merge work with a more recreational, relaxed lifestyle.

Where does the maturing population want to live? A joint survey conducted by Allstate and Harris Interactive indicates that four out of ten Boomers intend to move during their retirement years, with nearly one third expecting to downsize their housing. Seventeen percent say they will move closer to relatives, and 14 percent want to relocate to warmer locales. The survey also indicated that individual circumstances play a much larger role in decisions, rather than the real estate market itself.

A recent AARP survey revealed that 85 percent of the respondents want to remain in their homes as they age, with four out of five homes being owned free of any mortgage indebtedness. This suggests that people will strive to live independently as long as possible and, if feasible, rely on in-home services to manage medical conditions associated with advancing age.

The building boom in assisted living facilities and nursing homes during the early 1990s offers many more options than were previously available to less physically independent people. The American Seniors Housing Association reports a significant decline in the number of assisted living and nursing home institutions under construction since 1998, an indication that supply has caught up with demand, especially because of the number of people who are still able to live independently.

Recent Census Bureau statistics (2002) indicate that of the nation's 97.5 million households, 3.9 million, or about 4 percent, are multigenerational. That is, at least three generations. This also means changing lifestyles. The young seniors may become the caregivers to the youngest generation (small children). Older, less physically or financially independent seniors may have moved in with their adult children, with those adults now becoming the senior adults' caregivers. Multigenerational living means that everyone has to be suitably accommodated under one roof.

Population Shifts

The population in the United States is more mobile than in other advanced industrial economies. According to the Census Bureau, the average American moves 12 times in a lifetime.

Population shifts are driven primarily by employment opportunities, but today's younger generations are also more inclined to explore new venues for their climatic, recreational, or cultural appeal than their elders were. Even though the nation's population continues to grow, some parts of the country have experienced population decline. These shifts create opportunities for real estate companies in areas with population increases, but challenge other communities and their real estate companies to find ways to remain vital.

Culturally Diverse Population

As the population grows, so does its cultural diversity. Recent Fannie Mae Foundation statistics indicate that by the early 2000s, foreign-born households had jumped by 4.3 million over the 1980s, which accounts for 31 percent of the nation's overall household growth. Foreign-born owners account for 20 percent of the new homeowners. The increasing diversity of our population is due to an influx of temporary residents working for international corporations as well as to immigration.

The National Association of Home Builders anticipates that immigrants will fuel the housing market during the next ten years, accounting for about two-thirds of the market's projected growth. Harvard University's Joint Center for Housing Studies indicates that the 10 million immigrants who came to this country in the past decade will be the next wave of homebuyers. The National Association of REALTORS® expects that by 2010, more than 50 percent of the first-time homebuyers will be minorities, with Latinos being the largest segment of the minority population.

All of this suggests that opportunities abound for real estate companies that are prepared to serve a culturally diverse clientele. But this means that only those companies that understand the uniqueness of cultures and have a staff that is familiar with multinational customs and language can benefit.

Anyone who has traveled abroad has experienced first-hand the wonder, and the isolation, of different customs and unfamiliar languages. It's striking to note that people in many countries are fluent in multiple languages, with English often being the second or third language studied by young people during their formal education. It's also not uncommon to find public signage, restaurant menus, and the like in English as well as the local language.

Turning the tables, one quickly sees that this land of opportunity is also one that has been somewhat lax in its development of multilingual and multicultural understanding. While language is the most obvious hurdle for immigrants, even among English speakers, differences in customs, taboos, and business etiquette pose daily challenges.

A resource for preparing a real estate company's sales staff to serve this population is the cultural diversity training and certificate program that has been jointly developed by the National Association of REALTORS® and the Department of Housing and Urban Development (HUD). The National Association of Hispanic Real Estate Professionals, recently formed by Latino licensees, is currently developing curriculum to help all licensees serve the lucrative Latino market.

■ CONCLUSION

Hopefully, the obvious conclusion is the importance of strategically positioning a company in the local business environment. Although there's some uncertainty associated with that environment, with the watchful eye of management a company can be less vulnerable. How well a company does is a function of how well management analyzes the factors in the local environment that have a bearing on its operations and how pragmatic and perhaps bold management is when predicting the future.

■ DISCUSSION EXERCISES

Discuss the most dramatic economic, political, and social changes in your area that have affected the real estate business recently. What have you observed about the adjustments real estate companies have made to cope with them?

Have any real estate businesses in your area failed or dramatically changed their operations recently? What do you think were the causes?

What conditions in the business environment in your area impact other businesses more than they impact real estate companies? Impact real estate companies more than other businesses?

CHAPTER SIX

ANALYZING THE MARKET

Who are the consumers of your company's services?

What do they really need a real estate company to do for them?

How well is your company positioned to serve today's consumers now?
And in the future?

———————

After analyzing the general business climate, the next step is a market analysis. This is the part of the situational analysis that looks specifically at the consumers of real estate services and answers questions like: Who are they? Where are they located? What services do they need? Where do they go to get those services?

Lest someone say, "I already know the answers," the flaw in that line of thinking is that a marketplace changes. Not just in the number and profile of consumers but also in the where and how they get their needs satisfied (in other words, consumer behavior). This is also where a company's competition figures into the equation. An analysis will generate quantified answers, the facts and figures, that business planners need to develop quantified projections for the company.

A critical piece of the market analysis is an assessment of the company, that is, the internal environment. This reveals how well the company does in the marketplace by comparing what is learned about the consumers with what is learned about the company. This tells the company what it should continue to do, do differently, or cease doing entirely.

The cease-entirely decisions are often the ones that companies struggle with most. Like a favorite old shoe, companies get comfortable with the old, familiar activities that were once the foundation of their success. But because companies do not have unlimited human or financial resources, they can rarely afford to keep adding to their agenda without eventually shedding some of their "old shoes." A market analysis can help make those hard decisions.

■ ANALYZING BUSINESS OPPORTUNITIES

Analyzing opportunities is really a process of looking at all the available options in the marketplace. While a company can't take advantage of every business opportunity, it's important to first consider all possible avenues. This is what stimulates creative thinking and helps an organization move forward rather than being restricted by old business patterns. Later in the process, options can be eliminated.

Geographic Markets

There are a variety of ways to look at the marketplace. One is geographically. Today's geographic market bears little resemblance to the local, neighborhood real estate market we once knew.

The mobility of today's population means that the once-loyal customer bases that brokerage companies could count on are moving to other communities. Even where population numbers remain the same, the shifting population means that customers don't stay in one place long enough to develop the depth of allegiance to local vendors that is typical when consumers stay in one community for a lifetime. The result is that most brokerage companies can no longer survive solely on business generated in a highly localized geographic market.

Consumers don't see the market in narrow geographic terms either. The mobile consumer can feed his or her thirst for knowledge or wanderlust in a variety of convenient ways. Technology, which affects the way multiple listing services operate and provides endless opportunities in cyberspace, brings the consumer to the doorstep of a state on the other side of the country or a country on the other side of the world.

The middle ground, between the most narrow and the broadest views of the market, is a regional approach. That region can be several communities or several counties, depending on the density of the population and the diversity of the properties. Although some real estate companies have tentacles (branches or affiliated corporations) that reach into many states, they, too, are regional specialists. A regional marketplace enables companies to foster customer loyalty or the patronage of past customers by serving a wider range of geographic preferences.

Multiple Listing Services.   MLSs have traditionally provided listing inventories for fairly narrow geographic areas, determined primarily by the locale of their members' businesses. Today, MLSs are repositories of vast amounts of data that reflect the members' expanded geographic markets and expanded scope of services.

- Local MLSs have merged to form large, regional systems to expand the geographic area for which listing inventory can be accessed.

- Real estate companies have banded together to form integrated databases, essentially structuring their own MLSs.

- MLSs have become multifunction information systems, providing mortgage loan information, competitive market analysis data, sample contracts, worksheets for qualifying buyers and estimating ownership and closing costs, investment analysis, online mapping, and tax records.

- MLSs are linking their listing inventories with Internet sites (the IDXs and VOWs that were discussed in the first chapter) to provide a wide geographic range of property information.

Because today's MLSs are highly computerized, they can assemble and distribute a much broader range of timely, useful information. Ultimately, the goal is to provide the resources companies need to meet the demands of today's consumers.

Technology Marketplace.   Today's marketplace has virtually no borders. The Internet has fostered a cybereconomy, delivering information, products, and services directly to the desktops and laptops of today's consumers virtually anywhere in the world. Cable television and satellite networks also deliver information and provide interactive communications.

Consumers can be interactive in the pursuit and evaluation of information and can view property listings located almost anywhere. Today, a consumer can electronically "walk through" a house in California on a virtual reality tour from the comfort of his or her home in New Jersey. The statistics about Internet usage in the first chapter leave little doubt about the importance of the Internet in people's lives.

Today's real estate companies and many of their individual salespeople have interactive Web sites, with approximately 60 percent of NAR members saying they have Web sites. Company sites also typically link to a variety of other real estate-related resources, including the National Association of REALTORS® Web site, *www.realtor.com*. The recent proliferation of vendors offering professional Web site design and other on-line sales and marketing tools is testimony to the enormous number of opportunities on the Internet.

Referral Networks.   Referral networks have been used for a number of years to serve broader geographic markets. A broker can refer buyers and sellers to a broker in another marketplace or to another real estate company whose scope of service is beyond that which a broker customarily provides. Some networks are independent; others are connected with national franchises and corporations. Companies also establish their own internal systems to funnel referrals between offices or departments.

Referral networks are advantageous because the added service a company can provide to a consumer also means added revenue for the company. Consumers benefit, as well, because referrals take the guesswork out of selecting suitable licensees to help them.

Referral networks also provide a number of additional services for their members, ranging from opportunities to network with other broker members and training programs for their salespeople to regional or national advertising programs. Some brokers feel this is an especially important feature because the network can provide market identity that the company could not otherwise attain for itself.

If state licensing laws permit, a broker may also be able to promote the company's listings in other states. For example, a broker from another state could expand the exposure of a unique listing by targeting potential purchasers or investors in your area. Or you could advertise a property located in another state that belongs to a buyer with whom you are currently working. By expediting the sale of your buyer's property, you can expedite the buyer's purchase with you.

While intercity referral networks are attractive, they are only as valuable as the cost-versus-benefit equation allows. Decisions should be guided by the answers to: How many referrals can be expected? Is there high turnover or a large transferee market in the area? Does the company need the affiliation to compete with other firms in the area? Will a national advertising campaign produce significant results for the company? What is the cost of affiliation compared with the costs of other networks?

In the final analysis, can affiliation with a commercial referral network do things a company and its sales staff can't do more effectively themselves? Is it a valuable addition to the informal networking with potential consumers and other real estate practitioners that the company customarily does?

Relocation Networks.   These may be part of or in addition to intercity referral networks. Though their ultimate purpose is to help people establish residence in another geographic area as they move within their companies or to other employers, relocation networks can be structured in a number of ways.

One way is through corporate relocation management companies, otherwise known as *third-party equity contractors*. These companies enter into agreements with large corporations to handle employee transfers. The relocation companies generally team up with reliable local real estate companies in each community in which their clients have an office or plant.

The downside of these arrangements is that the relocation company may expect the real estate company to provide services above and beyond those it normally provides.

■ For listings, services could include yard care, plumbing (winterizing), supervising painting and other cosmetic repairs, and providing weekly or monthly status reports of merchandising efforts.

■ For buyers, corporations may expect buyer representation (buyer agency) and perhaps other assistance to help a family relocate to a new community.

In order to accommodate these demands and retain relocation company business, the real estate company may decide that it's necessary to appoint a relocation director who is trained specifically to supervise these transactions and orchestrate the myriad of details associated with the services the corporate relocation company expects. The relocation director should assign referrals to the company's salespeople, not be an active salesperson himself or herself.

Another way for a real estate company to assist local employers is by developing its own contact network and structuring services similar to those of the corporate relocation companies. Some employers provide their own in-house relocation assistance to current and newly hired employees. Other employers do not provide any organized relocation assistance. Both of these cases are opportunities for a company to design programs tailored to meet the needs of employers and their transferees.

Any of these relocation arrangements offers the potential to generate additional income. They also can be costly, in some cases as much as 40 percent of revenue earned. Again, affiliation is worthwhile only if the additional benefits justify the cost. Additional staff time must be allocated to these services. Furthermore, and perhaps most significant, third-party equity contractors charge brokerage companies numerous fees for handling referral transactions that must be considered.

A contentious issue recently is the corporate relocation company practice of charging "after the fact" fees. These are assessed for servicing a buyer or seller who is the employee of a relocation corporation's client, even though no formal referral was established or disclosed at the time the salesperson began working with the individual. The Employee Relocation Council has begun to address the issue for its members with policies regarding this practice.

Service Markets

Another way to look at the marketplace is by services. While there are a number of ways to segment services, for the purpose of this discussion the focus is services related to various kinds of property.

Companies must make strategic decisions about whether to be generalists or specialists, that is, whether to offer a broad or a narrow range of services. In small or rural markets, a company is more likely to be a generalist, doing such things as selling and leasing residential and commercial properties, brokering industrial or recreational land, and appraising and managing real estate. Typically, this strategy is driven by the fact that there is not sufficient demand for any one or a select few services for a company to be profitable otherwise.

Being a generalist is demanding and requires considerable knowledge about many aspects of real estate. Unless the broker has that expertise, or can hire it, and can adequately supervise all of these activities, trying to be all things to all people can be very unrealistic and even disastrous.

Specialization has become as common in the real estate industry as it has elsewhere in the business world. This strategy is appealing when there is sufficient demand for a specialized service and the company has considerable expertise in that specialty. The company should not venture into a specialty just because there's a demand to fill, however. There's too much liability for the company unless it has the appropriate, skilled talent.

Even a residential sales specialty requires that the company decide which transaction services to provide. Services might be limited to marketing properties and following the transactions through to settlement. Or the company may serve only buyers or also provide mortgage brokerage and title or escrow services.

Niche Marketing.   The ultimate in specialization is niche marketing—targeting very specific or narrow segments of the market with specialized, focused services. Niche marketing appeals to consumers by satisfying a need for unique or distinctive expertise and offers some exciting opportunities for the company to be innovative and distinguish itself from the competition.

By looking at the local demographics of the population, the profile of land uses in the area, and the competition's target markets, business planners can identify niche opportunities. Look at census data and other industry and consumer research as well as any distinctive skill or expertise that members of the sales staff may have that would appeal to a specific niche market.

A market niche could be a specific kind of property, such as luxury homes, condominiums, resort, vacation or waterfront properties, ranches, farms, prestige properties, or new construction. Or the niche could be a specific consumer population, perhaps one that is underserved or one with whom you have unique commonality or particular sympathy.

The most obvious consumer niches to consider are the populations discussed in the previous chapter: senior citizens, baby boomers or their children, or international buyers. Or the niche may be singles, people with disabilities, or first-time buyers. The caveat is that when certain populations are targeted while others are ignored, the company can inadvertently violate the fair housing laws. Niche marketing must be done carefully to avoid discriminating against people in the protected classes.

There can be drawbacks to niche marketing. "Putting all of your eggs in one basket" if the market is too specialized or there's a sudden downturn in the targeted market may not provide enough business to sustain a profitable operation. A company can minimize its vulnerability by selecting several niches.

Niche marketing can be a viable strategy only as long as the company has the expertise to gain the confidence of the niche's patronage. Don't pick it just because there are business opportunities. A property niche requires considerable knowledge about its ownership, use, transfer, and any special laws that affect it. A population niche requires knowledge about its uniqueness and perhaps specialized services that population requires.

Beyond Residential Brokerage.   The real estate industry is much more than houses, though the residential business seems to get more attention, perhaps because of the housing market's high profile on the economic barometer. This does not suggest, however, that other types of property are not a critical part of the economy. They are, and they also demand very specialized services. From a business management point of view, however, the fundamental principles of running a company are universal, regardless of the type of property the company handles.

A real estate company may specialize in investment properties, commercial sales or leasing, industrial properties, commercial farming, real estate development, auctions, or property exchanges. Depending on the state's licensing laws, the company may also consider brokering businesses. Any of these specialties requires a wide range of expertise (and perhaps additional licenses) relating to the use and operation of a property, including government regulations and tax laws.

For example, serving real estate investors requires a broad base of knowledge about tax laws as well as real estate to help people make wise decisions about acquiring, managing, and disposing of their investments. That also means understanding the current laws governing exchanges. Or a company may specialize in real estate counseling. This endeavor requires sophisticated analysis of the investor's circumstances and real estate holdings and then providing educated, objective advice.

Agency Services

Another way to segment the service market is by the nature of the assistance consumers want real estate companies to provide. Do they want to be served as customers, or as clients? Furthermore, do they really understand the differences so they can make educated choices?

In the history of the real estate industry, few topics have prompted as much discussion as agency relationships. The industry has been buffeted about as state regulators, consumer advocacy groups, and the industry itself began challenging one of its most fundamental practices, that being the common law of agency.

When the client or principal was the seller and the customer was the buyer, the licensee's fiduciary obligations to the seller were very clear. Although some people would argue that licensees treated buyers more like clients than customers anyway, that still left buyers without formal representation. So, buyer agency emerged. This, too, should be straightforward; just turn the tables so the buyer is the client and the seller is the customer.

The discussion could end very simply at this point by saying "study the consumers in your marketplace and decide whether they want to be customers or clients." This falls into the "what services do they want" part of the market analysis. Then align company operations with the marketplace, consistent with the basic principle of a consumer-driven business. This would tell the company whether exclusive agency, serving either buyer-clients *or* seller-clients, is suitable.

The agency story gets much more complicated, though, because of the desire of brokerage companies to preserve client relationships with sellers while also adding buyers to their client lists. This would not be so problematic from a legal perspective if a company's client-seller and client-buyer are engaged in distinctly separate transactions and impervious firewalls could be built within the company's systems so that confidences and proprietary information of each client could be scrupulously protected.

Although the marketplace hasn't necessarily indicated that the consumer wants client services to sell a property and also client services to buy another one through the same company, that's what some brokerage companies have assumed. Or perhaps the companies are driven by profit motives. In any event, this strategy does appeal to the one-stop-shop preference of many consumers. However, it's not nearly as easy for a company to provide as might be assumed.

The next part of the agency story is that license law officials in a number of states have entered the fray with a regulatory solution: designated agency. This is a landmark development because real estate license laws have historically been rooted in the common law of agency, which steadfastly prohibits dual agency (though some states have permitted it with informed consent).

Designated agency is a construct that attempts to shield the principal broker from dual agency conflicts by permitting the appointment of licensees within the company to act as a client's exclusive agent.

Designated agency has received a mixed reception. Proponents welcome it as practical solution for resolving their dual agency dilemmas. Though they have found that, even with the regulators' attempts to protect client interests with internal company procedures, implementing the solution has meant navigating a maze of intricate situations in the real world of real estate transactions that don't fall into neatly prescribed procedures.

The critics see designated agency as an implausible notion that only creates more dilemmas, not the least of which is that designated agency is an attempt to circumvent or rewrite common law to suit a selected purpose that creates conflicting principles in law, which will eventually prompt litigation. It's also been said that designated agency is still dual agency dressed up in different clothes and does not properly serve the interests of clients on either side of the transaction because designated agency sets aside selected principles of the fiduciary relationship.

Regardless of where your state's law sits in the transformation of agency practices, one universal practice has emerged, and that is *agency disclosure*. While the legal details vary, the common purpose is to ensure that consumers are able to make reasonably informed decisions about the relationships they form with licensees.

Certainly, the laws that prevail in the state where the company does business are those with which the company must comply. It's possible that the law will undergo more transformations as agency practices are refined. In the meantime, the broker/owner must determine the company's agency policies and the company must develop services and systems to support those policies. In the context of a market analysis, the policy should suit the demands of the consumer.

- If state law permits nonagency, which essentially relieves licensees from all fiduciary obligations, the broker may decide to serve all consumers (sellers and buyers) as customers, rather than clients. This is a significant departure from customary practices, so consumers may not fully understand the implications of nonagency services.

- If state law permits both agency and nonagency relationships, the broker must decide for whom client versus customer services will be provided. Because consumers typically have preconceived notions about what licensees do, the broker cannot assume they understand the distinction. This is another persuasive argument in favor of agency disclosure laws.

- In states where the laws permit the full range of agency relationships, the broker has more complicated decisions to make: Does the firm represent buyers/tenants or sellers/landlords, or both in the same transaction? Is subagency permitted by state law? If so, how will this affect the company's policies?

- If state law permits designated agency, the broker has to decide, first, whether to use it, and if "yes," then how it will be implemented, particularly the internal procedures that are essential to protecting the interests of all concerned.

Serving Sellers. What do sellers want? The standard answer is that they want their properties sold at the best possible price in the shortest period of time, with minimum hassle and expense and maximum market exposure. The rest of the answer is not so predictable, and therein lies a major pitfall for a real estate company. One size, so to speak, does not necessarily fit all sellers.

An analysis of the marketplace will tell you whether sellers want a standard listing package, complete with agency representation, MLS and Internet exposure, company advertising, and the customary oversight of the transaction through to closing. Or whether sellers want a tailored plan, one in which the seller undertakes some activities (perhaps with the aid of the Internet) and the real estate company provides selected other services. Certainly, the fees that a seller is willing to pay in either case must be commensurate with the services that are received.

While not all real estate companies agree with the tailored plan of services, an increasing number of companies each year are adopting the a-la-carte approach to services. In some markets, real estate companies have joined forces with sellers to help them by doing such things as posting their properties in the MLS, helping them with their advertising, or agreeing to bring prospective buyers to the properties. *Agree* is the operative word, because these arrangements must be put in contract form, spelling out the terms of service the company will provide.

This then brings us back to the discussion of representation again. Not all contracts between brokers and sellers are necessarily agency agreements. Where state law permits, the broker may provide a tailored plan of services that does not include representation, if that is the seller's desire.

Otherwise, there are several kinds of contracts that are customarily used to provide representation. The brokerage company needs to decide whether to use open listings or one of the two types of exclusive listings. As a member of an MLS, though, that decision may have already have been made because it's not uncommon for MLSs to require the use of exclusive agency or an exclusive-right-to-sell agreement to inventory a listing.

Open listings are rarely satisfactory for either the owner or the broker. They create considerable controversy over procuring cause and, in the case of multiple brokers showing the property, who is entitled to a commission. Open listings may also mean that the owner misses out on some of the marketing or other services that would typically be provided under an exclusive arrangement. However, this objection can be mitigated to some extent by promoting these listings to buyer or tenant representatives.

The customs in the marketplace, practices of other brokers, and preferences of sellers should guide decisions about the type of listing agreements used. Company policy may be to enter into only exclusive-right-to-sell agreements or to provide alternatives in selected, unique situations. Even exclusive agency agreements do not eliminate controversy, but they may be tolerable in certain cases.

Serving Buyers.   What do buyers want? The standard answer has been that they want maximum service to help them select a suitable property and guide them seamlessly through all aspects of a purchase. Most want an advocate, someone to look out for their interests and provide advice and counsel in their decision making.

In today's marketplace, that answer is still valid, but there are some significant twists. One is the point at which buyers want to engage the services of a brokerage company. Buyers now can come to the salesperson armed with far more information about price, property, and process than they once did, all gathered from the Internet. As disarming as this might be for some salespeople, many more say that they can spend better quality and less quantity time with better informed buyers.

The part of the market analysis that studies buyer behavior must include a look at the way buyers use the Internet, the sites they visit (including the company's), and the services buyers really want from a brokerage company. This then leads to a study of fees, especially fee-for-service pricing. As revealed in the first chapter, today's consumers are looking much more critically at the cost of brokerage services, especially full-service commissions, and are forcing companies to offer a-la-carte plans or tailored services for buyers.

The other twist is the issue of representation, which until recently had to be provided by the buyer's attorney. Now, an overwhelming majority of brokerage companies provide that representation. Some companies have chosen to limit their business to buyer representation (known as *exclusive buyer's agents* or *EBAs*), and in fact, the professional council of buyer's agents continues to gain membership each year.

Bear in mind that buyers are not the clients and have no representation until an agency relationship is established. This happens by virtue of all the lessons one learns about agency and how relationships are established, both purposefully and inadvertently. Disclosure itself doesn't create agency.

Buyer representation agreements come in various written forms, similar to the options available in listing agreements, with similar advantages and disadvantages. Decisions to use an open agreement or one of two forms of exclusive contracts, again, rests with the broker and becomes the policy for the company and its salespeople. The preference in the marketplace must also be considered.

Defining *Your* Market

No market analysis is complete without a look at hard data, the numbers or quantitative evidence that can help make final decisions about market segments and services. While exploring the marketplace, several opportunities will draw your attention. To test assumptions about whether they will be good for the company, ask the following questions:

- How many potential users of the services are there?

- How many of those users can your company reasonably expect to capture (as compared to the other brokerage firms in the area)?

- How many properties of specific types are there in your area?

- How many of those properties are likely to sell during the next two to three years?

- How many of those sales can your company reasonably expect to capture?

Demographic data are particularly helpful in the quest for answers. Demographics reveal age, education level, income and employment, household composition, and whether people rent or own homes. These data are much more useful for assessing business potential than simply head-count, as in population density. The data also can be used to see how a broader or narrower geographic market would affect business potential.

Demographic information is available from a variety of sources. Although companies can engage their own study to identify potential markets for products or services, this is a costly venture. Information that is readily available in the public domain, such as census data, can usually serve the purpose. Local municipalities and school districts, utility companies, public and private social service agencies, and collegiate institutions are good resources as well. Often, these groups also do forecasting that may be useful for the company's purposes.

Study land uses. Zoning maps and community development groups and collegiate institutions provide a wealth of information for analyzing the number of properties in various land-use classifications. Compare this data with the needs of various segments of the population.

The trends that develop over time are especially helpful for identifying marketplace potential. Track the changes in the demographics and how the land uses accommodate those changes. If one segment is growing more rapidly than the supply of suitable property, for example, there will be greater demand than there is supply. The reverse is also true.

Finally, look at sales data. The register of deeds (or the office where real property transfers are recorded) and MLS statistics not only reveal the number of various types of properties that have transferred but also sales prices. By adding the sales prices of the properties and dividing that total by the number of transactions, the average price of a transaction can be determined.

Separate that data by brokerage company. Compare the number, average price, and types of properties that each company (including yours) handled. Look at several years' data, considering the economic conditions that prevailed at the time, to help forecast average prices and numbers of transactions. (See Figure 6.1.)

The purpose of working through this process is to help identify target markets with sufficient business potential. Because the population profile changes over time, it's important to revisit this process periodically to be sure that the organization is still in tune with the marketplace.

■ ANALYZING THE COMPETITION

Firms jockey for position in the marketplace, striving to do business a little better than or a little differently from their competitors. Competition forces companies to press the limits of their creativity and provides consumers with the price and product or service benefits of a free enterprise system.

Competition is also a cleansing process, the survival of the fittest. The survivors have learned from their competitors' mistakes and how to take advantage of the opportunities their competitors create for them.

FIGURE 6.1

Analyzing Potential in the Market

$$\frac{\text{Total prices of properties sold in an area}}{\text{Total number of sales}} = \text{Average sales price in an area}$$

$$\text{Average sale price} \times \text{Number of sales transactions for one brokerage company} = \text{Gross sales volume}$$

$$\frac{\text{Number of sales transactions for one brokerage company}}{\text{Total number of sales in the market}} = \text{Percentage of the market}$$

Using these simple calculations, you can analyze the sales data by the types of properties being sold and the percentage of the market you or your competitors command by type of property or total volume. You can then begin forecasting goals for your company.

The way competitors compete is by scrutinizing what each other is doing. So an important piece of a company's market analysis is a look at the competition. (Consider, too, that the competition is looking at you as well.)

Consumers also watch the competition, though the way they see competing companies and the competitors see one another is different. Consumers often see little distinction between the services each real estate company offers. The *absence* of a service is often more noticeable than the services that *are* offered. On the other hand, the industry sees more differences than similarities. Perhaps that is because the industry tends to attach more importance to certain aspects of a company or its services than the consumer does.

The challenge is to differentiate between your company and the competition in ways that are meaningful to the consumer.

Market Share

It's conceivable that the market opportunities your company identifies are ones that your competitors are looking at, too. This suggests that an important part of a market analysis is a study of not just the opportunities but capacity in those opportunities.

This is why it's called market "share." A company can't be successful by specializing in condominiums if there are only a few developments in the area and one broker is already very competent and successful in that specialty. This is not to suggest that a company must avoid markets that are already being served. But it's much easier to succeed, at least initially, by targeting a market in which there are ample opportunities.

It's also conceivable that a company has identified a unique opportunity because it matches with a unique talent the company has that the competition does not. In this case, the company will be the one-and-only who is serving a particular target market. That may be the good news (no competition) but it may also be a sign that the strategy could be less lucrative or more risky than it appears. Studied risk, however, does not discourage entrepreneurial business people.

Analyzing market share is not an occasional event but an ongoing activity for most brokerage companies. Tracking the company's market share compared to its competitors provides key pieces of information for gauging company performance throughout the year.

Competitive Edge

Many of the decisions a company makes about *how* to serve its target markets are influenced by what the competition does. Should it join a franchise or a referral or relocation network? Where should sales offices be located? Should the company buy billboard advertising or a paid info-mercial on television?

Should the company do any of these things because the competition *does?* Or because it *doesn't?* When looking at the competition, pay closest atten-tion to firms that are similar in size to your company and serve similar target markets. Trying to go head-to-head with a large company's financial resources is not very feasible for a small company.

Attend any professional conference or convention, open any trade publi-cation, or even check your e-mail and you'll find an incredible array of marketing and advertising tools, communications devices, and sundry other tips, tools, and programs promoted to enhance your business (all at a cost, of course).

Here's another cost-versus-benefit analysis. While it's tempting to buy into every attraction, the cost can far outweigh the benefit if the consumer sees little value or the company's competitive position is not enhanced appre-ciably. Decide which ones are absolutely necessary to stay in the running and defer those that would be merely nice enhancements until you have discretionary dollars.

Affiliations.   Begin by looking at your competitors' affiliations. Are the majority connected with franchises, national corporations, or networks? How many are independent? Is MLS membership necessary? A company doesn't have to do what everyone else does, but it should not eliminate options that are needed to be competitive. Most of these organizations have production statistics and cost comparisons from other, similar markets to use in an analysis. Also, talk to brokers who have relinquished their affiliations with organizations you are considering. Their experiences can be very telling.

Location.   Study the locations of other offices. There's more method than madness in the selection of office sites. Cheap office space may be available off the beaten path. But your competitors will benefit from your being in business more than you will if they are more accessible to or within the travel patterns of the clientele you intend to attract. Is the area saturated with offices, particularly in relation to the number of potential customers in a targeted market?

Marketing Strategies.   Study the advertising and marketing strategies of other firms. Advertising and promotional strategies are designed to promote the company as well as to showcase it above the competition. Just because someone else has a billboard doesn't necessarily mean that's the tool for you, however. It is too costly to "buy" the market, so you have to make wise choices. The services of public relations or advertising professionals are invaluable when assessing marketing strategies.

Consumer Services.   In addition to the types of agency and nonagency services being offered, look at the competition's services, such as home warranty or guaranteed buyback programs, decorating or furnishing allowances, cross-purchasing or affinity programs, or closing cost credits, to name a few. Here again, the point is not to mimic the competition, but to assess the competitive merits of various services.

Be innovative. A new tip, tool, or process that you've learned about that the competition has not yet embraced may be something to consider. New ideas are refreshing, but they are also untested. What attracts a consumer in one part of the country could fizzle in another, so it's important to think about local consumer behavior. If a very unconventional approach is being considered, think about why no one else is doing it. It may have been tried before, but with disastrous results. Or it may have been an idea ahead of its time, which means the time could be right, now.

Recruiting Advantages.   Typically, a competitive analysis focuses on the external marketplace. But a company also needs to think about how its marketplace strategies affect the ability to attract and retain salespeople. Salespeople are the ones who are most directly affected by what a company does to rise or fall against the competition. They also know what services their personal followers expect.

While this is not to say that a company should be dictated to by the sales staff, it does say that the salespeople have considerable insight and as much (if not more) at stake in the decisions companies make to enhance, add, or eliminate a service. When the competition offers a tool or process that is especially effective and your company does not, that ultimately affects recruiting and turnover.

■ ANALYZING YOUR ORGANIZATION

This is the internal environmental analysis that an organization must do. It is captured during the discussion of the market analysis because the company is an integral part of that marketplace. Often, the most valuable lessons a company learns about itself are the result of looking at the consumers and competitive forces in the marketplace. Gathering some consumers in a focus group (perhaps past customers) is a good way to find out what they think.

Before a company can convert the information learned in a market analysis into a meaningful and achievable action plan, it needs to take an objective and critical look at all of its current structures, systems, and processes. The result may be a reaffirmation that the company is doing the right things or a sober awakening that the company is not properly aligned to do the things the market now indicates are right.

Ask the following questions:

- How do the company's current services align with those the market analysis indicates are suitable? With the services offered by the competition? Which services generate profits and which ones do not? What services should be added, eliminated, or altered?

- How effective and efficient is the organization's current structure? How well does each office, division, and department function within itself and within the entire organization? What systems and procedures need to be enhanced or eliminated to make the organization function more efficiently? What changes would be needed as a result of the market analysis?

- What is the financial position of the organization? Does its income meet its needs? Meet projections? Or is the company running at a deficit? Is the available cash sufficient to fund operations? Or does the organization have to rely on outside sources of funding? Is the budgeting process adequate to manage the company's financial affairs? What does the organization need to do to enhance its financial position or fund initiatives that are critical to its success?

- Are the right people doing the right jobs? Are there positions that should be added or eliminated? Are there personnel changes (management, staff, or sales personnel) that should be made to better align talent with responsibilities? What personnel changes would be needed as a result of the market analysis?

- What is the physical condition of the offices? Of the equipment and technology? Are there improvements that will increase the efficiency of the company's operation or enhance its image?

- How well do the salespeople perform? What is the per-person production? What are their strengths and weaknesses? What should the company be doing to enhance their performance?

- Has the company gained or lost salespeople? Why? Are the company's recruiting efforts working? How many salespeople should the company have on staff?

- Has the company met its previously stated objectives? Its production forecasts? What is the company's market share and is it on target with projections? Has the company gained or lost ground? Why?

These are some of the most critical questions that need answers before deciding what to commit to a plan. Notice that this analysis is another informational exercise, often requiring quantified numbers. The answers to these questions are useful throughout the year as management monitors company performance as well. Involve the salespeople, too. They have the front-line perspective that isn't necessarily revealed by statistics.

■ CONCLUSION

The market analysis, along with the analysis of the business climate, arms the company with the information it needs to take the next step: decide how the organization should respond to seize opportunities and prepare for the challenges that lie ahead. The information will guide decisions about target markets and services and the ways the company will position itself in the competitive environment. Virtually every decision, from the development of the business plan and financial projections to the development of marketing and advertising programs, will be affected by the information gathered during this process.

■ DISCUSSION EXERCISES

Discuss the methodology you would use to analyze the marketplace. What do you already know, and what do you need to find out, about the consumers and the property in your area? What sources of information would you use?

Discuss the methodology you would use to analyze your competition. What do you know, and what do you need to find out, about the firms and their services that affect your company?

What innovative services or business strategies not currently prevalent in your area do you think would work?

Discuss the methodology you would use to analyze your company. What internal procedures already exist to gather the information you need? What systems should your company implement to give you the quality, reliable data you need?

7

DEVELOPING A PLAN

In what way, if any, will the mission of your organization change in the coming years?

What should be the company's priorities or principal efforts?

How should those be reflected in a business plan?

Business planners can form some notions about what the company should be doing while analyzing the business climate and the marketplace. But notions are vague and don't provide sufficient guidance for a company. It's like embarking on a trip without a specific destination in mind. Even when you have a destination, you need a map to get you there. A plan identifies a specific destination for the company and the methodology for reaching that destination.

If your company has paid little attention to planning or has a formal-looking document (a plan) that the management team hasn't seen for a while, that's not particularly unusual. Companies short-circuit the planning process for a variety of reasons, most of them related to time, money, and talent. Those who do allocate (or acquire) the necessary resources often lack the systems or procedures needed to make the plan a living document, an integral part of the company's operations.

Yes, planning does take time and money. But the amount of company time and money devoted to planning is relatively small in comparison with the benefit of ensuring that the company uses its resources for the right things. This pays enormous dividends, especially if the company avoids financial calamity. Even companies hanging on by a thin thread will spend money for a sound business plan so that they can get back on track.

With respect to talent, sound business planning does require some skill. That's not to say that the company can't do it in-house. The company may have the personnel that can lead the process and develop good plans, similar to the framework discussed in this unit.

But if that talent doesn't exist, the company has to be willing to seek the help of outside counsel, such as a business-savvy associate, a professional planning consultant, or a resource from a local college, university, or association of business professionals. Often, the fresh perspective of an outsider is very beneficial. The amount of time company personnel can devote to special projects and the organization's financial situation will influence the division of labor between in-house and outside personnel.

■ PLANNING RATIONALE

Several general concepts about planning are important to keep in mind. They affect the way plans are developed as well as the way plans are used.

- The *purpose of a plan* is to direct the organization's financial and human resources to those selected activities that will yield the greatest return on investment. Conversely, plans prevent the organization from diverting its resources to activities, regardless of tradition, that produce meager results. A plan tells the organization how to "work smart."

- A properly constructed plan tells the organization *what* it wants to accomplish and provides a general framework for *how* the organization intends to do this. Plans turn aspirations into concrete expectations. Plans contain specific goals, which are measurable, and provide a methodology, including timeframes, to tell the organization how to accomplish them. Specificity provides benchmarks so the organization can determine whether it's accomplishing what it set out to do.

■ A plan helps the organization be *resilient*. Organizations must be responsive, but they also must resist the temptation to abandon course at the sight of each intimidating change. With thoughtful forecasting, the company will have a plan that empowers it to function in the contemporary environment. By anticipating changes and restructuring activities, if necessary, the organization can keep pace with contemporary times and stay on course during turbulent ones.

■ The *foundation* of a plan is an analysis of the past, present, and likely future. A plan is only as good as the information gathering and filtering processes (the situational analysis). These are the exercises that scour the external and internal environments to learn as much as possible about the company's business and evaluate the factors (and their cause and effect) that will have a bearing on the company's business in the future. *Under*estimating the competition and *over*-stating the company's abilities (including revenue) are common pitfalls that must be avoided.

■ Planning activities must be *integrated* throughout the organization. This means that planning must occur at all levels of the organization. After upper management defines the long-range plan, lower levels of management plan activities around the goals for which they are responsible. A business plan is of little value unless all units of the organization are working in concert with one another.

■ Planning requires *commitment* from everyone in the organization. This means people must "buy into" the plan. Otherwise, they will stride off on their own paths, which defeats the purpose of having a plan. People are more likely to be committed when they see that the plan evolved from a deliberate, logical decision-making process. Engaging people from various levels in the organization not only provides multiple perspectives but also gives people a sense of ownership, which enhances commitment.

■ A plan must be *implemented*. Unfortunately, the planning documents in some organizations are stowed in a file drawer as soon as they are typed, never to see the light of day again. Some organizations use the documents for awhile and then stray off on some other path, as if the documents never existed. But an organization cannot afford to squander resources on projects that are not utilized.

■ Planning is the most fundamental management activity. From this flows virtually every business decision that is made. A plan is also useful for building credibility with people outside the organization. Lenders, suppliers, and potential business affiliates want to see that the company has a thoughtfully prepared business plan and use it as part of their decision-making processes.

■ A business plan is only a management tool. It should not take the fun out of being in business or stifle enthusiasm or creativity. In fact, a properly designed and implemented plan should have a positive effect on the organization. Be flexible! If a plan doesn't materialize as expected during the first year, don't give up. (This is where leadership's entrepreneurial spirit is an asset.) Because a plan is reviewed periodically, the company can make adjustments if necessary and set more realistic or achievable goals. It's difficult to anticipate, especially for a new business venture, how long it will take to reach certain plateaus.

■ YOUR BUSINESS PLAN

The information gathered from the situational analysis is now used to actually develop plans. Pertinent information that must be considered revolves around that which has been learned about the

■ business environment,

■ marketplace (consumers and competitors),

■ company's services and compatibility with demand,

■ organization of the company's sales and marketing activities (strengths and weaknesses),

■ company's human resources,

- organization of the company's operating structure and technology systems, and

- company's financial position.

There are various levels of planning, some more comprehensive and long term than others. The beginning point is a long-range blueprint (a master plan, in a sense) for the organization. A typical long-range plan spans three to five years. In recent years, organizations have found that a three-year timeframe is more feasible because of the dynamic environment. Formally, this is known as a long-range, general, or strategic plan.

The point is best made by saying that "Good long-range planning allows the company to be a meaningful specific rather than a wandering generality." Some organizations don't plan farther out than one or two years. But that's typically not a long enough period to implement a plan and gauge performance, especially of new endeavors. It takes time to solidify the company's position with a new target market or to reap the benefits of a franchise affiliation.

Furthermore, without a long-range plan, the temptation is far too great to shift course each year when instant results do not materialize. Valuable human and financial resources can be expended in one direction, only to be diverted in another direction and then another. Although organizations must be responsive to change, these must be deliberate and thoughtful responses.

Would you rather push a rope or pull a rope to get it from one place to another? It takes little effort to push one end of the rope. But when you do, where does it go; how many turns does it take? Isn't it more productive to take hold of one end and pull the rope? In doing so, you can control where it goes. But you have to know in which direction to head. And the longer the rope, the longer it takes for the tail to line up behind the leader.

Organizations are like the longer rope. Many facets of an organization have to be aligned in position behind the leader (the plan). The larger or more complex the organization, the more cumbersome the process. If the plan calls for some dramatic changes, there's the very element of change that an organization's culture and its people may not readily adjust to. All of this simply strengthens the argument in favor of a longer-term plan.

Planning terminology can vary. Professional strategic planners have individual preferences and sometimes put their own spin on terminology. The important thing to remember is what each part of the plan should tell you. Figure 7.1 shows how the pieces fit together.

Mission

The development of the long-range plan begins with the answers to several important questions.

- What is the company's purpose for being in business?

- What specifically does the business do?

- Where should the company be in the future that is different from where it is today?

The answers define the **mission,** the organization's fundamental purpose for existing. *This is the foundation on which the business enterprise is built.* Defining a mission is a thought-provoking exercise that involves a critical assessment of the organization to validate its basic reason for being and, most important, a vision of its reason for existing in the future.

These thoughts are then crystallized into one or several concise sentences that become the **mission statement.** These words, very simply, tell what the organization is about. Everything it does must support the mission, and if something doesn't, then the organization shouldn't be doing it. The mission statement is a critical first step in developing a plan because everything else that follows must support the mission.

FIGURE 7.1

Outline of the Components of a Plan

Mission Statement	
General Objective	General Objective
Goal	Goal
Strategy	Strategy
Tactics	Tactics
Strategy	Strategy
Tactics	Tactics

General Objectives

Next, expand on the mission statement by identifying **general objectives.** Perhaps the best way to characterize these is by the terminology that's currently in vogue: initiatives or competencies. They crystallize what the organization needs to focus on to accomplish its mission in the contemporary environment. Essentially, *general objectives*, *initiatives*, or *competencies* (whatever you choose to call them) become the organization's priorities during the timeframe of the plan (three or five years).

The number of general objectives is typically a function of the size and complexity of the organization and the capacity of its human and financial resources. For a fairly small organization, two general objectives are likely most feasible. Larger organizations typically don't choose more than four. It's possible, though, that even a very large, complex organization will choose only one or two competencies so that all efforts are mobilized in a very focused way.

To demonstrate what general objectives or initiatives look like, consider this:

> The situational analysis reveals that one of the most critical issues is the role of technology in everything the company does. The analysis also reveals that the company, which had been a leader in the first-time homebuyer market, has been losing market share. Yet, that population has been growing and with the low interest rates and proliferation of incentives for first-time homebuyers, this target market has great potential.
>
> Converting this to objectives, one might be "to fully integrate the use of the latest technology throughout the organization." Another objective might be "to make homeownership a reality for first-time buyers throughout the metropolitan area."

Notice that these particular initiatives or competencies affect the entire organization. Even the one that focuses on a target market suggests that the company's public relations messages, marketing and advertising themes, mortgage department activities, and perhaps other parts of the company, in addition to the individual sales offices, will have a role to play. Although these illustrations have companywide impact, the organization can establish objectives that are less broad, in which case a particular department or group of sales offices becomes a priority.

The mission statement and general objectives tell what the company *aspires* to do. But they do not provide specific direction to tell the organization how to accomplish that.

Think about planning the same way you would describe a sports game. First, you identify the game and the general theme of the game (the mission statement and general objectives). Now, you have to tell people what the object of the game is; these are the company's goals. Then, describe the series of plays that will get the team to the goal; these are the strategies the company will use to reach its goals. And finally, lay out the sequence of steps that will be needed to execute plays; these are the tactics that implement the plan.

Goals

The next step is to spell out the goals of the "game." Each general objective is supported by a number of specific **goals.** These are the end results the organization wants to achieve. They break down the aspirational or futuristic nature of the general objectives into manageable accomplishments and show how the organization intends to achieve its objectives.

Goals must be translated into specific words that tell precisely how to focus the organization's resources. They have four characteristics:

1. Specific or identifiable

2. Measurable (quantitative)

3. Attainable

4. Framed in time (beginning and completion dates)

Words like *increase, maximize, decrease,* or *minimize,* with nothing more specific or measurable, do not provide any way to determine whether the organization is on target. Specific goals would say "increase by 100 transactions," "increase by 25 percent," or "$500,000 in gross commissions." You may hesitate to make such precise statements because they represent a commitment that is easily scrutinized, and failure is obvious. But specificity is needed to give the organization readily identifiable *outcomes* for measuring the results of its efforts.

Timeframes also add specificity. If you want to increase your activity in a particular service by 100 transactions, do you mean in one year, two years or six months? A timeframe serves as a benchmark for determining achievements. A lack of timeframes can leave the organization floundering just as badly as if it didn't have any goals. An accomplishment that is significant enough to be a goal has to be achieved in a timely fashion.

Goals must challenge the organization to move forward, but they also must be attainable. The object is to make the best use of a company's resources, not to frustrate the effort with unrealistic expectations. Goals must be properly aligned with the capacity of the organization's financial and human resources. Or a part of the plan must be devoted to enhancing resources or systems to accomplish a goal. The best way to set realistic goals is with the information gained from the situational analysis. The business environment, the marketplace, and the company's past performance all affect future accomplishments.

Before setting a goal related to revenue or number of transactions, evaluate past production figures. Then, decide the amount of gross revenue you want to generate. Convert this figure to a number of transactions by determining the previous average commission and dividing the new gross figure by that amount. Now, decide on the distribution of listings and sales; compare these figures with previous activity. This, then, tells you whether the gross income or transaction projections are realistic.

Using other historical data, you can set goals relating to such achievements as the percentage of the market share you want to capture, the volume of business generated by various types of properties, or the volume of business generated from rentals and sales or other services.

With verifiable, measurable goals the organization has data with which to assess the organization's accomplishments during the plan's three- or five-year life. If the goals were unrealistic or unanticipated changes in the marketplace occurred, the company may have to revise the quantitative measures and the time frames in subsequent years. But don't change the numbers in the plan just to make your organization look better. The harsh reality may be that the organization is really straying off course. Face the facts and do something about it.

Strategies

After setting goals, the next step is their supporting **strategies.** These prescribe the methodology for accomplishing each goal. Long-range planning is otherwise known as *strategic planning* because it provides not just goals but also the strategic methodology for accomplishing them. Remember the game analogy: people need to know what steps to take to "score." Strategies provide those directions.

Strategies get to the heart of the hard decisions needed to convert goals into game-winning accomplishments. Look at what the organization currently does and decide what it needs to continue doing or do differently or new things it needs to do. Also consider the obstacles or roadblocks the organization could encounter and how will it overcome them. All of this reveals what the company needs to do to align systems (including technology), processes, procedures, and, most important, the human and financial resources in concert with the goals.

The strategy part of a plan is also where the phase-out of an activity that is no longer suitable is addressed. If certain customary activities no longer contribute to the achievement of an objective, they should be discontinued.

Figure 7.2 shows how goals and strategies support a general objective. If you have decided that one of the company's niche markets is vacation properties and second homes, for example, a portion of your business plan could be developed following this format.

Not all goals may be production-related. An earlier example about a general objective relating to technology could be supported with a goal about upgrading the company's computer system and strategies to make that happen. Another goal about an interactive Web site with strategies to build or enhance it could be suitable. An accompanying strategy may also be to reduce the amount of newspaper advertising.

Similarly, a goal to establish a new business unit, such as a relocation department, or to open a branch office by a certain target date could be supported with strategies to make the necessary preparations and plan the allocation of resources to that end. Or a goal to trim back a certain operation could be supported with strategies to assimilate those activities and personnel elsewhere in the organization.

FIGURE 7.2

Goals and Strategies

General Objective—To provide real estate services relating to vacation properties and second homes.

    Goal—To obtain 48 listings of properties suitable as vacation properties or second homes within the next 24 months. (Now you need to define strategies to get these listings.)

        Strategy—Assemble the professional knowledge necessary to identify suitable properties, including buyer's preferences, lifestyles, and desirable amenities.

        Strategy—Train the sales associates to identify and list suitable properties.

        Strategy—Develop a network with developers of these properties.

    Goal—To close 36 sales transactions within the next 24 months. (Now you need to define strategies to acquire the sales.)

        Strategy—Train the sales associates to work with potential buyers.

        Strategy—Develop marketing and advertising programs to promote these properties to the target population.

        Strategy—Develop an outreach program to target potential buyers in other geographic areas.

    Goal—To increase vacation- and second-home market share to 40 percent of the company's total sales production within three years.

        Strategy—Establish a business unit within the organization to provide a wide variety of services to people who own or desire vacation properties or second homes.

Contingency Plans

Because planning involves forecasting, the more futuristic the forecast, the fewer variables there are that can be predicted with great certainty. While most situations in the business environment, the marketplace, or within the company don't occur without some warning, circumstances can arise that could send a company scurrying to adjust.

A company can be prepared to make necessary adjustments by developing **contingency plans.** Not all master plans have this component. Companies develop contingency plans when there are significant indicators that a change in circumstances is a distinct possibility but not yet certain or close enough on the horizon to be incorporated in the plan.

Contingency plans are simply alternative goals and strategies that will be implemented in the event they are needed. It's impossible to move forward when the company is busy circling the wagons in a time of crisis. Contingency planning is a proactive measure that prevents the organization from being thrown for a loop and protects against knee-jerk reactions in the heat of the moment that could divert resources in careless or uncontrolled ways. It takes a little extra time to wander down the "what if" path of a major exodus in the job market, for instance, but it's an ace in the hole (which the competition may not have) that could pay enormous dividends.

Putting All the Pieces Together

A business plan is unique for each organization. Plans are not "packaged programs" that someone else has developed. Nor can you "borrow" another organization's and make it yours. If your organization is inflicted with the "just give me the words" ailment, it won't have a plan that supports *your* company's mission and general objectives and goals, strategies, and time-frames or measurements that are suitable for *your* organization in *your* marketplace.

A major benefit of planning is the *process itself,* that is, the discussions that ensue as various viewpoints, creative ideas, and possible solutions are shared. In other words, a plan is not a document that the broker prepares while sitting alone in the backroom, even in a small organization. Planning is a participatory exercise that fosters teamwork and engages people who have a stake in the outcomes in ways that enhance the plan's implementation. No doubt, all of this looks familiar in the context of the first unit's discussions.

The players in the process certainly include senior management and perhaps also a cross section of representatives from other levels in the organization, including sales staff. In a small brokerage company, the broker and perhaps a sales manager or selected salespeople are involved. The leader of the project could be a designated member of senior management or an outside consultant.

While the design of the actual planning meetings can vary, generally they consist of tasks first being assigned to gather the research in the situational analysis. This premeeting preparation is key to jumpstarting the program. It forms the basis of initial discussions as people react to the discoveries and reach consensus on the major impacts on the organization. These will eventually become the basis of the general objectives. Because they go hand-in-hand with the mission, the mission statement must be visited (or developed if the company doesn't have a clearly defined one) to decide whether it is still viable. Then goals and strategies can be developed.

This can be a very efficient exercise, the bulk of the work being accomplished perhaps in a two-day retreat. Once the situational discussion concludes and mission and general objectives are codified, the goal and strategy parts come together rather quickly, building on the ideas that were offered in the earlier discussion. Conducting planning meetings requires strong leadership so that discussions flow freely, but stay on point, and eventually achieve consensus. That may also mean helping people with divergent views, self-protecting instincts, and other bones they want to pick—make some concessions.

When all is said, someone commits the plan to writing, circulates a draft to all the participants to be sure it says what everyone agreed to and once everyone agrees, then it's ready to go. The planning document generally includes the

- table of contents;

- executive summary;

- summary of the situational analysis, the key factors that show the rationale behind the plan (which is just as useful for future reference as the actual plan);

- mission statement;

- general objectives/initiatives/competencies; and

- goals and their respective strategies.

The final item that is written when the planning document is assembled is the executive summary. This is a several-page report that is really a condensed version of the plan. The summary is the part of the document that outsiders (lenders and investors) typically see, so it must capture the essence of the plan. The summary includes a brief history of the company; its current activities, particularly its distinguishing features and services and position in the marketplace; and important factors about its financial position. Key risks and opportunities are also included, along with general objectives (or competencies) and significant goals to indicate what the company intends to do about them.

■ IMPLEMENTING A PLAN

Notice that after all is said, it's not done. The written document is only the beginning. The plan needs to be converted into action. This is the part of the process that brings the plan to life by defining activities and, most important, charging people with the responsibility for accomplishing them. The plan continues to live as an annual short-term, or business, plan is developed and management monitors the company's performance.

Tactical Planning

Using the game analogy again, tactics tells the team how to execute the plays of the game. *Tactical* or *activity* planning directs the workflow under the strategies.

In the strategies illustrated in Figure 7.2, there is still more the company needs to know about what to do. In the training strategy, what is the plan for developing and implementing the training? In the strategy relating to marketing and advertising, what specific marketing and promotional activities are needed? If a new business unit is to be created, what must be done to assemble the necessary money and personnel and define the work for the department?

When do any of these things have to be accomplished? Are the necessary resources and talent readily available in-house or are there activities that need to be outsourced?

Tactical planning answers these questions. In doing so, it breaks down the plan into manageable pieces of work. Otherwise, the scope of the task can look overwhelming. (No wonder organizations just shove the document into a bottom drawer.)

This phase of planning also identifies responsibilities. Normally, the work units that are affected by the strategies are responsible for the tactical or activity planning. They're most familiar with the work, and because they are accountable for accomplishment, they need to be engaged in the process. A sales office that is charged with achieving a production quota is the work unit that should decide how to reach it. Even though this is typically a participatory process, the manager is ultimately responsible for the outcomes, which includes seeing that resources are not diverted to counterproductive activities.

The Business Plan

A business plan is the company's work plan for the year. It comes together very easily because it is simply an extrapolation of the goals and strategies that were benchmarked for completion that year, perhaps with some refinements, and makes them priorities. A business plan can also include new strategies that may be needed to address situations that have emerged that can threaten the attainment of goals in the master plan.

The mention of refinements means that projections of numbers, dollars, and timeframes when the plan was first developed may need to be revised. Because there are more "knowns" than conjectures since the first planning discussions, the next 12-month period can be forecast with greater certainty. Projections may be revised downward because of developments in the business climate, the marketplace, or the company so as not to frustrate the organization. But it's also permissible to revise projections upward. If the company is ahead in the game, keep it winning.

The business plan typically becomes the working document that managers at all levels in the organization use to monitor progress throughout the year. Many of the quantitative measures can easily be segmented by quarters so that management has readily identifiable benchmarks. It's a lot easier to manage by quarters than it is to figure out how to make up for lost time in the last few months of the year.

Along the way, management can also identify activities that should be restructured or new strategies that could be recommended for the next year.

Back to the Long-Range Plan

By reviewing the long-range plan when the business plan is prepared each year, management can gauge the company's progress and the validity of the long-range plan. In so doing, management can determine whether the company is still on the right course or needs to revise the plan to respond to changes within the organization, the marketplace, or the business climate.

The long-range plan can be easily updated with each year's review, essentially recasting the plan for three years by adding a new third year each year. This does not mean that the company keeps changing courses or moving the goalposts farther away. It means that the essence of the plan can be used to build the next one, essentially providing continuity as the company moves forward.

Look at the assumptions from the situational analysis and evaluate which ones are still valid and those that need to be revised. (This is where the most recent company performance data are helpful.) From that, the rest of the components of the plan can be considered and tweaked as necessary. As goals or strategies are accomplished, they can be replaced with new ones as appropriate. This way a company can be flexible, continue to grow, and respond to change without getting jerked off course on a whim. Even the most comprehensive planning processes typically build on the previous plan.

■ CONCLUSION

With some thoughtful design and practice, planning will become as routine as any other business activity. A sound long-range plan becomes the foundation for the company's operations. Other phases of planning simply bring the plan to life by defining activities needed to implement the plan and giving the company's "marching orders" for the coming year. An annual review of the long-range plan forms the basis for the next plan. This way management is constantly providing the vision for the organization that will help it prosper in the future.

■ DISCUSSION EXERCISES

Identify one general objective and then develop appropriate supporting goals.

Prepare several strategies that could be implemented around these goals. Are the strategies identifiable, measurable, attainable, and framed in time?

Using one of your strategies, define appropriate tactics or activities.

IN CONCLUSION
OF UNIT TWO

Armed with a business plan, a manager is prepared to move on to the other management functions. This can be done with some assurance that the right course has been charted, particularly because of the amount of research that went into the development of the plan. The company has its marching orders and it is now up to management to guide all the other systems, procedures, and resources accordingly.

■ THE SCENARIO

Having read this unit, what is your analysis of the following scenario?

One bright Thursday morning, the managers of the company's 15 sales offices gathered for their monthly meeting with senior management. (That's the broker of record and the three regional managers who oversee the sales offices located within their geographic areas.) The hottest item on the prepublished agenda was "revenue projections for the coming year."

For the past week, the sales office managers had been scrambling through their files trying to figure out what "number" they will put on the table when it's their turn to tell the assembled group how much money each of their offices will bring into the company next year.

While senior management is sitting in eager anticipation of what the office managers are going to say on Thursday morning, the office managers are struggling to figure out how to cope with their assignment. They could briefly review year-to-date production and pick a number so that they have something to say at the meeting. They could analyze the past several years' income and expense statements and come up with a conservative number, then look like heroes when their offices exceed projections later on. Or they could be really gutsy, predict record-setting accomplishments and impress everyone on Thursday morning with their go-getting, winning attitude. Then they can deal with the consequences next year when they fall short.

By the conclusion of Thursday's meeting, each manager's projection has been recorded on a flip chart. The managers had not offered, nor were they asked for, a rationale for their projections, so it's conceivable that they could have used any one of the above-noted methods to come up with their numbers. Nevertheless, after the sums on the flip chart were totaled, senior management took the managers to task by saying that the grand total did not live up to senior management's expectations.

The meeting ended with both the office managers and senior management leaving totally frustrated over what should have been done to project next year's revenue.

■ THE ANALYSIS

The discussions in this second unit should shed some light on the debacle in the Thursday morning management meeting.

The purpose of the monthly meeting, that being to solicit input from the sales office managers with respect to the next year's revenue projections, is a worthy participatory exercise. The best people to state the case are those who are most familiar with the work of their respective offices. It's also better to have the people who will ultimately be responsible for accomplishing a goal participate in its development. The fact that people left the meeting feeling frustrated, though, says everyone should have known what the expectations were.

If senior management had developed a business plan for the coming year, the office managers should have been told what it was, rather than being told after the fact that they were off-base. If senior management didn't have any plan, but rather expected the meeting exercise to at least produce a revenue goal for next year (a questionable notion, at best), then no one should have been disappointed. If senior management expected to gather information to use in developing a plan for the coming year, then the input should have been respectfully accepted, even if it wasn't what management wanted to hear.

The fact that the office managers were thrashing around in a variety of modes as they prepared for the meeting says they were ill equipped for the task. They lacked the necessary information and a uniform and skillful methodology to produce valid numbers. It also appears that revenue-projecting exercises don't get their due respect. It could be because they are uncomfortable or because sales managers don't feel their voices will be heard anyway, so there's no point in wasting a lot of time and effort. Maybe the real source of their frustration is that senior management is out of touch with the realities of life in the sales offices and the industry.

While there are several ways to engage senior and office managers in planning exercises and produce useful outcomes, the hardest thing for either level of management to cope with is not being on the same page of the program. Office managers want to have input, but they also need some direction. In other words, when the organization does not have a master plan, the individual units within the organization don't know what they need to be doing.

■ SUMMARY

Throughout this unit we have developed the various stages involved in the planning process. Depending on whether you are the broker/owner, a senior manager in a large organization, a sales manager, or a department manager, your involvement in these phases will probably be different. As a guide for understanding your function in the process, the following summary is provided.

- Analyzing the Business Climate:

  - The broker/owner along with senior management conducts the analysis and may use outside resources.

  - Other managers could be invited by the broker/owner to participate. Beyond that they need to understand how the analysis impacts the planning process.

- Analyzing the Market:

  - The responsibilities are similar to those described above.

– Other levels of management, such as a sales manager, can provide valuable insight about the marketplace, the competition, and the current state of the company.

■ Developing the Plan:

– The Long-Range or Master Plan

The broker/owner and senior management are primarily responsible for developing the long-range plan and any contingency plans. Though other levels of management may be invited to participate in the development of the long-range plan, the owners and senior management are primarily responsible for implementing the plan.

– The Business Plan

The broker/owner and senior management are primarily responsible for developing the business plan.

All levels of management are responsible for monitoring their areas of responsibility to accomplish the business plan.

– Tactical Planning

All levels of management and possibly others in the organization are involved in planning the activities that are needed to accomplish certain strategies prescribed in the long-range plan.

ORGANIZING THE ORGANIZATION

Once there was a day when "Here's the desk; Here's the phone; Good luck, you're on your own" said just about all there was to say about where a real estate salesperson would be working. Indeed, it was an office, with a desk or two and some phones, and maybe a Girl-Friday type who ran the broker's office while he and a few salespeople hit the road, armed with sheer determination and gut instinct, to drum up business.

That real estate deal could just as well have been written on the back of a used envelope or a diner napkin. Not many laws to worry about that could send anyone to a court of litigation. High-tech was a car with air-conditioning. Multilist was a pile of listing sheets in a binder that had to be sorted through to replace the outdated with the new. Training was what the salesperson learned at the arm of the broker. Company information systems were the pages in the bookkeeper's ledger.

No, not novel fiction. And from a business management point of view, not a lot about a company that had to be planned or organized, either. Unquestionably, all of this bears little resemblance to the industry today. It does make a point about the reasons for walking a meticulous path through today's business management study.

The plan that was formed in the previous unit now needs organization, the who, what, where, and how decisions that make the company do what the plan says are the right things to do. Like planning, organizing is an ongoing activity. With each year's business plan and each major overhaul of the long-term plan, the same decisions have to be visited so that as plans change, so do the organization's structure and systems. Otherwise, the company's progress is as hamstrung as it would be without any plan at all.

The organizing function essentially groups activities and resources so that a company can operate effectively and efficiently. To do this, the company needs

- structure for the its ownership, business alliances, and human resources;

- physical facilities, properly provisioned with communications and information systems;

- financial structure to properly manage the company's financial resources;

- policies and procedures to prescribe how business is conducted; and

- marketing and advertising with which to generate business.

The blueprint for the company's structure is the company's plan. In bringing the plan to life, the organization also takes on its own personality. While there may be some general boundaries to guide decisions and, certainly, some hard lines drawn by law, the organizational structure, facilities, policies and procedures, and marketing and advertising strategies are individual to each company. The company must also pay heed to the contemporary environment and make the most of the present-day tools and technology. The chapters in this unit are devoted to organizing the company so that it is prepared to accomplish its mission.

If you are the broker/owner or a senior manager in a large organization, you will be responsible for the major legal and financial decisions. This will also include company policy. If you are a sales office or department manager, you most likely will have some authority to make financial decisions and to develop operating systems within your office or department.

CHAPTER EIGHT

8

STRUCTURING THE ORGANIZATION

How are the real estate companies in your area structured? Their ownership, affiliations, staffing, departmental systems, and the scope of authority of their sales managers?

What has changed in recent years? Why?

The structure of an organization is essentially the framework for a company's operations. The legal form of ownership, professional affiliations, organizational chart (the way activities are grouped), and chain of command (the hierarchy) all provide structure so that the organization can function.

The operating structure will vary, depending on the kind and scope of work the company does (back to its plan) and the company's stage in its life cycle. The start-up company is in the *birth* stage, typically characterized by a fairly modest scope of work (and most likely, a tight budget) and an efficient, though streamlined, operating structure so that it can get on its feet.

Once the company has survived the most vulnerable first one to three years, it can become more ambitious. In organizational life cycling this is known as the *growth* stage. As its name implies, the company expands the work that it started doing and/or stretches into new markets or endeavors. This is typically the most energetic time in an organization's life. Depending on the nature of the work it does, how well it's tailored to the marketplace, and the aggressiveness of its leadership, this stage can be short lived or endure for five or ten more years.

Organizations also have a *midlife*, though not a crisis. If there's to be one, the crisis is more likely to arise during a company's most aggressive years (the growth stage), when making the right decisions at the right time can be most challenging. This is not to say that the organization that reaches midlife can't also be vulnerable, but this is the point when the company's gradual growth is typically rooted in a very solid market position, which can also be enhanced with the addition of a new venture. Eventually, the company will reach stability (neutral growth).

And then there's the *maturity* stage, which is characterized by long-term stability. Companies can succeed and be profitable during their midlife and mature years, but they can be vulnerable if they become complacent. These are the companies that struggle most with the "That's the way we always did it, and it worked" attitude. Midlife and maturity should suggest that the company has the experience to be smart about doing business in whatever the prevailing environment. If a company uses that to its advantage, it can endure. Otherwise, it will discover the last step in maturity: *decline*.

The framework or operating structure of a company (and a company's plan) must change as the organization cycles through the various stages of life. Ownership may be reconfigured, adding new owners or severing relationships with current ones. Business affiliations may change as new alliances are adopted or existing ones are discontinued. Operations may expand to include new business sectors or scale back to reduce the number of services. In essence, operating strategies must empower the organization to function.

■ LEGAL OWNERSHIP

One of the most fundamental decisions is the "who" and the "how" with respect to the company's ownership.

The broker may be the sole owner of the business or join forces with other owners. The salespeople may have an ownership position in the company, an increasingly more common practice. The lone worker or one who employs only one or two salespeople may feel comfortable being a sole proprietor. However, other forms of ownership may be preferable.

Because these decisions have complex legal and tax implications, the advice of professional counsel is strongly advised. State licensing laws may specify certain ownership positions for the responsible broker and officers of a corporation, which must also be considered.

Sole Proprietorship

In a sole proprietorship, the broker is the sole owner. The broker hangs out a shingle, personally reaps all of the rewards of being in business, and bears all personal liability for its losses. The sole proprietor has exclusive command over the business, without the entanglements of other owners, so the success or failure of the enterprise is attributable to one person.

Presumably, the owner embarks on this venture because he or she has certain technical (as in real estate) and business expertise to make this a worthwhile endeavor. While it may be appealing to own a business and "run it the way I want to," the sole owner does not have the benefit of the expertise or advice of other stakeholders in the business. There is also enormous liability because a sole proprietorship does not offer any personal shield, meaning that the owner has essentially put all of his or her assets and creditworthiness on the line for the business.

The longevity of the enterprise and the livelihood of anyone who works for the proprietor rest with the owner. If the owner becomes incapacitated or dies, the business is vulnerable unless the owner has given legal authorization or prepared a plan of succession to cover these eventualities. (State license law may stipulate certain procedures.)

Often, proprietors see their businesses as valued legacies for family members. Without the technical expertise or commitment to perpetuate the enterprise, however, the business may not endure. Deloitte & Touche statistics indicate that only 35 percent of family businesses survive under the second generation.

Corporations

A corporation is a sole legal entity created under state laws of incorporation. Although it is an association of one or more persons (as stockholders), a corporation is regarded as having an existence and personality of its own. It is treated as a single individual that has legal capacity to contract and otherwise conduct its affairs as prescribed by the articles of incorporation.

A corporation may be closely held, meaning that the shares of stock are owned by relatively few people, all or most of whom are directly involved in the corporation's business. Or the corporation may be publicly owned, meaning that the corporate shares are publicly traded in accordance with securities and exchange laws.

Corporate structures are appealing for several reasons.

- *Limited liability.* Liability incurred by the corporation becomes an obligation of the corporation, not of the individual owners. Unless a shareholder has signed a personal guarantee for the corporation's obligations, actions for damages, judgments, or bankruptcies will not affect the person's assets. Only the amount of the stockholder's investment in the corporation is at risk.

- *Perpetual existence.* Because a corporation is a legal entity that exists indefinitely (until and unless it is properly dissolved), it technically never dies. Any officer who dies, retires, or resigns can be replaced.

- *Centralized management.* The stockholders elect a board of directors that, in turn, elects a slate of officers. The officers are responsible for the general affairs of the corporation. At least one of the officers, the licensed broker, is directly responsible for the real estate brokerage activities under state license law.

- *Transferability.* The corporate stock may be transferred freely from one stockholder to another.

- *Lack of income limitations.* A corporation may have an unlimited number of stockholders and is permitted to earn an unlimited amount of income.

One of the major disadvantages of a corporation is that profits are taxed twice: once at the corporate level (before dividends are distributed) and again as dividends are distributed to the stockholders. Salaries paid to the officers are not considered profits, so they are taxable only to the individuals who receive them. Losses may not be passed on to the stockholders, but may be applied to the corporation's future earnings. Any capital gains realized by the corporation are passed on to the stockholders as ordinary income.

Brokers who incorporate have customarily retained their ownership positions in closely held or private corporations. Recently, some brokers have taken their corporations public and circulated offerings of their stock on the major stock exchanges. Motives vary for doing this, including the ability to infuse cash into the corporation and to give staff, particularly managers and salespeople, an ownership stake in the company.

Any corporate strategy should be evaluated with the help of an accountant and a corporate or tax attorney, particularly because corporate and tax laws are constantly changing.

S Corporation

The S corporation offers the same first four advantages of a corporation and overcomes one of the major disadvantages, the double taxation. Income, losses, and capital gains are passed directly to the stockholders. They, rather than the corporation, pay taxes (or deduct losses) on their personal tax returns.

There are restrictions on an S corporation. The number of shareholders is limited to no more than 75 owners. Not more than 25 percent of the income may be generated from passive investments, such as stock dividends, rental of investment properties, and interest from money deposits. If the S corporation is engaged primarily in real estate brokerage activities, these restrictions may not be burdensome. But it is easy to make mistakes, jeopardizing the S corporation status, without professional advice.

A recent development in the real estate industry is that individual licensees are incorporating themselves or as sales teams under a corporate umbrella. These strategies raise a multitude of issues, not the least of which are real estate licensing and agency concerns that must be resolved in accordance with state law.

General Partnership

A partnership is an organization formed under a state's Uniform Partnership Act in which two or more co-owners engage in business for a profit. All of the owners are general partners and share full personal liability for the debts or other obligations of the partnership. The partnership itself does not pay taxes, although it does file an information return, reporting the income it distributed to each partner. The partners are responsible for paying their own individual taxes. Losses or capital gains also are passed along to the partners.

A partnership can hold a real estate broker's license, provided each partner who is engaged in the real estate business is also a licensed broker. Because the partnership does not enjoy status as a sole legal entity (like a corporation), it does not have a life of its own. The death, withdrawal, bankruptcy, or legal disability of any of the general partners will dissolve the partnership. It is advisable to seek counsel before forming a general partnership, including assistance in writing a partnership agreement.

Limited Partnership

A limited partnership is a venture in which one person (or a group of people), known as the general partner(s), organizes and operates a partnership. Other members of the partnership, the limited partners, are merely investors. These individuals do not have responsibility for or any say in the direction or operation of the partnership. They share in the profits from the efforts of the general partner and are liable for losses only to the extent of their investment. General partners, however, have unlimited liability and their actions are closely regulated by state and federal agencies, including the manner in which limited-partner investors are solicited.

Limited Liability Companies

Personal liability and corporate income taxes are the two most persuasive issues that affect the choice of ownership structure. Many states have laws that enable businesses to operate as limited liability companies (LLCs).

The investors in LLCs are members, rather than partners or shareholders, holding membership interests (rather than stock) in the company.

LLCs may be an appealing alternative to S corporations and limited partnerships. Some of the restrictions that are imposed on an S corporation can be avoided. An LLC partially limits the liability that otherwise exists in a limited partnership, provided the appropriate steps are taken to accomplish this. Regulations and fees for establishing LLCs vary considerably from state to state, so professional guidance is essential.

■ MODE OF OPERATION

Once the most desirable form of ownership is determined, the next issue to consider is the mode of operation. That is, whether the company is going to be independent or affiliated in some fashion with other organizations. Generally, the competitive advantage or disadvantage and the benefits and drawbacks for the company influence this decision.

Independent

An independent business appeals both to owners, who want maximum freedom to guide their affairs, and to consumers, who want to do business with people who totally own and operate their own companies. In this mode of operation, the business enterprise is totally self-reliant. This go-it-alone strategy means that the company's success is due to its efforts alone. This also means that the company confronts its struggles alone as well. There are no supportive benefits such as those available when companies are affiliated with one another.

Franchise

A franchise is essentially a "packaged program" for a business, presumably a proven formula for running a business that provides a tested product or service that has appeal or acceptance in the marketplace. The owner of the franchise authorizes franchisees to engage in this patented or copyrighted business, with the expectation that the franchisees will make money for themselves and for the owner of the franchise.

Franchisees are independent business owners who, at the same time, are affiliated with other companies who are part of the franchise's network. The most common reason real estate companies choose affiliation is it provides them more power in the marketplace than an independent company could otherwise achieve for itself. Companies choose franchises based on the principal focus of the franchise.

- **Marketing and advertising:** While all franchises provide brand name or identity, that brand identity is the primary focus of many franchises. The appeal is their professional marketing and advertising programs, typically including television, radio, or print media campaigns; Web site connectivity; and brochures, newsletters, signs, and other marketing tools. National franchises also have the purchasing power to assemble coupon and merchant-discount programs and other cross-marketing strategies.

- **Target market services:** These franchises' primary focus is specific consumer services, such as counseling owners who want to sell their properties themselves or services associated with buyer agency. The primary advantage of consumer-service-oriented franchises is the technical expertise they offer to the franchisees. These franchises appeal to companies whose business focus is similar to the franchise's focus.

- **Business operations:** These are the franchises that provide operating structures, such as the 100 percent commission companies and the pyramid ownership plans. The appeal of these franchises is that they offer greater financial benefits to the salespeople than are customary in other kinds of organizations.

Ultimately, brand-name recognition is the primary benefit of a franchise. This can be a blessing or a curse for a company, though. It's not uncommon for consumers to remember the name of the franchise rather than the name of the individual firm. So a company needs to promote its individual identity while also linking itself with the franchise. Some franchises grant exclusivity or limit the number of franchisees in geographic areas, while others do not. This means that a company may not achieve the power in the marketplace that was expected.

A franchise's power in the marketplace is also a function of the success or failure of the individual franchisees. Franchises often provide business development expertise to protect the reputation of the brand and franchise revenue. Frequently, there are also training programs and seminars for the salespeople and leadership and management programs for the brokers.

Franchise affiliation provides a logical connection for referrals with other franchisees around the country. However, this association can also be a drawback. If consumers have had unsatisfactory experiences with one franchisee, they may resist referrals to others (though these may have been just isolated events). It's best to become acquainted with other franchisees to decide whether this is a desirable group with whom to affiliate. It's advantageous, though not a necessity, to share similar philosophies of doing business.

One of the downsides of affiliation is the franchised service or product itself. Not all franchises are successful everywhere. The brand may not have the power in a particular marketplace that it commands elsewhere or it may have had a storied past after franchisees in an area started up and failed or disassociated from the franchise.

Franchises can also be costly. The entrepreneur who dreamed up the franchise and took it out for a test drive shares it with a profit motive, not out of a sense of generosity. So there are costs involved. These must be analyzed in conjunction with the benefits that could be anticipated from the affiliation.

When evaluating costs and benefits, consider the initial franchise fees (which can be very expensive and, for an established company, will include costs to convert signs and other signature materials) and the fees that are owed during the term of the franchise contract. These may be predetermined, monthly amounts, regardless of the company's production. Or they may be based on transaction activity, collected either periodically or out of each transaction.

Once convinced that the benefits warrant the expense, the company must decide how to foot the bill. Generally, the company pays the initial fee but ongoing costs of affiliation may be borne solely by the company or shared with the salespeople. Salespeople will resent the financial obligation, however, unless they feel the franchise affiliation benefits their production.

National Corporations

A number of national corporations have been attracted to the real estate business in recent years. Often, the goal is to strengthen their operations by engaging in diverse but compatible enterprises. The ability to link the products and services of these enterprises in cross-marketing programs is an additional enticement.

National corporations typically purchase existing local real estate firms, selecting those that meet certain criteria for size or market share. The terms of the agreement with the corporation will determine the structure of the company under the corporate umbrella, the broker/owner role and responsibilities in the organization, and the degree of financial independence (or dependence) the company will have.

Once the business is sold to a national corporation, the broker/owner essentially becomes a manager. While this means relinquishing some prestige and decision-making authority, the attractive trade-off may be the power of the corporate name along with advertising and promotional programs and strategies to enhance the company's internal operations. Depending on the financial arrangements, the company may also realize an infusion of cash with which to enhance its brokerage activities.

Local Affiliations

In recent years, local brokerage firms have sought ways among themselves to strengthen their competitive advantage and achieve cost efficiencies. They do this by forming an association, corporation, or local franchise and pooling financial resources for such expenses as training, marketing, and advertising programs and secretarial and accounting services. They can also pool expertise, as professional sales teams, to offer complementary services such as land development, commercial leasing, and property management. Because each of these ventures is structured individually, there is no standard financial arrangement.

Collectively, brokers can increase their power in the market by capitalizing on the market share of each firm and creating local name recognition for new affiliates. But companies need to consider the image and success of the associated firms. The rising-star company may be providing greater benefits to the weaker firms than it will reap in return. On the other hand, jointly capturing a larger share of the market benefits everyone.

An informal way brokers can achieve cost efficiencies is to share office space, housing their independent operations under one roof, and share rent, common facilities such as conference rooms, and secretarial and accounting staff. Because several brokers are working out of the same physical location, consumers may not see the businesses as distinctly separate enterprises. It's important to be sure that the arrangements meet any office requirements prescribed by state license law.

There are several downsides to shared-office arrangements, unless eventualities are properly addressed ahead of time. One is the liability for one broker's unpaid bills that could become the responsibility of the other brokers. There is also the possibility that controversy will arise over entitlement to customers. In addition, litigation between a consumer and one of the brokers could unexpectedly draw another broker into the proceedings, simply by virtue of the affiliation.

Affiliated Business Arrangements

An affiliated business arrangement (AfBA) is a network of interrelated companies, owned by one holding corporation, that offer services tied to a real estate transaction. The most obvious is mortgage lending, though title insurance, settlement services, or property inspections are also possibilities.

For years real estate brokers have sought ways to enhance the services they offer consumers. Today, this strategy is even more important to satisfy the consumers' quest for seamless transactions. AfBAs provide the interrelated services consumers desire and provide the operational structure real estate companies covet to coordinate and control a transaction. The linkage of services through AfBAs also links sources of revenue.

While AfBAs are appealing, significant capital is needed to set up separate companies, and no one should venture into these arrangements without considerable legal oversight, in light of antitrust concerns and the Real Estate Settlement Procedures Act.

Multiple Listing Services

The discussion of affiliations would be incomplete without once again mentioning multiple listing services (MLSs). Regardless of whether the company is independent, a franchisee, or part of a national corporation, MLS membership may be an important facet of its operation. Depending on the strategies in the company's business plan, MLS membership may be important not only for serving consumers but also for the company's competitive position in the marketplace.

■ MERGERS AND ACQUISITIONS

The distinction between a merger and an acquisition is more academic than real. In practice, companies combine in very individual ways under legal arrangements that suit their specific purposes. The allure of an alliance is also individual, though the intended gain is efficiency and/or effectiveness for the organizations. Your company may be searching for an alliance or yours may be the company being courted by another. In either case, the goal is to combine forces in ways that are a "win-win" for both organizations as they become one.

For the company being pursued, joining forces with another may provide additional financial resources with which to aggressively pursue selected company objectives or may result in greater power in the marketplace. Depending on the role the broker/owner would have, this may be an opportunity to relinquish some management responsibilities and concentrate on activities in which she or he has particular expertise or interest. Or this may be the most suitable way to phase into retirement.

For the company doing the pursuing, joining forces with another may be the most suitable way to expand operations or gain managerial or staff talent or other assets to strengthen the organization or its position in the marketplace. If a company's business plan calls for adding new products or services or expanding geographic territory, purchasing an existing company that offers these features is one way to accomplish those goals.

Although a company could expand by opening a new office or starting a new division, acquiring another business could accomplish the same purpose more efficiently. An existing business has an established presence in the marketplace, experienced personnel, a physical office site complete with furnishings and equipment, and possibly a franchise affiliation. All of these assets take time and money to establish. The business also has a proven cash flow, which is an advantage if financing is needed to acquire the company.

Even though an acquisition eliminates some of the unpredictable variables associated with starting a new enterprise or opening a branch office, this strategy is not without risk. Often, the motive for acquiring a real estate business is to capture its sales talent. However, the market position of the acquired business can quickly deteriorate if that talent is lost, making this a very costly recruiting exercise. In fact, upheaval is often seen as a prime opportunity for others to court the company's personnel.

In the corporate world, some people have gained celebrated reputations as merger and acquisition specialists because of their keen ability to evaluate business enterprises, find good fits, and orchestrate successful transitions. This is not to say that a company in quest of an alliance can't go it alone, but it does make the point that these projects require considerable skill to forge a happy and profitable match.

Evaluating a Business

Any merger or acquisition requires that the company principals be astute consumers. The win may be for the company being acquired if its owners are unloading problems and frustrations. But the venture is not a win for the company that now shoulders the burden of worn-out equipment, a staff of malcontents, a franchise affiliation that is more costly than beneficial, an office location that is no longer viable, or more debt or other liability than was anticipated. Several questions to consider:

- Why is the business for sale? Are the current owners just ready to retire or are they bailing out because they can't make a go of the business any longer?

- What are the business's primary assets (or appeal)? What are its liabilities?

- How much is the business really worth? Is the profit overstated or understated? Has the owner deferred expenditures that should have been made? (The profit will look better than it really should.) Or is the business incurring expenses that should be trimmed? (The profit won't look as good as it could.)

- What is the reputation of the business in the marketplace? In the case of a merger in which both companies will retain some identity, will the association portray a positive message?

■ How well is the company managed? Is it a well-run organization that just needs the power in the marketplace that can be achieved with affiliation? Or is it a lingering organization that can be made better with more astute oversight?

Evaluating or appraising a business is a difficult task. Like any appraisal, the validity of the evaluation is a function of the quantity and quality of the information that is available. (Not all business owners freely open all records for perusal or accurately state the true state of affairs.) Also, like any appraisal, there is some amount of subjectivity involved, even in quantified measures. And after all is said in the appraisal, the value and the price of a business may differ, depending on the motivations of the parties.

Frequently, real estate brokers have the expertise to evaluate a business. However, because their view of the venture may be less than objective when they are directly involved in the merger or acquisition, the advice of an accountant who can expertly assess the company's financial statements is a wise addition to the decision-making process.

Return on investment (ROI) is the most widely accepted valuation approach—expressed as present value returned on investment, internal rate of return, or financial rate of return. In any case, these theoretical approaches to value require a large amount of financial data to produce the numbers with which to analyze an investment. While working through the analysis, also consider that the business being analyzed may not continue to be the same business, so any of its assets could be worth either more or less after the merger or acquisition.

Look closely at all aspects of the organization, especially those that made the company attractive in the first place. Determine the value of that which is being purchased—the name, current listings, pending sales, all or some of the company's services (property management or mortgage business), office equipment (or leases), employees or salespeople, contracts (such as advertising, franchise, or multiple listing service), or office location. Sometimes, all a purchaser wants is the sales unit, leaving the seller with the rest of the business assets and liabilities.

Goodwill.   The length of time the company has been in business and the way it's integrated into the new organization will affect the value of the company's name and goodwill. The quality of listings and volume of sales transactions may improve or decrease. Because the salespeople have a significant bearing on these aspects of the business, a mass exodus can seriously jeopardize the value of goodwill or the quality of the listings and sales.

Organizational Culture. Because business cultures and management philosophies differ, the effect of new leadership on the overall operation of the current firm must be considered, including the

- planning philosophy,

- organizational structure and business systems,

- staffing or personnel assignments and supervisory responsibilities,

- training and professional development programs,

- allocation of financial resources and financial management systems, and

- management styles.

Certainly, the more compatible the organizations are in these regards, the more attractive the acquisition or merger will be. That's not to suggest that dissimilar organizations can't blend successfully, but any transition takes time while people learn to function under new business philosophies, management styles, and operating systems. The greater the differences, the longer the transition period and the time before the venture reaches its financial potential. Highly divergent cultures and business philosophies are often not good candidates for these ventures.

The success or failure of a merger or acquisition rests in the hands of the people who work for the organization. When cultural and philosophical differences are great, considerable retraining may be needed. It's also likely that people will resist the merger, take matters into their own hands, and find other places of employment. All of this has cost implications as well.

Transition

The structure of the merger or acquisition will dictate a number of things. It may be that little will change, other than the name of the acquired company. Or the change may be more dramatic, with closure of the acquired company's offices and the assignment of personnel to other offices.

Or the newly blended organization may be a fully integrated merger of leadership, systems, and personnel, all doing business as a new entity under a company name that is a blend of the previous companies' or a name that reflects a fresh start for both companies.

Regardless of the specific arrangements of the venture, the companies need a transition plan. The outward things people see (like company name and signature) are a minor part of the story. The companies need to ensure that business runs smoothly so that the venture proves to be financially rewarding in as efficient a timeframe as possible. A transition plan needs to address several things.

- **Containment:** Even before the legal documents are signed, rumors start circulating. One could hope they are harbingers of excitement and positive outcomes, but invariably rumors thrive on the negative, which can threaten relationships with staff (particularly salespeople), customers, clients, and others in the business community.

  Companies need a plan to contain the news until they are ready to make their formal announcement and to retain staff and business relationships. In other words, they need to maintain control and assure everyone that all is well.

- **Organization:** After the closing and formal announcement of the venture is not the time to decide how the companies are going to do business. A smooth transition requires a well-thought-out plan for leadership and assignment of responsibilities, operating policies and procedures, business systems, and the allocation of personnel.

  The object of the exercise is to design an efficient operating structure during the transition period. This is an interim plan that enables the organization to get up and running while it phases in various changes that will become permanent.

- **Launch:** Two audiences are affected by the merger or acquisition: the internal community (the workforce) and the external community. The company needs a good marketing plan to convey the message of its new identity to these two audiences. This requires considerable advanced planning so that the organization is armed with signage and promotional materials and is prepared to capture the minds and hearts of its audiences when it makes the public announcement.

The initial kickoff is a fast-paced, high-energy time, typically beginning with an exciting event for company staff that is then followed with announcements to current customers and clients (they should not hear the news third-hand) and, finally, the community at large.

Once the company is prepared for the fanfare and has a road map to get business underway, the hard work begins. During the first two weeks after the fanfare, the company needs to get staff on board with the company's services and business policies and procedures. Much of the success of the new venture depends on the way leadership, especially of the acquiring company, conducts itself. People are often skeptical or feel insecure, and they certainly resent being steamrollered. The more respectful and patient leadership is and the stronger the partnership between management and staff, the smoother the transition will be.

A well-known fact of mergers and acquisitions is that duplicate systems, redundant personnel, and divergent business philosophies mean that some people may not retain their jobs. The new company's production policies may mean that marginal salespeople will be terminated; duplicate administrative departments mean that excess personnel must be assimilated elsewhere in the organization (sometimes by demotion) or let go. People may leave rather than wait for management to decide their fate. Unless management has a plan for retention and succession, the organization may lose the very people it wanted to keep.

■ INTERNAL STRUCTURE

An internal operating structure is essentially the organization of work. In a single-person organization, the structure is very simple—one person is the organization and is responsible for all facets of its operations. As the scope of work grows, the structure of the organization becomes more complex. Work has to be properly organized so the company can work efficiently. The process of structuring work involves a series of steps.

1. Begin by identifying all the work required by the company's business plan.

2. Group interrelated tasks associated with that work.

3. Assign those collected tasks to work groups. (Groups generally have certain primary functions that relate to administrative, operating, and product or service activities.)

4. Convert that work into job positions. (Analyze the relationship and scope of work that can reasonably be accomplished by an individual, considering the time and effort involved.)

5. Determine the roles and responsibilities associated with each position. This becomes a job description for the position.

6. Identify the skill sets or talent needed to perform each job and discharge the responsibilities of the position.

Essentially, this process arranges work in a rationale or logical scheme; it tells the company what needs to be done and who is needed to do it. A real estate company's work may be grouped by property type (residential, commercial, etc.) or by services (brokerage, property management, appraising, etc.). There may also be groups that provide administrative support and manage the information systems. As the organization grows larger or more decentralized, its efficiency becomes more dependent on these work groups.

A start-up company obviously goes through this process from scratch. But organizations revisit the process periodically to ensure that work is arranged efficiently and the human resources are properly aligned. Are there better ways to group work? Are there job positions that should be added, eliminated, or reconfigured? Are the skills and talents of current personnel properly aligned with their jobs? Or are some workers better suited to other jobs? This process also forms the basis for recruiting, hiring, and training.

One-Person Organization

If you are a one-person business, you are the broker, salesperson, and manager. A one-person organization is a singularly self-directed enterprise whose scope of work is a function of that which one person can accomplish. This also means that the growth of the enterprise is self-limiting. Obviously, this is a small enterprise that operates at the will of one person, who can work as much or as hard as he or she chooses, and is dependent solely on the revenue that can be generated by one person.

Although the organization structure is simplistic, that does not mean that the work is simplistic. Although there are no other people to supervise, the chief one-and-only person has all the other responsibilities of running the business, from managing its financial affairs and market and advertising activities to delivering the core services of the business. This means that the person needs multiple business management skill sets and either must make time to devote to multiple tasks or must outsource certain functions to expert professionals.

One- to Ten-Agent Organization

A one- to ten-agent organization is a small, centralized operation. (See Figure 8.1.) The broker/owner role now includes supervisory responsibilities. This means that skill sets are required to supervise the organization's human resources in addition to those required for the other business management responsibilities.

Obviously, with more hands on board, the capacity of the organization expands. More work can be accomplished and the company can sustain more consistent operations and generate a steadier stream of revenue than when the company is totally dependent on one person's efforts.

Growth means that the cost of doing business increases and the organization becomes more complex. Increased cost of facilities, information systems, and other support services that today's salespeople expect can be disproportionately expensive per person until the organization grows closer to the eight- to ten-agent size, unless a very small number of salespeople are highly productive. There is also the likelihood that nonselling staff and other clerical support will be needed to assist with administration functions.

FIGURE 8.1

One- to Ten-Agent Organization

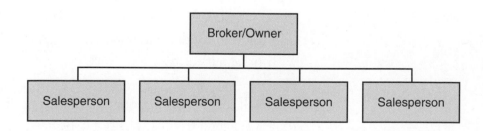

All of this means that there are more human variables to manage. As soon as one salesperson is hired, the broker becomes a sales manager. Typically, one-tenth of the broker's time is devoted to this activity. With each additional salesperson, another tenth of the broker's time is added to sales management activities. As the sales staff grows, the broker has less time to devote to sales activities and may eventually become a full-time sales manager (unless one is hired).

Monolithic Organization

A monolithic organization is a highly centralized operation, functioning as a single (mono) unit, with work being structured to flow from one singular source of authority at the top of the organization. The one-person and one- to ten-agent organizations are monolithic in the sense that one person at the top of the organization (the broker/owner) is the chief in charge of the entire scope of the organization's work.

As human and financial resources permit, the scope of work expands, with the result being that work is grouped in more focused ways. Hence, there may be a number of work groups (departments or divisions) that are responsible for accomplishing various goals in the business plan. Some are directly responsible for delivering the company's core services, and others are responsible for administrative functions that support the salespeople and the internal operation of the company. (See Figure 8.2.)

The distinguishing characteristic of a monolithic organization is that work is highly controlled by the top of the organization. This is normally the broker/owner or president. Authority flows from this position to the next level of senior management, then from senior management to department or division managers. The managers at each level are responsible for directing their work groups, but they do so only within the limits authorized by the immediate superior. Decision making is highly controlled by one or only a few individuals in upper management, leaving subordinate positions with little authority.

The skill sets or talent required for each position reflects the scope of work that is assigned to those positions. Because the work becomes more focused the lower the position on the organization chart, skill sets become more task oriented. A training director in a monolithic organization has little influence over other aspects of the company's administration, so this position is likely

FIGURE 8.2

Monolithic Organization

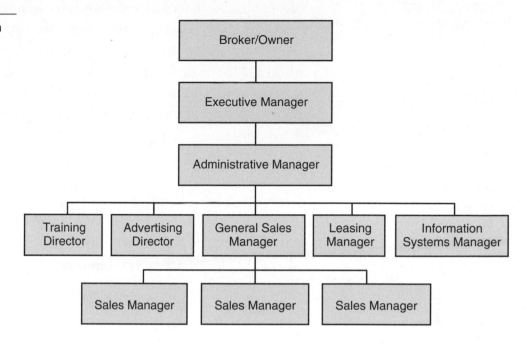

to require only very specific training skills. Broader business management skill sets would be required of the top three positions in Figure 8.2.

Although nothing about the formal organization chart changes, the physical efficiency of work and the control over human factors can differ, depending on whether all work groups are housed under one roof or at scattered sites. The most important consideration, though, is that physical space must comfortably house the scope of work and provide flexibility, so that as the organization grows, people are not working in overcrowded, morale-defeating conditions.

Housing all of the company's operations in one location can be efficient, reducing the facility cost per person and function and enhancing the coordination of activities among departments. It's easier for senior management to supervise all activities, though taken to the extreme, highly controlling management uses centralization to keep everyone under the one-roof microscope. Multiple facilities can also be efficient, though, with sales offices being strategically placed for their purposes and administrative functions housed elsewhere.

Decentralized Organization

A decentralized organization consists of a number of work groups or departments, but, unlike a monolithic organization, there are fewer layers of management at the top of the organization. As demonstrated in Figure 8.3, authority is delegated from the top of the organization to the next management level. The managers or directors of those work groups have the authority to direct their groups' activities, operating essentially as individual business units.

Decentralized operations are often viewed as more functionally efficient. With fewer levels of management to bog down the process, organizations can be more responsive or resilient. Managers or directors can freely direct the work for which they are responsible, essentially making the calls rather than waiting for direction from intermediaries.

Frequently, the work groups are structured as individual **profit centers.** This means that each unit functions on its own financial platform and is expected to produce enough income to cover its costs of operation plus make a profit for the company. Work units that are responsible for a company's core services (like sales divisions or offices) are often set up as profit centers.

Typically, administrative functions are centralized. Setting up accounting and information management, marketing, and training departments for the entire organization, rather than duplicating these activities in each work unit, is more cost-efficient and standardizes certain activities that are necessary for the organization to run smoothly. That standardization, however, does not mean that administrative departments ignore the needs of other business units. Processes and procedures must be tailored to support the various requirements of these units.

FIGURE 8.3

Decentralized Organization

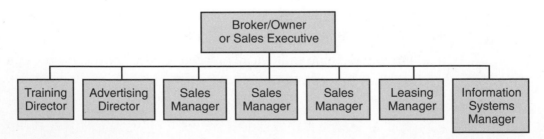

The challenge in a decentralized organization is to achieve the proper balance between autonomy and control. While each work group functions independently, all units must function as a unified organization, operating under the same business philosophy and company policies and procedures. Decentralized organizations maintain order by fostering teamwork among the managers or directors of the various business units and by selecting individuals who can exercise prudent use of authority.

■ CHAIN OF COMMAND

The organization of work involves an orderly organization of responsibilities so that people know exactly the scope of work for which they are accountable. People also need to know exactly who their superiors are so they know from whom to take direction. Otherwise, work evolves in a chaotic manner, lines of authority become vague, and people wind up asserting themselves in places they don't belong.

By establishing a formal hierarchy, an organization charts the chain of command or the path that authority travels to provide an orderly process for making decisions, issuing instructions, and commanding or directing work. In real estate organizations there are typically two types of authority.

- *Staff* authority, which is given to the people who are responsible for support services, the work groups providing administrative support. These groups contribute *indirectly* to the achievement of the company's objectives. They provide services such as accounting, marketing and advertising, training, purchasing (materials for the operation of the business), and maintenance.

- *Line* authority, which is given to the people who are responsible for contributing *directly* to the achievement of the company's objectives. These include work groups such as the sales offices or the property management, leasing, or new construction departments.

The organization's chart shows very clearly how each position functions within the context of all other positions in the organization. Positions that are connected by direct lines of authority must directly interface with one another. Positions outside those direct lines often have some degree of interdependence, though no authority to direct one another's activities. A sales office manager often interfaces with accounting and marketing departments, but has no authority to direct process or policy in those departments.

Job Descriptions

The way to put the meat on the bones of an organization chart and expressly state how positions function is with job descriptions. A **job description** converts the scope of authority conferred on a position by describing the responsibilities of the position. The description also shows how the person in the position is to interface with superiors, subordinates, and others in the organization when there is no direct line of responsibility.

A job description tells people where they fit into the big picture of the company: to whom they are to report; the positions that report to them; and exactly what their responsibilities are versus the responsibilities of others. A properly written job description is not a recital of chores or tasks associated with a job, but rather describes the activities for which a person is *accountable*. This tells people what the critical elements of their jobs are within the organization and provides a basis for assessing performance.

Don't assume people know what a job entails. In the case of salespeople, it's tempting to say, "They already know what to do . . . get sales and listings." But that's not a suitable job description. Are they responsible for meeting production goals or complying with the law or company policies? Furthermore, it's not appropriate to chastise a person for failing to properly discharge responsibilities if he or she hasn't been explicitly told what they are.

Job descriptions provide a tool with which to identify skill sets required for the positions. Basically, "what does a person need to be able to do to handle the responsibilities for which he or she is accountable?" Typically, the larger the scope of responsibility, the more diverse the skill sets are. Job descriptions are also used to periodically evaluate the assignment of responsibilities within the organization and identify more efficient assignments if necessary.

Informal Organization

Regardless of the way positions appear on a chart, most organizations have an informal structure. This is because work overlaps and doesn't always fit neatly into a chart. Often, this means that systems or processes are needed to facilitate the flow of work outside the formal chart so that the organization can function as an efficient enterprise.

■ **CASE IN POINT . . .**   According to the formal organization, the manager of a sales office is responsible for managing that office's advertising budget, and the salespeople in that office operate under the manager's directives with respect to listing advertising. That's straightforward.

Then, along comes a listing that is assigned to one of those salespeople by the manager of the relocation department, who is responsible for all aspects of a listing, including its advertising, that comes through the relocation network. Now, there are two separate authorities for managing listing advertising and two separate bosses the salesperson has to follow, depending on the source of the listing.

This is a prime example of the way work doesn't always fit neatly into a chart. Obviously, the goal is to get the listings advertised. But authority must be clearly delineated so that the office manager maintains control over the aspects of advertising for which that position is responsible, while also facilitating the work for which the relocation director is responsible. Most importantly, the salespeople need to know which boss's directives to follow in which situations.

The major challenge in managing the informal structure of an organization is maintaining order. The formal structure typically provides direct lines of reporting, with one boss and one person's directives to follow. The order of the organization in this case is very clear. Order can begin to unravel when lines of authority become blurred or people have multiple bosses. Conflicts arise over accountability (easy to pass the buck), and multiple and perhaps conflicting directives are, at best, confusing and, at worst, result in undesirable actions.

Processes or systems are needed to clearly provide for cases in which people are permitted to work outside the formal structure and the authority bosses have in those situations. Otherwise, people will create their own informal structure. Sometimes they do this anyway, regardless of the company's formal or sanctioned informal structure.

- People shop for decisions, seeking the answers they want to hear, regardless of whether the person they seek out is the boss or has the authority to make the decision. In these cases, all people want is someone to concur with a course of action they wanted to take.

- Some people want to exercise more authority than they've been granted, so they manage work or decide matters that are beyond their scope of authority. While people sometimes take on more responsibility than they've been authorized for laudable reasons, the disruptive influences are those who do so with some self-serving purpose or agenda.

- When people don't agree with a company policy or procedure, they may give directions or make decisions that are beyond their scope of authority primarily for the purpose of countermanding or derailing company procedures.

- When management fails to provide decisive leadership, people leap-frog over the immediate supervisor and go to the next higher-up or take it on themselves to decide a course of action. These are cases in which management has failed to do its job or hasn't responded in a timely enough manner for people to do their jobs.

- When company processes or procedures are inefficient or impractical, people will ignore them or find their own, better ways of doing things. A supervisor's approval or authorization from another department's supervisor that seems unnecessary or unduly restricts the flow of work will be circumvented.

Management is responsible for preserving order and chain of command, which includes fulfilling the responsibilities for which the managers are accountable and refraining from interjecting themselves into other managers' areas of responsibility. People work outside the formal organization structure for a variety of reasons, any of which should be management's wake-up call that work is not properly organized, that the wrong people are in positions of authority, or that the people in positions of authority are not fulfilling their responsibilities.

■ **CASE IN POINT . . .**   As the broker of a small company, you hire a sales manager who, among other things, is responsible for assigning referrals. A salesperson approaches you directly with a plea for a referral, feeling that you'll be receptive because the two of you have previously had a close working relationship.

If you intervene, you undermine the authority of the sales manager. This can also be interpreted by the salesperson as your public acknowledgment that the manager has not properly done his or her job. Ultimately, the chain of command unravels because you've authorized the salesperson to ignore it. To preserve order,

- you could ask the salesperson to raise the issue with the manager (and if the salesperson doesn't, it could be that the salesperson was seeking preferential treatment from you), or . . .

- you could approach the manager along with the salesperson and inquire about the status of referral assignments.

Either approach demonstrates to both the sales manager and the salesperson that you respect the manager's authority. Your intervention also demonstrates that you are responsive by addressing an issue that, if ignored, could mushroom into a major problem. A disgruntled salesperson could turn other salespeople against the company's referral system. (Repeated queries about referrals, however, could indicate a more serious problem that should be addressed with the manager.)

■ CONCLUSION

Giving structure to an organization gives it the orderly form it needs to execute the business plan. The broker (and other owners, if there are any) must decide the most suitable form of legal ownership and appropriate business affiliations. These involve decisions about the degree of independence or interdependence the company and its principals will have with other organizations.

As the scope of work grows or becomes more complex, the company can get disorganized, or even become dysfunctional. Organizations need an internal structure that groups work in a logical, efficient manner and a chain of command that clearly defines the path of decision-making authority. Job descriptions tell people the breadth and limits of what they are expected to do. Just as the business plan provides a blueprint around which the company is organized, the structure of the organization provides a road map for assembling the tools for the business and allocating its resources.

■ DISCUSSION EXERCISES

Chart your current organization. What is its formal structure? What activities is each work unit responsible for accomplishing? What personnel are assigned to each work group and who is the supervisor?

What is the informal structure of your current organization? How does this differ from the formal organization? What problems, if any, arise from people working within the informal rather than the formal structure of the company?

Select a position in your company and prepare a job description for that position.

CHAPTER NINE

STRUCTURING BUSINESS SYSTEMS

Where should the office(s) be located?

How will it be designed?

What technology is needed to support the work that people do?

Just as people need housing, a company needs a physical plant or facility in which to do business. While that facility may be as humble or state-of-the-art as resources allow, it needs to be sufficiently efficient so that people can do their jobs. At the very least, the basic "house."

That basic facility, today, is not the desk/phone office of yesteryear. For all companies in today's business world, technology plays a major role in the way people do their jobs, companies manage their information, and the public interfaces with the organizations. This has altered virtually everything companies used to think about the where and what of their offices.

One thing that has not changed is the need to project an image of the company. This is the "dress-up" space the public (and a potential recruit) sees that showcases what the company thinks of itself and instills confidence that this is a good place to do business. Impressive corporate headquarters, the monuments of stability or affluence, can accomplish this. For real estate companies, the people they need to impress (the consumers) have less reason to visit the tower of power and are much more likely to meet the company in the sales office.

While the seat of the company and the sales office may be one and the same, the two have distinctly separate functions. In business management parlance, there's something known as backroom operations. This is the behind-the-scenes administrative function that the public doesn't and has no need to see. With today's technology, that function revolves around a computer system, which can be connected, operated, and managed virtually anywhere.

All of this says that facilities have to be tailored to suit the work. In so doing, the company creates environments that are conducive to efficient operations and makes the best use of its financial resources. As a company's plans change, the facilities change as well. Although a new office site or updated décor, furnishings, or equipment might look tempting, only those that support the organization's plan and priorities are appropriate to consider.

Significant financial resources are committed to a company's facilities and systems, which means the company needs to be a smart shopper. Many resources are available to help evaluate physical needs, design facilities, and automate a business so that the company gets the best value for its dollar.

■ YOUR OFFICE

Because real estate is essentially an office business (as opposed to a manufacturing operation), the primary facility need is office space. Picking the right location, right-sized space, and the right furnishings and equipment is a function of the purpose of the office, not just today, but for the not-too-distant future as well. The office space should be flexible enough to accommodate change. Otherwise, the company could fall victim to the "penny-wise, pound-foolish" trap. The cheapest choice at the outset could be more expensive in the long run.

Another model of the past that is quickly being recast (among others mentioned in this book) is the form and function of an office. The best way to characterize this is by saying that the purpose of an office has flip-flopped. Instead of being the place people go to work as they have in past years, the office is a place that supports *wherever* they work. This evolution is not unique to the real estate industry. Nearly every business activity has workforce populations who have disengaged from the company office.

While real estate companies may have differing policies about homeofficing, a nationwide trend is that the sales office is no longer the salespeople's primary base of operations, except as required by a state's licensing laws. This trend is driven primarily by the increasing use of technology. (See Figure 9.1.) As you consider the following discussions, keep in mind that the location, site, size, and design are all affected as more salespeople have fewer reasons to use the company's office.

Location

If the quest is for sales office space, the starting point is the market analysis.

- Where are the company's target markets located?

- What are their consuming patterns?

- Does the office need to be within the traffic patterns (vehicular or pedestrian) they are likely to travel?

- How likely are they to be "walk-in" business for the company?

FIGURE 9.1

REALTOR® Use of Technology

Web site (either their own or the company's)	60%
Mobile phones or pagers	68%
Computers (either at home or the office)	100%
E-mail	94%
Digital cameras	85%

Source: E-mail poll conducted by the National Association of REALTORS®.

■ How important to the salespeople is the proximity of the office to those consumers?

Think about the fact that as companies expand their geographic view of their businesses, the neighborhood sales office becomes less important than the company's ability to interface with consumers electronically. While the virtual office has not replaced the physical one, the Internet office place creates fewer reasons for consumers to actually set foot in the company's buildings. This also means that a longer distance to travel on occasion may not be a major deterrent.

Add to consideration the part of the market analysis that looked at the competition and market shares.

■ Where do the company's most significant competitors have offices?

■ How much potential business is there in those locations?

■ Does the company have to be located in the same locations to preserve or increase market share in its target markets?

■ How much name recognition does the company have in the target market area?

There's a common fear that if a company does not have a presence where the competition is located, the company will lose. But if there's not enough business to support everyone, it may be better to chart new territory. On the other hand, if there's a concentration of other brokerage firms in an area, that could indicate they've identified an area with great potential.

If the purpose of the office quest is to open a branch office, the value of the company's name recognition in the area should be considered. This is not to say that a company shouldn't blaze a trail into markets where it's not well known, but the company does need to factor a marketing and advertising program into the cost. Salespeople should not be expected to bear the entire cost of self-promotion when the company relocates them to a new office.

Office space for primarily administrative purposes should support the operation of the company's various business units. There's no need to pay the price for a prime location when the work has low public profile. The important consideration is the efficiency with which work units and their managers must interface with one another. The supervisor of the marketing department is better off being located in the same place as the staff that person supervises.

Site

Armed with that analysis, the actual site selection can begin to take shape. Notice that all of this amounts to the company going through a buyer qualification process before starting its "house hunting." (Practice what the industry preaches.)

Visibility of a sales office (and its signage) is important if the company expects a lot of consumer traffic. The office doesn't have to be on a main road, but at least it must be in a place where consumers can find it before they get lost to the competition. While a free-standing building may provide the most visible office and signage (and ownership opportunity, if that's a consideration), higher density sites (shopping centers, malls, office complexes) are not necessarily inferior, depending on the actual space and sign placement that is available or permitted.

The person who goes office shopping doesn't always see the same things that a consumer sees, particularly if the shopper is familiar with the area. The barrier in the middle of a four-lane highway without easy access from the opposite side of the road may not raise a red flag to the person who is accustomed to contending with it. An out-of-the-way location that is difficult for anyone who's unfamiliar with the area can be a constant source of aggravation for the person who has to give directions.

How important is parking? Even a commercial brokerage company located in a central business district can frustrate consumers when parking can't be easily located. Suburban sites, especially in malls and office complexes, can be equally frustrating. Before signing a lease or purchasing a building, visit the site at various times of day and on different days of the week to get a good sense of capacity.

Consider, too, the parking for staff, especially as the needs may peak and wane dramatically according to work patterns and schedules of office events. Otherwise, the office manager can become a parking lot attendant trying to keep spaces intended for customers free from salespeople who "just stop by for a minute."

Size

The change in purpose of today's office has a great effect on the amount of square footage needed. While the work an office supports can be accommodated in a variety of physical configurations (which also affects the amount of floor space that is needed), the first consideration is the nature of the work it has to support: people, equipment, and public image.

A real estate sales office today is primarily an informational and support center. This means accommodating management and support staff (which may also include a salesperson's assistant) and office and telecommunications equipment. Because this office is typically the only place where the consumer actually meets the company (the image space), an attractive reception area and comfortable conference rooms are a priority.

With more people working at home and the fact that they can easily carry the contents of their desks in smaller and smaller electronic containers, there's less and less they need in the brokerage office. Of course, a lot of this depends on how technologically advanced the company's operations are. If contract files reside in the company's database, they can be accessed through a secure Internet connection or by e-mail attachment.

This means that there's minimal reason for the sales office to provide desk space. Most companies have not abandoned the desk space concept entirely, but they at least provide several workstations for those occasions when salespeople do need company resources. The challenge is to match space available with anticipated need. Otherwise, a lot of floor space sits idle on occasion or people are clogging hallways at other times. The best guides are the company's workplace policies and the work patterns of its salespeople.

One strategy for managing workstations, which is used in a number of business enterprises, is known as **hotelling.** As its name implies, it's a reservation system (though without the fee). With a phone call, e-mail, or interactive Web site calendar, the salesperson can reserve a workstation for the desired time or in another office site that has availability. Because of the unpredictable nature of the real estate business, this system has to be quickly responsive.

If the company views the office as the principal working headquarters for the sales staff, significantly more space is required. A rule of thumb is approximately 100 square feet of floor space per salesperson, depending on how the space is configured. Partitioning single offices will require more space than an open or bull pen arrangement.

Calculate desk cost to see how many salespeople are needed to cover this overhead and make a profit. A very expensive site can be a self-defeating proposition for the manager if the anticipated number of salespeople is an impracticably large number of people for one person to supervise. A larger support staff would be needed as well.

Use the checklist in Figure 9.2 to identify which areas are essential for the company and those that are desirable or optional. Don't overlook the importance of public areas, such as reception areas, conference rooms, restroom facilities, and refreshment centers. The back office space (staff, equipment, and supplies) should not be the leftovers, but a pleasant environment that promotes maximum efficiency.

When selecting office space, it's also wise to consider how training programs, sales meetings, and other group events will be accommodated. The worst place to conduct these is at desks or workstations. Electronic capability is also needed so that audio and video conferencing and satellite delivery can be used. Renting outside facilities on an as-needed basis may be more cost-efficient than setting aside space that will be used infrequently.

Unless the company has someone on staff who is skilled in designing office space, the services of a professional space planner are an invaluable resource to help select the most cost-efficient space, identify areas that can be used for multiple purposes, and plan flexibility for future expansion or contraction.

Legal Issues.   Several legal issues must be considered before signing on the dotted line of a lease or purchase agreement. One of these is the state licensing law and any specific office requirements. In most jurisdictions, even if the requirements are minimal, the facility must be inspected before the office can be opened for business. Local zoning ordinances must also be checked to be sure the intended use is in compliance and that signage

FIGURE 9.2

Space Area Checklist

	Essential	Desirable	Optional
Reception Area			
Customer			
Receptionist			
Display Area			
Desk Space			
Management			
Salespeople			
Personal Assistants			
Secretarial			
Accounting/Bookkeeping			
Advertising/Promotions			
Research/Data Collection			
Others			
Work/Equipment Area(s)			
Computer(s)			
Fax Machine(s)			
Copy/Duplicating			
Telecommunications			
Conference Area(s)			
Filing			
Storage			
Office Supplies			
Signs, Promotional Materials, etc.			
Records			
Coat Closets			
Rest Room(s)			
Coffee Bar/Kitchen			
Training/Audiovisual			
Library			
Children's Play Area			

and parking requirements are satisfied. Any necessary occupancy permits must also be obtained.

The facility must also comply with the Americans with Disabilities Act (ADA). Because a real estate company provides services to the public, the office (regardless of whether it's owned or leased) must be accessible to people with disabilities. Or the company must be prepared to provide accommodations that will enable a person with a disability to access the company's services. The company also has obligations as an employer under ADA.

Consider ADA *before* selecting the office space rather than after moving in. Some sites may be readily accessible; others may require considerable, costly retrofit. An architect or someone versed in the law can review the facility and recommend the most suitable ways to comply with ADA. Architectural or structural barriers pose the greatest challenge. ADA provides acceptable alternatives in the event that altering the structure to overcome barriers is an undue hardship.

Entry barriers (which can be overcome with a ramp or call button at a suitable height for a person using a wheelchair) are not the only considerations. If the public is customarily given access to rest rooms, refreshments, and other comforts in the office, these, too, must be accessible by people with disabilities.

Design and Décor

Now comes the task of designing and decorating the office. Figures 9.3 and 9.4 provide some preliminary ideas for a floor plan. Figure 9.5 provides a checklist of things to consider at the remodeling, decorating, and furnishing stages. Some companies use similar floor plans and décor, including the company's signature color scheme, in all of their offices to reinforce their image and provide added efficiency for people who have occasion to work in several office locations.

Public Areas.   The reception area is where the company is introduced and the public forms its first impressions. This is a sensory experience, not only by sight but by sound, smell, and feel as well. A calm, inviting atmosphere, free of distractions from the hubbub in the "backroom" and harsh paging systems, creates a professional welcome. (Provide the receptionist, staff, or floor person a suitably inviting workspace as well.) Think about how visitors will spend their time in the waiting area and provide comfortable seating that is stocked with informative or promotional material and perhaps an interactive video display.

FIGURE 9.3

**Sample Office
Arrangement**

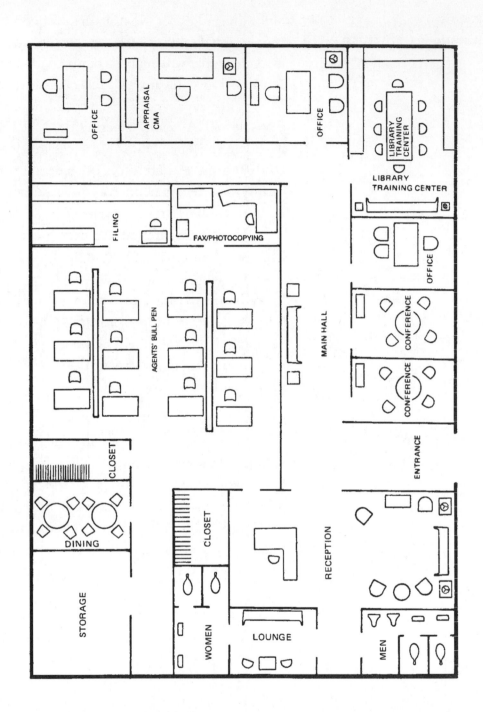

FIGURE 9.4

Additional Office Layout

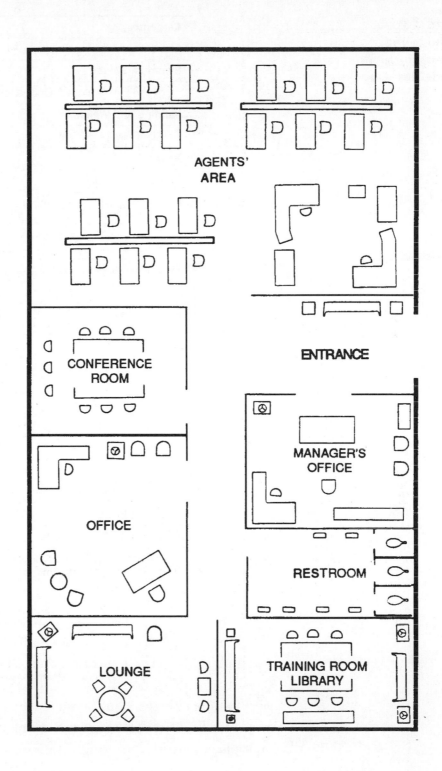

FIGURE 9.5

Remodeling, Decorating, and Furnishing Checklist

Carpentry
Partitions, Paneling, Shelving, Doors
Electrical Service
Lighting and Switches, Outlets for Equipment
Painting and Wallpaper
Walls, Ceilings, Moldings
Plumbing
Rest Rooms, Kitchen
Heating and Air Conditioning
Communications
Telephones, Fax Machines, Modems
Floor Coverings
Carpeting, Tile
Window Coverings
Blinds, Drapes
Furnishings
Desks and Chairs
Vinyl Floor Mats
Credenzas and Filing Cabinets
Typewriter and Computer Stands
Conference Room Chairs and Tables
Reception Area Seating and Receptionist Unit
Pictures, Plaques, Clocks, and Bulletin Boards
Lamps and Wastebaskets
Workroom Table/Counter, Supply Cabinet

Conference rooms are as important showcases for the company as the reception area and should be similarly comfortable and distraction-free. The public should not have to walk through staff work areas to get to conference rooms, nor should salespeople have to entertain customers at workstations or desks. Equip conference rooms with telephones, computers, and video facilities. These are not optional expenditures if the rooms serve multiple purposes for meetings, closings, and additional workstation space.

Décor can be as upscale or modest as resources permit. Two things to keep in mind, however. One is safety. The pretty ceramic-tiled floors on a wet day, the curled floor mats, or the frayed carpeting can be a lawsuit waiting to happen if someone slips or trips and falls. The other issue is practicality. Very cheap could be very expensive in the long run if the décor can't withstand high use, abuse, and repeated cleaning and then has to be replaced. Also think about how child-friendly and ADA-friendly the environment is.

Work Areas.   Regardless of how much floor space is devoted to work areas, the space should be separate from the public areas and support an efficient flow of work and the interaction of people and systems.

Think about how work activities are grouped. The sales-support staff and the salespeople should be readily accessible to one another, and the administrative-support staff should be readily accessible to the broker or manager. Equipment and supplies should be conveniently located for the people who use them. Areas like the broker's and/or manager's office, kitchen, and restrooms serve both public and private purposes and should be readily accessible without having to trail through the backroom work area.

Mapping the space for the sales staff involves more than simply allocating square feet on the floor for desks. A trend in office design, including in the corporate world, is the *open office*. This resembles the corral or bull pen arrangement that has been used for a number of years in the real estate industry.

The appeal is that, without barriers of the walls of individual offices, people can more freely interact with one another, which inspires creative thinking and joint problem solving. Because not all workers are in the office at the same time, this environment is especially helpful for fostering teamwork and camaraderie when they are present. The open arrangement also means that less floor space per person is needed and space can easily be reconfigured as needs change.

This communal environment has its critics, however. For the most part, they object to the disruption and distraction that can interfere with concentration and privacy (particularly on the telephone) that can affect client confidentiality. This environment also reveals to management the less flattering aspects of human behavior that fail to respect others' business leads and personal belongings, all of which add to the things a manager has to manage.

In companies where separate offices have been viewed as a status symbol, the communal, classless environment may be difficult to adjust to and may seem like a demotion. A lesson can be learned from a president and CEO of a major Fortune 500 company who was so committed to the benefits of the open environment that he insisted that he and his senior advisers work in open offices (just like the rest of the company's workforce). Granted, the workstations are mahogany-framed glass, but the space is not otherwise any larger or more prestigious than that of anyone else in the company. Private or confidential work is done in small conference rooms.

Equipment and Furnishings. Floor planning requires some thought about the configuration of the hardware and furnishings that will eventually be put into place. While today's technology is less dependent on the hardwire connections than previously were required, an office customarily uses more permanent and, in some cases, much more complex systems than residential users do. In fact, today's sophisticated systems are appealingly accommodated in buildings that are *blackwired* (institutionally outfitted with the connectivity to support electronic communications).

Regardless of the connectivity and accompanying power sources that are required, the placement of those utilities and the furniture and equipment must be compatible with one another. Otherwise, the wire jungle becomes a tripping hazard or the power source is across the room from where the photocopy machine should be. Although utilities can be moved, it's cheaper to think about their placement before hardwiring an installation, rather than discovering later on that it's misplaced.

An office can be furnished in variety of imaginative ways to create an appealing décor. Furniture comes in a variety of qualities at a variety of prices. Often, better quality, used furniture is less costly than new, inferior furniture. And while small desks are less expensive, they are unsatisfactory if most of the work surface is occupied by a large phone set and a computer.

■ COMMUNICATIONS AND INFORMATION SYSTEMS

A major piece of today's business systems is the technology devoted to communications and the management of information. While there are many tools (and fun gadgets) individual salespeople and managers can consider for their personal use, the focus of this discussion is on the company. What does it need to communicate and to manage and process information quickly, efficiently, and accurately? And affordably?

One of the best ways to answer these questions is with the help of a systems analyst. Computer, business equipment, and telecommunications specialists are all possible resources. A person who is familiar with the broad range of available options can help avoid the inefficient, troublesome, or overpriced options and help select the ones that best serve the company's purposes, at the best price.

Future capacity should also be considered. In many cases, spending more, initially, will offer considerable savings in the long run. Inexpensive or used systems may be available, but they may also be outdated or incompatible with other technology currently in use. Another trap for the penny-wise and pound-foolish.

Today's communications and information systems can be seamlessly "connected." A faxed document can be converted for transmission by e-mail. Computers can send text to a pager or cellular phone and vice versa. Even real-time chat can be done on-line via e-mail or video camera. The integration of systems contributes to efficient operations as much as their separate components do.

Computer System

The centerpiece of a company's information management system and its communication system is its computer system. This may be as state-of-the-art or as basic as financial resources and operator expertise permit. The typical computer system is an assemblage of a number of hardware and software components so that the system can serve multiple purposes for multiple users in a variety of locations at the same time. All of this is possible because of the connective network that enables the system to serve both internal and external users in the communication and exchange of information.

Today's offices are information centers. This means that companies must assemble, manage, retrieve, and store vast amounts of data. These are no longer paper, file-cabinet tasks, but electronic ones. A critical function of a manager, that being to monitor the company's activities, requires a volume of information. Because of technology, that information is readily available and can be massaged in a variety of ways to tell management what it needs to know.

This is not to say that computers have eliminated paper. We've not yet reached that point. But a computer can house far more than can be stored in desks and filing cabinets. Virtually anything that users (that is, management, salespeople, customers and clients, and the public) must, need to, or would like to know can reside in the company's database. Granted, not all data is available to everyone. (There must be proprietary and secured access.) But this makes the point that the quantity of information that a company stores can be as vast as the computer system's capacity will allow.

The scope of information that is available isn't limited by the capacity of a company's database, though. With external resources, via the Internet, any of those users can be linked to a wider world of information than people can imagine. This also says that the company must have its own Internet presence (Web site) so that the company is part of the cyberspace network.

Software

The way the company's information is captured, dressed up for impressive presentation, and distributed is the function of software programs.

One of the best ways to make hardware-systems decisions is to first decide what the company wants that system to do. That's more easily decided, especially for novices, by first looking at software options. Although software can be custom-designed, this is rarely cost-efficient for a small organization. And with the wide range of commercially available software, that's not really necessary. It's also better not to take the chance that customized software could be friendly only to the designer or incompatible with other software the company wants to use.

A consultant can help evaluate information management and communication needs so that suitable software can be selected, along with the basic operating system that will support those programs. Talk to other users of software being considered because they might see products differently from the way an experienced computer person does. Also evaluate the technical support offered by the software manufacturer. How readily accessible and affordable is it? The person (or people) using the software will greatly appreciate this resource.

Internal Applications.   Begin by looking at the management of a *financial* database. The most obvious activity to commit to electronic management is the accounting function. This can be done with spreadsheet, money manager, or more sophisticated accounting software. Once that financial data is available, though, it can do much more than simply reside as electronic ledgers. Pairing that data with either task-specific or multifunction software can tell management just about anything it wants to know about the company's activities.

Office management software, especially that which is designed specifically for real estate companies, can be used to monitor transaction activity, pending closings, and listings about to expire; track business by region, office, or salesperson; project cash flow for the coming months; and monitor the performance of salespeople at any given time. Real estate trends in the area can be monitored as well. (Some programs offer as many as 38 assessments of a company's operations.) All of this information is readily available for market analysis purposes, too.

Word processing software is a must for today's company as well. It serves the obvious purposes of doing what typewriters do. But the advantage of word processing (aside from the superior ease with which documents can be typed) is that correspondence, reports, routinely used forms, and the like reside in the company's electronic system. They can easily be retrieved for reference, reuse, edit, or distribution. A word processing program is also the essential companion to a wide variety of other text-oriented software, like real estate contract programs.

Virtually any word a company wants to write for a promotional flyer, address label, or training program manual can be expertly crafted on a program like WordPerfect™ or Microsoft® Word™. A desktop publishing program, which takes a slightly more skilled user, has powerful design, layout, and graphic capability that can turn out very professional-looking presentations such as brochures and newsletters. A company can handle many of the print functions that it previously sent out-of-house.

A word processing program also becomes the resident "file" for text (words) documents the company receives (e-mailed attachments, information downloaded from the Internet, and the like). This is an essential feature so that text can be retrieved and cycled back through the electronic network to internal and external users.

While financial management and word processing software are the essentials, real estate companies may also equip their computer systems with software that is specifically real estate-service oriented. For the most part, these are programs that salespeople, transaction coordinators, or personal assistants use. The list of available options is lengthy, but, for instance, loan qualifying, comparative market analysis, mortgage analysis, contact management, transaction management, mapping, and listing management programs are available.

Several management issues arise, though, when companies do venture into service-related software. One is that considerable dollars can be spent on intriguing programs that don't get used. Either the salespeople aren't as intrigued as the person who made the purchase or the salespeople have their own programs. Or the software isn't user-friendly. Good software choices can be made with some thorough preliminary investigation.

Another, perhaps more financially risky, issue is *copyright infringement*. The purchaser of a copyrighted program (the company) is the only authorized user. While the program can reside in the company's system for in-house use, company personnel must be clearly prohibited from downloading those programs onto their personal computers. Pirating programs seems to be an offense that few take seriously, but that doesn't excuse the action, and an aggressive enforcer can create untold misery for all involved. Suitably direct company policies can minimize potential problems.

External Application.   The heart of the company's external connectivity is the link of its computer system to the Internet. While there is a hardware component of an on-line connection, the basic operation is a software function. Two components for Internet use are essential: the connection and the navigation.

Today, there are more options for connection than a person can keep track of. Many on-line services continue to promote themselves with the distribution of free CDs to get users logged into their systems. Telecommunications and cable TV companies are also promoting Internet connections.

The choice is primarily a function of the cost of connection time and the ease of access. The experience of other users, especially the frequency of downtime (inability to access) and dropped connections (inability to stay on-line), is very helpful. Also look at an on-line service's e-mail program. Other users can report their experiences with such things as ease of use and spam (unsolicited e-mails, which are often advertisements but can also be circulated for nefarious purposes).

Once on-line, an Internet browser, such as Netscape or Internet Explorer, is needed to get around the Internet. A browser is generally part of the computer's basic operating system.

For a company to establish its own Internet presence, it needs a Web site. Because a Web site is part of a company's image making as well as its information and communication systems, a site's design is very company specific. This is where a professional resource that has combined technology and Internet marketing expertise is very helpful. A company can't simply open a site and forget it. The site requires human, hands-on involvement to update the contents of the site and links with other sites and to monitor activity on the site.

Connectivity also means that the company's system is vulnerable to intervention. Company personnel can access or alter data they are not entitled to, and outsiders can do the same. Incoming data can come loaded with other data that plant nasty annoyances, delete data, or totally disable system functions. These are the viruses that can be time-wasting frustrations or paralyzing events. Unbeknownst to the company, it often keeps the virus alive by sending it to another system as data is transferred.

Two "must" software purchases build *firewalls* (security) and provide *virus protection*. Firewalls can be constructed around selected files or systems to protect against unauthorized access and tampering. Client information and sensitive company operations data deserve particular attention. Antivirus software (which may also have firewall components) intends to insulate the system from viral attacks. These programs are not fail-safe, however.

A diligent procedure for downloading updated virus definitions and routinely scanning the system is needed to make the programs effective.

Hardware

The physical hardware decisions fall into place fairly easily after the software investigation. That's also when the users will be identified (by jobs the software supports) and where they are located. Decisions must also be made about the amount of hardware that will be available to the sales staff and the workstation connections for personally owned hardware. The professional systems adviser can help assemble the appropriate hardware system (central processing unit, monitors, keyboards, connections, and peripherals, such as printers and scanners) and design the layout.

Connectivity also becomes a hardware systems issue. The number of company sites, the number of people at each site, and the capacity of the various Internet connection services will affect hardware and hardwiring requirements. Connection by telephone line affects the selection of modems (speed being a big factor because of line usage costs), though modem choice is less significant when the faster broadband, cable connections are used. Keep in mind that fees for connecting business and residential customers are typically different.

Shopping for hardware carries caveats similar to other shopping ventures, the major one being that cheapest could turn out to be most expensive, especially where technology is involved. A several-generations-old system is only as good as it still is today, and it may not be satisfactory to run tomorrow's software. Even the best price for the latest generation system at one vendor is not necessarily the most cost-effective expenditure if the warranty or technical support is inferior to another vendor's.

Technical Support. If technical support is at the other end of a busy signal or an expensive long-distance phone call (no 800 number), or a two-week wait at a drop-off repair counter, the company loses valuable time and money. Often, companies budget for technical support (either in-house or an outside resource) so that they have readily available assistance to unravel the inevitable hardware and software glitches. This support is also helpful for setting up procedures to manage the system and recommend enhancements when they are needed.

Preserving Data. As advantageous as it is to store all the company's data and documents on a computer, that database is vulnerable if there's a hardware or software failure. An essential part of managing the system is a routine plan for backing up or preserving data. This can be done on CD or tape (no need to put additional paper in the files), performed as frequently as the database changes significantly. It's also important to protect backup files from fire and theft, which is generally done by securing CDs or tape off-site. The company can be in for untold distress if the guts of its records are lost, especially if the time comes to defend a lawsuit or answer to a regulatory agency.

Voice Messaging

As important as an e-mail address is today, there are still times when people need a telephone. But that, too, has gone high-tech.

Although a source of frustration on occasion, automated answering systems with voice messaging have become standard operating equipment in business today. These systems are efficient, particularly because calls can be relayed without human intervention. Messages and phone numbers don't have to be transcribed, so the recipient hears exactly what the caller said. Voice messaging also minimizes phone tag, and provides 24-hour contact with remote access, and because mailboxes can be secured, confidences can be protected.

Other advantages (depending on the features the company chooses) include the ability to disseminate useful industry information or specific listing data through audio-text features accessed by a Touch-Tone phone. In multioffice organizations, systems can be used to connect offices through a central messaging center, an especially attractive feature in areas where toll costs could deter callers.

The downside is that overly long phone trees, with too many steps to reach the desired destination or a human being, or improperly designed menu options can unreasonably try people's patience or even turn callers away. The system isn't very efficient if the cost is a public relations nightmare or a loss of business. Some companies have abandoned the automated answering feature (or shortened it) so that callers can reach a human being, who can then direct the call to the appropriate person or mailbox.

Another downside is that people in the workplace have learned how to dodge the system. Nothing is as frustrating for a manager as to watch someone sit at a desk, ignoring the ringing phone and just letting voicemail answer the calls. That's also immensely aggravating (and potentially problematic) for the caller who has urgent business. People also are far too tempted to screen calls and many are not particularly diligent about emptying their mailboxes or returning calls.

Any of these problems can be minimized by monitoring the callers' responses to your system. The company can also establish procedures to ensure that salespeople respond to their messages.

Facsimile Machines

A facsimile machine is as common as a telephone in today's office. If the alternative is postal mail, fax is certainly faster, easier, and cheaper. When a printed document with a personal signature (like a contract) is essential, fax is a suitable medium.

While a fax machine won't likely be replaced any time soon, it has taken on more of a support role as it interfaces with other systems. Connect the fax machine with the computer system and faxes can be transmitted via computer, or documents scanned into a computer can be faxed. Connect fax machines with voice messaging systems and the company can set up a "fax-back" system. This is a totally electronic cycle of information, initiated by a caller's request for descriptions of listings or other information (using codes on a Touch-Tone phone). The computer responds with a fax of the requested information to the caller's fax.

Good quality, plain-paper fax machines can be purchased very reasonably today, as salespeople have also discovered for their home offices. Plain-paper is preferable to thermal because the document is better quality, which eliminates the need to photocopy thermal-paper faxes. Multifunction machines, combining telephone, fax modem, computer printers, and scanners in one machine, may be considered for their economy of space and efficiency in linking multiple communications through one unit.

Although keeping a fax machine stocked in paper costs money, the major operating expense is the use of the telephone line, especially for lengthy documents. Economies can be achieved with a no-frills phone line (unless the machine is linked to a voice messaging system). Fax machines don't need call forwarding, call waiting, and the like. Computer connections with rapid transmission modems or digital or broadband connections can shorten transmission time.

Communicating with People Who Are Hearing Impaired

Today's technology opens many avenues for people who are deaf or hearing impaired. Text Telephones (TTs), formerly known as TDDs, are typewriter-like units that display conversation in text on a screen. A TT "talks" with another text telephone or a computer so that people, regardless of auditory capacity, can communicate with one another.

This is an important tool for a real estate company. Under ADA, the company is required to provide accommodations so that people can access and partake of the company's services. Installing a TT in one or more of the company's offices or using other services the local phone company has to serve people who are hearing impaired are alternatives that should be explored. The company must also be prepared to accommodate people throughout a transaction, typically with oral or sign language interpreters. Local organizations that service this population can provide valuable assistance.

Communicating with People Who Are Visually Impaired

Technology also provides numerous opportunities for people who are blind or have limited vision. Large- or raised-print publications can easily be produced on computers and photocopier machines. Real estate documents and other print material can be converted to audiocassettes or attached to e-mail documents for users who have audio-supported computer software. A local organization that services this population can provide additional advice. The bottom line is that a real estate company is required under ADA to provide accommodations for people with visual impairments.

As a practical matter, any person who's discovered that aging eyes don't cope with small-print documents anymore will appreciate a large-print version. A little extra time at the copy machine to enlarge a document is just good business.

Multilingual Communications

A final, good-business comment, which could also have fair housing implications, is about communicating with people whose first language is not

English. As the population becomes increasingly diverse, multilingual services become increasingly important. While Spanish language documents are more prevalent in this country than once was the case, more can be done to enhance multilingual communications. Multilingual members of the company staff, translators at a local college or university, and multilingual materials on the Internet are all resources to help a company serve diverse clientele.

■ FACILITIES MANAGEMENT

Keep it clean; keep it safe; keep it well maintained; keep its costs under control. A very short, perhaps overly simplistic, way of saying what managing facilities is about. Without venturing into the full lesson on facilities management (which can be a professional specialty of its own), the point is to give a heads-up, especially to the office manager who is on site, to some things that deserve a watchful eye.

Depending on company philosophy, the clean-safe-maintenance-cost exercises may have different priorities. But cost-containment should not mean that the work environment is uncomfortable, unpleasant, or jeopardizes people's welfare. The Office of Health and Safety Administration (OSHA) has a number of things to say about the workplace environment that companies need to pay attention to. (The OSHA poster should also be displayed in the workplace.) Furthermore, there's just good common sense that is good business, regardless of legal implications.

Security in the Office   A fact of life today is that no place is 100 percent secure from a determined intruder. But steps must be taken to protect the facilities, staff, and customers and clients. The company may not see an office as a warehouse of salable equipment or a convenient route through which a person can easily escape with that equipment. If a collection of keys to the company's listings (including the addresses!) is readily accessible to the staff, that means that keys also are readily accessible to anyone else. A professional security firm should be called on to conduct a security audit of the facilities.

Beginning with the exterior of the building, the exterior, the parking lot, and all entrances should be well-lighted. Shrubbery should be trimmed to eliminate hiding places. Windows should be double-paned and double-locked. Exterior doors should be metal or thick wood and have double-side keyed dead bolt locks. Change the locks or alarm codes periodically to protect against lost keys and unauthorized entry. Don't overlook the roof to be sure that there are no hiding places or possible sites for entry.

Protect the listings. Code the addresses on keys and lock them in a secure location. Keep track of lockboxes so that you know the properties on which they are installed. Fortunately, lockboxes have improved considerably, making them less vulnerable to vandalism or unauthorized entry. Some have a system that tracks the entry each time the box is opened. Nevertheless, keys, keypads, and combinations do fall into the hands of unauthorized people on occasion.

Establish security procedures to keep the staff out of harm's way. Use sign-out sheets and call-in systems so that the whereabouts of staff outside the office are known and a threatening encounter can be detected. Establish a code or warning system so that a person can summon help and alert others to a danger. Identify a secure location in the office where personnel can go, and plan an escape route so they can get out in case of a problem.

Salespeople can additionally protect themselves by guarding the amount of personal information they distribute in promotional materials and being vigilant when scheduling appointments. An increasing number of companies are requiring personal identification from customers and clients before salespeople go into the field with them. (NAR has a program on personal safety that is very useful.)

Safety in the Office

Provide a safe environment for staff and the public. Their safety is not just a matter of legal liability but a practical consideration as well. Take steps to prevent accidents and prepare to respond to a fire or medical emergency.

- As soon phones are installed, program them with emergency numbers and be sure everyone knows how to use them.

- Be sure smoke detectors are installed in all the appropriate places. If the building has a sprinkler system, be sure it works properly.

- Purchase a first-aid kit and fire extinguishers, particularly for the workroom. Instruct everyone about how these items should be used so that people don't create more problems than they solve.

- Familiarize people with safety procedures. More injuries and loss of life occur when people ignore the alarms that were intended to protect them. Conduct fire and disaster drills (don't overlook weather-related emergencies as well).

- Secure handrails and clear walks and stairways of obstacles.

- Make certain the electrical service is adequate to accommodate the computers and other office equipment and appliances.

- Familiarize yourself with the labor laws in your state to be sure you comply with any safety requirements.

■ CONCLUSION

With well-selected facilities that are well provisioned with the equipment and other systems that a company needs to function efficiently, the organization has the physical tools for its trade. While all of this can be a significant part of a company's initial investment and continuing operating budget, the dollar is well spent when it enhances the company's image and the environment in which its people work. Because of the way people work today, the company's communications and information management systems are just as important (if not more so) as its physical plant.

■ DISCUSSION EXERCISES

Critique a real estate office with which you are familiar, considering its general location, its site, and its design or layout.

What communications and information systems do you consider to be essential for your business to run efficiently and effectively? Which are desirable and optional?

Outline the steps you would take to open a branch office.

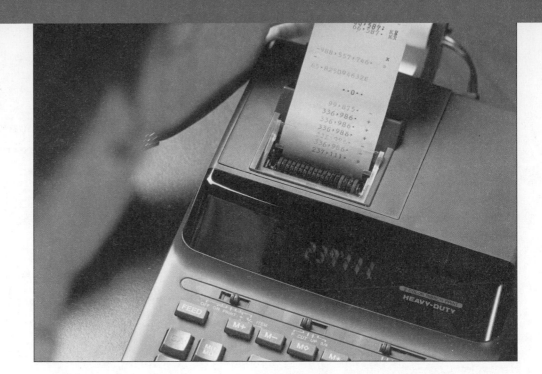

10

STRUCTURING THE FINANCES

How much money do you need to start a business? To keep it running?

What do you need to do to keep the company on a healthy financial track?

———————————

The two resources that companies depend on most are human and financial. Unless the company properly allocates its financial resources, none of the company's systems, processes, or people can accomplish what the company's plan says to do. In other words, the plan and the money have to be aligned.

The financial management people view their role, as holders of the purse strings, to be the controllers of what a company does. Others think the financial management folks ought to be paving the way "green," facilitating (rather than controlling) the company's operations. There's just so much money to go around. Alignment means putting the available money in the right places so the company can do the right things.

Business plans and financial plans go hand in hand. If a company intends to open a new office, upgrade its computer system, increase its promotion to retain position in the marketplace, or implement a more competitive sales commission plan, the company needs a financial plan to make these things happen, while also keeping existing systems and services operating. Financing and budgets are part of that financial planning.

■ THE FINANCIALS

The place to begin a discussion of finances is with an elementary guide to financial statements, commonly known as *the financials*. These statements provide a picture of an organization's fiscal condition, captured in a variety of ways, depending on the kind of statement.

Certainly, the principal owners and senior management must be able to interpret the statements, but even the lowest manager on the totem pole is expected to be able to decipher reports. Business planners, lenders, investors, or potential buyers (as part of their due diligence) also gain essential information for their decisions from the company's financials.

The platform on which financials are prepared is known as *double entry bookkeeping*. This is a system of capturing *debits* and *credits*, each offsetting the other, to result in an equal balance. Considerable expertise (the accountant's) is required to properly categorize and interpret data in accordance with legal and generally acceptable accounting practices. Novice business owners and managers especially (though often the most experienced, too) can benefit from a professional's explanation of what these reports reveal about the organization's financial condition.

Balance Sheet

A balance sheet reports the organization's assets, liabilities, and owner equity and provides a snapshot of the organization's general financial position as of the date it is prepared.

- Assets consist of what the company owns that either exist as cash or can be converted to cash in less than one year. Depending on the nature of the organization's business and current holdings, entries will be categorized as either current or fixed assets.

- Liabilities are obligations incurred during the normal course of doing business, including those to creditors. Tax obligations, employee benefit and mandatory pension programs, and restricted funds are also entered as liabilities.

■ Owner equity is the net worth of the business, the difference between assets and liabilities. This also includes net income and the equity financing provided by investors (as opposed to financing provided by creditors).

The entries on a balance sheet must balance. That is, total assets and total liabilities plus owner equity should be identical figures. An accountant can interpret the significance of the entries, though perhaps the most useful observations are gained by comparing balance sheets over several years' time, particularly the ratio of owner equity to liabilities. This is the number that owners or stockholders of the organization have the greatest personal stake in.

Income Statement

An income statement, sometimes known as an *income and expense* or *profit and loss* statement, is a picture of an organization's financial performance during a particular period of time. Twelve-month reports generally coincide with the company's operating calendar, stated as January 1 to December 31 or some other fiscal operating year. The income statement tells how the company got to the balance sheet.

The income side of the report reflects all of the income generated by the company in the ordinary course of doing business. The expense side reflects expenses incurred in generating that income. Each expense entry is charged against the income account that incurred the expense. A review of individual income and expense accounts reveals those that are most productive or incur the greatest expense. The total income over total expense is net income, commonly called (pretax) *profit*. If expense exceeds income, the bottom line shows a negative number.

Several accounting methods can be used to report income and expense. The *cash* method reports entries in the period they were paid. For instance, a sale in February that is collected in April is entered as *April revenue*. The *accrual* method reports entries in the period they occurred. That February sale would be entered as *February revenue*. The accountant can best advise which method is most suitable for the company. Regardless of the method used, however, the same principle must be applied to both income and expense entries. Shifting accounting methods requires very studious decisions, rather than simply using whatever method makes the picture look better.

There are also various accounting methods to treat inventory, which real estate companies are unlikely to have. An accountant can explain those procedures, though, if they apply.

Income. Depending on the company's primary and ancillary services and accompanying fee structures, income to a real estate company is most likely derived from

- *brokerage fees*—the commissions that are generated by the salespeople and those received from cooperating brokers, and fees generated from a-la-carte menus of services. Any commissions generated by the broker/owner and other managerial personnel may be included as well (though to get a true picture of sales staff productivity, these amounts are not part of that analysis).

- *additional service fees*—activities such as appraising or property management or fees for referrals, generated by referring customers or clients to other brokerage companies or to other business units providing services like insurance, title or escrow, and mortgage lending.

- *transaction fees*—administrative service fees collected from each transaction that are intended to offset a variety of internal operating costs (particularly salaries for support staff) associated with delivering real estate brokerage services.

Expense. Operating expenses fall into two categories:

1. *Fixed expenses*—rent, dues and fees, salaries, taxes and license fees, insurance, and depreciation (funding for depreciation on equipment, buildings, and automobiles the company owns)

2. *Variable expenses*—advertising and promotion, utilities, equipment and supplies, and cost of sales

Cost of sales includes commissions paid to the salespeople and brokers cooperating in the transactions, overrides paid to the sales manager, and fees attributed to individual transactions, such as MLS, franchise, and referral or relocation fees. Cost of sales is variable expense because expenditures fluctuate with production volume, commission splits and the number of cooperating broker transactions, and referral, relocation, and franchise fees.

Cash Flow Statement

A cash flow statement reports the cash position of the organization. It focuses on the company's cash-generating operations, showing the cash balance plus cash generated (receipts) and how cash is used (disbursements).

The purpose of cash flow statements is to show the organization how much cash it has for day-to-day operations. This is critical information because if the company does not have sufficient cash, it has to go outside the organization to fund operations. That means borrowing money or finding investors to keep the company running. The need for cash (from either source) can be a rude awakening, particularly because these ventures often require time to arrange and involve additional costs (and legal ramifications) that should be approached methodically, not in a crisis mode.

Cash flow statements have become popular relatively recently (1980s), primarily because many companies in today's business world operate on very lean cash positions. So cash has to be monitored very closely, typically on a monthly basis.

Whereas an income statement reports revenue and expenses, a cash flow statement reports receipts and disbursements. While these are driven by revenue and expenses, they are also affected by items that appear on the balance sheet, like accounts receivable and accounts payable as well as capital expenditures and debt service. Delays in collecting and paying accounts can significantly alter the company's cash position.

All of this makes a cash flow analysis an important part of management's financial oversight. The accountant can assist in assembling and interpreting an analysis. Important factors to consider are the amounts, due dates, and payment terms of receipts and disbursements and payment history of collectibles. A monthly analysis not only gives management a heads-up alert but also identifies where aggressive steps (like collections on accounts receivable) are needed to enhance cash position so that the company can meet its obligations.

■ FINANCIAL RESOURCES

Regardless of how diligent the savings plan or how ample the profit line, companies can rarely get up and running or continue to operate without outside resources. Financing is an integral part of the company's financial structure, rather than an isolated or short-term event. Those outside resources fall into one of two general categories:

1. *Debt financing*—loans

2. *Equity financing*—ownership interests

Planning and managing the use of outside resources is a critical part of management's financial oversight. Each of these resources has advantages and disadvantages as well as cost and timing issues. In this management effort, timing is everything. Too much money too soon unduly increases costs to the organization (either in interest payments or premature, diluted ownership positions). Too little money too late unduly stresses operations and can result in missed business opportunities or less prudent decisions in the chase for money. That last-minute money may be readily available, but at greater costs.

Financial Projections

The key to the wise use of outside resources is wise forecasting. A diligent analysis of past and present operations (back to the company's financials), particularly money-flow patterns, provides a basis for projecting future need. Financial projections must also accommodate any new strategic initiatives that are outlined in the business plan. Because of the cyclical nature of the real estate business and the time lag between signatures on the contracts and settlement, a cash-flow analysis is a key piece of this study. The object of the exercise is to anticipate the company's needs so that the necessary money is available at the right time.

Start-up companies have the added challenge that they have no history on which to base financial projections. New business owners can easily fall into the trap of underestimating the competition and the cost of doing business (though veteran business owners can be similarly afflicted). In addition to the obvious capital needed to put a business in place, companies need money to bridge what can be a wide gap between the first day of business and the time they break even—and the even longer time before they make solid profits.

Depending on how the company is structured and the affiliations and services needed to compete in the marketplace, the capital requirements of a real estate business will vary. Basic necessities, however, typically include

- legal fees (establish the business),

- accounting fees (advice and to set up books),

- telecommunications and computerization (equipment and installation),

- initial fees for affiliations (MLS, franchise, etc.) and professional associations,

- office space (buy or rent, remodeling),

- office equipment (facsimile machines, duplicating equipment, desks, chairs, file cabinets, etc.),

- office supplies;

- personnel (payroll and Social Security, workers' comp, unemployment, income tax withholding),

- graphics (logo, signs, stationery),

- promotion and advertising (initial entry into the marketplace), and

- signage (office and yard signs).

Depending on how the total cost of these items compares with the amount of money on hand plus that which can be gathered from other sources, additional expenditures could be considered. Or more cost-efficient ways to provide the basic necessities will have to be devised. Consider whether leasing versus purchasing items such as office space, telephone systems, or duplicating equipment is more feasible.

Start-up companies are most vulnerable when they lack the capital needed to operate until they break even. *Be conservative when estimating income and generous when estimating expenses.* A three-to-five-year span to the break-even point is a typical projection. In the meantime, companies have to withstand operating losses and may also have to make additional capital expenditures to be competitive.

Cash flow must also be factored into start-up capital requirements. A considerable amount of bill-paying cash goes out before an appreciable amount of cash flows in to minimize the drain on capital reserves. The first year is the most treacherous, though a company should expect to be totally capital-dependent for at least the first six months.

Procuring Financing

The first step in the procurement of financing is to engage an attorney and an accountant and make them an integral part of the decision-making process. They are also good resources to network with potential lenders or investors and make the necessary introductions. The local branch of the Service Core of Retired Executives (SCORE) may also have expertise that can help work through some of these decisions as well.

The decision-making process consists of evaluating financial projections and determining the appropriateness of debit or equity financing. One or the other is typically more desirable, depending on the purpose for which financing is needed, the amount, the urgency and duration of the need, tax consequences, the relationship the company's owners desire to have with others, and the creditworthiness of the company. All of these considerations have legal as well as financial implications.

Equity financing gives investors the opportunity to be part of an enterprise they feel has attractive growth or earnings potential, rather than sitting on the sidelines simply as note-holders. Generally, equity financing is desirable for capital expansion or improvements, rather than to cover temporary cash-flow requirements. Because equity financing involves restructuring ownership and possibly business operations (if the investors are going to have an active role in the organization), these are more complicated and time-consuming ventures to arrange and aren't suitable for quick responses to financial need.

Debit financing is preferable when the company's principals don't want to relinquish any ownership position, and it provides tax-deductible interest payments (a feature the accountant may advise is preferable). Depending on the size and quality of the company's assets and its credit standing, debit financing is generally more versatile, serving both long-term and short-term needs, and may also provide an open line of credit if the company is a worthy risk. Especially when dealing with a lender with whom the company has an established relationship, financing can often be arranged relatively quickly if time is a consideration.

Financing Portfolio

Regardless of the chosen resource, the company has to "package a worthy pitch," that is, a financing portfolio. This is especially true for the start-up company, which has to convince a lender or an investor that a business venture that doesn't yet exist, has no assets (collateral), and no proven track record is a worthy risk. Early-stage companies face similar challenges because they are still trying to prove themselves as viable enterprises. That said, however, it's usually easier for these companies to arrange debt rather than equity financing.

Unless debt financing can be arranged privately (family, friends, or business associates, with debt perhaps being convertible to stock at some point), the logical place to go is an institutional lender. Banks and the Small Business Administration are good sources, as are government incentive programs for emerging companies and, if applicable, programs for minority-owned businesses.

The first barrier is the office door of the bank officer, who is typically subjected to numerous business schemes and entrepreneurial ideas that are proposed as can't-fail ventures. That barrier is more difficult to penetrate if the proposing business owner has no established professional reputation or personal banking relationship with the institution. The known entity is more likely to get noticed, and if that connection does not exist, the introduction by other business owners (or the company's attorney or accountant) is often the key to opening that door.

A company that has a previously established relationship with the lender and is seeking a relatively small sum of money may be asked to simply complete a loan application that the lender can then process through a computer scoring system to evaluate the request.

Otherwise, a fairly comprehensive financing portfolio will be required so that the request can be scrutinized in detail and considered by a lending committee or potential investors. The portfolio should be easy to read, get to the point, and stand out on the pile of all the other applications on the lender's desk. It begins with an introduction of the company and the request in a three-paragraph summary of the merits of the proposal. The balance of the portfolio substantiates the request by

- educating the potential lender or investor about the business's industry and the marketplace;

- demonstrating the industry and business management expertise of the company's principals and that they are characterworthy (personal résumés and a list of references are typically part of this);

- describing the company's business and its operations, including a business plan, the financial statements, and budgets; and

- demonstrating that the company has a sound plan for using and repaying the money that is requested.

Ultimately, lenders and investors want to be able to assess their exposure or risk in the venture. They are rarely willing to bankroll a venture in which their risk is greater than the company's (or its principals') risk. This means that the company (or its principals, if they must personally guarantee the loan) must be willing to place a significant amount of capital or collateral on the line. For the principals, this means risking personal assets, which can have significantly more financial implications than simply funding their business.

Once the company gets the money, the relationship it maintains with the lender is as important at the one that got it the money. In a sense, the lender becomes a partner. Good communications with that stakeholder not only affects future borrowing power but also becomes a valuable safety net in the event all does not go as the company planned. Business owners are far too inclined to prematurely boast the good news about the company and drag their feet with the bad, but it's far better to tell the tales in reverse. Lenders respect a heads-up warning (that may eventually prove to be a nonevent) and a realistic assessment of the value of a company's accomplishments.

■ GENERAL OPERATING BUDGET

A general operating budget is an essential part of a company's financial structure. A budget serves the same purpose as a business plan, that is, it provides a road map. In this case, it is a map of how the company intends to allocate its financial resources in the context of projected income and expenses (normally for a one-year timeframe) to support the company's business plan. *Projected* is the operative word. These are forecasts, or targets, that are intended to keep the organization on track.

Budgets are more or less useful, depending on how realistic the projections are. They need to be based on quantifiable evidence and sound analysis of internal and external factors that affect income and cost of operations. Overly ambitious revenue or overly conservative expense estimates may make the profit forecast look good, but they don't provide management with the key indicators needed to monitor the financial health of the organization with any validity.

A balanced budget (one in which expenses don't exceed revenue) intends to help a company live within its means. If a sizable expenditure is required to accomplish a goal, the company has to find offsetting revenue to make this happen. The alternative is to construct a deficit budget, which says that the company expects to spend more than it makes. A deficit can be tolerated on occasion if an excessive expenditure has high probability of significantly enhancing revenue in coming years. But a company can't tolerate many years of deficit spending before reserves have been depleted or debt far exceeds the value of the business.

A general operating budget resembles an income statement to the extent that the line items are similar. (See Figure 10.1.) This helps the company measure actual income and expense entries against those that are budgeted. Companies commonly also prepare a variety of other, more specific, budgets to guide such things as departmental, office, or functional activities.

Gross Income

The information gathered during the situational analysis (both external and internal factors) can serve as the basis for developing realistic revenue projections. These targets may also have been benchmarked in the company's business plan. For budgeting purposes, the exercise is simply one of mathematically converting services to revenue. Transaction revenue can be determined by first multiplying the average sale price of a property by the number of transactions expected. The result is gross sales volume. Then, calculate the amount of income that can be expected from the gross sales.

Price-Setting Decisions. Before making this final calculation, however, the company must decide how to charge for its services. Price-setting decisions involve some of the most critical issues management must address but are ones that rarely get the attention they deserve. While any pricing decision affects the income statement, a motive to maximize revenue over time or maximize the number of unit sales to reduce unit cost will not have the desired effect if the price upsets other variables. In other words, you can't just put a bigger price tag on services and expect the bottom line to turn out better.

Pricing decisions involve determining what the market will bear and at what point a price increase will reduce volume or revenue. This essentially pushes the envelope on price, pushing price to its maximum level before it has a negative effect. Other variables affecting pricing decisions are competitive factors, the type of consumer (some being exceedingly price-and-value- or bargain-conscious and others being the boutique or concierge clientele), the power of company brand name or image, and the perceived value of its services' benefits. Unless all of these are considered, any price could have a self-defeating effect.

The practice of charging transaction fees offers several lessons about pricing. The companies that blazed the trail proved that the market (at least, in some parts of the country) would bear the price. This is also an example of segmented price, that is, the basic price of the service remains the same while a separate price is added. All were argued by the companies as necessary charges to cover expenses. So, other companies figured they could get away with charging the fees as well. Then the market was further tested when the price of transaction fees increased. The unknown at the moment is when or if the consumer will rebel.

Pricing decisions also come back to the commission versus fee-for-service decisions. An increasing number of real estate companies are including a-la-carte menus in their service repertoire. This involves another pricing decision: what fees are suitable for each service or should attractive prices be offered for "packages" of services. (*Real Estate, a la Carte*, by Julie Garton-Good, provides some helpful insight.) The companies that blaze the trail have the additional challenge of forecasting income without a track record or historical data as a guide.

There are also the alternatives of charging either hourly or contingency fees, similar to the way other professionals charge for their services. An hourly charge could be capped at some amount for a month's service. A contingency fee could be collected when an agency agreement is signed, and a performance clause could provide for the return of the initial fee if the company is unable to perform the stated service within a certain time period. The company could also include reimbursement for expenses in either of these cases.

Price must be based on sound business rationale, not based on the logic that that's what everyone else charges. Pricing decisions take into account legal restrictions. A company cannot afford to ignore the antitrust laws or state licensing laws (such as those that prohibit charging advance fees or being reimbursed for expenses).

Operating Expenses

The gross income forecast is next offset with a forecast of operating expenses. Fixed expenses (rent, salaries, insurance, and the like) are easier to forecast because these are already known. Variable expenses are more difficult and also require the most management to control. The caveat in forecasting variable expenses is that too often managers pad their expenses so they look like heroes when they come in under budget. Obviously, this does as much harm to the budget process as being overly conservative.

Because each company's business plan is different, operating expenses will reflect expenditures needed to implement the plan. Although the way these expenses are categorized may differ, depending on the accountant's design of the company's statements or the computer software program used, typical expenses that must be budgeted fall into the categories described below.

Cost of Sales, or Transaction Expense. This category of expenses includes direct transaction or service costs (commissions, referral and franchise fees, and the like) and expenditures made to assist a transaction to settlement, such as minor repairs or the purchase of an appliance. For the typical real estate company, this category of expense is one of its largest.

Once was the day when real estate companies used calculations of company dollar to determine the amount of money available for operational expenses. *Company dollar* is the amount of gross revenue that remains after cost of sales has been deducted. Today, companies more commonly use the format of an income statement and enter these costs as operating expenses because, in fact, that's what they are.

Marketing and Advertising Expenses. These include costs to develop marketing and advertising strategies and design the materials. Costs also include the placement or distribution of classified, institutional, listing, and recruiting advertising and signs (for sale, sold, and open house); advertising on television and/or radio; and listings in telephone directories. Web site design and maintenance may either be categorized as marketing or communications expense.

Occupancy. These are the "housing costs," which include rent, utilities, janitorial services, and trash/recycling removal. Depending on the terms of the lease, some of these expenses may be included in the rent. If the company owns its office building, mortgage payments, even though not considered a pure expense, must be budgeted.

Equipment and Supplies. These include the rental or maintenance of, as well as the purchase of supplies for, equipment such as computers, duplicating equipment, fax machines, and audiovisual aids. This category also includes postage (including overnight delivery) and packaging, shipping, bulk-mail permits, printing, office supplies, lockboxes, and kitchen and restroom supplies.

Dues and Publications. These include the broker's and the company's dues in professional and industry organizations and MLS and franchise fees; subscriptions for directories, newspapers, and magazines; and other dues for organizations such as the credit bureau and chamber of commerce.

Services and Fees.   These expenses include accounting and bookkeep-ing services, insurance (comprehensive business policy, workers' compen-sation, and errors and omissions policies), legal services, credit reports, computer consultant, and communications services, including basic, local and long-distance telephone service, fax and computer lines, Internet services, and paging services.

Salaries.   These are salaries for the broker (unless the broker doesn't take one), managers, secretarial and clerical personnel, and other employees, including the training director, relocation director, and transaction coor-dinator. Also included are employee-related costs such as medical and dental insurance and other fringe benefits.

Taxes and Licenses.   This includes real estate licenses for the broker and the company, business licenses, and taxes, including payroll taxes (income taxes, Social Security, and unemployment taxes).

Miscellaneous Expenses.   These include awards, incentives and con-tests, education, conferences and conventions, travel and entertainment, auto expenses, and petty cash.

Bank Charges.   This includes payments on debt and service charges on bank accounts and credit card services.

Repairs and Replacements.   These include the repair and replace-ment of equipment the company owns, which are expenses that must be budgeted for even though, in strict accounting terms, they are asset expen-ditures that are depreciated.

Reserve for Contingencies.   Companies need to plan for contingen-cies. The most fiscally sound way to do this is to budget an amount for contingencies, which plans for a certain amount of anticipated revenue to be allocated to fund the company's reserve account. In effect, this is a savings plan that causes the company to set aside reserves for unexpected expenses or for capturing opportunities that present themselves. It's tempt-ing to eliminate this line, particularly because it reduces anticipated net income (which means the company doesn't look as profitable), but prudent financial management suggests this is an important safety net.

FIGURE **10.1**

Income and Operating Expense Budget

GROSS INCOME

Commissions on in-house sales	$_____
Commission received from cooperating transactions	$_____
Referral fees	$_____
Other fees for service	$_____
Total Gross Income	$_____

GENERAL OPERATING EXPENSES

Commissions paid to salespeople	$_____
Commissions paid to cooperating brokers	$_____
Overrides paid to managers	$_____
Relocation and referral fees	$_____
MLS fees	$_____
Franchise fees	$_____
Other	$_____
Total Cost of Sales	$_____
Marketing and advertising consultant	$_____
Classified advertising	$_____
Institutional advertising	$_____
Direct mail	$_____
Brochures	$_____
Television/radio	$_____
Signs	$_____
Telephone directories	$_____
Other	$_____
Total Marketing and Advertising	$_____
Rent	$_____
Utilities	$_____
Janitorial services	$_____
Trash/recycling removal	$_____
Other	$_____
Total Occupancy	$_____
Equipment maintenance/supplies	$_____
Office supplies	$_____
Postage and overnight delivery	$_____
Packaging and shipping	$_____
Bulk mail permits	$_____
Printing	$_____

FIGURE 10.1

Income and Operating Expense Budget *(Continued)*

Lockboxes	$_____
Kitchen/beverage	$_____
Other	$_____
Total Equipment and Supplies	$_____
Professional dues	$_____
Membership fees	$_____
Subscriptions	$_____
Total Dues and Publications	$_____
Accounting services	$_____
Legal services	$_____
Computer consultant	$_____
Communications services	$_____
Telephone	$_____
Paging services	$_____
Computer information networks	$_____
Insurance	$_____
Comprehensive business policy	$_____
Workers' compensation	$_____
Errors and omissions	$_____
Credit bureau	$_____
Total Services and Fees	$_____
Managerial salaries	$_____
Secretarial and clerical salaries	$_____
Other	$_____
Fringe benefits	$_____
Total Salaries	$_____
Real estate licenses	$_____
Business licenses	$_____
Taxes	$_____
Income taxes	$_____
Social Security	$_____
Unemployment	$_____
Other	$_____
Total Taxes and Licenses	$_____
Awards	$_____
Incentive programs and contests	$_____
Education	$_____

FIGURE 10.1

Income and Operating Expense Budget (Continued)

Conferences and conventions	$_____
Travel and entertainment	$_____
Auto expenses	$_____
Petty cash	$_____
Other	$_____
Total Miscellaneous	$_____
Interest on loans	$_____
Bank account charges	$_____
Total Bank Charges	$_____
Total Operating Expenses	$_____
NET INCOME	
Total Gross Income	$_____
Less Total Operating Expenses	$_____
NET INCOME	$_____

Net Income

After projecting the income and deducting the anticipated expenses, the difference is the anticipated net income (projected profit) for the year. This can be a sobering moment if there's no profit or, worse, a deficit. The process of developing a budget is as important as the final product because it forces management to consider and reconsider its projections on both the gross income and expense side of the ledger and find the most cost-effective ways to allocate the company's resources.

The outcome of budget discussions may be a change in company policy. It might be that the salespeople will have to share advertising expenses (like purchasing their own signs or paying some of the costs to advertise their listings) or franchise or MLS fees. Or they may have to pay for the use of the copier, office supplies, promotional brochures, postage, or fax. Any of these options could improve budget projections and the way the company manages its financial resources, but they could have a negative effect on the company's human resources.

Unless the company has a 100 percent commission structure and assesses a desk charge, the company could find that its ability to attract and retain sales talent is jeopardized. Salespeople resent being "nickel-and-dimed," especially if carried to extremes with a three-cent charge for each envelope, 50 cents for a cup of coffee, or a dollar to the secretary for typing a sales contract. Although it's common in most areas for salespeople to share in some operating expenses, if a company's compensation and expense structure is seriously out of line with the competition, the salespeople will go elsewhere to work.

Profit Centers

Certain aspects of the general operating budget can be budgeted in greater detail. Similar to the way planning is done (the business plan for the entire organization being then broken down into more detailed plans at lower levels in the organization), each work unit (department or sales office) develops its own detailed budget.

When companies designate these work units as *profit centers*, this means that each unit is charged with the responsibility for generating the income it needs to cover its costs of operations and make a profit for the company as a whole. The budget process in this case generally begins with the work unit being charged with producing a certain amount of profit. The work unit then embarks on a budget process to figure out how much income and expense to project to reach that profit goal.

Variable Expense Budgets

A general operating budget cites categories of expenses that are allocated for specific purposes. To guide the use of these funds, variable expense budgets are needed to identify individual expenditures within those categories. These more specific budgets are particularly helpful for monitoring expenditures throughout the year.

For example, an amount designated for marketing and advertising is broken down into various marketing and advertising activities. It's not uncommon in large companies to delegate this budgeting responsibility to the marketing director, who then becomes responsible for deciding the best way to use the funds. Once the budget is formed, the manager also becomes responsible for keeping these expenses in line with the budget.

Monthly Operating Budgets

Monthly operating budgets are simply monthly benchmarks, typically one-twelfth of the year's projections for each budgeted line item. Most computer software programs can trigger these computations.

These numbers are useful for comparing the *actual* income and expense figures with the *budget* numbers to monitor performance throughout the year. The actuals may be ahead on certain lines and behind on others, particularly because of monthly variations, but next month the numbers may shift. The most important things to look at are the bottom line and income and expenses that appear to be significantly lagging or exceeding projections.

It's best not to change the budget during the year. While that might make management feel better, that doesn't change the status of the organization. Any expenses that seem to be getting out of control after three months should be evaluated (some may be seasonal), and damage-control measures should be planned. That's not to say that the measures have to be implemented, but at least there's a battle plan if expenses significantly exceed income.

■ ACCOUNTING

Financial management also means managing the company's financial data. These are essentially bookkeeping functions, typically involving income and expense ledgers, accounts payable and accounts receivable ledgers, and commission and payroll records, plus bank and escrow account statements. Because of the critical nature of this information, companies need specific procedures for collecting, posting, maintaining, and verifying financial data.

Once there was a time when accounting or bookkeeping functions were labor-intensive tasks. Today, even the smallest company can streamline this operation with automation (computerization). However, automation is only a tool. Management is still accountable for the financial affairs of the organization and must be able to rely on data systems that are structured according to generally accepted accounting principles. In addition, state licensing laws may specify very detailed procedures that must be followed.

Electronic Data Management

With the wealth of computer software that's available, it's possible to set up the general ledgers, accounts payable, accounts receivable, payroll records, commission records, property management accounts, bank accounts, and even balance the books, issue checks, and bill accounts at the same time. Don't rely solely on the software, however. The company's accountant should be involved in setting up the books and helping staff manage the software to suit the company's operation.

The electronic data become the foundation for generating the company's balance sheet, income statement, and cash flow statement and, along with the budget, can provide a wealth of information management needs to keep tabs on the company's finances. When it's time to file taxes or do a general audit of the company's books, the necessary data are readily available.

License Law Requirements

When making financial software selections, also consider the requirements of state licensing laws, particularly those that apply to the administration of escrow accounts. Separate accounts must be established for escrow money so that it is never commingled with the company's general operating funds. In addition, the laws establish procedures for making deposits and withdrawals to escrow accounts.

The laws usually specify detailed record-keeping procedures. Certain information relating to a transaction must be posted with each deposit to the escrow account. In some states, the manner in which bank statements for escrow accounts are reconciled is quite specific. Companies must also be prepared to produce records as required for inspections by regulatory agencies. (See Figure 10.2 for a sample trust/escrow ledger.)

Security

Protect the money and the money data. This simple statement says much about the systems and procedures a company needs to ensure that the company's assets and its records are secure.

As grand as electronic data management systems are, they are vulnerable unless steps are taken to protect and preserve the data. This is especially important when the computer system is networked throughout the company. Files can be password-protected and firewalls can be built (a software function) to limit access to confidential information and prevent tampering with the data by unauthorized persons either within or outside the organization. Only upper management and the accountant should be able to access the company's financial records.

Money is normally secured with internal systems of checks and balances. Selective access to checkbooks, inventory of company assets (including

FIGURE 10.2
Trust/Escrow Ledger

TRUST/ESCROW LEDGER

Street Address	Town	County	State	Zip Code	❑ Sale ❑ Rental

Seller/Landlord	Purchaser/Tenant
Name _____	Name _____
Address_____	Address_____
City_____State ___ Zip_____	City_____State ___ Zip_____
Telephone (Home) _____ (Work)_____	Telephone (Home) _____ (Work)_____

Miscellaneous Comments

Date	Received from/on Behalf of or Paid to	Amount Received	Received By	Check No.	Amount Paid	Balance

equipment and serial numbers), and records management procedures to keep track of funds and provide safeguards against misappropriation, internal theft, or embezzlement are essential. The fewer people who handle money, the fewer opportunities that can arise for funds to be diverted. Typically, highly centralized controls are employed, with only certain people being authorized to approve disbursements and even then with a paper trail of vouchers to hold them accountable.

In a real estate company, one of the greatest concerns is securing other people's money, that being the escrow or trust money, security deposits, rent checks, and other transaction-related funds. Procedures are needed to track funds from the time they are received (normally by the salesperson) to the time they are deposited and then disbursed. Because issues of state license law are involved, the company needs procedures to account for and verify that these funds are handled appropriately. The company should have zero tolerance for mishandling funds and develop specific termination policies for people who do.

■ CONCLUSION

Structuring a company's finances is a function of aligning its resources in the most cost-efficient ways to accomplish the company's business plan. Essentially, this means putting the right amount of money in the right place at the right time. This is a multifunction project that involves diligent study of the company's financials, forecasting need, and building in the proper safeguards to ensure that the financial resources are used wisely. Budgets are one of the most useful tools for keeping a tight rein on the organization's finances. All of this is an information function that rises or falls on the vigilance of management, as it monitors the financial health of the organization and takes the necessary steps to maximize resources and minimize expense.

■ DISCUSSION EXERCISES

Obtain a copy of a company's financials or an annual stockholder report and discuss what you learn from that information.

What issues relating to the marketplace and your organization would affect the development of a general operating budget for your company or a budget for your office or department?

Discuss the financial management procedures that are required by your state's license law, particularly those that address the management of an escrow or trust account.

11

BUSINESS POLICIES AND PROCEDURES

What are your company's ethical policies?

What business policies and procedures has your company adopted?
How effective are they? How are they communicated?

Returning to the game analogy that's been used before, people need to know the rules of the game so they know how to execute the plays. In a business organization, people need to know the what and the why of the company policies and the how, when, and who of the procedures.

The purpose of a company's "rulebook" is to support the structure and systems the organization creates to maintain order and control the organization. Business policies and procedures set forth the company's philosophy for doing business and the rules of fair play and ethical conduct, which arise from the culture that senior management creates, as well as the internal processes that prescribe how work is to be done and the day-to-day conduct of the company's people.

Policies and procedures evolve as a result of management's deciding the processes that are suitable for the company to work efficiently, project the image it feels is desirable, and protect the organization's assets.

While it isn't necessary to commit all of this to writing (it exists anyway), *written authoritative guidance is highly desirable*. It prevents misunderstandings, provides consistency (which is extremely important when certain matters of law are involved), and minimizes the amount of time management devotes to directing processes, solving problems, and resolving controversy. People can essentially govern themselves in most situations. The company's written rules are generally provided in

- a policy and procedures manual, the general operations manual that spells out the rules and processes that govern all of the company's operations;

- a personnel procedures manual, the human resource "bible" for managers that directs internal procedures governing employment and employee relations (this manual is meant for managers, not for employees); and

- an employee handbook, the general circulation communication to all people who work for the company that tells them the day-to-day rules of conduct.

Similar to the rulebook in a game, the company's rules must also provide sanctions for the offenders. In other words, the rules must have teeth so that people take them seriously and know that there are consequences for digressions.

Several rules about formulating rules:

- The principal owner(s) and senior management are responsible for business philosophy, ethical codes, and policies and procedures, though input from lower levels of the organization (especially those who are most familiar with departmental or office operations) is advisable to ensure that the outcome is efficient operations. In other words, adopt necessary policies and procedures but don't bog down the organization with cumbersome process.

■ Policies and procedures manuals, personnel procedure manuals, and employee handbooks are all individualized documents. While there are many resources (including on the Internet) to guide the development of these manuals, the actual substance must support the culture and organizational systems and processes of the individual company. These aren't documents that one pirates and then just changes the company name on the pages.

■ All policies and procedures, regardless of whether they are committed to writing or adopted in practice, must be able to withstand legal scrutiny. As necessary as the rules are for creating order, they can create considerable disorder if they violate the law or cause litigation. The company attorney must be an integral part of the development of policies and procedures.

■ Rules, once adopted, must be followed. Herein lies another legal pitfall. In the event of litigation, both the rules and the actual conduct are scrutinized. Despite all the legal, written words, the organization is defenseless if its conduct is not consistent with those words. As a practical matter, there's also little point in going to the effort of developing policies and procedures and then ignoring them. A good tool for management to manage risk, especially with the sales staff, is to obtain an acknowledgment that each salesperson has received a copy of the manual.

■ Like many other things management does, policies and procedures must be revisited periodically to ensure that they support the organization as it changes and to address issues as they emerge and laws change. This also means that the printed manuals must constantly be updated, including the elimination of outdated material. Looseleaf binders are most satisfactory so that only individual pages (including dates of revisions) can be replaced.

■ Finally, the project of developing rules for the organization's game is not as overwhelming as it may sound. Certain policies and procedures have evolved over time, are already in practice, and just need to be committed to paper. The things that management spends most of its time directing or resolving are prime candidates to be addressed in the organization's manuals as well.

■ BUSINESS ETHICS

A code of conduct is one of the most fundamental sets of "rules" that management needs to frame. The code sets forth the company's value system and the right or morally correct way for it to do business; in other words, the company's ethics.

Ethics involves morality and a set of beliefs that guides actions and defines behavior as good or bad, right or wrong, or morally approved or disapproved. Various groups and cultures as well as individuals develop their own definitions, and consequently, their own beliefs about what is right, wrong, good, bad, and so forth. So, too, do business organizations form sets of beliefs or creeds.

Although there is no one universal value system, that does not say that different sets of values can govern different parts of our lives, or one standard that governs personal lives and another one that governs business. Peter Drucker, in his book *Management: Tasks, Responsibilities, Practices,* argues that there is no such thing as separate ethics for business. One ethical standard must govern all areas of our lives. *There is not a different standard of right for making money.*

The fundamental ethical principle of professional conduct is "Above all, do no harm."

The Heart of Ethics

Why is it that Wall Street is rocked by scandals, students cheat on college campuses, corporate and government officials are forced to resign? Some people will say, "Don't these people know any better?" Others might say, "I'd do the same thing they did," "I'll not likely get caught," or "They must have had a good reason." Most interesting is that not everyone sizes up situations the same way.

The reason they don't arises from their personal value systems. Value systems are products of past experiences, family upbringing, cultural influences and traditions, and the lessons learned about the fundamental principles that guide morality. Ask a number of people what each one values most in life and the responses will vary from money or professional success to such things as freedom, health, family, prestige, respect, or loyalty.

Whatever a person values most becomes the priority that guides decisions and, therefore, behavior.

Because everyone doesn't come out of the "same mold," the challenge is to bring people with divergent value systems together. Society does this with rules. These rules fall into two general categories: *laws*, which are the rules established by government (including consequences for violators), and *ethics*, which are driven by morality, values, and principles of individuals in the group as well as the group as a whole. Conduct can then be described as legal or illegal, ethical or unethical. Because some laws may appear to be unethical, ethics may impose a higher standard for conduct.

Management in an organization establishes value systems, which can range from moral, social, and aesthetic values to economic, legal, and political values. The company's value system forms the culture of the organization and becomes the way a company does business. Michael O'Connor and Ken Blanchard, authors of *Managing by Values*, contend that values are extraordinarily powerful forces in shaping an organization and dictating business practices.

A real estate company must live within the framework of an ever-expanding body of law that is intended to enhance protection for consumers. While those laws tell people what is expected of them in a legal context, a company also needs to articulate the value system that governs its business practices so people understand what is expected of them and the principles that govern their behavior. That system forms the basis for the company's code of ethics. Committing a code to writing accomplishes the telling part, but equally important is enforcement, so that people actually practice what the company preaches.

Code of Ethics

The mention of a code of ethics to many in the real estate industry brings to mind the codes that are established by the industry's professional organizations, such as the National Association of REALTORS®. While these codes serve a useful purpose for the industry (though some would argue that they are not as effective as they ought to be), industry codes do not supplant the need for an individual company to establish its own code of ethics as well.

A code of ethics reflects the cultural values established by the principal owners and senior management for their company. The code essentially reflects the company's business philosophy and the value principles on which that philosophy is based. If the philosophy is similar to that of NAR, the base is the Golden Rule, "Do unto others as you would have others do unto you." This provides a guide for ethical conduct as the question is posed, "Would I want someone to act in this manner toward me?"

With a code of ethics, the company says that these are the principles we live by. Generally, these statements cover the company's relationships with both its consumers and others in the business community (including competitors), as well as internal relationships between boss and subordinate and among peers. Some statements are aspirational in nature and others are very specific, addressing practices as well as standards by which they are measured to guide conduct during the ordinary course of doing business. In a real estate company, these usually relate to the way the company delivers its services.

If the company subscribes to an industry code of ethics, then the company's code should support, rather than conflict with, the practices the industry code prescribes. Of course, the company can always impose higher standards of conduct for its organization as well.

Institutionalizing Ethics

Institutionalizing ethics means integrating ethics throughout the organization: (1) Clearly state the ethical conduct that is expected. (2) Establish systems within the organization to ensure that the behavior is consistent with the words. (3) Provide penalties for people who deviate from the code of ethics.

In other words, once the company adopts a code of ethics, the organization must be committed to *following* it. This requires the active participation of everyone in the organization. People must focus not only on the *results* but also on the *process* to achieve those results.

Ethical practices occur when the process is not compromised or bypassed to achieve a result. If a company's attitude is "I don't care how you do it, just get it done," this says that the result is more important than how the result was achieved. The ethical code becomes meaningless if senior management tolerates or ignores behavior that is contrary to the values it has established.

Although businesses need to survive financially, they need to decide what price they are willing to pay while pursuing a dollar. A commitment to ethical conduct is one of a company's most valuable assets. Doing what's right is not always the easiest course of action, nor does it always produce immediate financial rewards. But *there is simply no right way to do the wrong thing*.

A company can institutionalize its code of ethics in several ways.

- *Put the code of ethics in writing*. Ethical standards are meaningless when they are simply elusive intangibles. Written statements memorialize the code, leave no room for ambiguity, and provide evidence for enforcement. That is, as long as the words are specific. It's not sufficient to say, "integrity is expected of every salesperson." Instead, describe the behavior that exemplifies integrity. A code of ethics that is too vague is merely window dressing, rather than a meaningful script.

- *Communicate the code of ethics*. Everyone in the organization needs to be told what the code of conduct is. This can be done through training and orientation programs, pamphlets, letters, and, most important, by management's example. The company should also communicate to the public. This can be accomplished in brochures, contracts, and advertising. The actual behavior of the company's people, however, makes the most powerful public statement.

- *Demonstrate that the code of ethics is important*. All levels of management must lead by example to gain commitment from others in the organization. There is no such thing as two sets of acceptable behavior, one for management and another for those being managed. Management must be consistent, meaning that it's not OK to ignore the code in certain situations, regardless of the financial gain that would result.

The institutionalization of ethics is measured not only by actual behavior but also by how employees, customers, and clients *perceive* the ethics of the company. Because the managers are responsible for creating an ethical environment in the company, they can take a lot of the credit or share some of the blame for this perception.

■ *Enforce the code of ethics.* The most powerful way to institutionalize ethics is to confront violations. Unethical behavior persists when organizations fail to aggressively pursue enforcement. Often, enforcement requires the removal of barriers that discourage people from stepping forward and informing upper management about unethical conduct. Otherwise, the organization is functioning with a "code of silence," rather than a code of ethics.

Provide directives about to whom suspected unethical behavior is to be reported, how disputes will be investigated and resolved, and a series of penalties that will be assessed for violations. Then do it!

■ *Reinforce the code of ethics.* Constant exposure is essential for reinforcement. The code should be a centerpiece in workshops and seminars, either by devoting sessions exclusively to the topic or by incorporating the subject in other discussions. The failure of many sales training sessions is they ignore ethical behavior in the pursuit of successful selling behavior. Training should prepare people for the ethical dilemmas they might encounter and develop possible solutions for these dilemmas.

Ethics can be either managed or mismanaged. Some managers choose to simply ignore the issue, but those who do could suffer unintended and undesirable consequences. Because some unethical conduct is also illegal, the company's legal liability is significantly increased and the penalties can be costly.

■ POLICIES AND PROCEDURES

The various manuals that a company prepares are the handbooks that tell people "the way we work" in the organization. Certainly, the code of ethics makes statements about how to work, either in a separate piece or as part of other manuals. But all of these handbooks or manuals delve into the organization's work processes, describing the way the company's services are delivered and the way people and documents flow. Policies and procedures are especially valuable for

- providing ready answers for many of the dilemmas people face during the course of daily operations,

- setting rules by which everyone shall play,

- helping to resolve conflicts before they arise, and

- providing a risk-management tool for both the company and its staff.

Careful wording in written policies is extremely important. Litigation and employment disputes can arise out of accusations that policies created contracts (though that's certainly not the intention) and interpretations that policy statements are promises that the company failed to fulfill. Obviously, this is a good argument in favor of making sure that the company attorney reviews the company's words. Written policies should contain statements that management can make changes at its discretion at any time and has the right to interpret and administer policies as changing circumstances warrant.

Like ethics, company policy and procedures must be institutionalized. Everyone in the organization should have a copy of the general operations manual and the employee handbook and should be encouraged to refer to them. These are an essential part of orientation for new staff as well. Management must also stand behind the policies and procedures, enforce them consistently, and administer sanctions as warranted. Once a manager ignores some of the rules or permits some people to circumvent them, the order that the rules intended to create no longer exists.

Because a company's manuals are declarations that can have legal implications, not only the procedures but also the stated words must be framed within the law. The laws to be most vigilant about are those that affect real estate practices, antitrust, employment and the workplace, and civil rights. A real estate company that employs independent contractors must also be concerned about differentiating between workplace procedures for them versus employees.

Because the manuals reflect a company's philosophy and operations, the substance is individual. However, there are certain subjects or processes that are typically addressed, some of which apply to everyone who works in the organization and others that apply to selected personnel or departments. The format of the manuals and the arrangement of content are individual as well, with some being more detailed or appropriate for employee handbooks. A human resource consultant and the company's attorney are invaluable advisers in these projects.

General Business Policies

As a foundation for all that follows in a general operations manual or employee handbook, the place to begin is by describing the company: its mission statement, a brief history of the organization, and a description of its target markets, by geographic area and types of properties or services. This is also where the company's general philosophy of doing business is explained. All of these pronouncements affect everyone who works for the company and also tell the public who the company is.

The company's general operating structure needs to be explained, including the organization chart and relationships with superiors and senior management. Generally, these issues are addressed with policy statements that reflect the culture, workplace environment, and management style of the organization. Often, senior management also has an *open door policy*, which speaks about the accessibility of management, including the principal owner or broker, by everyone who works for the company. The purpose of these statements is to explain the organization's hierarchy and the way people interact with one another.

In a real estate company, the policy discussion must also address some very critical issues that relate to its services. Aside from the need to provide policy and supporting procedures (remember the how, when, and who), the company cannot afford to leave potential legal landmines unattended. The company has the right to expect that all workers, including independent contractors, conduct themselves in a legal and ethical manner.

Agency. The broker must clearly define the company's policy regarding law of agency relationships. The policy must state whether the firm represents buyers/tenants, sellers/landlords, or both as disclosed dual agents or as designated agents, and state a position about subagency. Procedures must be outlined to explain how fiduciary obligations are to be fulfilled, including disclosures. Detailed procedures, especially those that preserve confidentiality and loyalty, are essential, particularly if the company is practicing designated agency. If state law permits nonagency, policies and accompanying procedures must be defined accordingly. (Sample office agency policies are available from the National Association of REALTORS®.)

Antitrust.   Because real estate practices are constantly being scrutinized for antitrust violations, a company's policies must address the prohibited acts of price fixing, group boycotting, territorial assignments, and tying agreements. Policies should explain the business rationale for the company's fees and its various fee structures. Equally important are procedures that tell salespeople what they need to do and say in their representations of the company's fees to protect the company from antitrust violations.

Equal Opportunity.   The company should express its philosophical commitment to equal opportunity in *housing* and *employment*. Then, establish specific policies and procedures to ensure that everyone in the organization serves all customers and clients properly under federal, state, and local fair housing, civil rights, and disability laws. Personnel policies and procedures must be developed to ensure that practices coincide with all applicable employment and disability laws.

The company could also participate in affirmative action programs. An example is the Fair Housing Partnership Agreement that the National Association of REALTORS® and the Department of Housing and Urban Development have jointly signed. This is a voluntary program in which participants can further equal opportunity in housing by engaging in certain advertising practices and outreach programs in the community.

Real Estate Licensing Laws and Regulations.   A policy should state that all of the activities in the organization must comply with the state's licensing laws. Any procedure that is defined throughout the operations manual should support this policy. Because the company must not permit unlicensed employees to engage in activities for which licensure is required, procedures should address what unlicensed people can and cannot do.

This is also a good place to discuss the company's policy with respect to personal assistants (including whether they are licensed or unlicensed), employees of the company or a salesperson, and the specific activities they are permitted to perform.

General Workplace Policies and Procedures. A number of rules for the workplace and accompanying procedures tell people about the day-to-day life in the organization. These apply to everyone, regardless of their position in the company or their employment status (independent contractor or employee). Typically, these issues are included in an employee handbook, but the placement is not as important as the topics that are covered. Human resource supports are available on the Internet, but commonly suggested topics include the following:

- Equal employment opportunity (including cultural diversity)

- Nonharassment, including sexual harassment (between staff members, management and staff and employees/independent contractors, and customers and clients—see NAR's sample policy)

- Drug and alcohol use/abuse (what, where, and procedures if violations of policy occur)

- Smoking and nonsmoking (in the workplace and with customers and clients)

- Violence in the workplace and personal safety and security issues (including procedures to protect personnel and precautions for salespeople in the field, as well as the company's policy about acceptable self-defense measures; i.e., Mace™, firearms, etc.)

- Standards of conduct (including issues such as theft, conflict of interest, and violations of laws, ethics, and policies)

- Job enrichment and professional growth (workplace philosophy and opportunities)

- Confidentiality (company matters as well as client confidences and personal information to protect against identity theft)

- Public relations (image of the organization)

- Actions on behalf of the organization (who, what, and procedures)

- Nonsolicitation (prevent disruption in the workplace)

- Use of company property and equipment

- Computer, Internet, and e-mail usage (Some companies draft separate policy manuals for computer usage and Internet access.) Issues to address include

  - hardware systems (physical security of equipment);

  - user accounts, passwords, and protected files;

  - copyrighted software (permissible use and legal issues);

  - handling attachments and forwarding messages (e-mail);

  - computer viruses (defenses of company system, including scanning attachments and user CDs and disks);

  - use of secure sites when transmitting personal data, credit information, and the like to protect against identity theft;

  - prohibited activities (frivolous and personal use of internal network and Internet, including harassing and offensive content);

  - intellectual property-rights protection and Internet downloads (typically prohibited);

  - company monitoring of computer and Internet usage (including user waiver of right of privacy);

  - directions for handling system failures

- Emergencies (workplace as well as personal)

- Termination (independent contractors and employees, and grievance procedures for them)

- About the work day:

  - Office hours (including procedures for after-hours in the workplace)

  - Holidays (including accommodations for cultural and religious preferences)

  - Personal phone calls (including emergency procedures and reimbursement of charges)

  - Dress policy (general professional appearance)

Employee Policies

In addition to the items above, a number of issues are addressed in policies that relate specifically to employees.

- Categories of employment and related fringe benefits

- Employment of minors

- Employment of relatives

- Meal and break times

- Pay procedures

- Travel/expense accounts (if any)

- Overtime

- Absenteeism and tardiness

- Layoffs

- Disciplinary actions

- Resignation and discharge

- Vacation and leave:

    - Personal days

    - Vacation time

    - Sick time

    - Jury duty

    - Bereavement leave

    - Military leave

    - Family and medical leave (check requirements under the federal Family and Medical Leave Act of 1993)

A number of state and federal laws exist to protect employees and working conditions. The distinction between employees and independent contractors may not necessarily be relevant in these laws. The best advice is legal advice to be sure that all employment polices and procedures and conditions in the workplace comply with these laws.

Procedures for Independent Contractor/ Salespeople

Although salespeople often enter into independent contractor agreements with the company, that work status should be reaffirmed with careful wording in the company's policy and procedures (another argument in favor of engaging legal counsel). The policies and procedures should address the following:

- Sales teams (the way they are accommodated in the company, including notification to management about how the team has structured its relationship)

- Part-time agents, full-time agents, and home officing (including definitions, hiring policies, and the way they work)

- Referrals (procedures for distributing in-house leads and referrals between salespeople and referrals to other companies)

- Cooperation among salespeople in-house (including sharing customers and clients)

- Standards for servicing customers and clients (listings, sales, and other applicable services)

- Open house procedures (including sales procedures and safety precautions)

- Transactions:

  - Listing and buyer agency agreements (types, situations in which each is used, policy on written versus oral agreements)

  - Forms and contracts (policy for written and oral contracts, written disclosures; contingency forms, transmittal to company files and to contract signatories; record keeping)

  - Escrow money (tracking procedures, deposits and withdrawals, cooperating broker procedures, disputes)

  - Litigation and legal expenses

  - Settlement or escrow procedures

- Commission programs

- Insurance (coinsurance on autos, errors and omissions)

- Dues and fees (professional association, MLS, franchise)

- Education and designations

- Advertising and marketing procedures (who pays and for what, which publications are used, frequency, content and approval of copy even when salesperson is paying the bill, solicitation)

- Internet advertising (requirements of license law, copyright and trademark infringement, defamation, sexual harassment, racial discrimination, wire fraud)

- Telephone solicitation (including do-not-call-list rules)

- Telephone procedures (personal and business calls, phone log, who gets the lead on an inquiry, expectations for returning messages)

- Dissemination of information (about the company and its listings, including the nature of information to be discussed on the phone and who is permitted to disseminate what information)

- Lockboxes and signs (inventory control procedures, who pays)

- Postage, printing, and direct mail (who pays, limits, review of copy)

- Attendance (*recommendations* for floor time, sales meetings, training sessions)

- Parking at the office

- Salespeople selling and purchasing real estate for themselves

- Handling disputes (between salespeople, with customers and clients, with licensees in other firms)

- Termination (disposition of listings, leads, pending closings)

■ CONCLUSION

Many systems and processes need to come together so that an organization can function. The company's policies and procedures are one more of those systems. The purpose is to essentially tell people how the company does business and provide orderly processes so that the company can function efficiently. Not only are manuals of policies and procedures good reference materials to help people self-direct their work but they also provide a framework within which management can manage the daily affairs of the organization.

■ DISCUSSION EXERCISES

Does your company have a code of ethics? If so, are there conflicts between what the company preaches and the way it practices?

Illustrate a typical ethical dilemma that you encountered in daily practice. How was it resolved? Could it have been resolved differently? How?

Discuss typical problems that arise in your company and how these could be resolved by a well-written company policy and procedures manual.

CHAPTER TWELVE

12

MARKETING AND ADVERTISING

What media attract today's consumers?

What tools can you use to promote your company? Your services or your listings?

For a company to meet the service-related goals in its business plan, the company needs a plan to generate business. What any company wants to say to the consumer, basically, is, "Pick us." That's not a particularly inspired way to convey the message, so, obviously, some ways are better than others. Especially when competitors are pleading with the public to pick them.

Some people characterize advertising as a head game, meaning that whoever gets into the head of the consumer wins. Capturing that head takes some finesse, which means the company needs a skillfully designed marketing and advertising program.

There are many tools of the advertising trade that intend to attract attention, make an impression, and cause people to act. Traditionally, real estate companies have used their listings, generally in classified ads, to entice the consumer. The hope being that something about a listing would be appealing enough to prompt at least the action of a phone call. Of course, if the listings weren't appealing, then the company got no benefit from the ads. So, the company pushed for more listings, hoping that perhaps they would have the appeal that would prompt consumer response.

That's a very inventory-dependent way to do business, with the added drawback that the company can't control the design of its inventory the way a manufacturing company can. So, the next thing to do was expand on the message, the most common one being affiliation with an MLS. Then the company had a larger inventory at its disposal. All the company had to do was convince the consumer that the company was a preferable choice over other MLS members.

And so it evolved that companies learned that who they are, the services they provide, and especially the people who work for them are the features the company must promote. Consumers are interested in the *benefits* of such an association. They don't want to be just the means to an end—the sale or lease of a property. Consumers look for salespeople who can be their trusted advisers or helpmates, not just order takers, so the consumers' primary interest is the people they do business with.

Just as a company needs a business plan, it needs a plan for putting a face on the company and its services and getting that face in the right places to capture the minds of consumers. For real estate companies, whose fundamental business is sales, marketing to those minds is a central activity. This is a creative process, and one that benefits from the imagination and skill of professional marketing and advertising specialists.

■ MARKET IDENTITY

First, the company needs to make a statement about itself. That's its market identity, otherwise known as its *brand*. This is done with the name it chooses, the design of its logo, and the selection of a slogan. All of this becomes the company's *signature*, its identity everywhere the signature appears—the sign on the office, yard signs, business cards, letterhead, brochures, and Web home pages. That signature makes an even more powerful statement when affiliated companies are recognized under the same banner.

What's in a Name?

The name of the company tells a story. Because real estate brokerage is a personalized service, some brokers feel they can communicate that personal touch by using their own names for the company name. If the broker has a high profile in the community, name recognition can be a powerful draw.

A fictitious name can be just as powerful, though. It may relate to a specialty, a geographic area, or other special characteristic that distinguishes the company from the competition. Some people consider the alphabetical position of the name in the telephone directory. Even with franchise affiliation, the company needs its own identity. A clever or compelling fictitious name is fine, but one that sounds too frivolous or comical, while creatively daring, can turn out to be an uphill marketing battle. Test-drive a name to gauge the reaction of friends before formally filing a fictitious business name (FBN).

FBNs, which are registered in the state where the company does business, must first be approved before they can be used. Words in the FBN like *Bank, Insurance, Escrow, Trust, Federal, National, State, United States, Reserve,* or *Deposit Insurance* are often questioned. Names that are already in use or names that imply the existence of nonexistent partnerships or corporations will not be accepted.

Some states require a certificate of fictitious name to be recorded in the city or county where the entity will do business. The name is usually advertised in a local general circulation newspaper for a period of time before the certificate is issued. In most cases, a corporation is not required to file a certificate because the corporation as a legal entity is entitled to use its own name. For real estate companies, state license laws may require licensing for both the broker and the FBN.

What's in the Signature?

A signature is the shorthand, the "sound bite" that creates brand-name recognition. A signature makes a short but powerful statement with words, colors, and graphics that stick in people's minds. Think about company signatures that stick in your mind. Some are readily recognized by their color schemes (like real estate franchises). Others have their catchy slogans or logos, like the golden arches that are recognized worldwide.

There's more to the design of a signature than simply picking something that others aren't using. Think "signature that sizzles." Sizzle is the attention-grabbing, impression-making characteristic of a signature. Even the most conservative institution (like a bank) needs a sizzling signature. This is the art of creative design that professionals know best, that crafts a signature that matches the company with the behavior and age of the consumers the company wants to attract.

The design must also look smart in a variety of formats. One that looks good on a billboard may not look so fine when it's scaled down for a classified ad or a business card. Striking colors or screened backgrounds work for color print and a Web page, but may lose the punch in a black-and-white newspaper. While it may not be possible to cover all these bases, a professional can craft a design that suits the media that are most likely to be used.

Professionals can also help gauge consumer reaction to the signature and determine when the time comes to redesign it. As a company ages through its life cycles, it may need a new face that appeals to the contemporary consumer, the new swoosh or swirl that says the company is in step with the times. This could be a contemporarily stylish color scheme, a slogan that builds on contemporary expressions, or a graphic that looks especially 21st century. A new signature may be so bold as to bear no resemblance to the old, but, typically, something recognizable from the old signature is incorporated in the new so as not to lose identity.

When companies undergo significant change, they often need to change the signature. After the merger of two firms, the new company needs a statement. Depending on the merger's strategic direction, the signature may combine some recognizable feature of the previous two companies or cast an entirely new image. (For dishonorable reasons, a new name and signature may be used to shield the true identity of a company as it continues to prey with its nefarious schemes.)

■ THE COMPANY'S MARKETING PLAN

Now that the company has a signature, the company can be readily identified, from a listing ad or the promotion of its relocation service to the sponsorship jerseys for the girls' softball team. The next step is to develop a plan for using the signature to sell the brand and the company's messages.

A marketing plan (similar to a business plan) identifies the goals and the ways these goals will be accomplished. The plan begins with answers to "What does the company want to sell, who are the buyers, and how can they be reached?" The "what" answer becomes the focus for the company's message and needs to be more specific than the company wants to "sell its services." Typically, the focus relates to a priority in the company's business plan, which then becomes the theme for the marketing plan.

The "who" and "how" answers can be captured from the market analysis. Knowing who the target markets are, where they're located, and what their consuming behavior is, especially where they're most likely to see promotional material and advertising, tells the company how to match the right advertising tools with the targeted populations. The lessons learned in the market analysis about the competition should also be considered.

Think "purpose, population, and price." A company can't afford to advertise in every medium or to waste money on a message that misses the target. Some promotional tools and advertising media are most beneficial for institutional purposes (promoting the company) and others for promoting services or listings. Some reach broad audiences and others target more specific ones. The goal of purpose-price-and-population is to pick the venue that serves the purpose and reaches the desired population for the best price. Obviously, the most cost-efficient price is the one that reaches the largest number of people in the target population.

A marketing plan is a package program, meaning that each promotional or advertising activity supports the others. This also improves the cost/benefit equation. One ad alone, for instance, rarely produces significant results. A basic rule in marketing is repetition, "hit often." This means making public appearances on a number of fronts, a number of times. A short but intense integrated campaign, rather than a longer, drawn-out one (with less frequent appearances), provides greater benefit for the same amount of money.

Now, package a program. There's a long list of media options, some with bigger (and smaller) price tags. But with some methodical study and advice from a professional, the company can assemble a beneficial and affordable program. And it can have some creative fun in the process.

Internet

Because people have been turning to the Internet in staggering numbers, the Internet is today's high-tech mass-marketing tool. (In case anyone needs convincing, just look at the number of advertising banners.) Graphics and attention-grabbing animation put a new spin on the meaning of "billboard," in this case the cyberhighway's version, to promote a company's signature. The Internet also serves more specific purposes, through the poster's Web site.

A recent study conducted by Borrell Associates, Inc., a Virginia-based research company, says that the number of homebuyers searching for properties on the Web surged from 2 percent in 1995 to 50 percent in 2001, many of whom spend about six weeks looking at neighborhoods and prices before contacting a licensee. These on-line shoppers spend about two weeks working with a licensee before purchasing, as opposed to an average of six weeks for those who haven't done on-line research.

This along with the point that's been made repeatedly about the importance of Internet presence takes us to the next step: deciding what the company wants that presence to do. For the most part (at least at the moment), companies hook visitors to their sites with listing information (hence the development of IDX discussed in the first chapter). Then, the company can create an identity, promote its services, and provide links to other valuable sites.

Because visitors have no brand loyalty at this point, the ease with which they can use and navigate the site is the key to telling their computers to memorize it as a "favorite." The first step is to get the visitor to the site.

■ Choose an Internet service that will give you high traffic and is easily accessible via the popular search engines.

- Help the search engine (which is like a librarian) locate your site by selecting key words that people who are searching for information are likely to use.

- Place your key words or phrases on your page where the search engines are likely to find them(in the first several words on the page title). Don't lead off with a person's or a company's name, copyright notice, or welcome message. The general viewer won't find you.

- Provide descriptive information, or metatags, to describe the site in a search engine's index. The viewer of the page won't see these, but they help the search engines respond to the viewer.

- Register the site with the search engine's index and consider ways to link the site with others (with their permission) to maximize your exposure.

The site has to be distinctive so that it stands out above all others. There are many do-it-yourself software programs for setting up a site. Perhaps the best advice, however, is to include the help of a professional (or use the company's marketing adviser) to design the site. In addition to the ease with which people can navigate the site, visitors want meaningful information. Some of the marketing tools that are geared to consumer education (such as newsletters) can also be used on the site. Even the company commercial needs to be very benefit-driven. Otherwise, it will be ignored like all the banners and drop-down ads that people are learning to tune out.

The Internet can also present some challenges. A Web site requires constant monitoring. Cyberspace information has limited shelf life, just like a printed flyer. Informative messages can look embarrassingly out-of-date when interest rates or tax laws change. But the greatest vulnerability is the time-sensitive nature of property listings. The virtue of IDX is being able to tie into the MLS database, which is presumably up-to-date. Otherwise, the company must constantly monitor the posted inventory to remove sold or expired listings. Often, companies engage someone (either on staff or outside) as a webmaster to oversee their Web sites.

Vigilant monitoring is also needed to be sure that site content has not been tampered with or that the site has not been linked to another site that could be embarrassing. (There's no end to the creativity of cyberspace demons.) If the site is interactive and does not have automated response features, someone has to be reading that "mail" so that people receive prompt responses. Someone must also keep track of "hits" (contacts) so that the company can gauge performance of the site.

One of the most significant, and potentially litigious, challenges is dealing with protected ownership of information. Not all information is considered public domain. Domain names and site content are assets, considered to be *intellectual property,* that owners frequently protect by copyright and trademark. This is a two-way street: the company must be sure that it does not use the protected property of others (unless permission is given) and the company must be sure to protect its property with copyrights and trademarks. Listings are proprietary information and should be posted only according to the rules of the MLS.

Mass Media

Though the Internet qualifies as mass media, the conventional view of mass media has been television, radio, and newspapers. Usually they are used as institutional advertising, that is, to promote the company. But they may be used to launch a new service or promote listings.

Broadcast Media.   With today's fast-paced lifestyles, radio and television are major sources of information. A significant drawback is there's no tangible, printed piece to put into the consumer's hands. The secret is to capture the audience's attention in 30 seconds and then introduce or reinforce the message elsewhere. Professional media consultants can help tailor a radio or TV message to capture that attention. Because broadcast media can be expensive, the message needs to make a strong impact in a short time.

Select radio and television stations whose audiences match the company's target market(s). Stations compile audience profiles (sometimes by zip-coded demographics), which are useful for matching stations with target markets and also identifying the number of consumers that can be reached. Don't overlook cable TV stations. Their audiences are typically more localized (particularly true for community stations), but the stations are useful for reaching very specific target markets. Cable bulletin board services are good for promoting listings as well as other services.

A caveat about using audience profiles is that a real estate company can run into fair housing violations if it selects a station whose primary audience is not a cross-section of the population. This is not to say that the station should be avoided, but the marketing program should also include media that reach the general population.

The cost of airtime is a good indicator of the size of the audience and its value as consumers. Inexpensive time slots are available in both radio and TV. But unless there's great target-market potential in health care and other night-shift workers, the midnight-to-5-A.M. time slot may not be a wise choice. The time is cheap, though. A 60-second spot could equal (or be less than) the cost of a 30-second spot in prime time. Radio is generally less expensive than commercial TV at any time of the day. Some broadcast stations offer packaged time slots that include preferred time as well as off hours, which may be a good deal.

A company could also consider sponsoring an interactive TV or radio program. These are ambitious projects because someone in the company has to be responsible for the weekly program. Planning and hosting programs and arranging for and interviewing guests can be fun. But the fun can wear thin after several months if you start to run out of creative ideas or tire of the amount of effort involved. Even listing magazine shows can be ambitious. Although there's no "talk" involved, there are still production time and video costs to consider. Because listings must be current, there isn't much lead-time either. A public relations consultant who has experience with these projects is an invaluable production adviser.

Print Media.   Print media such as newspapers have been a staple in the real estate advertising arsenal for years, though that scene is starting to shift as greater numbers of people turn to the Internet. NAR reports that the Internet and the newspaper are about equal draws. It's doubtful that print media will be totally eliminated in the foreseeable future, but clearly print has lost some of its appeal.

All of this suggests that print media must be evaluated carefully, which can be done in similar fashion to broadcast media. Using circulation data and reader profiles, the print selection can be matched with target markets. The choice of print options ranges from the local weekly and shopper newspapers to the daily metropolitan and regional publications. Compare costs and circulation to your target markets. Publications that are free to the reader have wide distribution but they are also readily discarded. Investigate the actual results of other advertisers in these publications.

Newspaper advertising can be used in a variety of ways. Display ads can promote the company or a particular service. These can be expensive, so it's best to maximize the impact with a professionally developed message and layout. A paid advertisement, appearing as an editorial column, can provide timely and informative news the consumer can use. A commercial message is permissible because the company (as opposed to the publisher) prepares the content. Publishers rarely print commercial messages that are submitted in press releases. Even classified, listing advertising is also advertising for the company.

Newsletters

Although newsletters can serve many purposes, one of the most useful from the consumer's point of view is one that educates. A newsletter is an ideal way to satisfy the consumers' thirst for information with articles about emerging trends, changes in the law, recent court cases, and real estate-related government regulations, while promoting the company at the same time.

Be sure of the facts being published, and if interpretations of laws or legal cases are written, include a disclaimer. Editorial comments should be clearly identified as such. Because some opinions may alienate some readers, think seriously about whether that is a risk worth taking.

Considerable time is involved in preparing text. While it's tempting to reprint an article that appeared elsewhere or to reproduce someone else's writing, typically these can't be used without violating copyright laws. Be sure to get the author's and/or publisher's permission to use a work. Also monitor newsletters the salespeople may be circulating to be sure they are observing the same rules.

Copyright the newsletter and then put it on the Web site, in the company word processing program so the salespeople can e-mail it to their contact network, or offer it to a professional publication or a local newspaper or magazine.

Press Releases

Press releases also are informative. But what a company thinks is worthwhile information and what the newspaper or the television or radio station thinks may be two entirely different things. Media, particularly in large metropolitan markets, work for circulation or ratings. They want stories that capture people's attention, a subject they can relate to, be it timely, controversial, innovative, or human-interest-oriented. Because real estate touches people's lives in many ways, there are many stories a company can tell that will capture media and public attention.

The media can also spot a commercial disguised as a press release, and major media in most markets will not use the story. However, they may use a story that announces a major company event (a merger or new office opening) or a public information seminar. A change in company leadership or the election of a company staff member as president of a local service organization or professional association can catch media attention, especially if the press release is directed to the business editor. Promote the salespeople and their professional accomplishments in local newspaper columns as well.

An example of a personal press release appears in Figure 12.1. Notice the form it follows. Catch the reader's eye by presenting the most important information at the outset, including who, what, where, how, and when. Do so in a factual manner, without editorializing. Some publications edit the copy. So catch the editor's eye at the very beginning of the release because that could be the only information the editor chooses to use. Finally, prepare the release so that it can be e-mailed.

Brochures

The hard copy printed brochure that a company can put in people's hands has been a staple in the business world. Simply because it is in print on paper, a brochure endures before people's eyes (unlike the fleeting exposure of broadcast media) and can also tell a more complete story and the consumer benefits of the message.

Many different kinds of messages can be delivered in a brochure. A general brochure can tell the company story and its business philosophy and then explain the company's services and expertise. (Salespeople can do similar self-promotion brochures as well.) Or a brochure could spotlight a particular

FIGURE 12.1

Sample Press Release

FOR IMMEDIATE RELEASE WITH PHOTO

To: _____ Name of paper _____

Attention: _____

_____ Date _____

_____ Address of paper _____

Photo Caption: Peter Jay, president of ABC REALTORS®, is shown presenting plaques to each of the top three winners for 1999. From left to right are: Jay, Wendy Lewis, William Eltee and Doris Moore.

ABC REALTORS® HONORS TOP THREE AGENTS FOR 1999

HOMETOWN: Wendy Lewis, Willam Eltee and Doris Moore recently were honored at the ABC REALTORS® annual staff awards ceremony as the top three producers in the firm for 1995. The winners were announced by ABC REALTORS® president, Peter Jay, at a dinner held in their honor at the Hillswood Country Club in Hometown.

Lewis attained the firm's highest sales volume,more than $6,000,000, and first place in selling the most company listings. Lewis, who joined the firm in 1977, has consistently been a top producer in the company. She has served as a director of the Hometown Board of REALTORS® since 1988 and was elected as the 1998 treasurer of the board.

Eltee has been with the ABC firm almost two years. His production for 1999 neared the $3,500,000 mark. A graduate of Weston High School, Eltee attended Emerson State College where he majored in business administration and finance. He also has extensive experience in general contracting and new construction.

Moore, a seven-year member of ABC, achieved close to $5,000,000 in sales volume and was recognized as having the most closed listings for the year. Active in the Hometown board, she has chaired the Grievance Committee since 1993 and serves on the REALTORS® Community Service Committee.

In presenting each of the recipients with a plaque, Jay said, "I congratulate the three winners and want to extend ABC's thanks for their efforts and dedication over the years. We are very proud to have them on our staff."

# # #

---

aspect of the company services or its premier listings, or promote the company as a good career choice.

Brochures have to be both visually and mentally appealing. Professional-looking designs, layouts, and graphics can be self-developed with a desktop publishing program or with the advice of a graphics arts specialist. That great looking brochure also has to have equally sharp content. The message has to be told in a well-constructed, well-written way. If the company doesn't have someone on staff who writes well, then the job should be outsourced to a good copy specialist.

Several things to keep in mind about content: Think about how readers will react to the story being told. Most consumers don't want to be subjected to words that they don't feel are relevant to them. When listing professional accomplishments, tell how these benefit the consumer. Be truthful and realistic (don't make promises that can't be kept), and be sure that all content complies with state license law. And avoid a "brag sheet"; this only reinforces stereotypes of self-centered business people. Think about how industry jargon or designations are used. Unless they are properly explained or mean something to the general public, they only confuse the story.

It's discouraging to spend a lot of money on beautiful brochures that don't get used. So use them generously. Because per-piece cost drops as the size of the print run increases, larger runs are generally preferable. But it's even more discouraging to find many unused brochures that are out-of-date, so try to gauge the usage and prepare copy that has a long shelf life. Once the initial design and layout are done, minor copy or photo changes are relatively inexpensive to make (especially if an in-house desktop program is used).

If brochures are being distributed to people's homes, be sure distribution does not violate postal service rules. Personally delivered materials cannot be placed in a mailbox or other receptacle intended for U.S. Postal Service use. The offender can be subjected to the amount of first-class postage for the entire postal route in which the material was hand delivered, can be fined, or can jeopardize the company's bulk-mail permit. Before using bulk mail, investigate the regulations and follow the correct procedures to preserve the company's bulk-mail privileges.

High-Tech "Brochures"   Today's marketing plans are on the high-tech track with high-tech tools. The content is similar to that of any brochure, but can be delivered by VHS, CD, DVD, PowerPoint™, and depending on the format, can be attached to an e-mail, up loaded onto the Web, or carried on a salesperson's laptop. Digital photography only adds to the ease with which exciting and informative stories can be told.

Technology-supported marketing tools put the glitz and glimmer on a story. High-impact visuals and/or captivating audio make storytelling a sensory experience, the benefit being that a story makes a stronger impression. A 10-minute video can carry more punch and say more than a print brochure. High-tech tools also appeal to our TV- or CD-dependent way of life.

The greatest investment in these tools is the initial cost of development or production. This may involve professional assistance; an amateurish looking or sounding production does little to enhance company image. Once produced, the video or audio delivery is easy and affordable to duplicate. Then use it; distribute as any other promotional piece is used. And put it in the reception or conference area for waiting visitors to enjoy.

Telephone Directories

The real estate section of the Yellow Pages is one of the most frequently referenced headings; as many as 30 to 50 percent of the customers use this publication to locate a broker. (Wonder what happened to the business cards you distribute?) Although a business listing or display ad (which is very costly) in a telephone directory is not a sole promotional tool, it should not be overlooked. Because some directories are not published frequently (and many of us do not replace old editions), avoid information that could date the listing, particularly in display ads.

Outdoor Advertising

Billboards; taxicab, bus, and automobile signs; and yard signs fall into this category. The company signature can become a fixture in the landscape because these usually provide long exposure. (Yard signs should provide long exposure because they appear on many listings, not on the same one.) Because they are eye-catching, these tools are good for reinforcing the company's signature. But they are not suitable for lengthy messages because people must be able to grasp what the message says in about four seconds.

Novelties

There are literally hundreds of items on which the company can imprint its name, from combs and sponges to calendars, balloons, rulers, and bottle caps. These fall into the institutional advertising category. It is possible to imprint many of these items with the company logo and lettering style rather than plain type. If the company has a theme, select an item that reflects that image. These are useful items for recruiting programs or public seminars or for the salespeople to use as handouts.

Solicitation

One of the most effective marketing tools is personal contact. Certainly, one-on-one networking that is common business practice can reap great rewards. While general solicitation can also be beneficial, the company image can suffer if the solicitors are not careful about the manner in which such activities are conducted. Consumers have grown increasingly intolerant of solicitors who interrupt their lives uninvited (hence the flurry of strengthened "do not call" laws). Any solicitation on behalf of the company must be done in ways that are not offensive and must comply with the laws and the ethics that govern these activities.

The company should adopt strict policies to ensure that salespeople do not disrupt an agency relationship that a person has with another licensee. A salesperson should not engage in discussions about future agency relationships unless invited to do so. General solicitations to a geographic area or group, which may include individuals who are already clients of other firms, are not unethical. But targeting solicitations to another licensee's client that promote the same services that are already being provided by the other licensee is a problem.

Telephone Consumer Protection Act. The Federal Communications Commission has issued regulations relating to the Telephone Consumer Protection Act of 1991. These regulations, which became effective on December 20, 1992, govern the use of telephone lines for commercial solicitation and advertisement.

The legislation is intended to protect telephone subscribers who do not wish to receive unsolicited live "cold called," autodialed, prerecorded, or artificial voice messages and fax machine solicitations. Contacts with 911, health care facility, physicians, poison control, and fire or law enforcement emergency lines are prohibited. Also prohibited are contacts with telephone lines in hospitals, health care facilities, and retirement home guest or patient rooms as well as paging services, cellular telephones, or any other service for which the consumer is charged a fee.

According to the procedures in the regulations, the soliciting company

- may not telephone a residence before 8 A.M. or after 9 P.M.;

- must identify the business name and telephone number and the name of the person making the call;

- must adopt a written policy and maintain a "do-not-call list" of residences requesting that they not be called;

- must advise and train all personnel and independent contractors engaged in any aspect of telephone solicitation regarding the "do-not-call list" maintenance and procedures;

- must share the "do-not-call list" with an affiliated entity (one that a consumer reasonably would expect to be affiliated with the soliciting company based on the company's name);

- may not use an automatic telephone dialing system in such a way that two or more telephone lines of a multiple-line business are engaged simultaneously; and

- may not use a telephone, computer, or other electronic/mechanical fax machine device to send unsolicited advertisements to another telephone, computer, or electronic/mechanical receiver.

Company solicitors can be sued for up to $500 in damages for violations. If the company has established written policies regarding these procedures, they may be used for defending alleged violations. Note that these rules apply when the caller has no prior business relationship with or permission or invitation from the consumer to make contact. Consult a lawyer for further information and advice regarding compliance with the Telephone Consumer Protection Act.

Be sure that the company and sales staff faithfully observe the provisions of recent federal (and perhaps state) "do-not-call list" legislation. A case in Pennsylvania resulted in $34,000 in penalties for violation of that state's law. For more information, go to www.dontcall.gov

Harassment. Salespeople must use common sense about how aggressively they pursue prospective customers and clients. If people feel harassed, the net effect is they have been alienated. Unfavorable comments spread faster than the favorable ones, so not only has one potential customer been turned off but so have many others. Also be sure that any local solicitation ordinances, along with permit requirements, are observed.

Blockbusting/Panic Selling.   Any discussion of solicitation would be incomplete without a mention of blockbusting or panic selling. This consists of frequent efforts to sell real estate in a neighborhood by generating fear that people in protected classes are moving into or out of a neighborhood. The fair housing laws further define these actions as ones that include representations that real estate values are declining because of these transactions, which in fact have nothing to do with the intrinsic value of the real estate. Blockbusting or panic selling violates the fair housing laws.

News Columns

One of the best ways to showcase expertise, and the company in the process, is by writing a real estate news column for a local general circulation or a weekly or shoppers' newspaper, or for a business or professional publication. These may be either free or paid-for columns, depending on the publication. Figure 12.2 is a sample news column that was printed free as a public service.

The purpose of these columns is to provide informative, substantive content that is useful for the consuming public. Articles must be well written and present an accurate, objective portrayal of an issue. Typically, the author controls the content and, therefore, can protect the story from being slanted or distorted. However, the writer must be aware of editorial policies that could give the publisher final say in the content or permit the publisher to edit the writing. Otherwise, a carefully written article may not appear in print as the author intended.

Letters to the Editor

A faithful observer of current events may get sufficiently stirred by the public discourse in city council, on radio or television, or in the local newspaper that involves matters of real estate. Adding comments to the dialogue can perform a valuable public service, and public service is a good image-builder for the company.

There are some caveats, however. The purpose of speaking up is to offer professional perspective to the discussion. While the letter may be passionate, unsubstantiated, emotional ramblings or exceedingly controversial positions will not advance the cause and could alienate the company's clientele.

FIGURE 12.2

A Sample News Column

Real Estate

John Cyr

Foothills sprout subdivisions

A few years ago, when land developers subdivided many thousand acres of homesites in the Valley Springs area and sold them to buyers from other parts of the state, we in the real estate business marvelled at their success.

Unfortunately, many of the lots would not sustain septic tanks. (For a homesite to qualify for a septic tank disposal system it must pass what is called a "percolation (perc) test," which means that the effluent from the leach lines must be absorbable to a depth of at least the first four feet of ground area.)

It turned out to be true that many of the lots sold could not pass such tests and, consequently, at last count, many owners hold lots they can't build on using the conventional septic tank systems.

Many of us think the reason the developers were so successful in selling so many lots is probably because they met the needs and desires of people from all parts of the state who wish to escape traffic congestion, smog, drugs and crime. They would go almost anywhere within reason to get away from it all. That's why the hill

country looked so good to them, and still does.

The market for hill country property is still strong but the local authorities are now wise to the septic problems and have taken measures to protect buyers from buying unusable lots. Enter the subdividers who have solved the problem by installing sewer plants that meet all county specifications.

La Contenta Golf and Country Club near Valley Springs was one of the first to provide such facilities and it sold out in just a year or two. Now several experienced Stockton developers have followed suit and are offering homesites in hill country subdivisions that offer "state of the art" community sewer systems.

Tony Meath of Lockeford is one who has installed such a system in his Gayla Manor Subdivision located on Highway 88 just about 5 miles east of Pine Grove. Gayla Manor not only has one of the first modern sewer plants outside of a city plant to be built in Amador County, it also offers community water service, paved streets, street lights, and protective restrictions, among other ameneties. Although on the market for only a month or so Tony reports that over half of the 56 lots are already sold.

Another enterprising developer, Jimmy Winchell of G. M. Winchell & Sons has just finished improvements on Wallace Lake Estates, a subdivision adjacent to the small community of Wallace on Highway 12. (Next to Rossetti's Restaurant).

Wallace Lake Estates is a more ambitious project with its own sewer and water system to serve 300 lots but also offers paved

streets, TV cable, telephone, security gates, street lights and propane piped to each homesite. Also, they have reserved a 14½-acre site for a future shopping center.

The lots are a minimum of 10,000 sq. ft. and surrounded by 240 acres of scenic oak-studded hills with it's own private lake. Jimmy already reports sales of over 39 lots with little or no advertising. The prices of the lots range from $50,000 to $80,000 with no bonds.

Other, smaller subdivisions, for people who want more land around them are coming on the market in the Valley Springs-Burson area offering 3 to 5 acres in size with guaranteed percolation for septic tanks. Rosemarie Realty (Rosemary Mendonca of Lodi) is one of the developers and a group of investors from Northern California are putting together another subdivision tentatively named Shangri-La Valley Estates, which will be selling 5 acres and larger homesites.

Such subdivisions make good sense because instead of using up valuable high-production agricultural land in the valley, they use land that has little value for other uses. The only drawback to such developments is the distance factor. But for those people who can carry on much of their work out of their homes, they might just as well live in a more pleasant, less stressful environment.

John Cyr is a Stockton real estate broker, author and owner of John Cyr Realtors. Questions can be submitted to a rotating panel of experts by writing BusinessMonday, The Stockton Record, Box 900, Stockton, CA 95201.

Reprinted with permission of John E. Cyr. Courtesy of *The Stockton Record.*

Letters to the editor must concisely capture the point and should not be overly long (otherwise they won't be used). Also, consider how the tone of a message can change if the letter is edited (if that's the paper's policy).

Media Resource

Another public service and company image-builder is to become a resource for local reporters, broadcasters, and real estate editors. This not only provides them with a ready resource for their research but also a "sound bite" when they are looking for an expert's quote. Once a relationship is established, the media are more likely to be receptive to a heads-up announcement for a story or other comments the expert resource chooses to make. (This can also aid in gaining exposure for press releases and the like.)

Understand how the media work. Reporters are often crunched by tight deadlines so they need immediate access, and if the resource is not available, they'll move on to another one. They may be looking for guidance or background information for a story or for a quotable comment. Typically, reporters also have limited space or airtime for a story.

People are quotable because of their stature, their expertise, or their provocative or insightful comments. Normally, the resource is contacted by telephone, often with mention of the specific topic of interest. The resource can offer to return the call in several minutes and use that interim time to compile statistics or other pertinent information and to frame the points the expert wants to make on the subject.

This not only makes the resource sound particularly knowledgeable but also minimizes the likelihood of being misquoted or having off-the-cuff or embarrassing remarks memorialized in print or on the airwaves. Comments can also be clearly stated as "off the record," which the media must respect. If the media are looking for an official position, be sure that only the person who is authorized to speak on behalf of the company provides these comments.

Because the media look for sound bites that can be quoted in limited space or airtime, the speaker has to learn to make the point concisely. However, even a short, carefully worded remark can be further edited, which can distort the message. The meaning of the remark can also be skewed, depending on where the comment is placed within the rest of the story. Bottom line is the expert gets misquoted. All of this is simply a fact of life in the limelight.

■ MARKETING PROPERTIES

Unless the company exclusively represents buyers, marketing listings is a significant part of a company's promotional activities and one that the sellers expect the company to perform with utmost skill.

A National Association of REALTORS® survey on the home buying and selling process indicated that the most frequent concern cited by sellers was getting a sales price high enough to recover what they put into the property. Keeping their homes in showcase condition during the selling process, closing on time for a relocation deadline, and selling in time to buy the house they want were other major concerns.

Unfortunately, too many salespeople see the signature on a listing contract as the end of their responsibility to the company rather than the beginning of their responsibility to the property owners. Some of that is the company's fault if it focuses on quotas rather than on service. A property worth listing is worth marketing.

The marketing plan for listings involves as much common sense as advertising skill and knowledge of the laws that govern advertising practices. A rule of thumb: If this were my property, how would I want to see it showcased? In the best light, of course. This means a property that is really ready for show, a realistic listing price, flattering pictures, and appealingly descriptive words.

While some marketing strategies achieve higher results than others in different market areas, the goal is to get the listing in the public eye. A company's own statistics can be used to determine how that eye is most effectively captured in its market area.

Pictures

The "a picture is worth a thousand words" notion takes on new meaning for a company's advertising budget. A company can ill afford to spend money on an ad that showcases a tree or a brown hillside instead of the house, or a snowcapped roof when the tulips are fading into summertime. The company can make much more effective advertising expenditures with an investment in good equipment, a talented photographer (if the salespeople can't do well), and a policy that only timely photographs will be used.

Today's digital photography produces outstanding results and is particularly useful for the variety of electronic formats that are desirable today. Photographs can be attached to e-mails, uploaded onto the Internet, and compiled on video. They can also be used for interactive videos and virtual tours on the Internet.

Photos also tell a powerful story for the property owner's benefit. Owners like to see how their property will be showcased, but the pictures are also a tactful way to persuade them to do maintenance or repairs after seeing what the lens sees. Pictures also make nice memory gifts at closing or postcards that can be used for marketing purposes.

Advertising Copy

Regardless of where the words about the property appear (classified advertising, a Web site, or a script for a TV promotion), the price the company pays for exposure is worthwhile only if the ad copy is effective. While the listing salesperson is most familiar with the property and, therefore, presumed to be the best person to write the ad, that also presumes the salesperson (or assistant) has the skill to write effective copy.

There are a variety of solutions to the poor-copy problem. Figure 12.3 is a form on which a salesperson can prepare notes to guide the development of an ad, particularly the sections on the right side of the form. With the help of computer software or hints gathered from ad-writing seminars (including classes the company decides are necessary to offer), the salesperson can compile better copy. Or the company can use a copy specialist.

Salespeople, not ads, sell properties. But the copy still has to generate attention, interest, desire, and action (AIDA). The copy must communicate a message about a property or create a word picture. Numerous studies indicate that the three most important features in an ad are the neighborhood (location), the size of the property, and the price. Ads that don't provide the information a buyer is looking for are less likely to be read. And as a practical matter, while abbreviations are common, does everyone understand our shorthand? A 4BR, 2B, hse w/ EIK, FR, and 2 FPs can be a real puzzle. The ad needs to make sense to the public.

Certainly, good ad copy enhances the chances that the listing will capture the right buyer. But even readers who decide that the copy does not describe

FIGURE 12.3

Ad Copy Form

			WHAT MAKES THIS HOUSE DIFFERENT FROM ALL OTHER HOUSES ON THE MARKET AT THIS TIME? (USP—UNIQUE SELLING PROPOSITION)	
CLIENT'S NAME:		SP.:		
ADDRESS:		LED NO.:		
TOWN:		AGE:		
LIST PRICE:		LIST DATE:		
STYLE:		EXT.:	WHO DO YOU SEE BUYING THIS HOUSE?:	
ROOMS:	DR:	FAM. RM.:		
BR:		E-I-KIT:		
BATH:	FULL:	HALF:	LIST AN INDIVIDUAL FEATURE AND DESCRIBE THE BENEFIT OF THAT FEATURE TO A BUYER	
FINISHED BASE:				
FPLC:	WHERE:	TYPE:	SPECIAL FEATURE:	BENEFIT:
# GARAGE:		CENT. AIR:		
POOL:		DESCRIBE:		
PROP. SIZE:				
ITEMS INCLUDED:				
WALL TO WALL: _____		SELF CLEAN OVEN: _____		
REFRIG: _____		CENT. VAC.: _____		
WASHER: _____		INTERCOM: _____		
DRYER: _____		OTHER: _____		
SPECIAL INSTRUCTIONS AS TO ADVERTISING COMMITTMENTS:				
			1-Year Homeowner's Warranty Included: __Yes __No	

the property they want to see can be sufficiently impressed by the company's professional marketing skill.

Legal Issues. Ultimately, the responsibility for an ad is the broker's, regardless of whether the ad is paid for by the company or the company's salesperson. Monitoring the accuracy and legality of ads is a critical activity for management and, as the following discussion reveals, management needs to be looking at a number of things in those ads. *Monitoring advertising on Web sites, including the salespeople's own, is an especially important risk-management activity today.*

Superlative comments or opinions are permissible; misrepresentations of facts are not. If a house is described as "energy efficient," the typical reader is going to expect superior insulation or cost-saving features, not just ordinary construction. Brand names, such as Thermopane®, should be used only when the named product is actually used. A typographical error ("3 bedrooms" instead of 2) is untruthful, regardless of whether the error originated with company's salesperson or typist or the publisher who printed the ad.

The owner's position must be accurately represented. This means publishing only the price authorized by the owner (not unauthorized reductions) and not publishing information that could compromise the owner's negotiating position ("owner anxious," unless authorized by the owner) or violates the broker's fiduciary responsibility to the owner.

The state licensing laws may include provisions that further affect ad contents. Several important issues are revealed in the answers to these questions:

- Does the advertisement of a listing have to include the licensed name of the firm? The phone number? In the case of multiple offices, which phone number?

- What conditions or restrictions are imposed when salespeople include their names and phone numbers? What about personal voice mail and pager numbers?

- What are the procedures for advertising on the Internet?

- What are the requirements if the broker or a salesperson advertises property that is personally owned?

While financing terms may be appealing, the representations must comply with the truth-in-lending laws. General expressions, such as "owner will finance" or "liberal terms available," are permissible. But "only $1,000 down" is dangerously misleading and is permitted only if the specific loan terms are included (the amount of the loan, amount of the down payment, amount of the monthly payments, and length of the term).

Is the language nondiscriminatory? The fair housing laws prohibit making, printing, or publishing any statement that indicates any preference, limitation, or discrimination based on race, color, religion, sex, familial status, handicap, or national origin. If you're unsure about the language, consult the Fair Housing Advertising Regulations (*Federal Register*/Vol. 54. No. 13/ Monday, January 23, 1989/Rules and Regulations).

For example, language such as *whites only, Hispanic neighborhood, Christian home, adults only, adults preferred* or *older neighborhood, singles, no children, walking distance to the synagogue, one block from the Italian club*, and *good parish schools* are considered discriminatory. It is permissible to say *mother-in-law quarters, family room, walk to bus stop, bachelor pad, great view*, or *wheelchair ramp*. These are federal guidelines, so be sure to consult local and state legal references as well.

Classified Advertising

From the company point of view, classified advertising serves dual purposes. It promotes the listing to possible buyers or tenants and is also institutional advertising for the company. Many property owners, however, see classifieds as their right of entitlement for listing the property and expect the ad to contribute directly to an eventual sale.

One of the owners' most common criticisms involves the amount of advertising devoted to their listings. It may be that promises were made just to get the listing. Or perhaps no amount of advertising would be acceptable to an owner who's frustrated while waiting for a property to sell. Regardless of the reason, the company has to avoid the violated expectations that can cause negative public relations fallout.

A clearly defined promotional plan, including the company's classified policy, needs to be explained the owner at the outset. Then, periodic reports (including copies of ads that were run) to substantiate the advertising should be provided to the owner. Compiling these reports is a relatively simple task with today's computer software.

Multiple Listing Services

So as not to slight one of the industry's most useful marketing tools, MLSs are once again mentioned. Today, considering the number of people turning to the Internet, the MLS has taken on new significance, as member brokers can now offer Internet exposure for a property owner's listing. (Local MLS rules, of course, prevail.)

Many of the legal issues that have been discussed also affect promotions in the MLS. Inaccurate information about the property not only creates an unfavorable impression but also creates liability for both the listing and the selling firms. The vigilance with which management monitors all advertising applies to MLS entries as well.

Brochures and Fliers

A brochure can be useful for marketing a listing, though because of the expense involved, the truly elaborate ones are typically produced only for unique, boutique, or high-priced properties. A lesser version is a flyer, which is a nice supplement to the information that can be accommodated in the fields on an MLS feature sheet. Fliers are useful for other companies' salespeople as well as for prospective purchasers and tenants. Again, management should monitor the content of brochures and fliers to ensure they do not create legal problems.

Open Houses

Open houses have been another standard tool of the trade, though they have their critics. The customs in the local marketplace, the company's measured results, the price of the property, and the salesperson's feelings about their effectiveness all factor into the significance of an open house in a listing's promotional plan.

Open houses appeal to people's natural curiosity. Some owners don't want their properties to be fodder for that curiosity, while others see an open house as just one more way that could possibly produce that one sought-after buyer. Some owners sometimes measure the attentiveness of salespeople by their willingness to conduct open houses.

Salespeople have mixed views on the subject. A survey by Texas A&M University's Real Estate Center revealed that 59 percent of the responding real estate practitioners didn't think open houses helped to locate buyers for the properties. Forty-one percent of the respondents indicated that they hold open houses to appease sellers. Others who have studied the results of open houses suggest that the salesperson, rather than the seller, is the principal beneficiary, that they are great for self-promotion.

Owners must be informed about the results that can be realistically expected. Owners don't mind sacrificing their time and effort, but they get upset (as do salespeople) when open houses do not produce any visitors. Picking a good day and time for a public open house is a critical (maybe even a mystical) part of the success of an open house. A weekday evening during daylight savings time may work in some areas; in other areas, it may not. A decorated holiday tour of the company's listings may be appealing. Track attendance to determine the best strategy.

Open houses are joint projects between the owner and the salesperson and require careful planning and execution, regardless of whether they are conducted for other salespeople or the public. Owners hesitate to authorize open houses when they expect to be inconvenienced and are sometimes uneasy about opening their homes to strangers.

Safety of the Salesperson. Unfortunately, real estate salespeople have been victims of violent crimes while on the job. The company should insist that salespeople faithfully observe some basic personal safety rules so that their whereabouts are always known, that they have the ability to summon help (a cellphone or pager), and that they have an escape plan at the property. There's also safety in numbers, which is an argument for using several hosts, especially if the structure is large. Sign-in/sign-out registers, although not foolproof for identifying those with questionable motives, just might encourage such a person to leave.

Safety of the Seller. No one should be allowed to freely wander through a property unattended. Although sellers should be encouraged to tuck valuables out of sight, this does not guarantee that the owner's belongings are secure. Nor does the salespeople's presence, for that matter, but they must be vigilant observers and be guided by proper procedures to safely handle suspicious situations. Think about the artful thief whose hands are quicker than the eye or an unscrupulous visitor who's casing the premises for future reference. At the conclusion of the open house, the salesperson should account for every visitor (the reason for sign-out entries) to be sure no one is still lurking in or around the property.

Safety of the Visitor. Open houses can create liability for the company and the seller because people attend as invitees of the owner and of the brokerage firm. Salespeople must be alert to conditions that could jeopardize public (the visitor) safety to protect the interests of all concerned.

This lesson can best be told by a case filed against a New Jersey broker, in which the state's supreme court determined that agents have a legal duty to conduct a reasonable inspection of the property and warn visitors of discoverable physical conditions that may be dangerous. The basis of the decision was that the property's being held open constituted use as a place of business.

The company should insist that salespeople inspect properties for hazards and take precautionary steps (posting signs or colored tape or verbally warning visitors). Although this case set a precedent in New Jersey, it also provided evidence that could be used by courts elsewhere.

Yard Signs

Yard signs are site-specific ads as well as institutional advertising for the company. Granted, there are some properties, such as condominiums, where signs may not be permitted and there are also are ongoing controversies in some municipalities about the use of yard signs. Yard signs come in a variety of styles and design, some also with "take-one" boxes for flyers. And there are "talking signs" that transmit information on a limited radio frequency that people can either listen to while parked in front of the property or within limited drive-by range.

■ PROTECTING THE COMPANY'S IMAGE

Everything a company does and says affects its brand name and its relationship with the public. Unfortunately, a few missteps do more to hurt public relations than many good steps help, but such is the nature of business. The company's attentiveness to public perception plays a major role in its ability to generate business. In a word, this means reputation.

Marketing specialists do look at the company's reputation. As much as the marketing plan needs to match the business plan, there may be image-making efforts that will enhance other promotions or advertising the company does. Perhaps the company could do a better job of demonstrating its business philosophy, concern for community, or any one of a number of other company ideals that foster goodwill with the public.

Companies enhance their community stature by doing things like underwriting charity fundraisers and youth sports teams to volunteering to fix up or repair someone's home. Within their own institutions, companies enhance their reputations with their attentiveness to customer satisfaction.

This is a major reason that many business enterprises have customer service departments. Managers in real estate companies devote a considerable amount of time to these kinds of issues. While the company can't give away the store, so to speak, the little extra effort, or money if that's what it takes, returns invaluable goodwill.

A final comment about company image brings us back to a few other pitfalls (in addition to the earlier-mentioned legal issues) that management needs to be aware of.

- If you're going to promote yourself as an expert, remember that consumers have grown weary and wary of the hollow representations that are occasionally made in this business. Claims need to be substantiated.

- Targeting a message to the wrong audience is not only a waste of time and money but also can damage reputations. Have you ever received a mailing and wondered why? Perhaps it was addressed to a party who has long since moved from your address, or its subject matter was totally irrelevant to you. Whether it's this activity or others, carelessness raises questions about attentiveness to details.

- Do you claim to be "Number One"? Number one in what? We're all number one in something, but unless you're specific, this claim can be misleading. Do you mean sales volume, market position, or number of offices? Can you substantiate this claim? (State license law may speak to these issues as well.) A point to ponder—what are the actual *benefits* to a consumer for doing business with "Number One"?

- Use care when making comparisons between you and the competition. False or misleading statements about competitors are unethical. Knocking the competition looks desperate or unprofessional, neither of which will enhance reputations.

- Be *truthful* and *realistic* in your claims. Stating that you provide a "free service" when the service is contingent on some business benefit to you (like a listing or a commission) is not only unethical but also a flagrant misrepresentation. Offers of premiums, prizes, or merchandise discounts may be regulated by your state's licensing laws.

- Do you have an affiliation with a professional organization or trade group? The industry tirelessly promotes its organizations and professional designations and also vigilantly monitors unauthorized use of its trademarks, trade names or insignia, and designations. Unauthorized use may also violate state license law.

- Promote the company's equal opportunity service, regardless of a consumer's race, color, religion, sex, familial status, handicap, or national origin. Display the equal opportunity slogan and logo in all printed material and publications. When using pictorial or graphic representations of people in a community, neighborhood, or housing development, be sure that the human models represent a cross section of the population.

- Selective use of media (print or electronic) could lead someone to conclude that your services are available only to certain populations. Publications whose audience profile is a population protected by the fair housing laws can be used only as long as publications that have general circulation are also used.

- Can you select publications that target specific audiences by, for example, nationality, language, or religion? Yes, provided you also advertise in a publication with general circulation. For example, if you are fluent in another language, you may want to use this skill to assist individuals who speak that language. You are permitted to advertise in a foreign language or nationality publication as long as you also advertise in a publication that reaches the general population.

■ CONCLUSION

Marketing is a total program. Any broker who's weathered a newspaper strike knows the frustration when a major contact with the public is temporarily out of circulation. More than anything, this says that showing its face and making its statements in many venues and taking advantage of all the exciting opportunities offered by technology serves the company well. Perhaps the most powerful marketing tool a company has, however, is the people who work for it, from the salespeople to the receptionist and the person who removes the "Sold" signs from the properties. They are the ones who provide the services and really contribute to the image of a company.

■ DISCUSSION EXERCISES

What marketing strategies have been most effective in promoting your firm in your area? What did you try that didn't prove to be very effective? How have emerging technologies affected your strategies?

What marketing strategies have you found to be most effective in promoting your listings? What ways have you found to control the cost of advertising listings?

What, if any, legal problems have you observed in the way companies and listings have been promoted in your area?

IN CONCLUSION
OF UNIT THREE

The purpose of organizing is to properly equip a company so that it can conduct business efficiently and effectively. Every part of a company's structure—from its ownership and affiliations and physical facilities to its business policies, alignment of its financial resources, and marketing plan—contributes to that operation. With all of that in place, the company has the systems that enable the people who provide the company's service to do their jobs.

■ THE SCENARIO

Having read this unit, what is your analysis of the following scenario?

The managers of the sales offices were each given a budget for their respective offices. The revenue from the salespeople's activities must cover the office's expenses for overhead (rent, telephone and communications, computers, and other equipment), advertising, salaries for clerical staff, and compensation for the manager as well as the salespeople and legal advisers. In addition, each office shares in the cost of the company's central administration. These include the company's accounting, marketing, relocation, and training departments. Essentially, each sales office is expected to operate as its own profit center while also supporting the company's overhead.

Taking the assignment to heart, Sally decides that if she is responsible for her office's meeting all of these expenses and must also turn a profit, she must make some changes. The first thing she does is go shopping. The antiquated copy machine is replaced with a lease on a new, more cost-efficient and effective model. The outdated telephone system is replaced with one that is equipped with voicemail to minimize the time the secretary devotes to answering the phone and provide remote message access for the salespeople.

Next, Sally decides to institute a new advertising policy. Each salesperson is entitled to five listing ads per month at office expense. Additional ads must be paid for by the salesperson, though Sally has the right to review their content.

Finally, Sally looks at transaction revenue. She decides to set up a schedule of fees for services. Because the company provides both buyer-agency and services for selling properties, she identifies selected tasks that the salespeople perform for sellers and buyers. She then implements a fee-for-service menu of options that the salespeople can offer. Sally's notion is that charging for individual services rather than depending solely on full-service commissions would enhance revenue.

Sally feels very proud of herself because after the first quarter of the year, office revenue was ahead of projections and expenses were under budget. Her contentment, however, is short-lived.

When the office managers gathered with the broker and the heads of the administrative departments for a first-quarter review, Sally was asked to discuss what she had done to produce her results. It was then that she learned she had grossly overstepped her bounds. Office equipment must be requisitioned through headquarters because the company had a master contract with a vendor to provide all copier machines and supplies. The company also wanted the entire organization to be using the same phone system. Sally's fee-for-service menu was attacked because the company did not have any such policy to offer services under this pricing structure. About the only thing Sally did "right" was to exercise her authority over her office's advertising policy.

In a decentralized organization, one would think that the managers have total authority to run their departments or offices as they see fit, as long as they produce the results needed for the good of the whole. Apparently, that's what Sally thought, too. So, what pieces are missing here?

■ THE ANALYSIS

The discussions in this third unit should shed some light on Sally's situation in the scenario.

Obviously, the things Sally did produced positive results, at least in terms of efficiency and financial benefit for her office. Senior management could learn from this that the company could make some changes and the organization as a whole would very likely benefit, though the companywide financial impact would have to be looked at more closely. In any event, Sally's office essentially became a pilot program, even though senior management hadn't planned on test-driving new procedures, especially testing marketplace reaction to a different fee structure.

The way Sally exercised authority, however, gets to the heart of organizational systems. Clear lines of authority are established to create order. Obviously, there was disorder, though the fault is not known. If senior management had not clearly communicated to subordinate managers the scope of their authority, then senior management is at fault and should take steps to correct that. If the subordinate manager (Sally) took it upon herself to fix things she thought senior management was negligent in addressing, then she's at fault. Better she should have gone to the seniors with her observations.

Even in decentralized organizations there are unified systems that intend to create efficiencies for all the business units. Centralized or bulk purchasing usually achieves cost efficiencies. The notion that every office has to endure the headaches of a lousy copy machine or an antiquated phone system simply because all of them do suggests that the system is managing the company instead of the company managing the system.

Because the business units function as individual profit centers, the company could direct unit managers to plan equipment upgrades in their budgeting processes. Senior management must also then be prepared to tolerate slimmer or neutral net profit from the units.

Depending on whether you are the broker/owner, a senior manager in a large organization, a sales manager, or a department manager, your involvement in the various decisions and tasks involved in the organizing function of management will probably be different. As a guide for understanding where you participate in the process, the following summary is provided.

- Structuring the ownership, business affiliations, and human resources:

  - The broker/owner must decide the most suitable legal structure for the ownership and, perhaps with the assistance of senior management, decide the business affiliations for the company, chart the organization, and make preliminary decisions about the manpower requirements.

  - Other levels of management need to be familiar with the decisions that the broker/owner and senior management make and understand specifically where their authority or chain of command fits within the entire organization.

- Structuring the business systems, which include the company's physical facilities and communications and information systems:

  - The ultimate responsibility for deciding the location of offices and the design of the company's communications and information systems rests with the owners and perhaps senior management.

  - Lower levels of management may be invited to provide input into these decisions.

  - Depending on the scope of authority, a sales or department manager may be authorized to purchase office equipment and furnishings and design the physical layout of the office.

- Structuring the finances of the organization:

  - The development of the general operating budget, including the compensation programs, is the responsibility of the broker/owner and senior management. They may, however, solicit input from other managers.

  - Lower levels of management are normally responsible for the budgets for their departments or offices.

■ Developing policies and procedures for the company:

— The broker/owner decides the general business philosophy and ethics for the organization.

— All levels of management are typically involved in developing the policies and procedures to define the rules people are expected to follow in the general conduct of business.

■ Marketing and advertising programs:

— The chain of command in the organization determines the management level at which the major decisions about the company's general marketing plan are made and the level that is responsible for individual marketing strategies.

STAFFING AND DIRECTING

An organization's business plan and systems and facilities structures are hollow halls without people. The business management functions explored so far are designed primarily for the benefit of the organization's people. Planning gives them direction, guiding management's decisions and telling people what they need to be doing. Organizing gives order to the institution and assembles the necessary provisions so people can work effectively and efficiently.

Now comes the heart of the organization, the people who actually do the company's work. Managing the company's human resources is part of the job for any manager who supervises people. This is the staffing and directing function of management. *In a real estate company, human resource management is a primary job, especially for managers of sales offices.*

Human resource management involves

- recruiting, selecting, and hiring the appropriate personnel;

- creating a workplace environment that fosters professional competency; and

- coaching performance and resolving issues that threaten the ability of the company to accomplish its goals.

A multitude of issues and related tasks fall under these headings, ranging from processes that help management make legal hiring decisions and administer compensation (and perhaps benefit) programs to minimizing turnover, retaining valued personnel, and making prudent termination decisions.

Depending on the organization's departmental structure and hierarchy, a company's human resource policies and procedures may be directed by a human resource (HR) department or by senior management. But the person who is directly responsible for administering those policies and who has the greatest effect on the daily life of a company's worker is the immediate manager or supervisor. This is where that person's interpersonal skills (think back to Unit One) will make or break the worker's relationship with the company.

The chapters in this unit are devoted to the activities that are necessary to assemble, develop, and retain staff and create an environment in which they can be productive for the organization.

CHAPTER THIRTEEN

THE PRACTICAL AND LEGAL REALITIES OF STAFFING

Whom do you need to hire?

What qualifications do they need? And what do they get paid?

While building a sales force is management's primary staffing activity in a real estate company, the organization also has other personnel positions to fill. Today's real estate companies are generally supported by a number of administrative, secretarial, and clerical personnel. As organizations grow and become more diverse, they require more people with more specialized or diverse skills. And they need more managers as well.

Each of the management functions that has been discussed sets the foundation for the next one, and then the next, and so on. The company's personnel marching orders, or staffing requirements, come from the organizational process of looking at the work that needs to be done and the job positions that are needed to do it (Chapter 8). Now, all of this must be converted to specific talent.

The practical matter of staffing is that a company needs the best people it can hire who have the credentials needed to do the jobs and a plan to compensate people in ways that fairly convert their value to the company into pay. A company has just so much money to go around, so the company has to get the best talent it can afford. The legal reality of staffing is that a company must do this in ways that treat people fairly and equally in their respective job classifications.

■ PERSONNEL POSITIONS

Employment positions are typically characterized as full-time, exempt or nonexempt (a distinction that will be unraveled shortly), or contingent positions. These are temporary, part-time, or leased (on loan) workers and independent contractors (ICs), who are consultants and special-service contract workers.

The scope and permanence of the work influence decisions about whether the positions are filled by full-time employees or contingent workers. A real estate company whose salespeople are independent contractors and the staple of that company's workforce would not consider them contingent, though.

Clerical and Administrative Support Positions

These include receptionists, secretaries, transaction coordinators, data entry and computer-support personnel, bookkeepers, and others who are trained specifically to handle paper and process, the behind-the-scenes support a company needs to operate. Typically, these are full-time and part-time or temporary employees.

Let's begin with the receptionist. This is the person who makes the first impression for the company. Some companies put the floor-duty salesperson in this seat, but that person's primary job is to sell, not to entertain visitors, direct them to the person with whom they have an appointment, or go searching for documents they stopped by to pick up. Granted, there are philosophical issues involved in these task assignments, but a person who is trained to handle receptionist and other clerical duties is a far more suitable full-time host or hostess.

Secretaries and other clerical personnel provide essential services, but the company must be clear about whether their primary responsibility is to expedite paper and processes for the company or for the salespeople. If the salespeople think a secretary works at their beck and call to type contracts and letters or do mailings and the company expects a secretary to be handling company correspondence and other business, somebody's work isn't getting the priority it should. And the secretary is put in an untenable position.

Transaction coordinators are clerical personnel (hired by the company or a separate transaction-coordinating company) that are responsible for orchestrating the flow of paper between the time a sales contract is signed and escrow or title closes. Companies hire these workers to take the burden of tracking transactions off the salespeople and to provide the company with some quality assurance that transactions will proceed smoothly to settlement. These clerical personnel are the company's hires, not the salespeople's.

Data entry and computer support personnel are responsible for the high-tech data management functions in today's companies, although a company may outsource some of its computer support to a consultant. Bookkeepers support the company's financial management systems, though they may also be responsible for other clerical functions as well.

Personal Assistants

Personal assistants play an increasingly important role in today's real estate business, handling non-sales-related tasks for the salespeople. Management has to make some basic employment or staffing decisions about the part assistants will play in the company.

- Does the assistant work for the salesperson or the company?

- What are the specific tasks an assistant will perform?

- Must the assistant be licensed to perform these tasks?

- Is the assistant an employee or an independent contractor?

- Who pays the assistant, and who is responsible for withholding income tax and Social Security and paying statutory benefits such as workers' compensation and unemployment compensation for an employee?

- Who is responsible if the assistant violates the law?

- Who is liable if the assistant is injured at the company's workplace or while performing duties off-site?

The answers to these questions not only guide company policy with respect to the use of personal assistants but also direct the company's staffing needs. Obviously, there are a number of legal issues to consider, not the least of which is state license law. Even if the personal assistant is hired by a salesperson, the company can have some legal exposure for the assistant's conduct. The company needs to determine how a salesperson's employee is permitted to use office space, supplies, and equipment as well as the permissible tasks and code of conduct that is expected of an assistant.

Managerial Positions

Depending on the internal structure of the organization, there may be designated work groups that are responsible for activities such as training, marketing and advertising, recruiting, and accounting. These departments can be staffed as they would be in any corporation, though a familiarity with real estate may be helpful in some cases. These positions are typically full-time employees. Sales office managers are also part of the management team, typically as employees as opposed to contract workers.

Sales Force

The centerpiece of a real estate company's staff is its sales force. Assembling a sales force that is effective and cost-efficient involves several basic employment decisions:

- How many salespeople does the company need?

- Are they full-time or part-time personnel?

- Are the salespeople experienced or newly licensed?

- Are they employees or independent contractors?

The Size of a Sales Force. Some companies accumulate licensees while others employ a small, highly skilled staff. The former group sees the size of the market share they can control being related to the number of salespeople they hire. Consequently, they plan for large sales staffs, expecting that they will control a larger share of the market. The latter group sees a smaller sales staff as being more professional, more cost-efficient, and more easily supervised. If that's a staff of top producers, they will control a sizable share of the market anyway.

The fact is that any given market can sustain only a finite number of salespeople competing for a finite amount of business. This factor must be considered when working through any internal financial analysis to determine the appropriate size sales staff.

From an internal perspective, the size of the sales force is a function of cost and revenue and determining the break-even point. Basically, what does a salesperson cost the company (both in direct costs like compensation and in indirect costs of managerial time, training, telephone, advertising, and the like) in relation to the revenue he or she generates? Without a handle on these numbers, management cannot determine the profit benefit of the current sales staff, let alone a new hire. Remember that a new hire is more likely to function at the break-even (or deficit) position before becoming a profit benefit.

Sometimes, companies use *desk cost*, which is simply a rule-of-thumb calculation that divides expenses by the number of salespeople. For example, if expenses are $20,000 and there are two salespeople, the desk cost for each is $10,000 annually. If there are four salespeople, the desk cost is $5,000 for each one. On a 50–50 split, for example, each of the four salespeople does not begin to earn a profit until each has brought in a total of $10,000 gross commissions. This, too, is a break-even calculation, so there's no profit figured into the equation.

A major caveat to using the desk cost calculation is that it doesn't accurately portray break-even in today's real estate company. Typically, commission splits vary from salesperson to salesperson, and often the salesperson's share is significantly higher than the company's. Considering these variables, desk cost doesn't reflect the true cost of sales staff, and is therefore a less valid indicator of the number of salespeople needed.

Many more companies are learning to work more profitably with more streamlined sales staffs, primarily because of these financial revelations. The ability of management to supervise the sales staff (one that expands beyond 30 people is more difficult) and the size of the available pool of talent the company desires (and can reasonably expect to attract) also factor into the staffing decisions.

The Full-Time versus Part-Time Decision.   An employee can be designated as full-time or part-time within the context of the number of hours worked per week. There is no such distinction for an independent contractor (IC). Because ICs are service-for-hire workers, their employment is a function of the services they render. The IC determines how much time is needed to perform the services he or she has contracted to provide.

That said, many real estate companies refer to their IC salespeople as being full-time or part-time. This is not an employment issue but a production issue. A company can establish its own definitions, perhaps that a full-time salesperson is one who has no other employment or outside commitments and a part-time salesperson is one who does. But these definitions don't accommodate the salespeople who are good producers but have other careers, or the ones who fall within the full-time definition, but produce little. Better (and safer from an IC contract point of view) to categorize employment by production.

Regardless of whether a salesperson is an employee or an IC, production can be achieved by a full- and/or a part-time sales force. Sometimes full-time/part-time decisions are strictly philosophical, arising from notions that full-time people are more professional, more knowledgeable, or more committed and that part-time people are less so. Although these perceptions may be justified in some cases, they are not universal. Furthermore, some companies view part-time people as a unique asset because of their network of contacts in business and the community, though supervising part-time staff can be a balancing act so that they don't feel like second-class citizens.

The practical part of the matter is that salespeople may need their current jobs to survive financially, support their real estate careers and provide for their families, and preserve hospitalization or other benefits for a period of time. Although some managers feel that the best way to start a career is to jump in with both feet, this is unrealistic in many situations and could discourage an otherwise suitable hire.

Experienced versus Newly Licensed Sales Force.   Both have their advantages and disadvantages. The obvious benefit of experienced sales-people is they have a customer base and the skills to make a productive contribution immediately. But experienced salespeople can be expensive to recruit. The top producers command top dollar and top amenities in the workplace. While it's tempting to try buying talent with generous compensation, that strategy could backfire if these people are treated more favorably than current, equally desirable salespeople. Resentment could result in the departure of others on the sales staff.

New licensees require considerable indoctrination, training, and supervi-sion to get them started, which is a significant investment of time and money, and most don't begin producing for several months. All the while, they create expenses, with little or no revenue in return. Although their production will increase eventually (if they turn out to be successful), it usually takes several years for them to become established and about five years to be earning themselves a really good living. Figures 13.1 and 13.2 provide some interesting insight into gross earnings, relative to length of time in the business.

There are advantages, however, to building a sales staff with newly licensed people. The major one is they've not acquired any habits in the real estate business, so they don't have any bad habits to break. It's relatively easy to train a newly licensed salesperson in the company's way of doing business, which is sometimes a difficult retraining process for experienced people. As long as the company retains the newly licensed people, they can become

FIGURE 13.1

Median Gross Personal Income by Number of Years in the Real Estate Industry, 2000

Years in Real Estate Industry	All REALTORS®	Brokers/ Broker Associates	Sales Agents
1–5	$20,300	$38,800	$18,800
6–10	49,100	60,800	44,900
11–15	61,000	74,300	51,500
16–25	68,900	82,300	50,500
26 and over	65,900	78,500	37,200

Source: National Association of REALTORS®

FIGURE 13.2

Number of Years in Real Estate Business: Sales Agents, 1978–2001

Years in Real Estate	1978	1981	1984	1987	1993	1996	1999	2001
1	17%	15%	15%	19%	11%	13%	10%	11%
2	23	20	13	16	10	11	9	8
3	13	18	8	12	10	7	7	8
4	9	13	8	7	9	9	6	6
5	9	8	9	6	9	5	6	5
6–10	19	19	30	25	29	28	21	19
11–15	5	4	9	9	13	12	18	17
16–25	5	3	6	6	9	13	18	18
26–39	1	1	2	1	2	1	5	6
40 and over	1	*	*	*	*	1	*	1
Median Years	3 yrs.	3 yrs.	5 yrs.	4 yrs.	6 yrs.	7 yrs.	9 yrs.	8 yrs.

Note: Detail may not add due to rounding.

*Less than one percent

Source: National Association of REALTORS®

solid producers and a solid revenue base while the company nurtures more newly licensed salespeople.

Real estate companies are often just trading talent among themselves. And sometimes they are trading personnel problems as well. Not every salesperson is suitable for your company. The one who blames the company (rather than himself or herself) for lack of success is not likely to do any better in another company. On the other hand, a company may be giving talent an opportunity to flourish in ways that were not otherwise possible. Different work environments, management styles, and business philosophies suit different people. Some people are simply disruptive influences anywhere they work, though.

Regardless of how attractive and competitive the company's services are, the company is not likely to attract top producers who are content where they are currently working. On the other hand, they know their worth and if they feel they are being used to support the company and receive little reward or recognition in return, they will go elsewhere to work (and they will leave you if that happens in your company).

Employee versus Independent Contractor.   The employee-salesperson model, the one most commonly used in the corporate world, looks like this: A company evaluates business potential in target markets and sales territories and assigns the salespeople the responsibility for covering selected territories based on workload or call-rate capacity. Generally, the salespeople are required to make certain quotas, by contacts and closings. Compensation is salary, commission, bonus, or a combination thereof, complete with required withholding and statutory workers' comp and unemployment benefits. Often, employees also receive fringe benefits and are reimbursed some or all of their travel, entertainment, communications, and other out-of-office business expense.

The IC model, on the other hand, says that the salesperson earns commission according to rates stated in the contract and is responsible for all of his or her business expenses, which often include sharing some of the company's expenses. ICs have free rein to work wherever and however they choose (within the requirements of license law), though typically the contract provides for some mutually agreed-on amount of production.

From a company's point of view, the employee model has a number of advantages, despite the cost (like statutory benefits and administration of tax withholding). In a word, control. There is no freewheeling marketing and selling (as with an IC), but there is a shorter leash with which to manage and supervise specific tasks and hold people accountable. The payback to the company is presumably better production and better quality service.

The IC model is the tradition in the real estate industry, originally because of the cost benefit to the company and the notion that the sales staff would work harder as independent business people. The IC incurred a considerable amount of expense and the company reaped the majority of the income benefit, without any obligations for tax withholding or statutory benefits. This was another cost saving to the company, and the IC got the income tax deduction for expenses. This has been viewed as a less expensive way for a company to field a sales staff.

As a real estate company's cost of doing business increases, the advantages and disadvantages of the two models become less significant. More companies are choosing to go the employee route, buying into the added employee costs to gain greater control over the sales activities. Generally, these companies have smaller sales forces and are more selective about the caliber of the salespeople they hire. Often, those salespeople feel like they are part of a finely tuned sales organization.

A Way Out of the Full-Time/Part-Time Dilemma.   In some parts of the country, real estate companies set up separate subsidiaries called *license-in-referral organizations (LIFROs)*. These are licensed brokerage firms that hire licensed salespeople, but these people do not actually engage in any sales activities. Instead, they provide business leads (referrals) that the LIFRO then refers to the affiliated brokerage firm. LIFROs are a way to attract or retain salespeople who do not meet a company's criteria for full-time salespeople but who can contribute by referring business.

LIFROs normally exist where the licensing laws prohibit the payment of a referral fee to anyone who does not have a real estate license. A referral company is a legal conduit through which licensees can receive these fees when they are collected from the conventional brokerage firm. LIFROs have also been formed to avoid membership assessments by industry organizations for people who are licensed but act only as referral agents.

Job Qualifications

Before the company jumps on the recruiting bandwagon to fill any of these personnel positions, management needs another set of marching orders: the *job description* and the *qualifications* for the position. The job description (which was developed in the previous unit) describes the role and responsibilities of the position. The qualifications describe the *knowledge, skill sets, experience,* and *personal characteristics* that are necessary to perform that job and are a business necessity for the company. *Job relatedness* and *business necessity* are the criteria for complying with equal opportunity laws.

How do you know what qualifications are necessary? Use a *job analysis*, which is a process of analyzing all of the activities the job entails and determining what a person needs to know or to be able to do. If the company hasn't prepared its own, HR resources (on the Internet) can provide sample analyses for various staff and clerical positions, and real estate industry resources have similar ones for salespeople. All of these can be refined to suit the individual company. A job analysis serves as a benchmark to match work and qualifications, a strictly job-performance-based exercise.

One of the most useful ways to convert qualifications to a hiring guide is with a *candidate profile*. This says "Here are the absolute essential or minimum qualifications (knowledge, skill sets, and so forth) to perform the job, and here are the ones that would be helpful or nice to have." The more thought given to whom the company needs to hire, the more efficiently management can screen candidates. Generally, the first cut is based on the minimum qualifications, so think about the kind of candidate that may be eliminated (or slip through) at that point.

■ COMPENSATION MANAGEMENT

Pay is a significant factor in a company's ability to recruit, motivate, and retain personnel. Today's real estate company has more hourly wage and salaried workers, not just straight commission people, and more variations in personnel positions (managerial, administrative, clerical, as well as sales), all of which require that management think about pay in a new light. People's perception that the company's pay is inappropriate can seriously compromise a company's staffing efforts.

Compensation planning and administration is a function of the company's philosophy about paying people, the position of the jobs in the organization, and the accompanying qualifications and expertise or experience level of the people in those jobs. People need to feel they are being fairly compensated for their efforts and must also be able to earn a decent living. The company needs affordable compensation programs so it can stay in business. These are not necessarily opposing desires, but they are certainly ones that require some careful planning to satisfy.

Compensation plans reflect a company's philosophy about pay. The *entitlement* philosophy says that pay should increase with seniority or length of service to the company, without regard to changes in the industry or economy. The *performance* philosophy says that pay is solely a function of a person's outcomes or performance, with the result that pay can go up and down, perhaps dramatically. Both philosophies are impractical in their purest forms. A company can't endure the inflexible financial commitment of entitlement or administer a pure performance-based system accurately and fairly. In the real world, pay plans are variations on the themes of these philosophies.

The point of compensation is to *reward people for their value to the company.* The purpose of a compensation plan is to convert that value to pay. How much are people worth? Many of them are worth far more than the company can afford to pay, but as long as people feel they are being fairly rewarded and have a rich environment in which to work, the company has made a satisfactory statement. Most companies use a traditional compensation model to convert value to pay. The process involves

1. analyzing the importance of job positions in the company, the level of responsibility, and the sophistication of expertise (knowledge, skills, and abilities) required, all of which are revealed in job descriptions and job qualifications.

2. analyzing the pay structures of other similar organizations for similar jobs, as revealed from compensation surveys.

3. developing a pay structure for the organization, using job evaluation and survey data to classify jobs and pay grades (or ranges of pay) within the organization.

4. developing pay structures for individual positions, including a process to use performance appraisals to evaluate individuals.

5. institutionalizing the company's compensation program with communication, implementation, and monitoring.

The goal of this process is to align pay with the work people do, align the company's pay with the marketplace, and develop an affordable pay structure that the company can administer fairly.

Pay Plans

Pay comes in various forms. *Wages,* which are hourly rates of pay; *salaries,* which are characterized as annual rates of compensation; and *variable pay plans,* which are singular or combinations of base salary, commission, bonuses, or other benefit incentives. Remember that a real estate company has a number of personnel positions (not just the sales force) for which it needs a pay plan.

As much discretion as a company has to devise its own policies and pay plans, that does not necessarily mean that the company has free rein. Pay practices need to be grounded in a firm legal foundation, particularly to ensure that equal work gets equal pay in compliance with employment laws.

State labor and wage-and-hour laws may apply, and perhaps the Federal Labor Standards Act (FLSA). Pay attention to provisions regarding the employment of minors, minimum wage laws, and rules for overtime pay. Generally, full-time hourly workers are considered to be working a 40-hour week. Additional hours are considered overtime and must be compensated at one-and-a-half times the hourly rate for each hour of overtime.

Under the FLSA (a state law may be similar), salaried workers may or may not fall within minimum wage and overtime requirements. This is where the exempt and nonexempt distinction applies. The laws are very complex and should be investigated thoroughly, but generally salaried executives, managers, and administrative and outside sales personnel are *exempt*. In other words, work is performed for the stated salary regardless of the number of hours or workdays devoted to the job. *Nonexempt* salaried workers, like clerical personnel and laborers, are not exempt from overtime and must be compensated accordingly.

Variable pay plans link compensation with performance in some fashion. These plans are suitable for salespeople and executives, managers, or other professionals where individual performance or production, or contribution to organizational accomplishments can be measured. For employees (as opposed to ICs) there is a base pay, but the incentive in these pay plans is the reward for past performance or accomplishments, with the expectation that greater accomplishments will be forthcoming in the future.

The theory behind variable pay is that people are motivated by money, which means that bonuses, overrides, and higher commission splits are suitable incentives. But these also provide recognition, and when pay is tied to organizational accomplishments, people feel that they are stakeholders in the company, which fosters commitment. Companies can also demonstrate worth with benefits like expense accounts, profit-sharing or stock-purchasing programs, and pension plans.

Pay is a package comprising wage, salary, or variable pay and incentives plus other benefits a company may be required to provide (unemployment compensation and workers' compensation) or discretionary fringes like health care or life insurance, profit-sharing, and retirement plans. Some workers consider required withholding for income taxes and Social Security from employee wages to be a benefit.

Equity

Equity is the perceived fairness of what a person gets paid in relation to what a person does. People measure fairness in comparison with what others in the organization do and get paid (*internal equity*) and what people in other companies do and get paid (*external equity*). All of this is a function of perception, as well as fact.

Consequently, equity arises from how well the company aligns pay with work, aligns pay with the competition, and broadcasts to its workers exactly what the company's pay policies and structures are, all of which are part of the company's compensation management process.

In theory, a company can pay people whatever it wants to or can afford. However, people (especially salespeople) go shopping, looking for the best deal, and if a company can't provide that deal, in terms of money and work environment, then the company is not in a strong position to recruit or retain personnel. Industry surveys (the most current are available on the Internet), particularly those that are broken down by region and firm size, provide a starting point for evaluating market pay. Clerical, administrative, and managerial pay can be evaluated similarly.

A company can fix its pay levels to fall at the bottom, middle, or highest range in comparison with other companies.

- The bottom range says that 75 percent of the companies pay more. A company may choose this strategy when it is short of funds or the labor market is flush, but the likelihood is that the company will experience greater turnover.

- The highest range says that the company is near the top 25 percent compared with other companies. This is an aggressive strategy that is very attractive for recruiting and retaining top personnel and increasing productivity. But the company must be very selective in its hiring and vigilant about monitoring personnel performance so as to gain maximum financial benefit.

■ The middle range pegs the company in the mid-market, with 50 percent of the companies paying more and 50 percent paying less. This is a moderate strategy that has neither enormous competitive advantage nor disadvantage, but it keeps the company in the running and is the strategy many companies use, particularly because it is more affordable than the highest sector.

From an internal perspective, equity means that all people who work in the *same class of jobs* are compensated at the same pay scale. While the golden goose (the sales force) is valuable, other positions are also valuable, and pay must be commensurately aligned with the level of responsibility in the organization. Managerial positions are especially vulnerable to the equity comparison in this respect.

Secrecy is a major enemy to equity. Companies can go a long way to fostering an atmosphere of fairness by publishing pay policies and wage, salary, and commission scales (not what each person makes). People need to see where their pay falls within the big scheme of things and exactly how pay, and performance and promotions through pay, are evaluated. People may not necessarily like what they see, but they are far more content when they see a fair, rational method for compensation.

Justice

Like any other organizational policies and procedures, compensation policies must be faithfully, consistently, and even-handedly administered. Justice arises from the perception (again) that people are being treated fairly, that the rules management has laid out are being equally applied to each person in the same class of jobs.

One of the reasons pay is categorized in ranges is so people in the same job classification can be compensated according to performance, experience, or seniority (if that's a company policy). This means that individuals' pay can be different, depending on performance, expertise, or seniority, but pay must fall within the set range for that job classification.

Periodically, pay is adjusted, commonly on an annual basis, though a new hire's pay may be reviewed after an initial three- or six-month period. Management needs specific, stated procedures (that it faithfully follows) for reviewing personnel and increasing, decreasing, or sustaining pay. Performance reviews are the typically stated platform for assessing personnel. Company procedures need to state how performance will be evaluated so people know what is expected of them ahead of time.

Any time management favors some personnel over others with similar experience or production (or bends the rules for recruiting purposes), management is suspect. While the favored party may be happy, the rest of the company's workforce can feel that they too may be victimized by (or can manipulate) management. So much for justice. Furthermore, the company is ripe for accusations that equal employment laws have been violated.

Sales Compensation

Sales forces are typically compensated in the following ways:

- Straight salary, though that is usually done only for a short-term base period.

- Straight commission, which is a sell-to-earn plan.

- Salespeople can be employees or ICs. The vulnerability of a sell-to-earn plan is that it does not provide great financial security for the salesperson, hence a draw (advance against future commission) may be part of the pay plan. However, a draw may end up being an unplanned salary (a problem for an IC) if the salesperson does not earn sufficient commission to cover the draw.

- Salary and bonuses, which include base salary plus a range of bonuses or other performance incentives, including expense accounts, profit sharing, and the like (for employees). The larger the difference between the base and the bonus, the more incentive-dependent the pay.

The rationale behind the real estate industry's traditional IC, straight-commission model is the expectation that salespeople will be motivated to work harder and make more money. That harder work is often rewarded with a graduated commission split, with a larger share of the gross being the salesperson's pay. This is a worthy incentive only as long as the company doesn't play numbers games by deducting a variety of company expenses from the salesperson's share. A split may be attractive on the surface, but in reality the salesperson earns less. Baiting salespeople with such programs can result in their switching to the competition.

This IC, straight-commission model is clearly performance-based, but it also assumes that money is an enduring motivator, which is not necessarily the case once the salesperson pays his or her child's tuition for the term or has earned enough to vacation or visit the grandchildren. Often, workplace conditions and benefits like health care insurance, retirement, or profit-sharing plans mean more. Unless the salespeople are employees, fringe benefits must be structured meticulously to preserve the IC status.

Another challenge to the straight-commission plan is that today's real estate industry is no longer a straight-commission business. With more and more companies adopting alternate pricing models, company revenue is an increasingly complex mix of fees collected for a variety of services. The bookkeeping alone is a burdensome task using the traditional split methodology.

From a performance-based perspective, the question arises whether all fees earned for services are equally valuable to the company. Differentiating between those the company values more and applying a different split to them only adds to the calculation nightmares. Because the salesperson's job is to provide service, the salesperson is better compensated for the effort of delivering those services plus a bonus (rather than a split) on fees generated in excess of a base amount. This is a great argument in favor of paying a base salary to an employee-salesperson plus a bonus.

Managerial Compensation

Structuring appropriate compensation for supervisory and managerial personnel, senior management, and even executives is more challenging. By the definition of their responsibilities, their activities contribute indirectly to the productivity of the organization. This is not to say that their roles are less important than the people who directly generate revenue (the sales force), but it's more difficult to quantify the relationship between managerial effectiveness and company performance.

The way companies settle this quandary is by holding management *accountable* for certain performance objectives, standards, or outcomes within the company and then compensating according to the results. Pay is linked to the scope of responsibility and the position in the organization's hierarchy. The higher the position, the greater the significance of the scope of responsibility, the greater the accountability and therefore the higher pay. This is still a value to the organization conversion, based on the premise that ultimately all that happens can be directly credited to or blamed on leadership.

In effect, companies pay managerial personnel for exercising their judgment as they make decisions and administer the functions for which they are accountable. Experience (gained within and/or outside the organization) and sometimes seniority factor into pay, especially for senior management. Proven track records (presumably good judgment) engender respect, which is why corporations will pay dearly for that talent. The expectation is that good managers' value to the company is worth the pay.

A flaw in an accountability-based compensation plan for managers in lower levels of the organization is that they have less or little control over all the variables that affect the performance outcomes of the office or department they supervise. If they do not have the authority to select or hire the personnel they supervise, that only exacerbates the situation.

A sales office manager depends on the skills and abilities of others and, therefore, has no direct control over revenue, but yet is accountable for the office's achieving revenue objectives. If that manager's sales staff is less skilled or effective than other sales managers', the manager has more potential performance deficits to supervise. Often, greater effort is required to supervise the less-skillful or less-experienced sales force. If the manager's pay is based solely on office performance without consideration for these variables, then pay is not fair or equitable compared with other managers doing similar jobs.

Real estate sales managers look at equity and justice in pay the same way any other worker does. This says that a company's pay policies for sales managers must be devised following the process described earlier. These are best designed as employee (as opposed to IC) positions because of the level of control and accountability that accompanies these supervisory roles.

Sales manager pay can be structured as straight salary or as variable pay, a base salary plus an override, based either on the percentage of gross commission (before salespeople's shares are deducted) or on net profit of the office. The latter is an incentive for the manager who has authority for financial decisions to manage expenses. The net profit calculation, though, is affected by the commission splits of the individual salespeople, so an office of top producers with top splits leaves less for the company, and the net profit doesn't look as good as the gross volume would. To fairly compensate the manager, override percentages need to be structured with this in mind.

The debate over full-time managers and selling managers arises again when it comes to devising pay plans. There may be some financial realities (especially for a start-up or cash-strapped company) that require a manager to also sell. However, this should not take the place of fair compensation for the supervisory job the company expects the manager to do.

■ LEGALITIES OF EMPLOYMENT

In addition to laws referenced earlier, a number of other laws affect personnel policies and procedures and the workplace environment. The way companies recruit, select and hire, promote, and terminate people and the social and physical environment in which they work are all subject to an ever-expanding body of law, particularly as courts further interpret the laws.

Lest one say that the way out from under all of this is to employ ICs, the fact is that the laws don't distinguish between ICs and employees. The applicability of some laws, however, does differ, depending on the number of workers a company has and other distinctions that an attorney skilled in employment law can interpret for the company.

Equal Employment Practices

In 2002 the Equal Employment Opportunity Commission (EEOC) received the highest number of job discrimination complaints filed by workers against private employers in seven years. Complaints jumped 4 percent, with the largest increases being in allegations of discrimination because of religion, age, and national origin. Although race and gender are still the leading offenses, recent developments indicate that no class is immune from employment discrimination, especially in today's more culturally diverse workplace.

A number of employment laws are designed to protect against discrimination in the workplace. Among these are Title VII of the Civil Rights Act of 1964, the Civil Rights Act of 1991, the Age Discrimination in

Employment Act, and the Americans with Disabilities Act (ADA). In addition, there is the Equal Pay Act of 1963, the Pregnancy Discrimination Act of 1978, and the Family and Medical Leave Act of 1993. Most states and some cities or municipalities have their own employment laws as well, some of which are similar to and others more restrictive than federal law.

The best advice is not to devise any employment policy or procedure until all of the laws are investigated. The purpose of equal employment laws is to prevent the employer from basing employment decisions on factors that are unrelated to the actual performance of a job. This means that virtually every human resource management activity *must scrupulously guard against any conduct,* in purpose or effect, that treats people differently because of their race, color, religion, sex or gender, national origin, age, marital status, or disability.

Job application forms and job screening and interview procedures, selection and hiring procedures, training, advancement, pay, and termination of employment as well as recruitment, advertising, tenure, layoff, leave, fringe benefits, and responsiveness to conflicts in the workplace are all potential places for allegations of discrimination. Even when a company declares suitable equal opportunity policies and procedures, lax or inconsistent enforcement can also raise questions of discrimination.

Like complaints of discrimination in housing, allegations of employment discrimination are time-consuming to defend, even if no grounds are found, and costly if a company is found guilty. The public relations fallout in an industry that supports equal housing opportunities can also be damaging.

While information is essential for a manager to properly manage personnel, there is certain information that is *patently irrelevant* and should not in any way be explored in application forms, job interviews or counseling sessions, and personnel records. One of the virtues of the job qualifications that were discussed earlier is that they are clearly job based. Use those as a guide to avoid wandering into territory that could violate the law. Avoid all inquiries that relate to the protected classes and discussions that could be construed to tread into those areas, such as

- citizenship and origin of name or maiden name;

- physical abilities, or limitations or disabilities;

- education and experience that are not a requirement for the job (arbitrary qualifications could effectively be discriminatory);

- family matters (spouse, marriage or pending prospect, and children or pregnancy can lead to gender discrimination; ages of children can reveal worker's age);

- feelings about working with people (either in the workplace or consumers) who are older/younger, or another gender, race, nationality, etc.;

- availability to work on Saturday or Sunday (can be a religious issue); and

- childhood background (place where grew up and the like; can reveal nationality, race, etc.).

Antiharassment Policies

Cultural diversity in the workplace plus growing intolerance of certain gender-related conduct creates an environment in which management must manage not only uncomfortable and offensive but also illegal behavior. In addition to the equal employment laws previously referenced, there are least 11 states and more than 100 municipalities that have laws prohibiting discrimination based on sexual orientation.

Management's zero-tolerance of inappropriate behavior is not only a requirement of the law but simply the right thing to do. First, management needs to publish an antiharassment policy that clearly defines behavior that is not tolerated and establish a nonthreatening, open-door policy so that an offended person can bring the matter to management's attention without fear of reprisal. To support the policy, management needs a declared process to resolve the issue. Generally, this consists of

- appointing a member of staff who is the point person to investigate complaints;

- developing a plan to handle the individual complaint, including identifying the key people involved and the situations that need to be explored;

- interviewing the person who lodged the complaint, complete with reassurance that the person was right in stepping forward;

- informing the accused person of the complaint, complete with reassurance that the accused's side of the story is part of the investigation;

- interviewing any witnesses and the accused; and

- deciding on an appropriate course of action, which may include adjusting working conditions to separate the parties involved.

Document all that transpires. A company is defenseless without good records in the event of future misconduct. Typically, companies adopt procedures for warnings, followed by periods of mandatory leave and then dismissal for repeat offenders.

Safety in the Workplace

The company has valuable human resources that need to be protected. People also deserve as healthful working conditions as possible. The Occupational Safety and Health Act of 1970 says so, too. The issues that the law covers are varied, including ergonomics, lighting, and equipment layout. This law also addresses exposure to hazardous substances, substance abuse, and workplace air quality, which is where smoking issues fall. Certainly, these are legal issues that management must be attentive to, but there's also the practical matter that the more pleasant the working conditions, the better people perform for the company.

■ CONCLUSION

The foundation of the staffing function is the company's personnel policies and procedures. These guide virtually every event in human resource management. The discussions relating to personnel positions, requirements for jobs, compensation management, and the legal issues that surround all of these topics provide a platform on which to further develop lawful and practical policies and procedures for recruiting, selecting, hiring, and supervising personnel.

■ DISCUSSION EXERCISES

Select a job position in your company and develop an appropriate candidate profile for that position. How does what you developed compare with what currently exists? How did you arrive at the qualifications you've selected as appropriate?

Identify the pros and cons of hiring a sales staff of employees versus independent contractors. If you hire a salesperson as an employee, how would you structure the job and compensation?

Discuss your perceptions of pay (either as a salesperson or a manager) and the strengths or weaknesses in the way compensation is administered in your company, based on what you've learned in this chapter.

14

RECRUITING, SELECTING, AND HIRING THE STAFF

How do you select the best personnel for the company?

What can you do to recruit salespeople?

Staffing an organization is an expensive proposition. A considerable amount of management's time and the company's money is required to recruit, select, and hire personnel, just to get people on board. Then, there's the investment in training, supervision, and other workplace enhancements plus pay, benefits, and possibly litigation (injury on the job, wrongful termination, and the like) that add to the cost of the company's human resources.

All of this is a necessary cost of doing business, but a company cannot afford to be unwise about its expenditures. This means it must invest smartly, picking the right people for the right jobs and *keeping them*. Departures cost mightily in exit procedures and lost production plus the cost of rehiring and retraining replacements.

Although the staffing process begins with recruiting, perhaps the better beginning is at the back end of the employment cycle, that being termi-nations. Management cannot invest wisely in new hires unless it knows why people leave (one of several purposes for exit interviews). They leave voluntarily and involuntarily for a variety of reasons, all of which man-agement bears some responsibility for, including the original hiring deci-sions. The company may need to get its house in order first, rather than open the revolving door to new hires again, who will also leave.

The object is to be the employer of choice. Competitive compensation and referrals and marketing budgets for salespeople are only part of the attraction. People want a positive work environment, with career development oppor-tunities and strong, accountable leadership in the managerial ranks. People want to be associated with a well-run company that has a respected brand name, not only with consumers but also in the company's industry.

■ EMPLOYMENT PROCESS

Each personnel position needs to be filled by a methodical process and do so within a legal framework. The previous chapter's discussions about employment laws, job performance-based qualifications, and compensation management are major centerpieces of the employment process. Whether a person is an employee or an independent contractor has no relevance when it comes to recruiting, selecting, and hiring procedures.

Regardless of the position being filled, the process entails a series of steps that are designed to help management make intelligent hiring decisions. Some of those steps are more involved when the job position involves greater responsibility, specialized skills, and the core of a service business, the sales force.

The employment process consists of *recruiting*, which gathers potential applicants; *prescreening*, which is normally an application and preliminary interview or conversation; *formal interview(s)* and a *selection* step, which is when the candidates are evaluated; and finally, the *hiring* step, when an offer of employment is extended. Each step is a filtering process, with the object being to narrow the field of contenders and identify the most suitable candidate for the position. (See Figure 14.1.)

Recruiting

The company needs to be able to recruit from a position of strength, which is why company image is so important. Recruiting is the process of assembling *a pool of candidates or applicants* for consideration. The company's business reputation and its workplace environment play a vital role in attracting the best people to that pool, which then gives management good candidates to consider. Recruiting can begin internally or externally.

Internal resources are people who are already working for the company who may have a personal interest in the job position or know of people outside the organization who would be suitable. Remember that creating opportunities to step up in the organization is an important part of the company's professional development. A managerial position may be just the opportunity a real estate salesperson has been waiting for. Some companies have policies that job opportunities will be offered internally before going outside. If that's the case, don't violate the policy.

One external resource is the Internet. Some companies post career opportunities on their Web sites on an ongoing basis. Various other external resources are used, depending on the nature of the position (full-time or

FIGURE 14.1

Employment Process

Step	Activity	Purpose
Recruiting	Generate a pool of candidates	Gather applicants for consideration
Prescreening	Application and preliminary interview	Gather preliminary information to determine whether to pursue the next step (Decision Point 1)
Formal Interview	Formal job interview(s)	Gather sufficient information to make a decision whether to hire an applicant (Decision Point 2)
Selection	Review information gathered about an applicant	Determine whether applicant is suitable for the position (Decision Point 3)
Hire	Make job offer and establish personnel file	Ensure new hire and company are properly prepared to begin a working relationship

temporary) and the sophistication of the expertise required. An employment or temporary placement agency may be suitable. Or the company can post its job opening in trade journals or classified ads. Sometimes the most effective are the activities of management and their one-on-one contacts with others in the business community. (Tactics for recruiting salespeople will be discussed later in the chapter.)

Any job posting should include a *brief* description of the key credentials the company is looking for. Although it's not fatal if everyone who sees a job posting replies, it's desirable not to waste people's time (including management's or the HR department's) with wild-goose chases.

Prescreening

The purpose of prescreening is to gather basic information to decide whether an applicant meets the minimum requirements for the position (as outlined in the candidate profile) and would be a good fit for the company. This is a quick weed-out step, from which management can develop a short list of applicants to further evaluate.

Prescreening can be done with an application form, a short telephone or videoconference conversation, a brief face-to-face meeting, or on the company's Web site, where an applicant completes a series of questions. Any one or several of these prescreening methods can be used, in whatever way best suits the company, but the object is to be efficient.

An application gathers basic personal information such as name, telephone number, address, education and experience (that are applicable to the job position), former employers, license information (if applicable), and references. Frequently, there are also several questions that require brief written answers, an exercise useful not only for the content of the responses, but also for evaluating communication skills.

A preliminary interview or conversation is an informal exchange of information for both management and the applicant. (The applicant is narrowing the field as well.) While it's permissible to tell a *short* story about the company, the purpose of the exchange is to learn about the applicant. Although the setting is informal, casual get-acquainted chats can easily wander into forbidden territory. Stay focused on topics of conversation that are clearly job-related, and do so in ways that cannot be construed to violate employment laws.

The important point is that the company must establish a prescreening process that it faithfully follows. Failing to give the telephone inquirer whose name or speech characteristics sound "different" or "foreign" the same consideration as anyone else can be problematic. If every candidate is expected to complete an application form or converse personally with someone in the company, then that's the rule, and all applicants must have an equal opportunity to be considered before the first cut is made.

Formal Interviews

The candidates who survive the prescreening step now move to the formal interview step, the most important information-gathering part of the process. The list of candidates may be as long or short as management desires, depending on the quality of the applicants and their suitability for the position. It's possible that no candidates are suitable. Don't proceed if that's the case. Go back to the recruiting step rather than waste time with candidates who don't meet minimum qualifications.

Formal or structured interviews are face-to-face, two-way exchanges and, depending on the job position or the number of candidates, can involve several interviews to gather sufficient information and narrow the field. This is not the time to "tell and sell" the company's story, but the time to gather information to determine how the candidate might perform on the job.

A formal interview is also the forum for the candidate to learn what the job entails (from the job description). One of the most common complaints is that the job didn't turn out to be as it was represented. The company needs to present a realistic preview of the job, and must also be careful not to convey any message that could be construed to be a commitment or binding contract.

Conducting a good and legally proper employment interview requires some skill, which means learning to explore the right topics in the right ways to gain useful information. For an interview to be productive, the interviewer needs a plan.

Prepare the Interview.   After reviewing the applications and any notes taken during preliminary interviews, topics that should be explored can be planned and prepared in a script for the interview. A script is essential for keeping the interview on the track of job-related conversations, and when multiple candidates are to be interviewed, it provides a uniform basis for evaluating each one. Both of these are important points with respect to equal employment law, but they also enhance the quality of the information that can be gathered.

A script also helps the interviewer run a professional interview (which impresses candidates) and concentrate on responses instead of thinking about what to ask next. The interview generally consists of the following elements:

- **Introduction**—The icebreaker time to put the candidate at ease. An opening question could be something like, "How did you become interested in our firm?" or "What do you know about our company?" Observe appearance and the ease with which the candidate communicates.

  Then set the stage for what follows by saying, "Certainly it's in your interest as well as ours to get to know one another. First, I'd like to get information about you, then I'll be happy to answer any questions you have about the company and the job position." Then tackle the list of scripted topics that relate to the items below.

- **Work experience**—In addition to items the candidate wants to expand on that are in the application, this is a time to explore: "What have you done best? Less well? What were your major accomplishments? What were the most difficult problems you've encountered in your jobs? How did you handle them? In what ways are you most effective with people? Why have you changed jobs (if this is applicable)? What are you looking for in a career, and what are your goals and aspirations?"

  These reveal skill and competence, motivation, attitude about work and employers, interpersonal skills, initiative, and problem-solving ability.

- **Education**—In addition to any particular education the candidate wishes to highlight, explore: "What were your special accomplishments? How did you choose the course of study? How has what you learned related to your career? How do you feel about additional education, or what would you like to study next?"

These reveal the level of accomplishment, professional interests, and potential for growth and development.

■ **Job-related skills and professional assets**—The time to explain the job and for the candidate to sell himself or herself with answers to, "What do you think are your major assets or best qualities for the job? What strengths do others usually see in you? Why are you a good person for this company to hire? What are your shortcomings or areas that need improvement? What qualities do you want to develop further? What training or additional experience do you need or would you like for the job?"

These reveal not only a candidate's job skills but also professional development issues.

■ **Closing**—The conclusion of the interview, in which the interviewer summarizes the discussion and says, "I've enjoyed talking to you and you've given me a lot of valuable information to help make a decision. Before you leave, are there any questions about the job, our company, or anything else that you would like to know?"

This indicates what the interviewer has learned and because candidates are narrowing the field as well, this gives them an opportunity to ask any questions about issues that have not been explored.

Conducting Interviews.   By their very nature, employment interviews are stressful. A one-on-one interview is less stressful, though, than panel interviews, in which the candidate meets with a group of people, or serial interviews, in which the candidate is passed from one person to another, each of whom has a separate interview agenda. Simulation or audition interviews are the most stressful, putting the candidate on the spot with a skill demonstration or problem-solving exercise. The choice of interview styles typically depends on the nature of the job.

The best information is gathered in a structured interview when people feel at ease and can be candid. The use of first names (if that's acceptable company practice), comfortable seating (without the interviewer stationed behind a desk), and a private setting that is free of interruptions create an atmosphere in which conversation can flow freely.

Work through the script in a conversational way, and keep the following in mind:

- Don't talk too much (notice there's no company commercial in the script) and listen beyond the words that are spoken. Ask open-ended questions (who, what, where, how, when) to encourage the candidate to talk.

- Play down any unfavorable information. Don't disagree; otherwise the applicant will try to retreat and say what the person thinks the interviewer wants to hear.

- Don't telegraph the correct answer with a statement such as "We are looking for highly motivated people. How would you describe yourself?" There's little point in asking that question because the candidate has already been told the answer.

- Watch, listen, and take notes. The interviewer should be able to learn what is needed in about 45 minutes.

- Above all, avoid questions or topics of conversation (discussed in the previous chapter) that could violate employment laws.

Bring the interview to a close by telling the applicant what happens next. "Thank you. We'll contact you in (a time period) with our decision" will suffice. If appropriate, tell the candidate that people will be invited for second interviews. If the candidate is not likely to still be in the running, suggest that the person feel free to interview elsewhere. (Candidates rely on the company to determine whether they are suited for the job.) The formal interview is the last information-gathering step and is not intended to conclude with a job offer. However, there are times when the interviewer (provided the person has authority to extend an offer of employment) may feel that such a step is appropriate.

Selection

Don't hire quota. Hire quality. The purpose of the entire process is to select the best match for the job and the organization. Although the interviewer forms some impressions during the interviews, selection is not a rush-to-judgment exercise, but the final filtering step of the employment process.

The right person is the one whose knowledge, skills and abilities, and goals, values, and expectations fit the job. The right fit for the organization is the one who is motivated, creative, and flexible and will work well in the organization's culture. Converting all of this to an employment decision requires a quantifiable assessment according to certain established selection criteria.

Those criteria can be specific knowledge, skills and abilities related to the job analysis, and more generalized characteristics that are predictors of job performance. A company can compile profiles of the people who currently perform the jobs and draw conclusions about personal characteristics that contribute to a specific job's performance in that organization. Or the company can use industry profiles for certain jobs, such as the attributes commonly attributed to successful real estate salespeople (motivation, initiative, and the like).

The point is that criteria related to the job and the organization must be established and become the platform for evaluating each candidate. One way to evaluate is with a *rating system* in which each candidate is scored, perhaps on a scale of five to one (one being least favorable), on each criterion, based on information gathered in the formal interviews, and then those scores are tallied. The totals provide a quantitative view of each candidate that management can then use to rank hiring preferences or decide that none of the candidates is suitable.

Also, envision the candidate working for the company and the kind of training and supervision the person would need. An axiom in human resource management is that a bad selection will not be fixed with training and will make the job of supervising all the more difficult. It's far better to be very selective than to try to press-fit a new hire into a job.

Some companies use additional means of assessing candidates. These may involve knowledge- and skill-oriented tests (perhaps computer skills) or personality tests (Minnesota Multiphasic Personality Inventory and Myers-Briggs are two widely used ones). The caveat is that any assessment must be job-skill related or verified as a reliable predictor of performance so as not to be construed as an unfair or unlawful way to eliminate job applicants.

Companies usually also check business and personal references that were provided on the application form. (The ethical and professional reputation of a salesperson is something to consider.) If the application does not include the most recent employer, this is an issue to ask the candidate about. In some states a criminal-background check is required for licensure, or the company may desire to perform one (as long as it does not have a discriminatory effect).

Regardless of what the company's criteria are and the manner in which it assesses candidates, the company must *evaluate all candidates in the same manner*. The process must be defensible from an equal employment perspective or the company could have significant legal exposure. The point is to analyze information for predictors of job success and then make a well-informed job-placement decision.

Hiring

The person who hires is also the one who usually fires. The hiring person should be totally committed to the person who is finally selected, to minimize the likelihood of having to do an about-face and show that person to the door. And the new hire also should be committed to the company.

When an offer of employment is extended, make sure that the selected hire knows what the company expects (for a salesperson this includes expenses like errors and omissions insurance, MLS and franchise fees, and the like). Also, the company's compensation plan and work rules should be described *before* he or she accepts employment. If there is a three- or six-month probationary period, that should be clarified as well. Each new hire should be given (and sign a receipt for) copies of the employee handbook and the company's procedural manual.

For the most part, the actual hiring process is an administrative and paperwork exercise. A variety of forms, including W-4 forms for employees or W-9 forms for others, information for unemployment and workers' compensation (depending on state law, may also be an issue for ICs), and others that relate to fringe benefits (hospitalization and the like) must be completed. If the new hire is a salesperson, the appropriate license forms must also be completed.

In essence, the process assembles a *personnel file*, which includes a variety of other information the company attorney may recommend (and avoids information that should not be retained), along with the original employment application. Because the hiring decision has already been made, certain personal information can be gathered, though it becomes part of a *confidential* file and cannot be used in management's later decision making. Several examples include closest family members for contact in an emergency, a copy of a driver's license, and citizenship information so that the company has proof the new hire is authorized to work in the United States.

If a real estate salesperson is an independent contractor, the IC and the company must enter into an agreement that specifically proclaims that this is the nature of the relationship. Federal tax laws require that the salesperson must be a properly licensed practitioner, that the gross income must be based on production rather than on the number of hours worked, and that the work must be done pursuant to a written agreement. Because the IRS scrutinizes claims of independent contractor status, it is essential to meet at least these three requirements.

A sample form that can be used for a model in preparing an IC agreement appears at the end of this chapter. Legal counsel should review any contract to ensure that it complies with prevailing federal and any state laws. Once the contract is signed, though, the company and the IC must demonstrate by their working relationship that indeed the salesperson is an IC. Managerial actions that control the way an IC works may violate the IC agreement and result in litigation, income tax problems, or unemployment compensation claims.

■ RECRUITING SALESPEOPLE

A brokerage company is only one of several in the area all competing to recruit the top producers and newly licensed salespeople. And those people are out comparison shopping, looking at how all the companies stack up against one another. A company is recruiting, and the salespeople are selecting.

The earlier discussion about the brand name of the company as a potential employer is very apropos when the time comes to recruit salespeople. They want a workplace where they can get maximum support so they can be most productive. This doesn't mean just providing good clerical and technological support and appealing marketing and commission programs, but an environment that is energizing, rather than somber, tension filled, or contentious. The responsibility for creating that environment falls squarely on the shoulders of the managers who supervise that workplace.

Don't confuse recruiting with selection. Even though recruiting salespeople is highly competitive, a company must *qualify* the people it selects. Recruiting salespeople is like prospecting for customers, meaning that the sales manager will make many contacts before making a contract, or in this case, selecting the right person to hire—the "hire quality, not quota" mantra.

Quota figures into recruiting only to the extent that management must analyze the company's recruiting history to determine the effectiveness of various recruiting strategies and the number of contacts that were needed for the company to select the most suitable salespeople. Unless the plan is to reduce the sales force, management also needs to look at the annual rate of attrition to determine the number of people that have to be brought on board each year to maintain, let alone expand, the sales staff.

The end result of these analyses plus the factors explored in the sales force discussion in the previous chapter give management its marching orders for developing a suitable recruiting and hiring plan for the year. Unfortunately, many managers see recruiting as something to do in their spare time (which never materializes). Or they embark on an aggressive campaign only after they lose a number of salespeople. A company's cash flow and profitability cannot withstand long periods of drought between departure and rehire. In that sense, recruiting is, again, like prospecting for customers: an ongoing activity.

There are many ways to network with potential salespeople. Some of them are more likely to reach unlicensed prospects; others will reach either newly licensed or experienced agents. And some ways take longer to generate a pool of candidates than others.

Recruiting Experienced Talent

Obviously, the place to find experienced talent is the competition, the most vulnerable companies (unfortunately) being those around which rumors of pending changes and discontent circulate. Interestingly, real estate companies seem to have a double standard about recruiting: "It's okay for me to recruit your salespeople, just you stay away from mine." Before sending recruiting letters to another company's office, think about the chain of events that could negatively affect yours.

Recruit a Manager.   Because good sales managers often develop a loyal following of good salespeople, some companies see recruiting a manager as a good way to also attract experienced sales talent. However, this strategy may not work as intended if the manager's contract prohibits soliciting or recruiting salespeople from the former company for a period of time after the manager departs. The result would be no recruits and perhaps a costly legal battle with the manager's previous employer over a disputed nonsolicitation clause.

Network the Industry.   The most desirable way to get experienced salespeople is for them to initiate the contact. The visibility and professional stature of the manager are strong draws for that contact. A presence where salespeople gather, meet, or do business creates opportunities for them to become acquainted with the manager and for the manager to converse with them. Any overture is an opportunity to tell the company's story and perhaps plant a seed that will be beneficial eventually. Respect people's allegiances, though. Knocking the competition or soliciting at every closing or open house will turn people off.

Mobilize Ambassadors.   Current salespeople are also great ambassadors. Good salespeople like to work with others who are just as dedicated and hard-working as they are. The real estate business is one of unique relationships. Salespeople are fierce competitors who also frequently cooperate with one another. When they see others in action, they can identify those who would be an asset to the company. Some companies offer enticements like bonuses or prizes for salespeople who recruit others to join the firm.

Recruiting Unlicensed Talent

One of the most pressing questions for prospective licensees is "How do I select the right broker?" Frequently, they are advised to

- interview with a variety of companies—several small, medium, and large, some with franchise affiliation and others that are independent—and attend career nights;

- talk to friends in the business to get the practitioners' perspectives on various companies; and

- talk to people who recently have done business with real estate companies to find out what they have to say about various firms.

A company who desires newly licensed people wants to be in the running for consideration in this list. (And you may have noticed that managers scramble over one another trying to lure this talent, even while people are still taking their prelicense classes.)

The pool of possible new talent extends beyond the classroom, to virtually anywhere managers and salespeople meet people. Real estate is a popular topic of conversation, and those conversations can reveal interests and attitudes that may very well be those of a future real estate licensee. Don't overlook past customers and clients, too. The company could even establish a bonus or shared commission program to compensate the salespeople for recruiting this talent as well.

Advertising

A variety of media can be used (radio, TV, newspapers, Web sites, which are a big source of recruits) to spread the word about a career. Traditionally, advertising in the help-wanted section of the newspaper has been a popular way to post sales jobs. A recruiting tag on other promotional messages, though, may be less expensive.

Select advertising media and tailor the message in the same way as any other advertising, that is, identify the target audience and promote the message where that audience is likely to see it. Advertise consistently enough to be effective, but not so aggressively that people wonder if something is wrong in the company. One ad on the same day of each week for a period of time will be more effective than one that appears only sporadically. If the target is newly licensed salespeople, time an advertising campaign to coincide with peak times that real estate classes are scheduled. Also, monitor the competition's recruiting ads (they monitor yours). A sample recruiting ad appears in Figure 14.2.

Be careful about advertising overly attractive enticements (a luxury car, a trip, or the promise of earning exorbitant amounts of money). Because consumers also see recruiting ads, they may think twice about paying the price for the company's services if they think it has large sums of money to pay salespeople.

Be sure that the language in the ad is not discriminatory. The phrase "experienced salespeople only" could have that effect if a housewife has been home raising her children or a minority person has not had the

FIGURE 14.2

Sample Recruiting Ad

A *SUCCESSFUL* CAREER
STARTS HERE!

Join a winning team of professional real estate salespeople.

We support your success with

* Free career counseling
* Tuition assistance
* Sales Training Program
* Generous commission program
* Company paid advertising

Visit any of our offices or call our career counselor at
555-SELL (555-7355)

ABC REALTY

opportunity to gain experience. Phrases such as "equal employment opportunity," "previous training not necessary," or "experienced or inexperienced invited" make a public statement that the company provides hiring opportunities to everyone.

Recruiting Brochures

A recruiting brochure is intended to make an impression on people who contemplate working for the company in the same way sales brochures make impressions on consumers. A recruiting brochure (print or perhaps CD) is a tangible memory minder that is also an important companion to other recruiting strategies. Follow the suggestions for preparing a sales brochure in Chapter 12, and the result will be a similarly appealing professional statement about a career with the company. Content should also include answers to the typical questions people have about the industry and a brokerage company. (Think back on your own experience for a guide.) A self-evaluation exercise is also a helpful inclusion.

Career Seminars

People attend seminars with a variety of motives, ranging from curiosity about the business or just toying with the notion of a career to seriously looking for an employer. From the company's point of view, the seminars are an opportunity to explain the real estate business and showcase the company in the process. The expectation is that the program will stir sufficient interest to entice a number of attendees to pursue the matter with the company.

Just as people have various motives for attending, seminars are conducted for a variety of reasons as well.

- Local educational institutions may sponsor seminars so that their students can explore career options and begin planning what they will do when their course work is finished.

- Educational institutions may use seminars to stimulate interest in the industry as a way to get people enrolled in their classes. Companies appear as a public service and showcase their career opportunities in the process.

- A franchise may conduct a seminar to promote the franchise's advantages for the salespeople. Member companies showcase themselves as well as provide testimonials.

- A company may sponsor its own seminar. In the previously mentioned formats, the company contributes to the program agenda developed by someone else. In a company-sponsored program, the company controls the agenda for its specific purpose.

Attendees sometimes see company-sponsored seminars as nothing more than glitzy commercials, masquerading as career nights. A program billed as a *career* seminar should be delivered as such. Explain real estate careers, presenting a completely objective discussion of the options. Then explain how the company fits into the picture. If the intent is to conduct a recruiting seminar, plan and promote an opportunity for people to learn why the company is a superior place to work. Promote advantages, but don't knock the competition.

One of the major criticisms of these seminars is that people feel they weren't given realistic information about how much money they will make and the amount of effort (and length of time) it takes to turn a fledgling job into a very profitable career. Showcasing success stories is one thing, but the extraordinary tales can be deceiving. Figure 14.3 provides an interesting breakdown of gross income.

The goal of career programs is to generate a pool of people to interview. Because the percentage of people attending a seminar who have the desire or ability to become real estate salespeople may be small, the audience needs to be large enough to justify the preparation time and expense. National companies and franchises provide guidance and support materials for these events, or the following information can be used as a guide.

- Select a central location that is convenient for the people the company wants to attract. If the purpose of the program is to recruit for the company, the office showcases the actual work site, but this is appropriate only if there is a suitable professional conference or meeting room. An off-site facility is better for a true career (as opposed to a recruiting) program.

- Select a facility that can accommodate a range of group sizes. Hotels and conference centers provide a professional atmosphere and the flexibility to adjust seating as reservations or attendance requires.

FIGURE 14.3

Gross Personal Income of REALTORS®, 2000 (Percentage Distribution)

	All REALTORS®	Brokers/ Broker Associates	Sales Agents
Less than $10,000	15%	6%	22%
$10,000–$24,999	15	9	19
$25,000–$34,999	9	8	10
$35,000–$49,999	13	12	13
$50,000–$74,999	14	16	13
$75,000–$99,999	10	13	8
$100,000–$149,999	11	17	8
$150,000–$249,999	7	11	4
$250,000 or more	5	8	3
Median Gross Income	$47,700	$73,400	$34,100

Note: Detail may not add due to rounding.

Source: National Association of REALTORS®

- Promote the career night with flyers and press releases, advertising, and Web site postings to announce the event at least seven days in advance. Request reservations and provide a telephone number or e-mail address. Designate a person to handle contacts, distribute tickets, and follow up contacts a day or two before the program to verify attendance.

- Confirm the room arrangements. The virtue of reservations is they help gauge the number of people attending. Add 10 percent to accommodate people without reservations, but be prepared for no-shows as well. If the room is too large, people get the feeling that the event is not well attended.

- Arrange for projectors, screens, easels, sound systems, registration tables, and a podium. Be prepared to cope with potential (that invariably turn out to be real) problems with malfunctioning equipment. Also be sure the atmosphere is comfortable; minimize distracting noise and erratic temperatures.

- Plan refreshments. A beverage and light snack are an icebreaker and create an opportunity to mingle with the attendees before and after the program. Name tags are also a nice touch.

- Prepare literature. A packet for each guest should include general information about real estate careers and specific information about the company, including its career brochure.

■ Plan and conduct the program. In a recruiting seminar, showcase the company's services for consumers and services for the sales staff. Invite a few people from the company to speak about their special areas of responsibility or expertise. A career seminar should also include a brief discussion of real estate ownership, its economic importance, and interesting market statistics.

■ End with a question-and-answer period and an invitation for attendees to contact the company's recruiter or a sales manager.

■ Follow up with thank-you letters or telephone calls to attendees.

■ Plan the next career seminar. When these events are conducted on a regular basis, the company gets more mileage out of advertising and planning expenses. School directors and previous attendees also know when to expect the event and can refer others to a program.

Licensing Courses

Brokerage companies and franchises often operate real estate schools as a way to recruit salespeople for their companies. But the students pay to be educated. Before deciding to open a real estate school, investigate state laws and procedures for operating a proprietary school. Providing quality education requires specialized expertise, and running a school may be a more significant (and expensive) undertaking than is warranted just to create a pool of recruits.

To protect the educational integrity of the classroom, some state licensing authorities prohibit solicitation of students or the dissemination of class rosters. Even if state law permits these activities, some educational institutions prohibit them to protect the confidentiality of their students. Consider this: If you recruit a prospective licensee and refer that person to an educational institution, you'd be upset if another broker or the instructor tried to scoop that recruit from you.

Because of their industry expertise, managers are often invited to be real estate instructors. This is a good opportunity to share that expertise, though managers often underestimate the time and talent required to prepare and instruct an educationally sound program. If the purpose for teaching is to recruit students or gather student rosters, consider the earlier point about scooping other brokers' referrals to the institution. Even if the educational institution does not have a policy about its instructors recruiting students, remember that the entire class is expecting to learn. An instructor who favors some students (as potential hires) over others can disrupt the educational process.

Trial Training Sessions

Because training and professional development are important to recruits, give them a preview of what the company does with a trial training session. This can be promoted via a newspaper ad or direct mail to the real estate schools. The audience will likely include members of the public who are curious about the business as well as people in various stages of licensure.

Scholarships

Scholarship programs for prelicense or degree courses benefit deserving students and provide considerable public relations benefit to the company. It's important, however, that the company not be directly involved in actually selecting the recipients. The company can commit the funding and also set guidelines for the award (merit or financial need). Then the educational institution should take over and screen applicants and determine the recipients. Any deeper involvement can tarnish the company's public relations, particularly with applicants who are not awarded a scholarship. The company can reenter the process by participating in an award ceremony. In return for the company's generosity, the recipient may consider it for possible employment.

Direct Mail

Direct mail can be a useful way to distribute a recruiting brochure or its cheaper cousin, a flyer. A rule of thumb is that mass mailings generally produce about a 2 percent response rate. Keep this in mind when investigating costs of print and postage (bulk rate is preferable) and mail-house service if the mailing is not prepared in-house. This may not be a worthwhile expenditure, but if it produces one qualified prospect to interview for every ten respondents, then it is useful.

■ SELECTING SALESPEOPLE

The process of prescreening candidates, conducting formal interviews, and then selecting sales staff is no different than it is for any other personnel position. Several additional points to keep in mind when selecting sales staff include:

- Prelicense courses are designed to a minimum level of proficiency for licensees to protect the public interest. The courses are *not* designed to develop successful business and selling skills or to identify suitable personality traits. A license could be just as easily a license to fail. A company can minimize this possibility by hiring people who are suitable for the business and providing professional training.

- One of the attractions for IC salespeople is the ability to control their daily work as well as their income. This is also the feature that contributes to failure. Human beings, by nature, are not particularly disciplined. People rely on others to create structure, or they have to make a conscientious effort to create it for themselves. Unless people can plan, prioritize, and manage their time and activities well, they will not succeed in an unstructured environment.

- Salespeople must also be able to withstand pressure while maintaining their composure, cope with rejection without feeling demoralized, and empathize with their customers and clients without losing their objectivity or letting their own self-serving interests interfere.

Many people with different personalities may match the profiles that are commonly suggested for salespeople. Typically, companies look for traits that other successful people possess. But those may not be so significant, given differences in individual personalities. What is important is how well people can adapt their personal skills to the situation. Selection is a judgment call. No one will always make perfect selections. Every manager, on occasion, has been surprised that the least likely person turns out to be a superstar and the most likely person to succeed quickly falls by the wayside.

■ CONCLUSION

The future of the company rests in the hands of the people it hires. Therefore, it's incumbent on the manager to make the right personnel choices, from identifying the skills and attributes that are needed for a position to developing a pool of talent from which to make the right selection. Selecting a new salesperson involves more than just spending 20 minutes with anyone who is interested in selling real estate and then making a job offer. Selection errors consume far too many company resources and make victims of people who deserve better treatment. A methodical selection process provides the information needed to make appropriate choices, which benefits both the company and the candidates.

■ **DISCUSSION EXERCISES**

Discuss how brandworthy your company is as an attractive employer. What are its recruiting strengths and weaknesses?

What recruiting techniques do you think are most effective in your area?

If you've had experience conducting employment interviews, discuss ways to conduct a successful interview. As an interviewee, discuss your experiences during employment interviews.

NEW JERSEY ASSOCIATION OF REALTORS® STANDARD FORM OF
BROKER-SALESPERSON
INDEPENDENT CONTRACTOR AGREEMENT

©2001, New Jersey Association of Realtors®, Inc.

1 THIS AGREEMENT, is made and entered into this _____ day of _____, 20_____, by and between

2

3 _____ (hereinafter referred to as the "Broker"),

4

5 having its principal office at _____,

6

7 _____, and _____

8

9 (hereinafter referred to as the "Salesperson"), residing at_____

10

11 _____

12

13 **WITNESSETH:**

14 WHEREAS, Broker is engaged in business as a real estate broker trading as _____

15 _____, with its principal office at

16 _____, and as such is duly licensed to

17 engage in activities including, but not limited to, selling, offering for sale, buying, offering to buy, listing and soliciting

18 prospective purchasers, and negotiating loans on real estate, leasing or offering to lease, and negotiating the sale, purchase or

19 exchange of leases, renting or placing for rent, or managing real estate or improvements thereon for another or others; and

20 WHEREAS, Broker has and does enjoy the goodwill of the public, and has a reputation for fair and honorable dealing

21 with the public; and

22 WHEREAS, Broker maintains an office in the State of New Jersey equipped with furnishings, listings, prospect lists

23 and other equipment necessary, helpful, and incidental to serving the public as a real estate broker; and

24 WHEREAS, Salesperson is duly licensed by the State of New Jersey as a real estate salesperson; and

25 WHEREAS, it is deemed to be to the mutual advantage of Broker and Salesperson to enter into this Agreement; and

26 WHEREAS, Salesperson acknowledges that he has not performed any acts on behalf of Broker nor has he been authorized

27 to act on behalf of Broker; and

28 WHEREAS, the parties acknowledge that they deem it desirable to enter into an agreement in compliance with the

29 provisions of N.J.A.C. 11:5-4.1;

30 NOW, THEREFORE, in consideration of the foregoing premises and the mutual covenants herein contained, it is mutually

31 covenanted and agreed by and between the parties hereto as follows:

32

33 1. **SERVICES.** Salesperson agrees to proceed diligently, faithfully, legally, and with his best efforts to sell, lease, or

34 rent any and all real estate listed with Broker, except for any listings which are placed by Broker exclusively with another

35 salesperson(s), and to solicit additional listings and customers for Broker, and otherwise to promote the business of serving

36 the public in real estate transactions, and for the mutual benefit of the parties hereto.

37

38 2. **OFFICE SPACE.** Broker agrees to provide Salesperson with work space and other facilities at its office presently

39 maintained at _____,

40 or at such other location as determined by Broker at which Broker may maintain an office. The items furnished pursuant

41 to this Paragraph 2 shall be for the convenience of the Salesperson.

42

43 3. **RULES AND REGULATIONS.** Salesperson and Broker agree to conduct business and regulate habits and working

44 hours in a manner which will maintain and increase the goodwill, business, profits, and reputation of Broker and Salesperson,

45 and the parties agree to conform to and abide by all laws, rules and regulations, and codes of ethics that are binding on,

46 or applicable to, real estate broker and real estate salespeople. Salesperson and Broker shall be governed by the Code of

47 Ethics of the NATIONAL ASSOCIATION OF REALTORS®, the real estate laws of the State of New Jersey, the Constitution

48 and By-Laws of the _____ Board/Association of REALTORS®,

49 the rules and regulations of any Multiple Listing Service with which Broker now or in the future may be affiliated with,

50 and any further modifications or additions to any of the foregoing. Salesperson acknowledges that it is his responsibility

51 to familiarize himself with all current Code of Ethics, the Local Board/Association By-Laws, the rules and regulations of any

52 Multiple Listing Service with which Broker is now affiliated, the Rules and Regulations of the Real Estate Commission and the

53 License Law of the State of New Jersey. Broker agrees to maintain copies of all the foregoing and to make the same available to

54 Salesperson. Salesperson agrees also to abide by the rules, regulations, policies and standards promulgated by Broker.

55

56 4. **LICENSING AND ASSOCIATION MEMBERSHIP.** Salesperson represents that he is duly licensed by the State of

57 New Jersey as a real estate salesperson. Salesperson acknowledges that Broker is a member of the _____

58 _____ Board/Association of REALTORS®, the New Jersey Association of REALTORS®

59 and the NATIONAL ASSOCIATION OF REALTORS®, and as a result thereof, Broker is subject to the rules and regulations

60 of those organizations. Salesperson agrees to be subject to and act in accordance with said rules and regulations. If Broker

61 requires Salesperson to become a member of any real estate organization, then Salesperson agrees that he shall become a

62 member thereof and shall pay all applicable fees and dues required to maintain said membership. As a result of Broker being

63 a member of the aforesaid groups, Broker and Salesperson agree to abide by all applicable rules, regulations and standards

64 of such organizations, including, but without limitation, those pertaining to ethics, conduct and procedure.

65

66 5. **COMPENSATION.** Salesperson's sole compensation from Broker shall be in the form of commissions. The

67 commissions for services rendered in the sale, rental, or leasing of any real estate and the method of payment, shall be

68 determined exclusively by Broker. Commissions, when earned and collected by Broker, shall be divided between Broker

69 and Salesperson after deduction of all expenses and co-brokerage commissions in accord with the Salesperson's Commission

70 Schedule attached to this Agreement as Schedule A which is an outline of compensation to be paid by Broker to Salesperson

71 during the Salesperson's affiliation with Broker.

6. **MULTIPLE SALESPEOPLE.** In the event that two (2) or more salespeople under contract with Broker participate in a sale and claim a commission thereon, then and in that event the amount of commissions allocable to each salesperson shall be divided in accordance with a written agreement among said salespeople. In the event that the salespeople shall be unable to agree, the dispute shall be submitted to and be determined by Broker, in his sole discretion.

7. **RESPONSIBILITY OF BROKER FOR COMMISSIONS.** In no event shall Broker be liable to Salesperson for any commissions not collected, nor shall Salesperson be personally liable for any commissions not collected. It is agreed that commissions collected shall be deposited with the Broker and subsequently divided and distributed in accordance with the terms of this Agreement.

8. **DIVISION AND DISTRIBUTION OF COMMISSIONS.** The division and distribution of the earned commissions as provided for in this Agreement which may be paid to or collected by the Broker, but from which Salesperson is due certain commissions, shall take place as soon as practicable after collection and receipt of such commissions, but in no event more than ten (10) business days after receipt by the Broker, or as soon thereafter as such funds have cleared the Broker's bank.

9. **RESPONSIBILITY FOR EXPENSES.** Unless otherwise agreed in writing, Broker shall not be liable to Salesperson for any expenses incurred by Salesperson or for any of his acts, nor shall Salesperson be liable to Broker for Broker's office help or expenses, or for any of Broker's acts other than as specifically provided for herein.

10. **ADVANCES.** Broker may from time to time and in his sole discretion make advances to Salesperson on account of future commissions; it being expressly agreed, however, that such advances are temporary loans by Broker for the accommodation of Salesperson which are due and payable on demand or as otherwise agreed to by the Broker, and are not compensation. Upon notice to Salesperson, Broker shall have the right to charge interest on any and all advances made to Salesperson, either at the time of making the advance or thereafter, at a rate chosen by Broker in his sole discretion, but not in excess of the maximum rate permitted by law. Upon receipt of payment of commissions, Broker shall credit the account of Salesperson (first toward interest, if any, and then toward principal) with the portion of such commissions due Salesperson. If at any time, the advances made to Salesperson together with interest thereon, if any, exceed the credits to his account for his share of commissions collected, then such excess shall be owing by Salesperson to Broker and shall be due and payable upon demand. After such demand, interest at the maximum rate permitted by law shall accrue upon the amount due Broker, notwithstanding the fact that any or all of the advances made to Salesperson have initially been interest free or at a reduced rate of interest.

11. **REAL ESTATE LICENSES, BONDS, DUES AND FEES.** Salesperson agrees to pay the cost of maintaining his real estate license, dues for membership in the NATIONAL ASSOCIATION OF REALTORS®, the New Jersey Association of REALTORS®, the local Board/Association of REALTORS® and other dues and fees related to the rendering of services by Salesperson as a real estate salesperson.

12. **AUTHORITY TO CONTRACT.** Salesperson shall have no authority to bind, obligate, or commit Broker by any promise or representation, either verbally or in writing, unless specifically authorized in writing by Broker in a particular transaction. However, Salesperson shall be and is hereby authorized to execute listing agreements for and on behalf of Broker as his agent subject to Broker's office policy.

13. **CONTROVERSIES WITH OTHERS.** In the event any transaction in which Salesperson is involved results in a dispute, litigation or legal expense, Salesperson shall cooperate fully with Broker. Broker and Salesperson shall share all expenses connected therewith, in the same proportion as they normally would share the commission resulting from such transaction if there were no dispute or litigation. It is the policy to avoid litigation wherever possible, and Broker, within his sole discretion may determine whether or not any litigation or dispute shall be prosecuted, defended, compromised or settled, and the terms and conditions of any compromise or settlement, or whether or not legal expense shall be incurred. Salesperson shall not have the right to directly or indirectly compel Broker to institute or prosecute litigation against any third party for collection of commissions, nor shall Salesperson have any cause of action against Broker for its failure to do so. In the event a commission is paid to Broker in which Salesperson is entitled to share, but another real estate broker disputes or may dispute the right of Broker to receive all or any portion of such commission, Salesperson agrees that Broker may hold said commission in trust until such dispute is resolved or sufficient time has passed to indicate to Broker in his sole and absolute judgment that no action or proceeding will be commenced by such other real estate broker regarding the subject commission. In the event Broker shall pay any commission to Salesperson and thereafter, either during or subsequent to termination of this Agreement, Broker shall become obligated, either by way of final judicial determination, arbitration award or good faith negotiation, to repay all or any part of such commission to others, Salesperson agrees to reimburse Broker his pro rata share thereof. In any such instance, Broker agrees to keep Salesperson reasonably informed of any proceeding.

14. **OWNERSHIP OF LISTINGS.** Salesperson agrees that any and all listings of property, and all actions taken in connection with the real estate business and in accordance with the terms of this Agreement shall be taken by Salesperson in the name of Broker. In the event Salesperson receives a listing, it shall be filed with Broker no later than twenty four (24) hours after receipt of same by Salesperson. Broker agrees, but is not obligated, to generally make available to Salesperson all current listings maintained by its office. However, all listings shall be and remain the separate and exclusive property of Broker unless otherwise agreed to in writing by the parties hereto.

15. **DOCUMENTS.** Broker and Salesperson agree that all documents generated by and relating to services performed by either of them in accordance with this Agreement, including, but without limitation, all correspondence received, copies of all correspondence written, plats, listing information, memoranda, files, photographs, reports, legal opinions, accounting information, any and all other instruments, documents or information of any nature whatsoever concerning transactions handled by Broker or by Salesperson or jointly are and shall remain the exclusive property of the Broker.

16. **COMMUNICATIONS.** Broker shall determine and approve all correspondence from the Broker's office pertaining to transactions being handled, in whole or in part, by the Salesperson.

17. **FORMS AND CONTRACTS.** Broker shall determine and approve the forms to be used and the contents of all completed contracts and other completed forms before they are presented to third parties for signature.

18. INDEPENDENT CONTRACTOR. This Agreement does not constitute employment of Salesperson by Broker and Broker and Salesperson acknowledge that Salesperson's duties under this Agreement shall be performed by him in his capacity as an independent contractor. Nothing contained in this Agreement shall constitute Broker and Salesperson as joint ventures or partners and neither shall be liable for any obligation incurred by the other party to this Agreement, except as provided herein. The Salesperson shall not be treated as an employee for Federal, State or local tax purposes with respect to services performed in accordance with the terms of this Agreement. Effective as of the date of this Agreement, Broker will not (i) withhold any Federal, State, or local income or FICA taxes from Salesperson's commissions; (ii) pay any FICA or Federal and State unemployment insurance on Salesperson's behalf; or (iii) include Salesperson in any of its retirement, pension, or profit sharing plans. Salesperson shall be required to pay all Federal, State, and local income and self-employment taxes on his income, as required by law, and to file all applicable estimated and final returns and forms in connection therewith.

19. NOTICE OF TERMINATION. This Agreement, and the relationship created hereby may be terminated by either party hereto with or without cause, at anytime upon three (3) days written notice. However, this Agreement shall immediately terminate upon Salesperson's death. Except as otherwise provided for herein, the rights of the parties hereto to any commissions which were accrued and earned prior to the termination of this Agreement shall not be divested by the termination of this Agreement.

20. SERVICES TO BE PERFORMED SUBSEQUENT TO TERMINATION. Upon termination of this Agreement, all negotiations commenced by Salesperson during the term of this Agreement shall continue to be handled through Broker and with such assistance by Salesperson as is determined by Broker. The Salesperson agrees to be compensated for such services in accordance with Schedule B attached hereto.

21. LIST OF PROSPECTS. Upon termination of this Agreement. Salesperson shall furnish Broker with a complete list of all prospects, leads and foreseeable transactions developed by Salesperson, or upon which Salesperson shall have been engaged with respect to any transaction completed subsequent to termination of this Agreement in which Salesperson has rendered assistance in accordance with the terms of this Agreement. Except as expressly provided for in Paragraph 20 of this Agreement, Salesperson shall not be compensated in respect of any transaction completed subsequent to termination of this agreement unless agreed to in writing by the Broker.

22. DUTY OF NON-DISCLOSURE. Salesperson agrees that upon termination of this Agreement, he will not furnish to any person, firm, company, corporation, partnership, joint venture, or any other entity engaged in the real estate business, any information as to Broker or its business, including, but not limited to, Broker's clients, customers, properties, prices, terms of negotiations, nor policies or relationships with prospects, clients and customers. Salesperson, shall not, after termination of this Agreement, remove from the files or from the office of the Broker, any information pertaining to the Broker's business, including, but not limited to, any maps, books, publications, card records, investor or prospect lists, or any other material, files or data, and it is expressly agreed that the aforementioned records and information are the property of Broker.

23. COMPENSATION SUBSEQUENT TO TERMINATION. Upon termination of this Agreement, Salesperson shall be compensated only in accordance with the appended Schedule B.

24. ESCROW DEPOSIT. All contracts of sale shall be accompanied by an escrow deposit in an amount as determined by Broker. Salesperson will, at all times, require purchaser or prospective purchasers, to put up such escrow deposit unless a higher or lower sum shall be mutually agreed to by Broker and Salesperson. Salesperson is expressly prohibited from accepting a smaller escrow deposit, a post-dated check, or agreeing not to deposit an escrow check, unless such action has been expressly authorized by Broker.

25. AUTOMOBILE. Salesperson agrees to furnish his own automobile, pay all expenses in connection with the operation and maintenance of said automobile, and that Broker shall have no responsibility therefor. Salesperson agrees to carry throughout the terms of this Agreement public liability insurance upon his automobile with minimum limits not less than _____ (\$ _____) for each person and _____ (\$ _____) for each accident, and property damage insurance with a minimum limit of not less than _____ (\$ _____). Upon request, Salesperson agrees to furnish to Broker certificates certifying as to such insurance prepared by the insurance company.

26. ASSIGNABILITY AND BINDING EFFECT. This Agreement is personal to the parties hereto and may not be assigned, sold or otherwise conveyed by either of them.

27. NOTICE. Any and all notices, or any other communication provided for herein shall be in writing and shall be personally delivered or mailed by registered or certified mail, return receipt requested prepaid postage, which shall be addressed to the parties at the addresses indicated herein, or to such different address as such party may have fixed. Any such notice shall be effective upon receipt, if personally delivered, or three (3) business days after mailing.

28. GOVERNING LAW. This Agreement shall be subject to and governed by the laws of the State of New Jersey, including the conflicts of laws, irrespective of the fact that Salesperson may be or become a resident of a different state.

29. WAIVER OF BREACH. The waiver by the Broker of a breach of any provision of this Agreement by the Salesperson shall not operate or be construed as a waiver of any subsequent breach by the Salesperson.

30. ENTIRE AGREEMENT. This Agreement constitutes the entire agreement between the parties and contains all of the agreement between the parties with respect to the subject matter hereof; this Agreement supersedes any and all other agreements, either oral or in writing between the parties hereto with respect to the subject matter hereof.

31. GENDER. When used in this Agreement, the masculine shall be deemed to include the feminine.

228 32. **SEPARABILITY.** If any provision of this Agreement is invalid or unenforceable in any jurisdiction, the other
229 provisions herein shall remain in full force and effect such jurisdiction and shall be liberally construed in order to effectuate
230 the purpose and intent of this Agreement, and the invalidity or unenforceability of any provision of this Agreement in any
231 jurisdiction shall not affect the durability or enforceability of any such provision in any other jurisdiction.

232 33. **MODIFICATION.** This Agreement may not be modified or amended except by an instrument in writing signed
233 by the parties hereto. Any modification to this Agreement between the parties after the date of the Agreement shall be of
234 no effect unless such modification is in writing and is signed by both Broker and Salesperson.

235
236 34. **PARAGRAPH HEADINGS.** The paragraph headings contained in this Agreement are for reference purposes only
237 and shall not affect in any way the meaning or interpretation of this Agreement.

238
239 35. **SURVIVAL OF PROVISIONS.** The provisions of this Agreement shall survive the termination of the Salesperson's
240 services under this Agreement.

241
242 36. **COPY RECEIVED.** Salesperson acknowledges receipt of a fully executed copy of this Agreement, duly signed by
243 Broker and Salesperson.

244
245 IN WITNESS WHEREOF, the undersigned have set their hands and seals, or if a corporation, has caused this
246 Agreement to be signed and sealed by its duly authorized corporate officer, the day and year first above written.

247
248 WITNESS:
249
250 _____   _____
251 WITNESS: (Broker)
252
253 _____   _____
254   (Salesperson)
255
256
257
258
258
260

SCHEDULE A

SALESPERSON'S COMMISSION SCHEDULE WHILE AFFILIATED WITH BROKER

Salesperson shall be entitled to receive the following percentage as his portion of the commission earned by Broker as a result
of closed sales, listings, rentals, leases, after deducting all expenses and co-brokerage commissions:

SALES TRANSACTIONS

1. _____% for written listings produced by Salesperson.

2. _____% for written listings produced and sold by Salesperson.

3. _____% for selling property listed by co-operating broker.

RENTAL/LEASE TRANSACTIONS

1. _____% for written listings produced by Salesperson.

2. _____% for written listings resulting in a signed lease agreement.

3. _____% for signed lease agreement listed by co-operating broker.

ADDITIONAL PROVISIONS (IF ANY):

SCHEDULE B

SALESPERSON'S COMMISSION SCHEDULE AFTER TERMINATION OF AFFILIATION WITH BROKER

The rate of compensation to be paid by Broker to Salesperson pertaining to transactions which close and on renewals which occur subsequent to the termination of Salesperson's affiliation with Broker is as follows:

1. AS TO SALES TRANSACTIONS
A. Listings

As to written listings which have been produced by Salesperson prior to the date of termination, Salesperson shall be entitled to receive the following percentage of his portion of the commission pursuant to Schedule A for each such transaction, upon collection by Broker.

(I) _____% if a contract of sale has been executed by all parties and all contingencies contained therein have been satisfied as of such date;

(II) _____% if a contract of sale has been executed by all parties but any contingencies contained therein have not been satisfied as of such date;

(III) _____% if a contract of sale has not been executed by all parties as of such date.

In the event a listing originally produced by Salesperson expires, and is renewed after such termination date, Salesperson shall be entitled to receive _____% of his portion of the commission for any such transaction upon collection in full by Broker.

B. Sales

As to transaction in which a prospective purchaser has been produced by Salesperson prior to the date of termination, Salesperson shall be entitled to receive the following percentage of his portion of the commission pursuant to Schedule A for any such transaction, upon collection by Broker:

(I) _____% if the title has closed, but the commission has not been collected as of such date;

(II) _____% if a contract of sale has been executed by all parties and all contingencies contained therein have been satisfied as of such date;

(III) _____% if a contract of sale has been executed by all parties but any contingencies contained therein have not been satisfied as of such date;

(IV) _____% if a contract of sale has not been executed by all parties as of such date; but thereafter a contract is executed by all parties.

2. AS TO RENTAL TRANSACTIONS
A. Listings

As to written listings which have been produced by Salesperson prior to the date of termination, Salesperson shall be entitled to receive the following percentage of his portion of the commission pursuant to Schedule A in any such transaction upon collection by Broker:

(I) _____% if a lease agreement has been executed by all parties as of such date, but the commission has not yet been received;

(II) _____% if a lease agreement has not been executed by all parties as of such date, but thereafter, a lease agreement is executed by all parties.

B. Leases

As to rental transactions in which Salesperson has produced a prospective lessee prior to the date of termination, Salesperson shall be entitled to receive the following percentage of his portion of the commission pursuant to Schedule A upon collection by Broker:

(I) _____% if a lease agreement has not been executed by all parties as of such date, but the commission has not yet been received;

(II) _____% if a lease agreement has not been executed by all parties as of such date, but thereafter, a lease agreement is executed by all parties.

3. ADDITIONAL PROVISIONS (IF ANY):

NJAR Form-134-Schedule B-1/91

CHAPTER FIFTEEN

PROFESSIONAL COMPETENCY

What should a company do to orient new people to the organization?

What can a company do to nurture the professional skills of people who work for it?

———————————

Once people are hired, the job of a manager really begins. This is when the manager's ability to provide leadership, cultivate talent, and create a favorable workplace environment is tested. The manager's focus at this point is to direct the professional accomplishments of the people who do the organization's work. This is the directing function of management.

Directing is not a matter of barking orders. All that was discussed in Unit One about a manager's leadership skills, management style, and ability to effectively manage human behavior and communicate come into play. These are the tools managers use to help people rise to the occasion and be productive.

This also means that management must give people the tools they need. The concept that a company's people are its most valuable resource takes on additional meaning because the organization also invests mightily in them. Not just in the wages, salaries, and other compensation but in the time and money an organization spends to indoctrinate people into the company's business and provide the training, skill enhancement, and personal development needed to help them do their jobs. The end result is competency for the organization and professional growth for its workforce. Hence the chapter title, "Professional Competency."

Each person on staff has different needs at different times to be proficient and to grow professionally. This is where management's ability to properly assess needs is important (another information-gathering exercise for the manager). One occasion may require half an hour of the manager's time to help someone solve a problem. Other occasions may require more in-depth discussions or formally structured forums, typically where a group of people could benefit from an exchange of information or the development of specific knowledge or skill sets.

■ ORIENTATION PROGRAMS

Once people come to work for the company, they are no longer outsiders. Regardless of how enthused people are about coming to work for the company, they often feel some twinge of apprehension and strangeness. Management must now help them move into the organization and become an integral part of the company's team.

The first way in which a company invests in its personnel is by orienting them to the organization. The introduction people get during the selection and hiring process is basically a brief overview. The next step is to open the rest of the book about the company. People can't help the organization accomplish its goals unless they know who the organization is, what it intends to do, and how it functions internally. In other words, tell them where they have come to work. An orientation program serves this purpose and creates a sense of belonging.

A standardized approach for indoctrinating new staff ensures that people have been properly informed about how to work in the organization.

Orientation programs can be conducted in a group setting if a number of people join the company at the same time. Or the broker and the immediate supervisor can present the orientation story, one-on-one, to the new hire. Regardless of the format, the substance is essentially the same.

- *An introduction to the company.* This includes a brief history of the company, its philosophy of doing business, and a general outline of the work that the company does. People need to see the big picture, the organization chart of the various departments and offices, so they know how the company operates and where their positions fit into that picture.

  How to work in the organization is covered with an explanation of the company's policies and procedures, daily office procedures, benefit and compensation programs, and professional development opportunities.

  The introduction to the company part of the orientation program is meaningful to any new hire, regardless of the job the person has in the organization.

- *The specific procedures that apply to the person's job.* For a salesperson, this part of orientation explains how the salespeople are expected to serve the company's customers and clients and all of the procedures for handling the various aspects of a real estate transaction. This includes internal procedures for handling paperwork and escrow funds, fiscal matters concerning negotiations of fees and cooperative transactions and the way the sales staff works together, and how the support staff functions.

  For all other positions, similar information tailored to the specific responsibilities and tasks of those jobs is explained.

Although this is a fairly comprehensive story to tell, it intends to avoid the "I was never told that" kind of problems that could arise later on. Granted, there is a learning curve that managers must patiently coach people through until they are more familiar with the company's way of doing business. But orientation sows the seeds that make a manager's job of managing easier.

Orientation should include an introduction of the upper echelon of the company. These are the individuals for whom people really work, and new hires deserve an opportunity to put names to faces. The broker and representatives of senior management should at the very least make a cameo appearance. Orientation is often one of the few occasions that people, especially in sizable or diverse organizations, see senior management.

Assessing New Hires.   Just as a new hire needs to be oriented to the company, management needs to learn more about the new hire, to gain some insight into the person with whom the manager will be working. Companies often conduct preemployment interviews (the meeting with the immediate supervisor or manager before the new hire's first official day on the job) for this purpose.

Assessing new hires resurrects the discussion of job skill and personality assessments. The policy in some companies is to assess after a person has been hired, rather than incorporate assessments in the hiring selection process. Generally, these policies arise out of concerns that assessments create more legal liability than they provide defensible predictors of job performance.

Once a person is hired, however, the compilation of a variety of assessments can be useful to identify talent and the education and training that would be beneficial. Obviously, these would be tailored to the skills required for the specific position (mathematical or computer skills, for example). For salespeople, there are interactive programs, such as the simulation-based Success Profiler, that can be used to do this.

Because of cultural or verbal bias or the lack of correlation between what is tested and a person's potential for success in the job, some assessment instruments are more valid than others. Regardless of the instrument used (if any), the supervisor should manage the person, not the data.

Business Plans for Salespeople.   Orientation for salespeople, regardless of whether they are newly licensed or experienced, also should include the development of a personal business plan. This formulates sales goals as well as a plan of activities to promote their association with the company. Some companies provide announcements that can be mailed to the salesperson's network of contacts, which are then followed up with items such as the company's brochure, newsletter, or giveaway novelty. Salespeople may also develop their own self-promotion material as well.

■ TRAINING PROGRAMS

The mention of professional competency typically brings to mind education and training. Often, these are seen as one and the same, but they are really two different exercises. Education builds knowledge; training develops skill by converting that knowledge into action. Consider this: the courses required before a person gets a license are, for the most part, knowledge-based. They do not ordinarily take this knowledge to the next level, that being to develop the skill needed to use the information to its greatest advantage.

Unfortunately, brokers or managers sometimes say to their salespeople, "Forget what you learned in school. I'll teach you what you *really* need to know." However, this statement overlooks an important fact—salespeople need a wide range of both knowledge *and* skill to be successful.

All of this being said, the word *training* may not necessarily be the appropriate way to describe what actually happens. This is not to say that a company cannot conduct educational sessions, but because the company benefits when people learn to use that knowledge, training is the necessary step to that end. Training intends to cause people to behave in certain ways. The happens when people

- become motivated to adopt the behavior;
- learn to process information and experiences;
- develop knowledge, skills, values and attitudes, or creative ideas; and
- transfer learning into application.

The obvious benefit is that enhanced proficiency means enhanced productivity. But companies also benefit when skill development supports the company's business philosophy and minimizes legal liability. Training can happen in a variety of forums, from the formal training session to an office sales meeting or a manager meeting one-on-one with a person.

Before any training is designed, the company needs to decide who needs to be trained, what subject matter needs to be covered, and how best to deliver that training.

Whom To Train

Some training topics benefit all people within the organization, including management (the new phone, computer system, and organizational topics), and other topics are more job-specific. This may be remedial training to renew proficiency (revisiting listing-presentation or buyer-qualifying techniques, for example) or proactive training that develops new techniques or strategies related to a new company service or recent legal development.

Managers. Some companies don't give much thought to management training, but managers (including brokers) should be able to develop their business management skills. Unless the company has a large enough management corps to warrant developing or conducting these programs, management can attend seminars, courses (which you may be attending now), and programs conducted by professional organizations.

Sales managers also should attend the sales-training program from time to time. Managers are at a great disadvantage when they don't know what is being taught (or are not up-to-date) and can't help implement and reinforce what the salespeople learn. The manager also needs to be giving all salespeople the same, not conflicting, directions. A critique of the program is also helpful for the person responsible for the training so that the content can be tailored to suit the needs that managers identify from working with the salespeople.

Experienced Salespeople. Some part of a company's training needs to appeal to the needs of experienced salespeople. One size doesn't fit all, because their skill levels are different from those of newly licensed salespeople. Training for the veterans can sharpen stale or outdated skills, help them integrate the company's sales practices into their methods, and bring them up-to-date on current laws and trends. Sessions comprising solely experienced people help them build rapport with one another and also acknowledge their seasoned expertise.

New Associates.   Newly licensed salespeople can be timid, feeling ill equipped to tackle their new jobs, or they can be overcharged, heading into the field before they know what they're doing. Neither case does the company a service, but the solution in both is to give people the tools they need and groom them as valuable professionals. Training sessions for newly licensed associates suit their novice state and preclude their being dissuaded by the skeptical (or cynical) views that some veterans are inclined to freely share.

Administrative Staff.   Secretaries, clerks, and other administrative personnel also should be involved in training programs. Any information about the inner workings of the organization, as well as tools to help them in their specific jobs, can be the subject of various training sessions.

What To Teach

What do they need to know? What skills do they need to develop? Effective training is based on a job-skills analysis, the same analysis that was used to develop position qualifications for hiring (Chapter 13). An analysis answers the "How do you know people need to know this?" question so that the company makes the best use of training money and time for both the attendees and the people doing the training.

Because business methods and organizations change, companies also reanalyze jobs from time to time to see how skill requirements may have changed and identify skill sets that deserve training attention (which may also resolve performance problems that management has had to contend with). As the legal and business environments change, risk reduction issues also change. Don't overlook the analysis for clerical, secretarial, and computer positions, too.

The remainder of the discussion concentrates on sales training, but many of the principles are applicable regardless of the skill purpose. A very important point to keep in mind, however, is that no training program, regardless of how good it is, will fix every problem an organization has. Training has one specific focus: *to affect behavior in people so they perform their jobs more effectively.* Training will not correct problems that are rooted in defective company policies or procedures, inefficient systems, negligent management, or misaligned financial resources.

Keys to Effective Sales Training.   Sales training over the years has been built around the modeling approach. That is the "just give them the words" scripts of what people should say in various sales situations. Modeling presumes that the script is fail-safe, that scripts can be delivered by anyone and sound natural or genuine, and that there's a canned answer for every situation. People become dependent on the memorized lines (and have to try to remember all of them) and don't learn to listen, size up situations, and think on their feet. While this training strategy may give the novice a few comebacks to get started, the person really hasn't learned much else.

Sales training is most effective for the trainees and the company when:

- Sales is approached as a business (as opposed to signatures on a contract) and training develops professional, ethical, and legal behavior.

- Salespeople learn how to relate (and listen) to people as individuals, to deliver the personalized services that today's sophisticated consumer expects. Success in sales is about building relationships.

- Salespeople are encouraged to develop their personal strengths and professional expertise. Not everyone is good at both listing and selling, and people should not be subjected to a guilt trip because of that.

- Training is institutionalized, which means that the workplace (especially the supervising manager) supports and reinforces what is learned. Otherwise, people retreat to old ways or attitudes, and training benefits last about as long as the sessions did.

- Training appeals to what the salespeople think they need to hear so they tune in. The company needs to sell benefits (yes, in training, too) so that people feel their time is well spent. Management should also periodically ask what the salespeople think they need.

- Program objectives are clearly defined, along with specific behavior the trainees are expected to adopt at the conclusion of the program. This tells how the program should be designed (content, forum, presentation and handout materials, learning exercises, and the like).

The content of sales-training programs falls into several general areas.

■ Basic real estate information, including economic trends and changes in demographics and lifestyles, environmental issues, construction, and development

■ Sales and listing strategies, including sales techniques directly related to activities that enhance services and produce revenue

■ Company policy issues, including new programs, services, sales tools, policy changes, or issues that need to be clarified because of recurring problems or disputes

■ Legal and risk-reduction issues, including recent litigation that affects real estate transactions and ownership and changes in federal, state, and local laws and ordinances

■ Motivational subjects, including kickoff campaigns for new programs and the new year's objectives

■ Personal development, including time management, personal business plans and goal setting, and technology skills

How To Deliver Training

Delivering training has three components: developing the curriculum (content), conducting the program, and evaluating the training's effectiveness. These are distinctly separate exercises. Curriculum or program development may be prepared by one resource, with someone else actually conducting the program, or the same resource may do both. Decisions about how to deliver training will be influenced by the nature of the subject matter, the expertise required to design the program, the financial resources that are available, the number of people to be trained, and the frequency with which a program needs to be offered.

Outsourcing.   The company can outsource the development or purchase a prepared program, and then have someone in-house (preferably someone with training or education expertise) conduct the program. Or the company can rely totally on outside talent. Delivering training, in this case, is relatively simple: schedule the classes, arrange the facilities, and bring the talent to you. Or send the people to the talent in regularly scheduled classes. (Some professional groups will schedule classes exclusively for your associates). These approaches are desirable when the company does not have in-house expertise to develop professional curriculum or when there's an appealing prepared program that suits the company's purpose.

Depending on how much influence the company has over the content of the program, the drawback of using outside talent and prepackaged programs is that trainees do not get the benefit of seeing the company's sales tools, business philosophy, and procedures in action. If the presenter is from out of town, that person may be unfamiliar with local laws or practices. While these problems are not insurmountable, they can cause conflicts and contradictions that distract from the program.

Sending people to outside talent may be the only practical way to do comprehensive training for one or a small number of people, however. Especially for a new-licensee program (unless the company has a large and consistent volume of new hires), it's important not to dampen their enthusiasm by making them cool their heels until the company gets a class together. A contingency plan is for the manager to do some one-on-one training with the new licensee so the person can perform certain activities until the next formal program is available.

In-House.   A company has more control over the entire delivery when both content and presentation are handled in-house. However, maintaining a training department is a major financial commitment. In addition to the materials and facilities costs, the company needs the in-house professional talent to develop sound curricula and presentation materials (including handouts) and to conduct the program. Trainers of this caliber, with the accompanying training or education credentials, are prized employees, who also command commensurate pay.

Even with an in-house training department, the company is likely to turn to outside resources on occasion. With today's technology, trainees can easily be networked with outside resources through audio and video conferencing. Specialized expertise may be required for some subject matter. Perhaps a "tired" topic can get a new life with a fresh perspective. For programs that deserve extra punch or prominence, outside "experts" can make a greater impact or generate greater credibility than in-house staff people would. It's also effective to go outside the organization for inspirational speakers.

Classroom Instruction.   People have been accustomed to learning in the kind of setting where they have sat since elementary school, that being the classroom. Organized classroom instruction offers a structured agenda with a leader who can keep the group focused and the discussions on track. Information is normally introduced in a lecture format, particularly for beginners. Once this is done, though, learning really occurs when people are engaged in both thinking and doing.

When trainees are gathered in a group, they can participate in learning exercises: skits, role play, brainstorming, and problem solving. These are worthwhile exercises, however, only when they suit the profile of the audience and are carefully planned. If people feel embarrassed or ridiculed, the exercises do more harm than good.

Location.   The facility must be conducive to learning and the classroom exercises that will be used. Professional salespeople want professional programs, conducted in professional settings. (The worst place to conduct programs is at the salespeople's desks.) Even an office's conference room can be problematic unless interruptions for phone calls or other business matters are strictly prohibited, especially so that the person with a self-imposed sense of importance can't grandstand. Regardless of where the program is conducted, all pagers and cellular phones must be turned off.

A training or conference room should provide comfortable seating, adequate work surface, an HVAC system that allows for maximum comfort, sufficient space to accommodate breakout groups or other learning exercises, and teaching aids (whiteboards, overhead projectors, PowerPoint™ presentations, VCRs, monitors, and perhaps, video-conferencing equipment). If this isn't available in-house, take the program off-site to a hotel or conference facility. Regardless of the location, accommodations must be available for speakers and attendees who have disabilities.

Some salespeople can find most any excuse to justify their not attending a training program. No matter what the location, not everyone will be pleased, and you'll have an uphill battle to encourage attendance if a previous program was shoddy or worthless (a persuasive reason for producing quality programs in the first place).

Trainers. The key to successful classroom training is the trainer. (The same can be said for a manager running an educational sales meeting.) The trainer must be able to take command and establish credibility, control discussions and keep them on track, and maximize the learning experience for each participant. The trainer should use examples effectively, without subjecting the audience to an endless stream of personal war stories, and facilitate discussions and exercises without allowing a few participants to monopolize the class. See Figure 15.1 for some practical rules for trainers to follow.

FIGURE 15.1

Rules for Trainers

Do

Project a personal interest in each student as a unique person.

Respect the student. Be tactful, fair, and objective.

Praise the students' accomplishments.

Set a good example by your appearance.

Demonstrate the competency students should achieve with quality examples and exhibits.

Relate the subject matter to real-life situations. The more relevant the subject appears to the students, the more interested and motivated they will be to learn.

Project a positive attitude and enthusiasm toward the subject to emphasize how it is important in the students' business.

Display integrity: "We don't cut corners, lie, cheat, or misrepresent at any time in any form."

Be modest and don't brag about yourself or your personal accomplishments.

Be prepared for each class. Follow a predetermined and logical outline.

Maintain student interest by planning a variety of learning activities.

Create a fast-paced and exciting rhythm with lectures, discussions, projects and case studies, videos, group sessions, or other techniques.

Use tone and volume of voice and physical mannerisms to keep student interest, but don't let them distract from the subject.

Create opportunities for students to share their personal knowledge and experience, but don't let anyone monopolize the discussion.

Use lecture and dialogue rather than straight lecture in classroom presentations.

Reinforce key points by summarizing periodically during the class session.

Use humor occasionally, but be sure that it will not be offensive to anyone.

Use theatrical devices or drama occasionally if they make a point, but don't threaten your credibility by appearing unprofessional. People should remember the point, not the method.

Strive to improve yourself. Use classroom evaluations to analyze your effectiveness.

Avoid rambling, illogical, or unproductive discussions.

Avoid telling the students: rather, show them what you mean. Remember that you make a stronger impression when you appeal to several senses.

Avoid gossip and don't slander the competition.

Avoid making promises that can't be fulfilled or exaggerating potential earnings.

Even if they have many years of experience in the classroom or in the business, trainers must prepare for each session, rather than talking off the tops of their heads. Simple things like organizing notes, following an agenda that is focused on the program's objectives, and assembling exhibits are essential for a professional program and managing time effectively (prompt beginning and ending as well). Reviewing topics to be sure that they are not disseminating information that is out-of-date or contrary to company policies and procedures will also solidify the trainers' credibility.

Handout materials are useful for the students to follow during the sessions, particularly when they include exercises for them to complete. Handouts are also a blueprint for implementing the classroom subjects in daily practice and a reference resource that can be used outside the classroom.

Twenty-First Century Learning.   Traditional classroom training has been facilitated by a live presenter, using participatory teaching methods between student and instructor and among students. Today, people can engage in totally independent computer-based learning, working at their own pace and time. A variety of training is available on CD and the Internet. (All of these methods are known as *distance learning*.) These can be used to supplement classroom programs or as stand-alone, self-training sessions.

One-on-One Training.   One-on-one sessions manager and salesperson-may be the only feasible way to cover a training agenda for one person or a few people at any given time. This training can follow content and presentation similar to that of a formal group program, with a specific agenda and sessions scheduled with the manager specifically for training purposes. A one-on-one training regime is also important for reinforcing or supplementing other training salespeople attend.

There's a difference between one-on-one training and on-the-job training, however. *On-the-job* training involves the salesperson and the manager working together in the field. Salespeople appreciate the manager's support, rather than going it alone, and it's reassuring to see the manager encounter real-life challenges in the field. This is also a way for the manager to gain insight into what the salespeople are doing, including their daily frustrations, and what's going on in the marketplace. The time spent together is also a good relationship builder.

However, on-the-job training is not a very satisfactory substitute for a formal training program for new licensees. Often, the lessons are disjointed, and if the manager has limited expertise or is out of step with the times, the training is not particularly constructive.

A form of one-on-one training involves *partners* or *mentors*. Team a newly licensed salesperson with an experienced one. The new associate benefits from the support of a mentor and the opportunity to learn from a voice of experience, and sometimes it's easier for two salespeople to relate to one another than for a salesperson to relate to a supervisor. A long-term bond can form, which can help the company retain both salespeople (but may also cause you to lose both if one of them decides to leave).

The manager should carefully select the individual who will act as a mentor. Look at the quality of the work to which the new associate will be exposed and minimize the formation of undesirable cliques. Look also for a mentor who is willing to assume this role. A mentor agreement with clearly specified duties and obligations and the time period for the assignment is important. The company should provide a shared commission arrangement so that the mentor doesn't feel used. That's also an incentive for the mentor to be attentive to the assignment.

Adult Learning.   Adult education and the process by which adults learn, or *andragogy*, is a specialty of its own and deserves a separate book. A useful publication on the subject is *How to Teach Adults*, by Dr. Donald R. Levi (see Bibliography). Regardless of whether the manager is leading classroom instruction, conducting educational business meetings, or working one-on-one with people, there are several rules to remember.

- Adults are very time- and benefit-oriented. They want their time to be respected (begin and end punctually) and the content to be substantive and worthwhile. They grow impatient quickly with disorganization and long-windedness.

- Most adults are not accustomed to being in a classroom or subordinate to an instructor, especially if the instructor is younger than they are. Adults are more likely to be anxious over their performance and need to feel respected. It's important to minimize intimidation and potential for embarrassment.

- It's possible to "teach an old dog new tricks," but the older the adult, the slower the adjustment to change. It takes patience and a little extra time to help adults adopt new behaviors. When working with a variety of age groups, this will be particularly evident.

- Adults, especially those over age 50, experience changes in visual, auditory, and motor skills. And some of those changes are different for men and women. Everything, from the level of lighting, glare, size of print-type, and colors in a room, to the frequency and volume of sounds and speech, is affected. Because the over-50 age group is growing, learning more about these issues has relevance to everything a company does.

- Adults have learned to think and analyze. They are less likely to accept facts without explanation and rationale. "Just do it because I say so" may work with children (well, some children) because they are conditioned to follow authority. But adults are more inclined to question and screen information. They also respond to stimulating and thought-provoking exercises.

- Adults have many life experiences from which to draw. They integrate new information by relating it to their experiences and finding correlation. Stimulating them to recall experiences helps them as well as others in the group to learn.

Evaluating Training

Because companies invest a considerable amount of money in training, they need to be able to evaluate the effectiveness of their expenditures. Asking participants to complete surveys at the conclusion of a session or program, surveying changes in attitudes, or administering formal examinations are common evaluation methods. The most obvious indicator of the effectiveness is reflected in changes in the company's operation, the volume of transactions, or the bottom line.

The caveat in focusing on the bottom line, however, is that training intends to affect behavior. And behavior rarely changes immediately. Companies must learn to be patient and give people the opportunity to try something new or different. The manager can be a tremendous asset by reinforcing the new skills that were introduced in training sessions and recognizing people's efforts rather than focusing immediately on results.

Reinforcing Training

One of the major failures of training is that, like a motivational program, training doesn't have a lasting effect unless it is reinforced. The responsibility for this aspect of training falls to the manager, which is why it's important for the manager to be familiar with the training curriculum. By coaching the salespeople one-on-one, conducting follow-up sessions, or devoting a sales meeting to a subject, the manager reinforces the training curriculum. This also showcases the company's commitment to the lessons being taught.

In the case of training programs for newly licensed salespeople, the tendency is to overload them with too much information too soon. It's tempting to tell them everything they'll ever need to know so they are prepared to handle any situation. But until new salespeople have had some field experience, much of the information they're exposed to has no relevance. It's more effective to develop some very specific skills that they can practice for awhile. Then bring them back into the training room and work with more technical information and develop more sophisticated skills.

■ BUSINESS MEETINGS

Another way companies develop people and their professional competency is in meetings. Conducting meetings is also one of a manager's most common activities. Go back to the lessons in Chapter 4 about all that a manager can learn about how best to give and gather information and how to plan and conduct worthwhile meetings. This is the time to put those lessons into action.

Meetings serve many purposes. They may be informational forums or opportunities for people to influence decision making or contribute ideas for the benefit of the organization (both of which are things that happen in a participatory workplace). Meetings are also opportunities to recognize accomplishments and foster teamwork.

Education and Information

Any information that affects the industry, the local marketplace, the company's customers and clients, or the company's staff falls into this category. There may also be legal developments or litigation issues, financing techniques, development trends, environmental concerns, a sales technique, or an in-house procedure or office system that deserve discussion or a formal presentation. The meeting could also be an extension of the company's training programs or address common weaknesses.

When planning these meetings, ponder these points.

- Do the salespeople need this information to be more effective and efficient? If they do, then the meeting is a valuable use of their time.

- If you don't provide this forum, can you be sure the salespeople will get the information otherwise? Volumes of good tips and information are disseminated at seminars, in professional and business publications, and on the Internet that not everyone (salespeople or managers) sees.

- Are the meetings repetitive? If the agenda is the same old thing, the meetings grow stale after awhile. Take some of the guesswork out of your planning by asking the salespeople for suggestions.

- Are there in-house procedures or office systems that could benefit all personnel (not just the salespeople)?

The manager doesn't always have to conduct the meeting. In fact, it's refreshing to hear a new voice from time to time. The company's training or marketing director, the broker, a salesperson, a representative from the company that's installed a new phone or computer system, a representative from the local school district or municipality, a local builder to discuss a co-op plan, the company's attorney . . . the list of possible speakers is endless.

Handout material is useful for informative and educational meetings. Unfortunately, everyone gathers an enormous amount of paper, most of which ends up in a useless pile on the desk or in a wastebasket. Establish a reference file in the office or scan it into your computer system so that a master set of the information can be accessed whenever it is needed.

As useful as these meetings can be, they are also forums in which discussions can wander into dangerous legal territory. Discussing company listings is permissible as long as information that compromises the principals' positions is not divulged (especially dangerous if disclosed dual agency or designated agency is practiced). Discussions of the company's service fees cannot be allowed to deteriorate into any activity that could be construed as price fixing.

Attitude and Recognition

A celebration can be planned around most any positive thing that happens to individuals or the company. While most companies have programs to award production, other accomplishments like obtaining a broker's license, a professional designation, a chairmanship or an office in a professional association, or participation in a community service organization are worthy of recognition.

Presenting individual awards in a public forum gives the achievements the recognition they deserve. The risk, however, is that the people who are never recognized tire of being ignored, so while the awardees get their strokes, others are being alienated. Management needs to think about ways to recognize worthy accomplishments by people who aren't always the top producers.

When the company has had a banner year, everyone in the company (down to the receptionist) should be recognized for their collective contributions. If it's the beginning of a new year, plan a rally to mobilize everyone around the company's objectives and financial goals. Or plan a social or athletic event just for fun.

Recall the comments in the first unit about how organizations benefit from team building. Companywide events build camaraderie and foster commitment to the company. (If you manage an office for a large company that doesn't have such an event, hold one just for your office.) Remember that all of the staff (management, support, and administrative personnel, as well as salespeople) play on the same team and should be included in these events.

Meetings of this nature should be upbeat and if the event is worthy of grand celebration, should be held offsite with great fanfare. People should look forward to participating, rather than feeling like they must attend a command performance. The informal, social time before and after the program is an important part of the affair. In large organizations, this is one of the few times everyone gets to "rub elbows" with senior management.

Plan icebreakers and activities to encourage socializing. Many of the people have nothing in common with one another, except that they work together. Give people something to talk about or a fun project, unrelated to business, on which they can work together. Remember, the point is for people to relax and have fun. This also shows that management cares.

Problem Identification

Any number of things can cause consternation in the workplace. Problem identification meetings give people an opportunity to air their concerns about the company, the office, or the business in general. These are prime information-gathering opportunities for management and should be convened several times during the year.

The purpose of a problem-identification meeting is quite clear—to create a forum for people to speak up. Announce its purpose and ask people to come prepared with issues they want to raise. The manager can set parameters (office procedures, the company's advertising program, a particular service the company offers) or state that any topic is welcome. Be sure to include the support staff in some of these meetings as well.

Managers are sometimes intimidated by this type of a meeting, fearing that it will become an unruly gripe session or a shouting match. But these meetings can be very constructive when conducted properly. The key to success is to set rules at the outset.

- Everyone will be given an opportunity to speak.

- Participants will be given a certain amount of time to talk.

- Specify that no evaluations, solutions, long-winded examples, or illustrations are permitted.

- Limit the length of the meeting (which is announced at the outset).

The manager's job is to create a welcoming, risk-free setting and then sit back, listen, take notes, and maintain order. The manager must maintain a nonjudgmental climate and respect people's viewpoints (don't try to argue someone into a change of mind). Generally, people feel freer to express themselves in a group (as opposed to one-on-one with the manager). But if it's likely that people will be hesitant about speaking up publicly, gather written submissions. Then, log them anonymously on a flipchart or whiteboard for the group to see.

The final step before the meeting concludes is to prioritize the issues and gain consensus about which ones should be addressed first. It's not uncommon that many of the issues are interrelated, so major problems are relatively easy to identify.

Perhaps the most important part of a problem-solving meeting is what happens after it's over. People welcome the opportunity to speak up, but they do so because they expect to get someone's attention. Don't brush them off. In other words, if you aren't interested in doing something about people's concerns, then don't ask what they are. Issues that fall under the manager's responsibility are ones the manager owns and must do something about. Other issues must be communicated to the appropriate people in the organization. In either case, people deserve feedback or status reports, especially if they're not going to participate in developing solutions.

Brainstorming

Organizations have a wealth of talent, untapped and often unknown until it's given an opportunity to shine. Brainstorming meetings give people that opportunity to tackle a specific problem or "noodle" an issue. The topic may be something the company brings to staff or one of the topics that was uncovered at a problem-identification meeting.

Brainstorming meetings can be very energizing and enjoyable. Define the issue and then just let the creative energies flow. With many minds in one room, an issue gets analyzed from a variety of perspectives. While it's particularly valuable to have the people who are affected by or most familiar with the subject to be involved, some others who aren't as close to the subject can offer a fresh perspective. One person's idea spurs others, with variations and refinements. The quality and creativity of the dialogue can be impressive.

The manager's job is to list the possible solutions on a flipchart or board and keep the group focused on the most important rule: *no criticism of the solutions is permitted.* Keep the group moving at a fast pace. When they've exhausted all the possibilities, take a break or close the meeting. If that's the end of the exercise, the participants need to be told what management intends to do with all the suggestions and who will make a decision (and when).

Decision Making

These are the participatory decision-making exercises that were discussed in Chapter 4. Decision-making meetings may be called to present a case that management brings to staff, or the meeting may be the next logical step after a brainstorming meeting to either make a decision or make a recommendation for management's consideration. It's important to clearly state at the outset which one of those is the assignment so that people know exactly what will happen with the end product of the meeting.

Generally, these meetings follow the classic decision-making model, with no more than 15 participants involved. (Any larger and it's difficult to reach consensus.) Depending on the nature of the issue, the manager can act as an impartial moderator or participate in the discussions as an equal with the others, in which case the manager has to guard against dominating the process. In either case, the manager is responsible for keeping the group focused on the outcome—a decision or recommendation.

The meeting ends with everyone reaching a conclusion they can live with, even if everyone doesn't fully agree. The goal is to arrive at consensus, not make decisions by majority vote. When the minority loses the vote, anyone who doesn't favor the decision is unlikely to support its implementation. Often, the course of action that has the fewest undesirable consequences is the one the group chooses.

In highly monolithic organizations, decision making, even about relatively insignificant matters, is rarely entrusted to anyone other than senior management or the broker/owner. If this is the culture in your organization, you're not likely to be conducting brainstorming or decision-making meetings.

■ RETREATS

Another forum for engaging people professionally and socially and fostering camaraderie is a retreat. While these require considerable planning and expense on the part of the company and commitment of time on the part of the people who attend, they offer benefits far beyond the program agenda.

Despite the fact that you're attempting to build a team, the reality is that salespeople rarely see one another aside from periodic staff meetings. This isolation is increasingly more common because of home-officing. A retreat is an opportunity to draw all of the full-time and part-time salespeople and support staff together. One of the reasons people enjoy professional meetings and education courses is the opportunity to brainstorm with other real estate professionals. When conducting a retreat, the company is creating such an opportunity within its own organization.

One of a meeting planner's greatest challenges is gathering a captive audience together without telephones, appointments, or office business to distract people. Take them to a conference facility and perhaps an overnight stay. Once people are totally immersed in the subject of the meeting, it's surprising how much can be accomplished, especially brainstorming and decision making. Give people a problem today and by tomorrow they'll have a solution, including a plan for implementation.

There are a variety of purposes that a retreat can serve. Wrap up last year and kick off the new year; develop a strategic plan; strategize the design of a new system, service, or department in the organization; develop a business plan for the year; or conduct management or sales training.

The purpose of the retreat will determine who attends and the length of the time for the program. The entire organization can be assembled for an educational forum or motivational rally (a miniconvention for the company), or assemble only management or certain department personnel. Planning the facilities, the program, food service, and other accommodations for a retreat is a major undertaking. But it's worth the effort to accomplish more in a shorter period of time than is possible in other forums.

■ PERSONAL INTERACTION

Although group forums offer many advantages, they are not a substitute for personal contact between the manager and an individual salesperson or other staff member. One-on-one interaction is an important part of professional development. Each person has individual needs, problems, and aspirations. The manager should not be hovering or micromanaging (overseeing every detail of every task) but does need to be accessible and attentive when called on. Seek out staff members periodically for personal consultation (a major subject of next chapter's discussion).

■ ADDITIONAL OPPORTUNITIES

The discussion to this point has focused on the internal environment the company creates to empower people to do their jobs. But there are a number of opportunities for people to enhance their competency outside the organization as well. In fact, a company that is committed to professional development encourages people to seek out these opportunities and often grants paid days off and/or subsidizes tuition and registration costs for employees to attend professional programs.

People gain as much from associating with other professionals with similar interests as they do from the actual education and training that can be gained. There are organizations and councils for brokers and managers, educators and trainers, marketing and advertising specialists, accountants, secretaries professional women, and business owners. People should be encouraged to explore opportunities beyond forums that focus on real estate.

The obvious forums for furthering education and training include colleges, universities, real estate schools, and professional organizations, but there are also self-training opportunities available online and through correspondence courses. Professional organizations conduct seminars, training programs, and more intense courses related to their members' activities, including designation programs.

The National Association of REALTORS® research group reports that salespeople who have designations from its institutes, societies, and councils earn more money. Most every real estate activity has related designations or organizations, including residential sales, buyer-agency, appraising, property management, nonresidential brokerage and management, counseling, and investment and international brokerage.

■ CONCLUSION

When people feel satisfied with their jobs, the place in which they work, and the progress they are making toward their career goals, they can be more productive for the company. Professional competency is about creating opportunities for people both to gain proficiency in the skills they need for their jobs and to influence their quality of life at work. The company that supports continuous learning opportunities is also able to retain key talent. Exposing the company's personnel to a broad range of business education and professional associations adds a dimension to the organization as well as to the individual jobs people do.

■ DISCUSSION EXERCISES

What are the most important things a new hire should know about your company that should be included in an orientation program?

From your experiences in training programs, what would you like to see your company do in the programs it conducts for new salespeople? For experienced salespeople?

Select one type of sales meeting and develop an agenda and a plan for promoting the meeting. Discuss your rationale for your selection and a plan for conducting the meeting.

From your experiences with sales meetings, either as a participant in a sales meeting or the person in charge of one, describe one of the best and one of the worst meetings. What happened that made the good one good and what made the other one bad?

CHAPTER SIXTEEN

16

COACHING
PERFORMANCE

How does the manager contribute to performance? And evaluate
performance?

How does the manager affect the retention of personnel?

A company flourishes when its managers build partnerships with the individual people on their staffs. This part of management's job is the interpersonal role of a manager (back to Chapter 3). The job is captured as "coaching" because, like an athletic coach or personal trainer, it provides feedback to help people develop their strengths and correct their weaknesses. In that sense, coaching is another way to deliver training and foster professional development.

The coaching role also requires a manager to be a leader, counselor, negotiator, and arbitrator. This is about management's taking responsibility for the workplace environment, solving problems, and negotiating solutions so that people can be productive. (The systems don't run people; people run the systems.) In human resource management parlance, this is the part of the job that's characterized as "people are a lot of work." But it's a very necessary part of management's function, all to the end of the company's goals.

The company needs a team that pulls together, but the team members also need to feel a sense of accomplishment in the process. When management provides feedback, people feel like something more than the means to the end, the company's bottom line. Managers who respect and value the people they supervise build trust and loyalty, which contributes greatly to the company being able to retain its valued resource.

While feedback is one of the most constructive ways to reward hard work, increase job satisfaction, and minimize turnover, management can do some (pretty dumb) things that are counterproductive. Making up different rules for different people, making up new rules for everyone because of the failings of a few, treating people as though they can't be trusted, and chastising poor performance when people didn't know exactly what was expected of them are but a few of the ways to upset the workplace. Best to think of these when setting foot in the office to resolve the latest problems.

■ MANAGING EMPLOYEES AND INDEPENDENT CONTRACTORS

Managing in today's real estate office involves supervising employees and, most likely, also independent contractors. It's important to understand the difference. From a management perspective, the essential difference is the degree of control that the company can exercise over activities, which has particular significance for preserving an IC relationship.

Step out of the real estate business and think about the working relationship that exists between employers and a large portion of this country's work force. The company directs the hours people are expected to work, meal times, allotments for vacation and personal days, meetings they are required to attend, and just about every other activity employees are expected to perform. This is a very structured environment, even in a participatory work culture, but one that gives the company control over the methods employees use to perform their jobs.

Independent contractors, on the other hand, work in a much less structured environment. An IC agreement is a service-for-hire contract in which the company engages the IC to achieve certain outcomes or objectives. The independent contractor controls the methods used to accomplish these objectives. A written contract, similar to the one that appears in Chapter 14, is used to define the responsibilities of the IC and the company, but the contract cannot unduly restrict the independent contractor's methods.

The end result of an IC agreement is that management cannot impose but can *recommend, suggest,* or *encourage* certain behavior. The IC is in control of conference or vacation schedules, daily activities (the number of sales calls, listing presentations, or open houses), and the properties and buyers the IC services. *The company can't have life both ways.* That is, it can't enjoy the financial benefits of hiring ICs while managing them as employees. One of the situations currently threatening the IC-employee line is the practice of pressuring their salespeople to do business with (or refer business to) the company's affiliated business enterprise.

Outsiders (those not involved in the real estate industry) look at the construct of staffing the core of a company's work force with ICs as a rather odd way to run a company. IC implies that workers are temporary, on board only as long as the contracts are in force, which is a challenging way to sustain continuity in operations and revenue. ICs are also considered organizational outsiders, yet in real estate companies ICs conduct business on the company's behalf and have a full complement of support services in the same way employees customarily do.

The point to be made is that the real estate workplace model is an anomaly (though traditionally it has been a successful one) that poses unique management challenges for companies whose sales force is IC. Sustaining the company's operations and revenue means assembling a stable army of independent workers and corralling that independence so that the company's services can be delivered in an effective and professional manner and achieve the company's goals.

The key is an *effective* (not controlling) manager, the coach who is engaged with the sales force and constantly strives to foster their professional growth. Some managers give up, feeling that ICs are so independent that there's little point in trying to supervise them at all. But the end result of that attitude is scattered or sporadic attempts by salespeople who receive little direction, motivation, or guidance. Managing ICs really requires the most astute people-management skills.

■ PERFORMANCE MANAGEMENT

The goal of management is to forge a psychological contract between the company and the individual workers, a key factor in the relationship between the company and both employees and ICs. The contract arises from the company's providing compensation, career enhancement, and quality in work life and the worker contributing his or her skill, reasonable time and effort, and extra effort when needed. The basis of a psychological contract is commitment, with both the company and the worker making a commitment to one another.

In this sense, performance is a two-way street. The company must uphold its end of the bargain by providing the leadership and supportive, energized work environment that attracted people to it as the employer of choice. The workforce has its obligations to discharge the responsibilities of the jobs for which they have been hired.

The two-way street becomes one way, though, as the ultimate responsibility for workforce performance is the company's (back to the company's part of the bargain). The company is responsible for removing barriers like inefficient company procedures, conflicts among workers, deficiencies in skills or abilities, or ineffective leadership that inhibits performance. Interestingly, a major barrier is the failure to articulate exactly what that performance should be.

Performance management consists of identifying performance criteria and then using that criteria to encourage, improve, evaluate, and reward performance. This is the basis of management's coaching and professional development efforts, advancement and pay decisions, and disciplinary actions or termination decisions.

Performance Criteria   Companies prepare business plans to direct company performance. The company's personnel need similar direction so they know what they are supposed to do to contribute to the organization's game plan. This is not a matter of handing a person a job description and saying, "Here, do this," or waving an IC agreement and saying, "Produce this much." A job needs to be broken down, much like a business plan, into specific outcomes or benchmarks that tell people what is expected of them.

Performance criteria generally have results-oriented and behavior-related components that are tied to a position's job description (including necessary skills and abilities) and the company's business strategies and priorities. Performance criteria must focus on the most important aspects of a job and then be linked with measurable outcomes so that the person knows the *standards* for satisfactory performance.

Not all outcomes are measured numerically, as in the production of "x" number of sales units. An outcome may be to follow required procedures or to observe the company's consumer service standards. The important point is to be specific, even if not numerical.

Performance standards must be developed for everyone in the organization, from the maintenance staff to the top executives and everyone in between. Typically, there are criteria for all personnel in the same job category plus specific criteria for individuals. The process of developing standards is as important as the end result, that being the written words. (Yes, put all of this in writing.) These should be developed from one-on-one discussions, generally at year-end in preparation for the coming year, between worker and supervisor (such as salesperson and sales manager). Several things to keep in mind about the process:

- Discussion of past performance is an opportunity to praise, listen to frustrations, and identify enhancement of skill or competency that can be incorporated in the coming year's performance standards.

- Targets for future performance must be realistic. High performance standards are desirable for professional growth and organizational accomplishments, but arbitrary or overstated outcomes set up a person for failure. Targets must be tailored to the capacity of each person and that individual's experience and skill level.

- The process of developing standards creates an opportunity to achieve buy-in, meaning that people support a plan they have an opportunity to influence. Often, people have valuable insights or suggestions for performance that the supervisor may have overlooked as well.

During the development of performance standards, several things about the people the manager supervises become very evident. Some are high or overachievers and will work toward commensurately high accomplishments, while others are focused on basic food and shelter or just want to still have a job next year. Others are hesitant to set their sights at any point out of fear of failure, feeling that if nothing's said, then any performance is a plus. The manager's job is to help resolve those underlying concerns so that collective individual performance achieves the company's goals.

People want direction and a fair shot at proving themselves, but setting performance standards can be intimidating. They represent commitments, and because they are written and someone else (the manager or supervisor) knows what they are, people can't wiggle out from under the obvious when the time comes to evaluate performance. Performance standards are only as constructive as management's willingness to support and encourage people to reach those targets.

Personal Business Plans

A personal business plan is a *holistic* approach to performance that incorporates job performance standards and professional accomplishments in a plan that resembles the structure of a company's business plan. Goals are converted to specific, measurable goals and strategies along with timeframe benchmarks for accomplishing the goals. Personal business plans are powerful tools for salespeople to self-direct and for management to coach performance. Managerial personnel often also prepare personal business plans.

Personal plans are developed one-on-one as part of the performance standards discussion. The process and rules for developing performance standards apply to personal business plans as well. (*Professional Real Estate Development* by Patrick Keigher and Joyce Emory, listed in the bibliography, is useful for developing personal business plans.) This is a team effort, with the manager providing guidance so that the company's issues are addressed in the development of each salesperson's personal plan. If the salesperson is an IC, *mutual agreement* over performance standards is essential.

From a production standpoint, the manager can identify what needs to be done based on the company's business plans and budgets. In the example in Figure 16.1, the total amount of revenue the office expects for the year is $350,500. Notice that for two quarters of the year, the example shows actual production in the previous year and the goals that ten salespeople are expected to reach in the coming year as the responsibility for the $350,500 is distributed.

Personal plans convert these production goals into individual accomplishments. Any number of other goals can also be developed in a salesperson's plan, ranging from improving the transaction fall-through rate to obtaining an industry designation. Plans help people manage their time by prioritizing activities so they can focus on those that directly relate to

FIGURE 16.1

Annual Office Production Goals, 2002–2003

Name	1st Quarter 2002 Actual	1st Quarter 2003 Goal	2nd Quarter 2002 Actual	2nd Quarter 2003 Goal	Total Year 2002 Actual	Total Year 2003 Goal
FORD	5,000		5,800		24,000	
		7,500		9,000		30,000
SMITH	8,000		4,700		29,000	
		8,000		5,500		35,000
ADAIN	5,000		6,000		30,000	
		8,000		8,000		37,500
DINKEL	7,500		8,000		34,000	
		11,000		10,000		40,000
FRANKS	5,500		4,200		26,900	
		6,000		6,000		30,000
RIGGS	9,500		9,500		48,000	
		10,000		10,000		50,000
KEAST	13,000		0		39,800	
		12,000		10,000		60,000
JONES	2,100		4,000		8,100	
		2,000		4,000		18,000
COSTA	5,500		3,300		25,600	
		6,000		6,120		24,000
BOWERS	0		3,000		13,000	
		6,000		6,000		24,000
COMPANY	10,766	130,500		127,500	278,300	350,500

achieving their goals. The manager's role is to support the implementation of a person's plan.

Performance Feedback

Providing feedback is management's coaching job. Perhaps the most important time a manager devotes to his or her job is the *hour* spent *each quarter* during the year with each person he or she supervises. Although this may sound like a Herculean task considering the scope of a manager's responsibilities, the one-on-one time with personnel is the most valuable. In fact, one of the manager's performance standards is often tied to quarterly meetings with each person on his or her staff.

Any one-on-one time is worth the time for building relationships, gathering information, identifying problems, praising accomplishments, and picking up on deficiencies. Performance feedback is essentially a periodic performance review, with the performance standards being the script or the talking points to gauge how people are doing and ways either they or management need to adjust so that people and the company will be on target at year-end. The point is not to wait until the end of the year to talk to people about what they should have been doing.

As in other management efforts previously discussed, management shouldn't ask what to do to support people and performance unless management is willing to take the words to heart and follow through. Or to at least investigate and then explain what's practical and impractical for management to do. The failure of management to provide feedback in this case is as counterproductive as failing to ask in the first place.

Performance Incentives

Some people can thrive simply on self-satisfaction, but people deserve the company's acknowledgment of their efforts. Incentives are ways for companies to recognize performance and in so doing, encourage people to keep going. Because people's motives for working and responses to recognition differ, companies generally employ a variety of incentives to reward and inspire people.

Incentives need to contribute to the quality of life in the workplace. The downside of some incentives is that they can have the opposite effect. Incentives that single out certain people can damage the team spirit companies try to build. Some incentives are so predictable that people come to expect them, which means they are no longer incentives.

Status.   The purpose of status incentives is to reward or inspire initiative or to give special skills or abilities an opportunity to shine. The company can do this in a variety of ways, such as by:

- Assigning a salesperson with exceptional skills to be a mentor or partner for a newly licensed salesperson (as was mentioned in Chapter 15).

- Asking a person with good writing skills or a background in publishing to be the editor of the company's newsletter.

- Assigning someone to oversee staff in the manager's absence.

- Inviting someone to make a presentation at a company meeting.

- Assigning a person to chair a special project task force or a problem-solving project.

These incentives are an effective way to foster professional growth, but they can disenfranchise equally skillful or deserving people unless management makes such opportunities part of the company workplace routine. Management must also guard against violating equal employment laws when selecting people for these opportunities.

Some special assignments deserve compensation. One of the gripes people have in the workplace is the tendency of companies to pile on responsibilities without giving people commensurate job titles or additional compensation. Status incentives are intended to encourage people to take initiative and develop recognition-worthy talents. The shining persons who are singled out as well as others the company is trying to inspire won't be flattered by the opportunity if they feel they are being used.

Pick people wisely. Some people will help themselves to more than the company intended once given the opportunity. The person who is just waiting to be sales manager for a day may not be willing to relinquish the position or could undermine the manager's authority once that day is over. A good idea could fuel office politics and power plays that could disrupt office harmony. Be very clear about the details of the assignment and the limits of authority.

Contests.   Contests intend to increase production with valuable recognition or reward to the victors. Not all companies agree on the value of sales contests, and indeed, there are some ways that contests can backfire.

Good-natured, spirited competition can turn into a nightmare for management if people are inclined to try winning at any cost. Unless the contest is structured properly and the manager is prepared to manage the situation, the contest can result in controversy over sales leads, an increased number of disgruntled sellers or buyers, or more overpriced listings than the company wants to advertise.

As companies try to foster team building and more salespeople are structuring their own sales teams, the playing field for contests changes. Pitting individual salespeople against one another can destroy the close-knit crew in a sales office, and unless all the salespeople are assigned to teams, production outcomes are not comparable.

Production contests tend to be biased, with the top producers typically being the same people who always win. The message to others is that their contributions aren't valuable so there's little reason trying to compete. Contests must be structured so that people with differing levels of experience or expertise can compete on similar levels.

Finally, there is the prize and the debate over whether the prize or the recognition is the incentive. Winning is recognition. A prize needs to be valuable (which usually also means costly), but it may not be universally appealing unless the company is willing to trade for equivalent value (the Caribbean or Hawaiian vacation for cash). An inexpensive or unique prize (the pressure cooker) has humorous value, and while fun is good for reducing tension and building camaraderie, that's a different goal than is intended for a true sales contest.

Awards.   Awards to the listing leader, the sales leader, or the outstanding customer-service person are typical, be they a nameplate added to a plaque in the reception area or a trophy that moves from desk to desk each month. While these are useful ways to recognize accomplishments, awards are so common that they suffer the predictability downside (the same people always win) and are little incentive unless they are also showcased for marketing purposes or backed up with a monetary award.

Award programs can polarize the sales force into two groups: the "outstandings" and the "also-rans." The "outstandings" compete with one another, trading a trophy back and forth. The "also-rans" don't even bother trying. Eventually awards can become meaningless, or even embarrassing to the person who constantly wins. This is not to suggest that the leader-of-the-month award should necessarily be eliminated, but consider other programs as well.

Job-Performance-Based Pay.   One of the options when the company develops its compensation policies is a job-performance-based, variable pay plan (which was discussed in Chapter 13). The assumption is that this plan is a reward for past performance and an incentive to perform well in the future. The major downside to performance-based pay is that people may work harder with good purpose than is reflected in their paychecks.

In the previously mentioned types of incentives, people are certainly entitled to fairly administered incentives. But when it's time to administer performance-based pay, the company has an unequivocal obligation to ensure that the pay is properly benchmarked to performance. The company can make or break its reputation as an employer of choice when paychecks are handed out, and it is in a vulnerable position with respect to equal employment laws unless it has defensible evidence to justify pay decisions.

Incentive pay must be based on the performance standards previously developed. Performance based on revenue production, which affects commission splits and bonuses, is relatively easy to gauge. Defects in the performance assessments are usually numerical rather than managerial and can be avoided with clearly stated numerical-based performance criteria at the outset and scrupulous record keeping.

Other performance must also be clearly measured against the performance standards, some of which may not be numerically stated. A standard that relates to company policies, customer service, improving on fall-through rate, and the like requires supportive evidence so that management can legitimately reward performance.

Negative Incentives. Some managers see fear, embarrassment, reprimand, and criticism as incentives for people to change behavior, that if an experience is sufficiently unpleasant, people will strive to avoid similar unpleasantness in the future. Yelling at the salesperson who hasn't had a listing in three months, and doing so in front of the entire staff, certainly lets everyone know what the manager thinks. But it's embarrassing to be the subject of ridicule, especially in front of others, and also insulting, as if the salesperson isn't already aware of the listing deficiency.

Negative incentives do more harm than good. At best, they work only momentarily. The subject salesperson may get out of the office in a hurry, *perhaps* to find a listing but more likely just to get out of the line of fire. Relationships suffer, including the manager's relationship with others in the office, and create an antagonistic atmosphere that takes far more time to repair than it took to create. Certainly, this does not provide the quality of life in the workplace and the respected leadership people want.

■ PERFORMANCE APPRAISALS

Performance appraisals, also known by various other names like *performance evaluations* and *performance reviews*, consist of a two-step process of rating individuals' performance and then communicating and managing with that information. Performance appraisals are generally viewed as formal, year-end activities that provide information for administrative purposes (such as compensation, advancement, and termination decisions) and for personal development (identifying strengths, weaknesses, and professional development).

Year-end performance appraisals focus on personnel performance, but the information also tells management and the company how they are doing and helps plan for the next year. The premise behind quarterly performance reviews is that they are tools for management to coach performance during the year and to monitor company performance and any necessary corrective actions that may be needed along the way to the year's end. There should be no great surprises when formal appraisals are done at the end of the year, other than perhaps how well people performed.

The basis of performance evaluations is the performance standards that were developed. The legal reality of evaluations is they must be clearly job-performance, not personality or character assessments, and must be fairly and equitably administered for each person. Otherwise, the company can have significant legal exposure when personnel decisions are made. The practical reality is evaluations provide much useful information for

- merit or performance adjustments in wages, salaries, and variable pay;

- identifying candidates for promotion (or demotion) to other positions in the company or for termination;

- identifying situations in which a person's skills are better suited for a different job in the company;

- determining whether management's expectations of people are unrealistic, which will be obvious if *everyone* is performing poorly in certain areas;

- determining job descriptions that may need to be revised based on changes in the marketplace, in the company's business plan, and in jobs of other personnel; and

- determining the effectiveness of training programs, hiring procedures, and company policies and procedures and any revisions that may be necessary.

Rating Performance

Rating is a process of evaluating performance in relation to the standards, which are benchmarks for satisfactory performance. Rating can be done independently by the manager (working through all of an individual's performance criteria), or the individual can prepare a self-evaluation. In either case, the criteria and the standards are developed at the beginning of the year, not dreamed up after the fact, and are tailored to expectations for each individual within an individual company. Sample performance evaluations and self-evaluation instruments that can be suitably tailored are available on the Internet.

One way to evaluate is with a rating scale, which is a process of determining numerical values for various levels of performance. These quantitative measures are used to rate each criterion, and then the scores are totaled.

- A scale of 1 to 5 would mean that a 3 is satisfactory and a 5 is the highest. This is a quantitative and straightforward method.

- A scale of 1 to 10 would peg satisfactory at 5 or 6 and a 10 at the highest. A 1 to 10 scale is a more finite assessment of performance, which provides more options but is more difficult to use and defend. (What's the measurable difference between a 6 or a 7, or a 7 and an 8?)

An alternative is to rate performance as "meeting expectations," "exceeding expectations," "outstanding," and "below expectations." This rating process is easy for people to understand and for managers to use (eliminating arguments over a rating of 6 instead of 7). After each criterion is evaluated, overall performance can be evaluated similarly. This rating method is preferable to the less defensible and more subjective "outstanding," "good," "fair," "needs improvement," or "poor" assessments. Does "good" mean a person met the standard for performance, which is a good thing? Or is "fair" satisfactory or O.K.?

As objectively and quantitatively as a manager tries to evaluate performance, subjective factors can easily influence ratings and result in the manager being more critical of some people and more lenient with others.

- The star producer has a lousy year. The tendency is to overlook this year's performance because of past production. Unless this year doesn't count for everyone, then the evaluation is not even-handed, though the people who did improve will resent the lack of acknowledgment.

- Managers often have better relationships with some people than with others, and some personalities are more likable or abrasive than others. But these are personality issues that have no place in objective measures of performance.

- There's a tendency to overlook people's weaknesses that are similar to the manager's and to be overly critical of people whose weaknesses the manager doesn't have. Managers who are perfectionists tend to be overly critical of everyone. Criticism isn't part of performance.

Often, there are variables (like economic conditions or dramatic changes within the company) that affect performance that are beyond the worker's control. These should have been identified during performance meetings earlier in the year so there should be no surprises. Management could be hardheaded and say that true professionals can rise above these situations, but that's unrealistic and unfair. Management must take these into account and not penalize people's performance ratings.

One of the most interesting ways to evaluate performance is to ask people to do *self-evaluations* using one of the rating systems previously described. Sometimes people are far more critical of their performance than the manager might be. Self-evaluations also reveal what matters most to people about their performance and provides insight that management may not have about what people are doing. Often, several open-ended questions are included so that people can express their thoughts about job satisfaction, pay, and the like.

Performance Interviews

The purpose of a performance interview is for the manager and the person to objectively discuss the performance evaluation, whether it be one the manager prepared ahead of time or the person's self-evaluation (and both may be used for interesting comparison). The outcome of the meeting is mutual understanding of the evaluation results and a plan for the coming year.

Although people may have some trepidation, these are not confrontational interrogation sessions. The manager must set a calm, objective tone for the meetings and put people at ease.

- Follow the performance standards "script." It is essential to keep these interviews on track to make efficient use of time. These meetings generally take about an hour.

- As each of the performance criteria is addressed, compare the assessments and learn from different perspectives.

- Don't dominate the meeting. It's the other person's forum to speak his or her mind as much as it is the manager's.

- Don't criticize! If the meeting is seen as the manager's opportunity to beat up on the interviewee, there won't be any constructive two-way exchange. The person will just bluff through the meeting until it's over.

- Don't dwell on faults. This is the time to praise accomplishments and develop solutions when someone is straying off track.

- Take notes and stay focused on information that is relevant to a person's job description so as not to stray into topics that could cause legal problems.

The company attorney can advise about legal and ethical requirements when conducting performance evaluations, documenting written and oral statements, and retaining records of the interview.

■ RETENTION

Presumably, the company's work environment that attracts recruits is the environment that will also retain them. But this means that management must continue to cultivate a supportive workplace. This also means that management has some lessons to learn from the people who do leave.

The keys to retention, regardless of the personnel position, are

- realistic job previews,

- good hiring selections,

- positive employer/employee relations, and

- opportunities for career enhancement.

Management is responsible for all of these. People resent being lured by attractive bait, only to find out later that they've been deceived. Although no one can fully anticipate what the working relationship will be, managers need to be honest and realistic when hiring people (realistic job previews) and provide a supportive work environment (career enhancement). The negotiator and arbitrator roles of management resolve conflicts and personnel problems that affect quality of work life.

Employee Relations

Employee relations is about quality of life with the company—the "keep them happy and they will work" mantra.

The most striking example of how well this plays has been showcased by a privately held corporation that operates in a campuslike facility, complete with tennis courts, fully equipped exercise facilities and spa, dining facilities with live piano music, and onsite childcare in which parents can visit throughout the day. Employees are provided meals, health care, and assorted other benefits and have maximum flextime work hours. This is the ultimate model of an employee- and family-friendly workplace.

When asked why the company treats employees so well, the CEO's comment is that this is the right way and it works. People are happy, healthy, relaxed, and highly productive. The company has a major investment in its employees, but the company also has low absenteeism and loses very few of its hires.

Certainly, this model is the exception, but there are elements of this model that are far more common in today's workplace. Companies are more family-friendly than once was the case, more concerned about the general welfare and health and safety of their workers, and more attentive to employee concerns. In short, today's workplace is far more compassionate.

One relatively simple thing management can do to enhance employee relations (and enhance psychological commitment) is to periodically do an *employee survey*. A survey requires some careful planning to elicit useful information, but it is invaluable for finding out what people think about

- compensation policies,

- workplace environment and morale,

- business ethics,

- potential for advancement,

- fairness or evenhandedness in the way management treats people,

- opportunities for professional development, and

- general satisfaction with the company, management, and their careers.

Surveys are essentially management's report cards. Even if there are things that the company cannot afford to do (like better pay or better benefits), there are things that management needs to be doing and saying to enhance understanding and improve the work environment.

Problem Solving

Ask managers in any real estate office how they spend most of their time and they'll say solving problems. Problems may be issues between the manager and a person he or she supervises or issues among workers. In either case, management's objective is to resolve the situation in a manner that is mutually satisfactory. Sometimes this involves a disciplinary meeting and other times the manager has to put on the counselor hat.

Management's Problem.   Recall the discussion in Chapter 3 about assessing behavior and the lessons about ways that managers can effectively address problem behavior. In a real estate office, the most common problems involve real estate transactions and breaches of company policies and procedures. But there are also morale issues (jealousy, commission disputes, personality conflicts, and cliques) that can turn a once positive, energized environment into an unappealing place to work (which is turnover in the making). In the most serious sense, the company could face litigation over employee discrimination and harassment.

■   **CASE IN POINT . . .**   The morning you discover that a salesperson has lost an earnest money check begins by hauling the person into your office. You slam the door and wave the company's policy and procedures manual under the person's nose. You vent: *"Don't you know any better than to be so careless? See what the manual says you're supposed to do with the check. Don't you know how much trouble we can all be in? What if the buyer backs out and we don't have the deposit in our account? I'll take that money out of your next commission check! Now, get out of my office and don't ever let that happen again!"* Okay! Problem identified; problem solved.

In this scenario, the manager identified what happened (the check got lost) and some of the difficulties that could result, but was the problem identified? Maybe the check was simply filed incorrectly by the secretary. Since there was no discussion, the manager doesn't really know what happened. The poor salesperson didn't get in a word edgewise (which may have been better than getting into a shouting match). The manager presented a solution, but it certainly was an ill-conceived one. This encounter missed the mark in a number of ways.

Identifying problem behavior is a necessary part of a manager's job. But managers need to approach this task with a purposeful, constructive plan. Serving notice to a person that he or she has conducted himself or herself in an unacceptable manner is only part of the process. The manager needs a solution or a course of action that corrects the situation and prevents it from occurring again. That solution must be acceptable to both the manager and the "offender," and if several people are offenders, each one must commit to the resolution.

Disciplinary Meetings.   These are commonly known as *disciplinary meetings*. Fundamentally, what the manager is doing is problem solving. An effective disciplinary meeting develops as follows:

- *Identify the problem* before scheduling a meeting. It's obvious that something happened, but the first step is to determine exactly what and identify the appropriate person with whom to address the problem.

- *Study the problem* before confronting the person. This slows you down long enough to gather the facts and describe the situation correctly.

- *Describe the problem* for the person from your point of view. ("As I understand it . . .") Presenting the problem in a descriptive fashion helps the person understand exactly the behavior that is observed. Don't be judgmental or accusatory or try to speculate why. Just provide a factual description.

- *Gather information from the person.* Ask questions. There may be information that you don't know. The meeting may end at this point if you learn that you misinterpreted the event. Be fair and give the person a chance to share some observations.

- *Keep the meeting objective.* This sounds difficult, but the purpose of the meeting is not to prove who's right or wrong, to pass judgment on a person's character, or to clobber a person's self-esteem. Minimize tension and defensiveness. "Yes, you did" and "No, I didn't" won't resolve anything.

- *Don't sugarcoat the problem.* This is not a meeting to praise and then sneak the problem into the agenda. The person needs to know precisely the point of the problem.

- *Agree that a problem exists.* The manager may be the only one who thinks there's a problem. Before the issue can be resolved, the "offender" must agree that this is an issue that needs attention.

- *Develop mutually acceptable alternatives* as possible solutions. The person must participate in this process. The manager is asking the person to change behavior, which means that a solution that is acceptable to the person is more likely to work. However, the manager has the right to veto alternatives that are unacceptable from the company's point of view. The manager must also be willing to contribute to the solution.

- *Agree on a course of action* and the time frame within which the correction will occur. Both of you must select the same course of action from the list of alternative solutions.

- *Agree on a follow-up meeting* at the end of the time frame to be sure that the problem is resolved.

- *Conclude the meeting* once you have agreement. Don't drag it out and cloud the issue.

- *Focus on one problem at a time.* It's tempting to unload on a person and find fault with everything he or she does. But this is not a gripe session. It's a problem-solving meeting.

- *Acknowledge the change.* A manager's job is to praise as much as it is to correct problems, so don't ignore the steps the person takes to correct the problem.

- *Document the proceedings.* Follow the advice of the company attorney as to proper documentation. A disciplinary meeting may be a prelude to more demonstrative discipline or eventual termination. Documentation is critical for the company to defend its actions.

Using this as a guide, how would you handle the scenario of the lost earnest money check?

The Employee's Problem.   The manager may be gliding through the day, feeling that everything in the office is under control. It may not be readily apparent that trouble is brewing, but it's best to be watchful of group dynamics.

- Do people hush as you stroll through the office?

- Is there a clique that huddled together over lunch, particularly after you announced a new office procedure?

- Is there a heated exchange in the back room or by the water cooler?

People must feel free to raise their concerns and *the sooner the better*. They may need a little encouragement like, "I notice that you seem to be . . . Would you like to talk?" or "How can I help?" And the manager has to be willing to listen and accept the fact that he or she may be the cause of a problem.

Give the person an opportunity to describe the problem without interfering or getting defensive. This can be a very emotional or delicate conversation for the person. If the problem is you, don't argue. If the problem is someone else in the office, don't take sides, make excuses, or defend the other person. If the problem is outside the office (with someone in another office, a customer, or the person's private life), listen.

If the manager is the source of the problem, the manager is responsible for the solution. The conversation needs to end with a description of what the manager intends to do to handle the situation and a commitment to that course of action. The manager only makes matters worse if the person feels that frustrations have fallen on deaf ears or that the manager is just placating him or her to get the person out the office.

If the problem is someone other than the manager, the decision is whether to intervene (the manager takes responsibility for the problem) or to help the person find ways to deal with the situation (the person owns the problem).

■ **CASE IN POINT . . .** The manager's dilemma is similar to that of a parent confronted with two children picking on one another. One child comes with a long tale about what his brother did to him. It could be the child just wanted to air his frustrations and he's totally content to run off and forget the matter or handle the situation himself. Maybe he wants you to go tell his brother off. But this means taking sides (one boy must be right and the other must be wrong) with the risk being that one person is alienated in the process of satisfying the other. Another point to consider is that maybe the reason his brother lashed out is totally justified. Intervention may be condoning unacceptable behavior.

Take this analogy back to the office and put a worker in the child's place. It's possible that all the person wants to do is vent frustrations or use the manager as a sounding board and does not expect the manager to take any action. Or the person may be asking for help, and if so, then the manager needs to be clear about what help is being requested.

If person A asks the manager to intervene in a problem with person B, remember that there are at least two sides to the story. Rather than risk a relationship with both people, it's best to help A find a solution first. Depending on the nature of the problem, the manager may decide to have a conversation with B to investigate whether there are also other problems that need to be addressed. B has to be approached objectively so that B doesn't feel that she or he has been the target of A's anger or ridicule. Don't betray confidences. If it's appropriate for the manager to be the negotiator and arbitrator, this means that the manager has to get out of the middle and help A and B find a solution that is acceptable to both of them.

■ RESIGNATION AND TERMINATION

A common law doctrine of employment is *employment-at-will* (EAW). This says that employers have the right to hire, fire, demote, and promote whomever they choose, and that employees have the right to quit whenever they want.

However, at-will is not nearly as simple as it sounds. At-will carries with it a covenant of *fairness* and *good faith* between the employer and the at-will employee, which means that if the employer breaches the covenant with unreasonable behavior, the employee can seek legal recourse. Employment is established by either express or implied contract, which arises from an employee doing the job. Long service and lack of job-performance criticism implies continued employment, which gives recourse to a dismissed employee under EAW.

Independent contractor agreements are typically at-will. Generally, very clearly stated language is included to proclaim the fact that the contract is at-will. This attempts to insulate the employer from claims of wrongful discharge. However, the carefully crafted words won't do much good if the actual practices are contradictory.

The bottom line is that the company door is not as free-swinging as at-will implies, though the scales are tipped in the employee's favor (a result of years of employer abuse). Plus there are equal employment laws to consider, which are also founded on the principle of fairness.

Resignation

The best a company can do to prevent people from resigning is to uphold its psychological commitment to the workforce. But once an employee has decided to leave, it's probably too late to convince him or her to stay. That's not to say that the manager shouldn't explore the person's reason for leaving and where he or she is going, however.

- If the person wants to change specialties or positions, consider finding a new role for the person in the company if that's someone management wants to retain.

- If the person wants to change companies, determine whether there's an internal problem or whether your company is losing its competitive edge over other employers.

Salespeople are more likely to leave because they are dissatisfied with the company's management of personnel (or lack thereof) than because of the company's commission split. According to a study conducted by Abelson & Co., 55 percent of the top producers were dissatisfied because low producers are not terminated, 35 percent cited conflicts with others in the office, and 18 percent cited conflicts with the manager.

To determine if a salesperson is producing a profit, establish the *minimum average production* (MAP) needed from each person. Begin with the desk cost and add a percentage that represents the minimum profit. Divide that figure by the number of salespeople. The result is the MAP, which can then be compared with actual production. Some people consistently fall below the MAP, some are average or above, and others exceed the MAP by a wide margin. Interestingly, the average real estate salesperson earns approximately $30,000 after expenses (according to industry consultants Swanepoel and Tuccillo), which suggests that "average" is not especially lucrative and also suggests that companies may need to be looking more closely at MAP.

As much as the manager may not want to lose a person, it's important to avoid getting into a bargaining position. If there are legitimate changes the company can make, that's fine. But playing favorites to keep people is as bad as playing favorites while they're working.

Sometimes, the person does management a favor by volunteering to leave. If this is the office malcontent or poorest performer, the manager is off the hook for not doing something about that problem sooner. If a person is truly miserable, do that person (as well as the company) a favor and let him or her go. Sometimes, people are just discouraged for the day. (How many times do salespeople "quit" when the business gets frustrating?) Rather than accepting a hasty decision, help the person over the hurdle before taking action.

Finally, graciously send the person on the way. The company that is truly compassionate and committed to professional development supports people's decisions to move on to new job opportunities.

Termination

The really difficult personnel decisions are the ones in which the manager must ask someone to leave. Termination represents failure. Even if the employee failed, the company (or the manager) is still responsible, whether by failure to properly hire, train, or coach. Some managers would rather sweep people out of the office instead of investing time in their professional development. But terminating a person because of the company's failure won't fix the problem.

Common reasons for showing people to the door include lack of productivity, violation of laws, violation of the company's ethics and policies and procedures, or because the employee is a serious personnel problem. Once the decision to terminate is made, the employee should not be surprised. The grounds are problem-oriented and in problem-solving and performance interviews and prior disciplinary discussions.

Companies are often hesitant to discipline out of fear of lawsuits. But managers also feel guilty, fear a loss of friendship, and are sometimes hamstrung by senior management. When companies establish personnel policies and standards of performance, they must enforce them. Often, real estate companies are hesitant to let salespeople go (the notion that one lost is a lost transaction). But, there's little point in expecting performance and then doing nothing when people don't measure up.

Termination is the absolute *final* step of the disciplinary process. The rules for discipline and termination are company policies and procedures that are also spelled out in the employee handbook. (Company rules and IC agreements must be in concert with one another.) The slippery slope out the door is not a direct shot, except in egregious situations. Even in these cases, it's safer to suspend a person from the office temporarily (rather than terminating) and then get direction from legal counsel. Never fire in a huff!

EAW case law provides considerable guidance for developing defensible policies and procedures, but even the practical matter of fairness says that people deserve some warning. Before codifying any policies, be sure that the company attorney has blessed them. Disciplinary and termination procedures generally provide the following steps:

- Investigate and document evidence of the behavior. A performance appraisal is a start. Because a manager can misinterpret behavior, further evidence is needed to verify whether accusations are justified. Investigation must be a fair and impartial inquiry, and all subsequent actions must be applied even-handedly. (In other words, the employer would do the same for any worker in a similar situation.)

- Communicate concerns to the person and describe the behavior. Also inform the person that the situation is serious enough to warrant termination. This is known as a *warning*.

- Develop a plan for corrective action, document the plan, and provide the support and assistance that is necessary to help the person correct the situation. This may be the end of the matter, but documentation should be retained so that if subsequent behavior warrants more serious action, the company has defensible evidence.

- Depending on the employment laws that govern the company (a factor of number of workers and state law), the company may be required to accept a rebuttal or explanation of the event from the employee's point of view and make it part of the personnel file.

- Subsequent behavior is handled following the same procedure as in the first event and may be disposed of with a *second warning* or perhaps a *suspension* for several days.

- Behavior that finally warrants termination should be communicated to the person along with the decision to terminate. This should be done privately and confidentially with a clear description of the reason for termination. Remain calm, firm, and professional. The chances are the person being terminated won't, but that's to be expected.

- Resolve the details for departure, including the date of departure and the way pending business is to be handled. Sometimes companies usher people out the door within the hour, though that's not practical, humane, or necessary unless the person's job position is such that the company is vulnerable to theft or sabotage.

- Protect the firm. Secure the facilities (change locks) and systems (change computer access codes and passwords), and take other actions that the attorney may recommend.

The company attorney is the best adviser, but the heads-up conclusion to this discussion is that disciplinary and termination actions create great liability for the company. The point cannot be repeated often enough about the importance of just cause, due process, and documentation. Without warnings (documented), evidence of the conduct (documented), and fair and even-handed application of rules and penalties, the company is particularly vulnerable.

Exit Interviews

One final and very important step, regardless of whether people leave voluntarily or involuntarily, is an exit interview. This step rarely gets the attention it deserves, but it provides extremely useful information for the company to evaluate its operations, especially personnel and management procedures. Because people who leave the company can be either its greatest advocates or greatest adversaries, one final conversation is an opportunity to promote the former and defuse the latter.

An exit interview is a debriefing session and a time to bring closure to the relationship. Regardless of whether the person resigns or is terminated, there are likely to be loose ends of business to tie up, but most of all, the session provides an opportunity for the manager to listen to what the person has to say. This meeting is usually conducted several days after the employee's last day of work, by which time some of the stress of decision day has worn off.

Regardless of the reasons for ending the relationship, exit interviews can be uncomfortable. The person who's eager to get on with a new job may be just as anxious about returning to the old employer as the person who's been fired. Some exit interviews will go better than others, but the manager must attempt to create an informal, relaxed, compassionate atmosphere.

The exit interview is the time to listen to what the person has to say about the manager, the company, and the way the resignation or termination was handled. This also tells the manager a little (albeit the sterilized version) of what the person will be telling the community about the company. Don't argue or be defensive, since that's not likely to change anyone's opinion at this point. Even when people have been asked to leave, they often just want to end the relationship as professionally as possible. Then send the person off with best wishes.

Then, sit back and learn from the experience.

■ CONCLUSION

The notion that work isn't supposed to be enjoyable or that the workplace isn't supposed to be pleasant (after all, this is work) says little about the way today's companies operate. Despite all of the difficult personnel decisions management has to make and all the legal issues that are part of the process, the most rewarding part of a manager's job is watching people thrive under the manager's direction. While some of those directions come in the form of formal performance criteria and are faced in performance reviews, the coach, teacher, and counselor part of the job is as energizing for the manager as it is for the people being supervised.

■ DISCUSSION EXERCISES

List at least three things you as the manager can do to help energize and empower your salespeople to be productive and develop professionally.

Discuss your experiences (positive and negative) either with conducting performance reviews or with being reviewed.

Select a problem that you are currently dealing with in your office and discuss how you plan to handle it.

IN CONCLUSION
OF UNIT FOUR

The staffing and directing functions of management are essentially human resource management functions. The organization is prepared to conduct business by recruiting, selecting, and hiring the appropriate personnel, who must now have a workplace environment that is supportive. That means a workplace that fosters professional competency and is free of the barriers that distract or inhibit performance. The responsibility for creating this environment falls squarely on the shoulders of the manager and tests the manager's ability to be a leader, a teacher, a counselor, a negotiator, and an arbitrator.

■ THE SCENARIO

Having read this unit, what is your analysis of the following scenario?

Dale, who is the manager of a single-office brokerage company, came to work one Monday morning after agonizing all weekend, trying to come up with some answers for that morning's meeting with his broker. This once productive and congenial office seemed to be crumbling around him, and Friday afternoon's announcement by two more of his salespeople that they were leaving felt like the final blow. Dale's broker told him that come Monday morning he better have a plan to turn things around and stop the hemorrhaging of the office's bottom line.

Dale was fairly certain that the broker wanted to hear a plan for hiring more salespeople. While that would certainly be appropriate, Dale also knew that there was more to the story that needed to be told. The more he analyzed the state of affairs in recent months, the more troubled he was by a number of situations that had gotten out of hand.

First, there is the office secretary. She is really a very good "Girl Friday," the sole staff person who acts as bookkeeper, telephone answerer, transaction coordinator, and personal secretary for Dale and, on occasion, the broker, whose primary activity is real estate development. At one time, she was a licensed salesperson in the office but because of changes in her personal life, she needed a job with regular working hours and benefits. Dale thought she would be an asset to his office because in addition to having broad clerical skills, she was familiar with the real estate business and the company's operation. Now, after a year and a half, Dale is contending with a secretary who thinks she is the sales manager.

Then, there is the high turnover in the sales staff. This situation had become increasingly problematic in the past six months. Dale was hired three years ago to manage the brokerage business so that the broker could devote more time to his other endeavor. Dale was previously a sales trainer with another real estate company, so when he came on board he instituted a training program and revamped the commission plan. The company successfully recruited salespeople, mostly newly licensed, and succeeded in retaining a core staff of about 15 highly talented, productive people.

That is, until recently. Now down to seven after Friday's announcements, with rumblings that another salesperson might leave as well, the broker's answer is just "hire more." Does the broker have the right solution? Or are there other steps Dale should recommend at his meeting with the broker?

■ THE ANALYSIS

The discussions in this fourth unit should shed some light on Dale's situation. His dilemmas are not atypical, as many sales managers have faced similar situations.

Dale's office problems are a lot easier to avoid than they are to quick-fix. It's very likely that hiring a few people immediately, assuming there is ready, experienced talent willing to step into the firm now, will have, at best, short-term benefit. Even at that, new hires need some settling-in time with a new company, so Dale's office won't feel the benefit of their production for a few months.

Recruiting will be difficult for Dale anyway. He may be able to encourage a few people to come to the company on the strength of his personal reputation as a good trainer. But, the professional grapevine has probably worked over the problems in that office, perhaps to the point that the word is worse than reality.

The first thing Dale should do Monday morning is talk to the salesperson who's rumored to be the next one leaving. What Dale needs to hear first-hand is the reasons for the discontent. The conversation may demonstrate management's attentiveness to the situation and could be a move that could retain the wavering salesperson. Even if the person's beyond retention and does leave, Dale still has some helpful information.

Of course, Dale should have been gathering information all along. Better observation of behavior in the workplace, periodic one-on-one meetings with the salespeople, and an exit interview when the first person took off would have given Dale the heads-up so that he could have nipped the problems in the bud months ago.

One could assume that one of the problems is the secretary, but the exact reasons may be a premature leap to a conclusion. Girl Friday may have taken it upon herself to be sales manager because the salespeople found her to be a better leader than Dale is. If that's the case, Dale should have wised up to that fact a while ago. On the other hand, Girl Friday could be one of those people who, once given a little authority (considering all the hats she wore), simply takes on more. Clearly, the lines of authority are blurred, in any case, and Dale needs to get that straight with Girl Friday.

Otherwise, Dale needs a plan to get to the root of the problems. The first step should be talking one-on-one with the salespeople who are still on board. The point of the meetings is to assess what people think about the company as a place to work and to learn how Dale and the company can support their work. Until this is known, anything else is pure speculation about the secretary, the company's commission plans or services, or Dale.

■ THE SUMMARY

Whether you are the broker/owner, a senior manager in a large organization, a sales manager, or a department manager, your involvement in the various human resources activities will differ. As a guide for understanding your role(s), the following summary is provided.

■ Recruiting, selecting, and hiring the appropriate staff:

- The broker/owner(s) and possibly senior management have previously determined the overall manpower requirements for the organization in the organizing function.

- The broker/owner is normally responsible for selecting and hiring senior management. The broker may also prefer to be an active recruiter for salespeople, depending on the size of the organization and the amount of other responsibilities that have been assigned to the sales manager.

- Either senior management or the broker/owner selects and hires office or sales managers.

- Sales and department managers are normally responsible for recruiting and selecting the staff whom they supervise. The procedures in the organization will dictate whether the manager or someone higher in the organization has the ultimate authority to hire.

■ Creating opportunities for the staff to develop professional competency:

- The broker/owner(s) and possibly senior management are normally responsible for making decisions about the nature of the professional development the company provides and committing the necessary financial resources.

- The department manager, specifically the training director, and the sales managers are actively involved in assessing training needs and developing the orientation and training programs.

- The sales manager is responsible for supporting training and the professional development of the staff in group functions such as sales meetings and in one-on-one involvement with the salespeople. In small organizations the sales manager also may be the trainer.

■ Coaching people to accomplish the company's as well as their own goals:

– Anyone who directly supervises people is responsible for coaching their performance, conducting performance reviews, and handling problems, conflicts, or other issues that directly affect the performance of the people who work for them. In small organizations, the broker/owner may also be the sales manager.

– Depending on the procedures in the organization, the person who supervises an individual may have the authority to terminate a worker. In some organizations this person may need the approval of an individual at a higher level in the organization to do so.

CONTROLLING THE ORGANIZATION

Once a company opens its doors for business and starts all the wheels into motion, the organization takes on a life of its own. It becomes an institution propelled by people, processes, and systems, all churning under the sheer force of their own momentum, the result being that many things are happening in a company at one time, regardless of its size.

Although the functions of management (planning, organizing, staffing, and directing) have been captured in this business management discussion under orderly headings, the real world is that managers' jobs are not so orderly that they can dispense with one and turn the page to the next management function. Management is occupied to some degree by all of these responsibilities all the time, simply because of the magnitude of the various systems, processes, and people the company has empowered.

It's easy for management to get caught up in the day-to-day details and lose sight of the fact that all the energies of the organization have to be controlled. Not that they have to be restricted, but that they need to be steered on the proper course. That course can be as entrepreneurial or as conservative as leadership's plan for the organization. Although most organizations won't stray so far off course that they will run aground in one year, it's easier (and wiser) to keep nudging a company in the right direction than it is to shift to a new course in a short period of time.

The controlling function of management does just that, makes sure that the organization is on course. Management does this by

■ monitoring operations and

■ managing risk.

The purpose of controlling the organization is to protect assets so that the company has the resources to promote growth. The controlling function is not something management does at the end of the year by looking at the latest financial report. Rather, it is a set of systems or procedures that are intended to keep activities on track and provide management with the information needed to periodically evaluate those activities. If management relies only on the accountant to report financial status and the lawyer to bail the company out of trouble, that intervention will be too little too late. It's far more prudent to detect problems early and take corrective action *before* the minus sign appears on the income statement or litigation arises.

CHAPTER SEVENTEEN

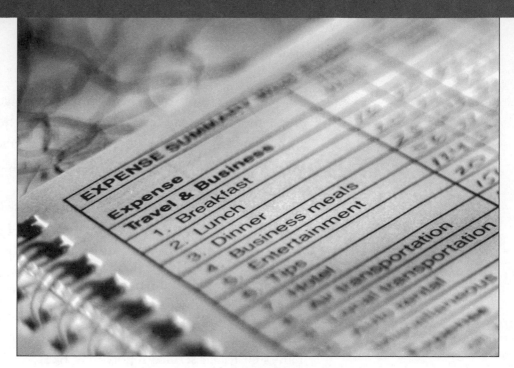

MONITORING OPERATIONS

Do you know how effective your advertising is? Are you over or under budget?

Is your income ahead or behind budget so far this year?

Are your customers and clients satisfied with your service?

The core of the monitoring function of management is information. For the most part, these are statistics and reports, the quantitative evidence that management needs to accurately assess the company's activities.

Today, this job is immeasurably easier because much of that information resides in the company's computer, and with the variety of software that is available, assessments of most anything management wants to know can easily be generated.

However, talk of computers is somewhat of a cart-before-the-horse exercise, because management must first develop procedures to collect the necessary information. Typically, information is gathered with the forms or reports that are the customary routine in the workplace. The success or failure of these procedures, though, is a function of how well they are designed. Management needs the cooperation of everyone in the organization to gather accurate information, so ease and efficiency are critical.

Once gathered, the information must be *used*. Time and money are too precious to bog down the organization with busywork. If the information is worth gathering, it's worth using. Information tells powerful stories that need to be read periodically throughout the year. Is the organization taking all the steps necessary to maximize income? Are expenses under control and as effective and productive as possible? And because the future of the company depends on its reputation with consumers, what does the company's customer service report look like?

■ MANAGEMENT OF INFORMATION

Business enterprises become repositories of huge amounts of information, often because of legal and regulatory requirements. One of management's responsibilities is to ensure that paperwork and data collection and retention procedures comply with the laws (especially relevant to license law). Guidance of legal counsel and an accountant is valuable for identifying bank statements; wage, salary, and salesperson compensation records; legal correspondence; tax returns; and other records that should be retained.

Lurking in those files and others is a vast amount of information that is very useful for monitoring the company's activities. The information that usually comes to mind is the financial data that can be assembled from general ledgers, accounts payable, accounts receivable, payroll records, and commission records plus various budgets. There is also a lot more information that can reveal the health or well-being of the organization.

The value of information is only as good as the data that are assembled. When the company selects software and powers up its computer system, decisions are made about what management wants to learn from the data. The object of data collection is to gather information that is

- accurate,

- complete, and

- timely.

Missing, inaccurate, or stale information skews the picture and can cause management to get exercised over bad news that really isn't all that serious or to rejoice over good news that really isn't that rosy. In either event, management can make faulty decisions because of faulty information and set the organization on an inappropriate course.

The information that is important to management is typically inconsequential to the people management counts on to fill out the forms. Forms and reports must be easy and efficient to use (keep paperwork reduction in mind), and procedures, including timeframes, for completing the documents must be established. Making the disbursement of a commission check dependent on a transaction file being completed (or some other conditional action) is one way to get people to cooperate.

A number of people, including salespeople and support staff, are likely to be handling documents, money, files, and computer input. An *office procedures manual* should be developed to

- manage the flow of information and paper, including *what, where, how, when,* and *by whom* forms, reports, documents, and data are processed.

- specify who has access to what data and files to ensure that accuracy and confidentiality (where appropriate) are protected. Procedures should specify what must remain onsite, what is permitted offsite (including in the salespeople's possession), and what information can be released (and by whom) to outsiders. Because of the increasing number of incidents of identity theft, it's important to ensure that personal information is protected in a secure environement.

- maintain and retain data, files, and records as required by law.

**Transaction or
Service Files**

Transaction files should be sufficiently complete to comply with license law, including contracts, disclosures, closing cost statements and escrow documents, and evidence that documents have been properly delivered to the signatories. These files must be retained for the time period required by law.

The company may also require other documents, reports, or correspondence to be included in transaction files. They are essential for defense in the event of litigation, but as a practical matter, they provide the information management needs to solve problems and resolve controversies so that matters don't rise to the point of litigation.

Because state license law is usually quite specific about the way escrow funds must be handled, transaction files should include a paper trail (like transmittal forms) to trace funds from the time they are received by the salesperson through each step along the way until funds are deposited (either by the company or a cooperating broker) and then released.

All of this documentation puts the company on sound footing with respect to legal issues, but transaction files also provide a lot of information about the organization's listing and sales activities. If the company is using transaction management software, the salespeople or support staff can easily assemble this information.

Listing Activities.   Management can monitor the effectiveness of listing activities by looking at the listing dates and prices in comparison with the results of the contracts.

- How long are listings on the market?

- What's the difference between the listing and the actual selling price?

- How many listings terminated or expired?

- What is the source of the listing contacts?

- Where are the listings located?

Management can gauge overall company performance as well as the production and effectiveness of individual salespeople.

Sales and Closing Activities.   When the pending sales files are compared with the closed transaction files, management can learn how well buyers and sellers are being serviced and identify the effect of conditions in the marketplace on the company's business. One of the most significant pieces of information is the cause of contracts failing to go to settlement. In many cases, the manager knows the stories intimately because these are problem transactions that the manager had to help nurture and defuse along the way.

- Were buyers not properly qualified?

- Are appraisals coming in low?

- Are there problems with home inspection reports?

- Are certain types of mortgage loans or lenders a problem?

- Did buyers feel deceived, or were there misrepresentations?

- Are contracts being lost because contingencies aren't being satisfied?

- Were there defects in the way contracts were prepared?

- How well were transactions prepared for settlement?

A seemingly smooth transaction can suddenly explode at settlement only because a minute but important detail was overlooked. If the company does not have a transaction coordinator on staff, all of these details become the salespeople's responsibilities. Monitoring settlements identifies tasks that are overlooked and procedures that are needed to correct problems. This is the final step in the transaction when the company's public relations are on the line.

Once transactions close, management has valuable information about the sources of buyers, the productivity of a referral or relocation network affiliation, the in-house versus cooperating-broker transactions, transactions in which a buyer was a client or a customer (depending on the company's policies), and trends in market values, financing, and the pace of the market.

License Records

Good license management procedures are critically important for the company to provide its real estate services. *No one* should be permitted to perform activities for which a real estate license is required until that license is properly issued. There are procedures for license applications, renewals, transfers, and departing licensees, as well as license requirements for the company's real estate offices.

Although a staff person could be assigned the responsibility of tending to the paperwork, the broker is ultimately responsible for seeing that all requirements are satisfied. The broker also should review the license records periodically to ensure that the company is in compliance with all of the requirements.

Personnel Records

Individual personnel files are important from a legal as well as a practical point of view. Personnel files become a history of a person's affiliation with the company and provide information managers need to know about the people are they are supervising. Personal data; employment applications; independent contractor agreements (if applicable); wage, salary, or commission records; manager's notes and reports from interviews with personnel; performance reviews; and other information the company lawyer recommends should be in the files. Because this is personal data, procedures are needed to limit access to the files to preserve confidentiality.

Closely related to this subject are the company's referral rotation procedures. One of the greatest sources of controversy in a real estate office is the distribution of referrals and leads. The company should have clear procedures (that are publicized and followed) for distributing and tracking referrals. Keep a master ledger as these assignments are made, and also record them in each salesperson's file so that authoritative documentation is available.

■ MANAGING WITH INFORMATION

Typically, senior management reviews the balance sheet, cash flow statement, and income statement, comparing the actual figures against the budget each month. Office managers, division managers, and other staff people usually are responsible for doing likewise, particularly as the reports relate to their areas of responsibility.

Monthly review shows trends in the flow of money and production activity, and by watching these trends, management can take corrective actions during the year if warranted. If there are major deviations from income or expense projections, these may be occurrences that management anticipated and had prepared contingency plans to address. Otherwise, the discussions later in this chapter that relate to maximizing income and minimizing expenses will be particularly useful.

Managing with information also means using what management learns to periodically review (perhaps quarterly) the company's business plan for the year. While a budget intends to keep the financial resources on track, the business plan intends to keep all of the company's activities focused. By looking at the year's goals in comparison with year-to-date company performance (service-related or other strategic initiatives), management can see which efforts are on track and those that need to be enhanced.

Although monitoring the organization is a management function, the company's workforce (especially the salespeople) can provide a lot of useful insight. Feedback gathered during quarterly performance reviews can elicit suggestions as to ways the company can work more cost-efficiently and effectively. These are also good topics for engaging people in problem-solving and brainstorming meetings.

■ MAXIMIZING INCOME

It's prudent management to strive to maximize income, regardless of whether the company is meeting projections or needs to take corrective steps to get back on track. Maximizing income should not be overlooked even if the company is ahead of projections, because that may not always be the case.

In a real estate company, the only place to look for income is its services. Depending on the company's focus, that most likely means sales or listings. And the best way to look at those services is from the perspective of quality, as in *the better the quality, the better the income*. It's also a far better use of time to move forward with new transactions instead of unraveling problems with transactions already logged on the books. Often, these are problems that could have been avoided in the first place.

Quality Service Standards

Without satisfied customers, companies don't have loyal customers or the image or reputation that fosters future business. Recognizing this fact, customer satisfaction is a major priority in most business enterprises. Merchants that consumers frequently patronize for their daily needs have more opportunities to satisfy their customers and develop loyalty. But developing loyal relationships with real estate consumers is more difficult, simply because real estate services are not patronized with great frequency. This says that a company has to give it its best shot when it has the opportunity.

That best shot comes when quality service is provided. This means that a company needs to define what constitutes quality service or set standards so that everyone, especially the salespeople, knows what is expected. (They have as much at stake in their success as the company has.) The standards will reflect the company's philosophy of doing business and the nature of the services it provides. Most importantly, quality service standards must become a priority in the company.

The 2002 Profile of Buyers and Sellers (based on 37,000 survey respondents who either bought or sold during 2001) published by the National Association of REALTORS® says a lot about the role of licensees and the link of services, especially for future business. The survey's findings include:

- Sellers of homes typically interviewed just one real estate salesperson before selecting the person who ultimately sold the property.

- Over half of the home sellers chose the salesperson based on prior interaction with the person or based on referral from friends, relatives, or another brokerage company.

- Seven of ten sellers of homes said they would use the same salesperson in future transactions.

- Forty percent of sellers used the same real estate person who assisted them in selling their previous home to help in the most recent purchase.

- Almost half of the homebuyers first find the home they ultimately purchase through the services of a salesperson. (Previously stated in the book is that 41 percent of homebuyers indicated that they used the Internet for property searches before they contacted a real estate company or salesperson.)

- The typical home search took seven weeks, during which the buyer visited ten homes.

- More than half of the homebuyers first learned about their real estate salesperson from either prior experience or referrals.

- More than eight of ten homebuyers received recommendations from their real estate salesperson about sources for other real estate-related services and/or products, with nearly 90 percent of them purchasing at least one product and/or service based on that recommendation.

- Two-thirds of the buyers said they would definitely use the same salesperson again in a future transaction.

The full report can be obtained from NAR's research division. The information is useful for determining who the consumers are, what they want, and ways that real estate professionals can improve their products and services for these consumers.

Servicing Sellers.   For the company that lists property or provides other marketing services for sellers, standards should be developed that make statements about how the company delivers these services. Think about the sellers' most common complaints so that they can be addressed as well.

- Salespeople don't return phone calls.

- Salespeople don't contact sellers frequently enough.

- Sellers don't know what the salespeople are doing to get the property sold.

- Salespeople make promises when the properties are listed that aren't fulfilled.

- The property took too long to sell.

- The settlement didn't go smoothly.

Converting these lessons into standards says that sellers should be provided with an explanation of the listing-to-sales process and what the company and the salesperson intend to do throughout. The better the communications, the fewer the problems. A comparative market analysis and a discussion about contemporary market conditions go a long way toward avoiding unrealistic expectations about prices and the time within which a property will sell.

Factor into this the fact that buyers are using the Internet to avoid paying too much for a property and, consequently, deal from a much stronger negotiating position after logging on to research comparable sales prices and the property's original sale price, mortgage balance, and property taxes. The buyer can also learn when properties are actually selling far below the listing price, which may not be information a seller (or seller's agent) is pleased to have known.

Service standards can incorporate such items as home warranty programs, referral or relocation services, or discount or cross-marketing programs that the company provides. For risk-management purposes, service standards should also include contract preparation and consumer protection issues such as agency, property, and lead-based paint disclosures.

Servicing Buyers.   Customer service standards for buyers are developed in a similar fashion, considering the services the company provides and the factors that influence buyers' choices of property and the kind of professional assistance they desire.

Quality service standards for buyers would also address agency disclosure and contract procedures, standards for preparing and negotiating sales agreements, and assisting the buyer through the transaction to settlement. These could include mortgage financing, home inspections or warranties, insurance, title and settlement services, and services such as referral and relocation and cross-marketing programs. Consumer protection and risk-management procedures, including procedures for documenting the showings, conversations, and negotiations with a buyer, should also be addressed.

Quality Control

Once the company has adopted standards, the next task is to monitor performance. This can be done in several ways. For internal quality control purposes, salesperson activities can be monitored with information in the transaction files. Another way is to incorporate quality service standards in the criteria used for performance reviews. While the most obvious are the salespeople's criteria, everyone involved in any aspect of customer service should be accountable for doing their part.

Customer Feedback.　The company's perception and the public's perception of the company can differ, so it's important to go outside the organization to evaluate the quality of services. This can be done using suggestion boxes or 800 phone numbers or inviting comments on the Web site. In one form or another, the point is to do a *customer service survey*. The object is to gather feedback about how the company and the salesperson performed. No one should conclude business with the company without an opportunity to critique the experience.

Keep several things in mind when conducting surveys:

- Survey questions must be short and easy to complete. Several yes/no queries, several scaled queries (met expectations, exceeded expectations, below expectations, etc.), and one or two open-ended questions should be adequate.

- Gather only information that the company plans to act on; otherwise, don't waste people's time.

- Develop a plan for reviewing the surveys and acting on the information. Customers appreciate the opportunity to speak their minds, but they become dissatisfied when the company doesn't pay attention to what they say.

In addition to a critique of services, gather suggestions for enhancements that can be considered for future planning.

Don't overlook feedback from people who have terminated their relationship with the company. The seller who terminates a listing or whose listing expires before the property sells should be given an opportunity to critique the experience. This tells management about corrective steps that might be necessary, but also reveals what the seller is broadcasting to the community about the experience. Simply the act of soliciting opinions can help defuse negative feelings.

Personnel Competency. One final comment about quality control—at some point management has to look closely at the competency of the salespeople and the manager. Monitoring activities are meaningless unless management acts on what it learns. These lessons can be factored into performance standards and management's coaching (with the salespeople and other personnel) and into the company's professional development and training department's activities.

Problem Solving

Management typically becomes the customer relations department. These are the irate phone calls from a seller who's disturbed because his house hasn't sold or from the buyer who's upset because her settlement is delayed. There are also the calls from another broker claiming part of a commission. Institutionalized customer service standards will minimize these calls, but there will still be occasions when conflicts arise.

Frequently, the source of the problem is miscommunication or a misunderstanding that can easily be resolved by a third person (the broker or manager). Although injured parties can pursue formal courses of action, many issues can be handled informally by the manager and even the salesperson. But there also are times when the disgruntled person demands the attention of company superiors. Often, the sales office manager is squarely in the middle between the salesperson and the disgruntled caller and, on occasion, between the salesperson and senior management.

The way management handles these situations will be either a win-win for the manager, the company, and the customer, or someone will be the loser. The goal is to resolve the problem so that everyone feels at least satisfied, if not victorious.

The first goal is to satisfy the customer or resolve the issue with the competitor. The earlier the intervention, the more likely the matter can be resolved informally (before it becomes a subject of arbitration or litigation). But before plunging headlong into the situation with a solution, get all the facts straight. Review information in the transaction file and talk with the salesperson involved. Resolution may be easily accomplished with phone calls to all of the parties. Or the situation may have to be rectified in a meeting with all of the parties.

Remember that at this point the company, management, and the salesperson are all on the same team and must present a united front to the public and competitors. Internal matters must be handled internally, so don't disparage one another in front of outsiders. Management must, however, be forthright and acknowledge mistakes. If the issue is suspected to be an egregious error of a legal nature, refrain from making any comments and seek legal advice about how to proceed.

Once the matter is resolved, then delve into the internal matters. Digressions from company policy should be handled one-on-one with the individual salesperson, and solutions should be developed to prevent problems from arising again.

■ MINIMIZING EXPENSES

Minimizing expenses does not necessarily mean cutting or eliminating valuable services for the customers or sales staff. As a practical matter, there's a limit to how much expenses can be cut before the company's operations are seriously compromised. More efficient use of financial resources can be achieved with certain cost-containment measures. The advantage of frequent monitoring is that areas where the company is over budget can be identified and management can take corrective action (a nudging exercise) before the company hemorrhages from overspending (the running-aground point). The following are cost efficiencies that can be considered.

Telephone

The cost of communicating can be significant, though it's cheaper to fax than it is to use postal mail. One of the best places to look for hidden expenditures is in the phone bill. Duplicate charges and charges for uncompleted calls often are hidden among legitimate charges. And today, there are numerous ways (no thanks to technology) that people can pirate access to an account and run up charges.

Managing communications expenses also means that the company needs phone log procedures (including the number, the name of the person called, and the purpose of the call) for long-distance calls, so that legitimate charges can be identified. Also discourage personal long-distance calls, even if the company is to be reimbursed (the company may or may not get the money). Caution people about the length of their calls (they may not realize how windy they are). Fortunately, personal usage is less problematic in recent years because of the number of people who have personal cell phones.

Take maximum advantage of cheaper calling times and other cost-saving programs. (A general circulation fax for promotional purposes can easily be done on nonpeak time.) Because of the competition among carriers, numerous discount programs and incentives are available. In the case of long-distance service, carefully compare costs in addition to per-minute rates to be sure the carrier selected is the best deal. Also warn staff that only an authorized person from the company is permitted to change carriers or provide information to solicitors.

Computers

The computer has taken on a major role in the company's communications system, and in many cases, this represents cost efficiencies for the company. E-mail, including attachments in lieu of faxes, has become commonplace. Certainly, this is less expensive than the cost of duplicating documents and sending by postal mail. In-house printing (business forms, flyers, letters, or even real estate contracts) can be more cost-efficient, especially when the time comes to revise the documents. All this being said, companies today have to constantly scrutinize the cost of Internet connectivity. These vendors, like telephone companies, have a variety of cost and associated efficiencies to consider.

Marketing and Advertising

Advertising is typically a real estate company's largest expense (25 percent or more in some firms) after cost of sales. Adding other costs associated with marketing makes for a sizable expenditure that must be carefully managed. Because a marketing program combines a variety of tools that complement one another, the effectiveness can be measured best only in terms of the total package. Public relations counsel can help set up procedures for evaluating the marketing program and then decipher the data.

The primary data with which to evaluate marketing are collected from consumers, though the quality of that data is affected by their perceptions. A consumer may indicate that a friend referred the person, but the person's decision to contact the company may have been reinforced by an ad. Nonetheless, companies should establish procedures to gather data about the source of initial inquiries and then include a line on the transaction report to indicate the source of contact that actually resulted in a transaction.

Phone logs or advertising registers are very important for identifying the marketing strategy that prompted the contact and then comparing the number of contacts with the cost (such as the cost of an ad) to determine the per-contact cost. Monitor the per-contact cost over the course of several months and look at the conversion to transactions to determine effectiveness. The company can also gauge the potential for income at different times of the year and seasonal effect as the volume of contacts fluctuates. But this also means looking at the conversion of contacts to contracts to be sure that the advertising is reaching the target audience and that salespeople are making the most of the contacts.

Yard signs, newspaper advertising, and the Internet were indicated in the NAR homebuyer and seller profile (according to the 2002 report) to be the most widely used marketing tools for listings. For a company that is trying to advertise a seller's property, this narrows the field with respect to property-specific marketing strategies. Of course, a company may find that some strategies are more or less effective in its marketplace, and in the final analysis, the point is to select the strategy(ies) that actually results in business.

As the Internet becomes an increasingly more popular (and effective) marketing tool, the company may have to rethink the distribution of advertising dollars, which gets to be a more pressing issue as the end of the year approaches. A major marketing program that started in January or an aggressive advertising campaign to capture the spring market may leave few dollars for the last quarter of the year. The Internet may be a much-needed cost efficiency so that the company can reduce the amount of classified advertising.

Other advertising cost efficiencies can be achieved in several ways:

- Proofread classified ads for typographical errors. Newspapers will usually give credit for these mistakes.

- Count the number of lines in the ads as they appeared and compare the number of line charges on the bills.

- Check the length of ads because it's possible that one or two fewer words can save an entire line charge.

- Check with the publisher to be sure that the company has the best deal. A package plan may be cheaper than running an ad for only two days.

- Look at the size of display ads. A half page may be just as effective as a full page, or a quarter page may do instead of a half page. The savings can be substantial as long as the quality or purpose of the ad is not compromised. Newspapers are also willing to negotiate attractive contracts.

The time may also come to retool the distribution of advertising and promotional costs between the company and the salespeople, as long as this does not negatively impact equity with the competition. The salespeople may be happy to participate if this means preserving or adding exposure. (Don't suddenly burden them with all of the advertising costs, though.) Engaging the salespeople in solutions, especially because their business is at stake, provides good suggestions and quells dissatisfaction as well.

Postage

Technology aside, companies still need mail. However, there are ways to economize. Put a scale in the office! Make the most of first-class postage. If the mailing is lighter than the maximum weight for one stamp, include a flyer or other promotional piece. For letters that need extra postage, keep the correct stamps on hand to avoid using two first-class stamps. Or rent a postage meter. The rental is not cheap, but it may be less expensive than incorrect postage or the cost of time spent stamping a large volume of mail by hand.

Use second-day delivery rather than overnight delivery when possible, and compare prices and services of various carriers. Some delivery services are very helpful in planning the most cost-effective way to send a parcel. Encourage people to choose packaging wisely, because a fraction of an ounce can push delivery cost into the next price category. It's also cheaper to fax the form someone forgot to include than to send a second overnight letter.

Don't scrimp on details that could cost money later. If proof that notice was served on a certain date is needed, get it. Certified mail isn't nearly as expensive as the legal problems that could arise in the future.

For mass coverage, consider bulk mailing. The price of a bulk permit each year and the extra attention needed to prepare the mailings properly are considerably less expensive than using first-class postage. The services of a mail house may be more cost-effective than the cost of a staff person to stuff envelopes or fold flyers, too. Plan bulk mailings sufficiently ahead of time to ensure receipt in a timely fashion, especially if they contain time-sensitive information.

Economies in the Office

The little things add up! Have the utility company do an energy audit if the company is paying utilities (consider energy-efficient lighting). Insist that the person responsible for stocking office supplies comparison shops to locate the most cost-efficient vendor. Even if a staff person has to do the pickup and delivery, the cost savings could be worth the company time. Buy in bulk, provided the stock has a long shelf life, and don't make all of the stock readily available, to discourage waste.

Use paper wisely. Don't skimp on the quality of the paper stock and graphics on the company letterhead, but don't use them for interoffice communiqués or scratch paper. Buy cheaper paper for this purpose, and scatter scratch pads generously around the office. Test recycled paper in the computer printer or duplicating machine. It's cheaper stock and a cost savings, as long as the quality of the printed product is not compromised.

The cost of duplicating keys for listings and rental units can add up. The cost of inconvenience and emergency locksmith services (because of misplaced or lost keys) can be even greater. If the company duplicates a large number of keys, the purchase of key-cutting equipment or even certifying someone on staff as a locksmith may be more cost-efficient. This could be a big plus for the company that does property management as well as sales.

Keep track of yard signs and lockboxes. Use a log to identify locations where these items are being used and the people who checked them out. Missing tools are as aggravating as they are expensive to replace.

Salaries and Benefits

It's tempting to cut support staff when the year and the money don't seem to be coming out even. But remember all the reasons for creating these positions in the first place. Consider ways to economize by outsourcing some tasks or activities. A contractor's service might be cheaper than salary and benefits for a staff person. Ask employees to participate in the costs of benefits such as health care. Before manipulating overtime hours and wages, though, check wage-and-hour laws.

Costs of Sales

The cost of sales on the income statement includes all of the costs for commissions and referral and franchise fees that are associated with the sales transactions. Before cutting commissions to control costs, remember the rationale for setting the pay schedules in the first place (back to Chapter 13). In the case of referral and franchise fees, track these over the long run to determine if there is sufficient added benefit to warrant the expenditure. Also consider the "after the fact" fees charged by the referral company in transactions when its client began working with the company without the benefit of the referral.

Pay attention to the number of in-house versus cooperating sales. Depending on commission arrangements with the salespeople and other brokers, one way to minimize costs is to encourage the salespeople to sell the company's listings. This strategy is only feasible, however, as long as it does not conflict with agency laws or compromise the quality of service provided to customers and clients. No one should be pushed into a property simply because of a company's profit motive.

■ LOOKING INTO THE FUTURE

The information gathered about the organization while monitoring this year's activities is critical when charting its course for the future. If all of this looks familiar, that's because it's the same kind of data that are part of the market analysis that is done in preparation of the company's business plans.

The point in the first chapter is the magnitude of change that keeps companies on their toes. The secret to coping with change is to be smart enough to stay the course and visionary enough to become a leader in a new industry of services or business methods. The structure of the organization is bound to change. If certain services are not as profitable as management would like, this may mean closing a division and concentrating on other activities.

The company may decide that the way to cope with change is to expand its horizons and grow the organization either vertically or horizontally. Vertical growth increases capacity in current services. Horizontal growth increases the scope or number of services or target markets the company serves. (See Figure 17.1.)

All of this cycles around to the next year's business plan and the process that was discussed in the second unit. Management that has been faithfully monitoring the company this year is already armed with a considerable amount of the information needed to chart a profitable path for the next year.

■ CONCLUSION

Monitoring the operations involves keeping in touch with all aspects of the business and controlling activities and making adjustments where necessary. Ultimately, the goal is to ensure that the company has a business to manage next year. There's nothing quite so exhilarating as to see the company exceed expectations. And there's nothing quite so unnerving as to discover that the company is struggling, especially if this is the firm's first year in business and reserves are dwindling. The information management learns about the company can be used to either praise progress or remedy faults. Controlling should not restrict the organization, but rather should inspire the company to grow by directing its resources to the most productive activities.

■ DISCUSSION EXERCISES

Discuss transaction management software that you use; share transaction tracking forms that you use or design a tracking system for your office.

Discuss ways to economize on expenditures in your company, office, or department.

What are your experiences with customer service surveys?

FIGURE 17.1

Growth of an Organization

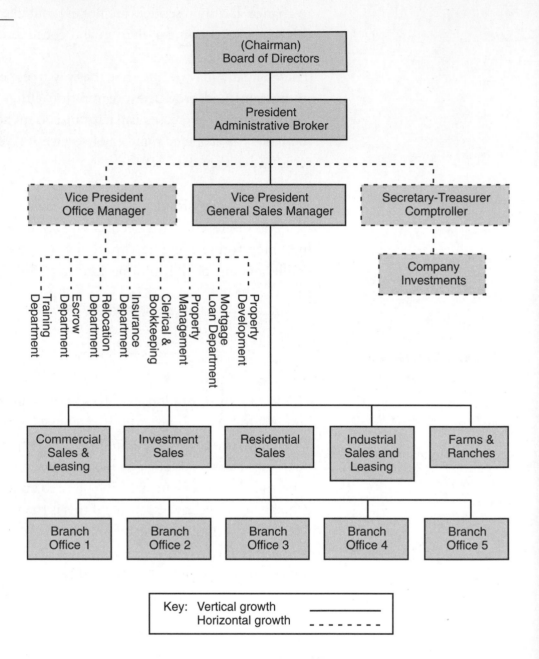

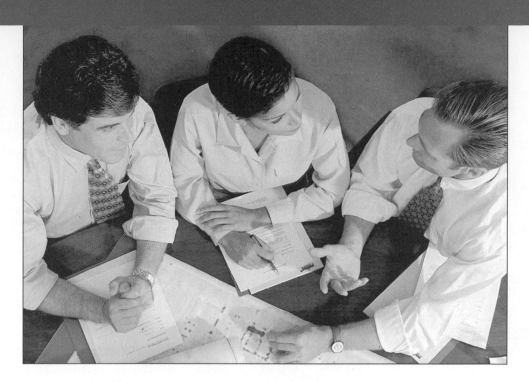

18

MANAGING RISK

What poses the greatest risk for your company?

What can you do to protect the company from these risks?

———————

Risk begins at the time you make up your mind to go into business and sign the partnership, corporation, and/or loan papers. It sits on the slippery doorstep of the office, in the seat of the first employment interview, and at your feet with the first employee you let go.

Step outside the office on a listing presentation and into a property with a buyer, the conference room to negotiate a sales contract, or a local eatery for lunch with fellow brokers and you're in the riskiest arenas of the real estate business. Add more salespeople, several employees, and a lot more buyers and sellers to the mix, and the risk to the company expands exponentially. In the broader context, look at current events and the potential for catastrophe and financial mismanagement.

This is not to suggest that one should be intimidated by risk, but rather to say that risk is a given in the business world. Virtually every business enterprise and profession has had to learn how to insulate itself from threats to their enterprises and navigate an increasingly litigious environment. Ours has become a nation whose court dockets are choked with lawsuits, and that's not likely to change any time soon. But litigation is only one of the bolts of lightning that can rock an organization's foundation.

■ PROTECTING THE INSTITUTION

There's a sense of comfort or complacency that can easily settle in when a company is making money, or at least keeping its head above water, and manages to put out the daily brushfires as they flare. It's not uncommon for organizations to feel that they are managing their affairs just fine, as long as the money and the brushfires are under control. And while these are not unimportant activities, there's more to consider about the health and well-being of the institution.

Brand

Call it brand, name, or goodwill, this is the company's reputation and prestige in the marketplace. While a company's product or service is associated with that brand, the *name* the organization attains gives it stature. In the corporate world, a company's brand is considered its most valuable asset. Though it's an intangible asset (distinguished here from the value of projected earnings when a company is sold), brand or name has enormous effect on a company's position in the marketplace and its future.

When a company first opens its doors, it works hard to establish credibility as a competent and trustworthy place to do business. As the company proceeds through its life's stages and touches more people, the company can continually enhance its reputation and demonstrate its trustworthiness. But that's also when a company's decisions, ranging from the way it manages its finances to the way it handles customers and treats workers, have the powerful potential to damage that reputation.

Protecting a company's name as a solid, trustworthy institution is crucial to the future of the organization (and yes, its future earnings). The reputation of the institution rarely rises or falls on singular events (even recent corporate scandals were tips on bigger icebergs). However, many good deeds are easily overshadowed by a few missteps in which consumers, investors, or people who work for the company feel that trust has been violated. Once the company's reputation declines, the organization is more suspect on all fronts.

Value the integrity of the institution. Demonstrate that with conscientious-to-a-fault customer service, especially to resolve complaints of the dissatisfied, and fair and honest dealings with the people who work for the company and with other professionals in the industry as well. Keep the inside house in order, which means prudently managed. All of this may sound like lofty ideals, but consider the jeopardy to the bottom line if the company's reputation declines.

Licensing

Any business enterprise that requires a government permit or license for a part or all of its operation is vulnerable if that privilege is suspended or revoked. Certainly, a real estate company is vulnerable in this regard, and perhaps more so than other business enterprises because the principal license (or licensee) under which the company operates is affected by the conduct of every individual licensee who is affiliated with the company.

Although the worst-case scenario of the principal broker sitting in a jail cell for fraud or drug trafficking would be a major disruption of the company's license, the company is far more likely to be affected by something one of its sales or broker licensees does. This falls under a very simple, though powerful, statement in license law that says the broker is responsible for actions of his or her underlying licensees. The phraseology may differ from state to state, but the effect is that the broker is ultimately responsible for supervising and exercising control over all conduct that relates to licensed activities.

The risk to the company increases with each licensee who comes to work for the company. It's a rare real estate company that says, "We can't hire any more licensees because we can't keep track of them." (Maybe it should.) Certainly, the more licensees who work for you, the better your supervisory and management skills need to be. Unfortunately, the larger the sales staff, the greater the likelihood that the manager knows less about what licensees do.

The company is also vulnerable when its business philosophy pushes the envelope to "make the deal" or when members of the sales staff are more focused on the deal and less on how they made it (all of these points having been made in earlier chapters). If that's the way of the company, then the company has to face the fact that the broker has considerable exposure and is subject to sanctions if the conduct gets crosswise with state regulations.

At the very least, allegations of violations distract valuable time and company resources during the investigation and defense stages of the enforcement process. Depending on the nature and severity of the transgression, the principal broker (and if there's a company license, the company as well) found in violation is subject to fine, suspension, or revocation of the license. Although a fine obviously has financial implications, the other two possibilities can seriously threaten the very existence of the institution.

The most apparent conclusion to all of this is that a company needs to take proactive, preventive steps. Some companies establish zero tolerance policies, refusing to hire anyone whose license has previously been sanctioned or who has a criminal past (more stringently investigated than criminal background checks by licensing authorities). The caveat about using criminal conviction and arrest records when making hiring decisions, however, is they could have the effect of disparately treating minority groups.

Companies can also put some grit behind the grin of their policies and procedures and employee handbooks. Pledges to observe all license laws, internal procedures to support those laws, and well-crafted company codes of ethics are meaningless unless the company institutionalizes procedures to sanction those who digress. The company shouldn't wait for the enforcement agency to make a routine inspection or sit in silent hope of dodging official notice that someone has filed a complaint.

The front line managers, the sales managers, are the company's most critical defense. They must be diligent (which isn't easy with the mobility of today's workforce) about investigating how people are conducting the company's business. Customer service reports and transaction report forms and one-on-one conversations with salespeople are useful ways to gather this information. The most important thing, however, is that management takes its responsibility seriously for supervising licensed activities.

Leadership

What happens if the broker, whose real estate license the entire entity depends on, dies? What happens if any member of the management team suddenly departs, whether by virtue of a better offer elsewhere, a change in career, retirement, a temporary disability, or a terminal illness? In other words, how resilient is the organization?

Although the institution may not fold (unless it's a sole proprietorship and there's only one principal), the organization can suffer or flounder temporarily while the leadership team restores its ranks. *The smaller the organization, the more vulnerable it is.* Confronting the reality that an organization needs to have a succession plan may sound like management has some ulterior motives in planning for people's departure. But planning for eventualities is simply good business.

This means that the organization needs, at a minimum, a plan for how responsibilities will be divided until a suitable replacement is found, or temporarily assigned if the vacancy is not permanent. Better still is a plan for identifying suitable replacements.

There's an axiom in management that says people should be grooming their replacements. While the most senior managers are responsible for developing a plan of succession for their positions, they also need to be looking at every position in the organization with an eye for talent that is waiting in the wings or that could be nurtured as replacements. Each sales office manager should be doing likewise as well.

While continuity is the purpose of succession planning, the added benefit is a work culture that fosters professional growth. The people who take on temporary assignments during vacations or other absences of their superiors or the companies that have management training programs (or encourage attendance at outside programs) have talent that can be valuable not just when the unexpected happens but during the normal course of attrition. Although the uniqueness of an individual is irreplaceable, there is other talent that can do a job, maybe differently, but maybe even better.

■ RISK MANAGEMENT CULTURE

Risk management means different things to different people. To some it means keep dousing the brushfires. To others it means keep the organization's vulnerabilities hidden, that if no one knows where the Achilles' heels are, the company will be OK (or at least the responsible manager won't look bad). And then, there are those who chalk up risk as an inevitable fact of life and budget for costs to bail the company out of problems.

Although a company can prepare financially (especially for lawsuits) by setting aside reserves for a litigation fund or, as many more do, purchasing liability insurance, these are measures in which the companies may be managing on hope—hope that the costs won't exceed their financial resources. But there are better ways to protect the company and in so doing, direct the company's financial resources to productive endeavors.

A *risk management culture* is an environment that infuses responsibility for managing risk in everyone in the organization, from the most senior to the lowest positions in the company. This is a *proactive* environment that focuses on identifying potential threats or anticipating crises and assembling the processes, structures, and tools to eliminate or minimize risk to the organization. In other words, the company takes a positive approach to risk by building offensive strategies.

When an organization fosters this culture, this says that risk management is a significant priority in everything the company does, an attitude or attentiveness that, when absent, creates vulnerability for the company.

The how-to of risk management involves a series of steps similar to any problem-solving process (identifying, analyzing, evaluating, and handling). Typically, someone in senior management is assigned the responsibility for being the risk management officer and convening people within the organization to periodically assess processes, systems, and tools from a risk management perspective and then preparing additional offenses as necessary.

Because many risks involve matters of law, the company legal counsel should be involved in the process. Often, the real estate industry's professional organizations have legal hot lines that can be helpful resources, especially for ways to handle certain risks as well.

Identify Risk

Risk arises primarily because of *ignorance, carelessness,* or *breach* of a company policy or procedure. Only the company can know where it's most vulnerable, and certainly, not all risks pose the same degree of consequence. There are, however, some things management should be looking for in its information systems, workplace relations, and external or public relations. Many involve practices that are fundamental simply because of the nature of the real estate business.

- **Advertising:** Legal and business risks arise in what is said and how the company's services, listings, and employment opportunities are portrayed. Equal employment and housing laws are a particular concern, but so also are the company's brand and reputation.

- **Antitrust:** These are issues that create vulnerability under federal and perhaps state antitrust laws. Price fixing (including company/broker practices and representations made by salespeople), group boycotting, territorial assignments, and tying agreements are all practices specifically prohibited.

- **Cultural diversity:** These are issues that relate to the legal awareness of rights and practices in the workplace and the marketplace, cultural awareness, and people's attentiveness (or lack thereof) to appropriate behaviors with respect to race, ethnicity, gender, and the like. These are management as well as customer-service issues.

- **Disability:** Practices that fail to enable people with disabilities to access the company's services and facilities and failure to properly accommodate these people in the workforce violate the Americans with Disabilities Act and perhaps similar state laws.

- **Employee-at-will and equal employment laws:** These are issues that arise from a number of employment laws that affect recruitment, hiring, training, advancement, discipline, and firing practices as well as pregnancy, family and medical leave, military service considerations, and wage and salary laws. Practices that target older workers (persons age 40 or older) and terminate any worker without just cause and due process in accordance with employment-at-will, or EAW, also create vulnerability.

■ **Fair housing:** These are practices relating to federal, state, and local laws that, whether by intent or effect, discriminate against persons seeking housing for sale or rent because of their race, color, religion, sex, handicap, familial status, national origin, and perhaps others as defined by state or local law. Failure to display equal opportunity notices as prescribed by a law is also a violation.

■ **Financial management:** Vulnerabilities lie in the way client funds are handled (license law issue) and financial obligations (debt payments or tax filings) are managed and the vulnerability of company assets (money and equipment) to tampering or misappropriation.

■ **Harassment:** A workplace environment that tolerates offensive behavior (including the jokesters and people who can't keep their hands to themselves) or fails to respond to allegations of harassment is vulnerable under equal employment laws, with sexual harassment being the most common issue. Offensive behavior with customers and clients is also problematic.

■ **Internet:** The vulnerability of the company's database to invasion or paralysis can cause major disruption in business. The misuse of intellectual property (whether by downloading, copying, or hyperlinking) either by the company or its staff infringes on copyright, trademark, or business method patents. A company that fails to protect its intellectual property also loses assets it thought were preserved.

■ **Property conditions:** These are the issues that relate to the real estate that is the subject of transactions, particularly conditions that statutory or case law has determined are material to a purchaser's decision. Vulnerability can lurk in misrepresentations or fraud, failure to meet the legal requirements for disclosure of property conditions, and the advice or recommendations salespeople provide relative to professional inspections or curative measures.

Vulnerability can also arise from the way environmental conditions are handled, common issues being

- asbestos,

- lead-based paint (including the Residential Lead-Based Paint Hazard Reduction Act),

- molds,

- PCBs,

- radon,

- toxic waste sites and landfills,

- underground storage tanks, and

- urea formaldehyde.

■ **Relationships:** These are the law of agency issues that affect the way customers versus clients are serviced, beginning with legal requirements for disclosure of relationships to the way salespeople handle fiduciary (or nonagency) responsibilities during a transaction. A company is also vulnerable with respect to practices involving relationships with other brokers and the relationships they have with their clients.

■ **RESPA:** These issues relate to practices governed by the Real Estate Settlement Procedures Act, including disclosures of settlement charges and affiliated business arrangements (AfBAs) and payments of kickbacks and prohibited referral fees.

■ **Workplace safety:** In addition to OSHA (safe workplace laws), civil actions could arise if workers or visitors to the place of business are injured on the premises. The company must also be vigilant about dangerous or threatening behavior.

A company can be vulnerable in any of these areas because of either a lack or inadequacy of a policy or procedure to protect the organization. Frequently, however, the organization has protective mechanisms that for a variety of reasons fail to work the way they were intended. In many cases, this occurs because management has fallen short on its enforcement responsibilities or allowed rules to be bent (or ignored).

Assessment of risk requires looking into all the chambers of the company's operations, beginning at the top with senior management and down through the activities of salespeople and support staff (transaction coordinators, personal assistants, secretarial, clerical, and receptionist) to the lowest position on the organization chart. Another place to look is the problems that are the brushfires management has had to fight. Yes, they represent a breakdown in the company's offense but they say here are loopholes that need to be closed.

Analyze Risk

This step in the process involves an analysis of the discoveries in the prior step. The purpose is twofold: One is to analyze how the threat occurs, that by understanding why it happens, possible solutions to prevent it become evident.

The other purpose is to analyze the level of risk to the organization. In other words, how serious the threat is from a financial, legal, or public relations point of view. This helps management prioritize its focus, to close the most dangerous loopholes first. Certainly, routine patterns or practices that are subjects of law and recent civil litigation should get management's attention. Legal counsel can also help evaluate the level of risk in these matters.

The analysis process also tests the organization's level of tolerance to risk and perhaps also reveals how committed management is to a proactive risk management culture. (An issue that would cause many sleepless nights for management in one organization could get a ho-hum response in others.) Risk tolerance gets tested every time management needs to confront the subject. Management will also discover that not everyone on the management team has the same tolerance level, some being more immune to risk and others being far more unnerved. The team will have to achieve consensus in this regard.

Evaluate Alternatives

This step identifies ways that the company can protect itself. What processes, systems, or tools should be created or enhanced? A range of possibilities may exist, or perhaps there's only one logical solution. Even if the risk is something that the organization can't do anything about, the organization can be proactive by planning suitable defensive strategies ahead of time.

Solutions can come in the form of more diligent oversight of company procedures and staff behavior, new or revised procedures, enhanced training of staff, better attentiveness to customer service, or perhaps allocation of financial resources to undertake a major initiative. Or a solution could involve a combination of these alternatives.

One of management's most useful tools is the company's policies and procedures manual, especially the way risk issues are addressed, and it can become clear written evidence about how processes are to work and people are to behave. While the benefits of a manual should not be underestimated, it's important to keep in mind that failure to enforce policies or to purposely engage in practices that contradict the company's ideals compromises the defense of the organization in the event of litigation.

Because one of the greatest vulnerabilities for a real estate company involves the transaction itself, particularly the way the salespeople conduct themselves, certain procedures become critically important.

- **Sales training:** A well-trained staff is one of a company's most powerful risk management assets. Perhaps this is all a matter of perspective, but training is more than how to sell and make money. Training should form a basis for ethical and legal conduct in the process (the legal liability and risk reduction issues) and foster a pattern of behavior in which consumer rights and laws are faithfully observed, absent the shortcuts that sometimes tempt salespeople (things like getting the disclosure forms signed after the fact or filling in the rest of the contact blanks after they're signed).

- **Discover, disclose, document:** The attentiveness of the salespeople to any condition about a property that could materially affect a consumer's decision is also effective risk management. A vigilant posture involves a process in which salespeople observe (within the limits of their expertise) and facilitate professional inspections to *discover* and *disclose* defects or environmental conditions and then *document* the disclosures that have been made.

  Documentation may be a legally required disclosure form, a professional report, acknowledgment of conditions in a sales contract or lease agreement, and/or a trail of notes and correspondence in the transaction file that document conversations between the salesperson and the consumer. In fact, any notes, including telephone and appointment logs, can close a window on risk, especially in the event of litigation.

■ **Customer satisfaction:** Attentiveness to customer service goes a long way toward insulating the company. Establishing quality service standards should contribute greatly, especially when those standards include educating buyers and sellers about the "rules of the game" when they begin working with the company. Minimizing violated expectations and educating consumers about certain laws, like fair housing, agency, and environmental and property disclosures, will avoid problems later on.

Although no one can prevent a person who feels harmed from pursuing his or her legal rights, many times these actions can be averted with management's attention to a customer complaint and attempt to resolve the differences. Yes, there are those disgruntled people who will feel no justice unless they see the broker in court, but from the company's point of view that should be the forum of last resort.

Handling a Risk

This is the step in which management decides on the most suitable course of action, implements it, and then follows up to ensure that the risk has been contained.

The most critical part of this process is assigning someone the responsibility for managing the risk. That person, generally a member of the management team, becomes accountable for directing company activities in the design of the process or procedure and then seeing that they are implemented.

Additional Offense

At the risk (pardon the pun) of sounding redundant, the importance of a lawyer and accountant can't be overemphasized. One of the most valuable lines in the company budget is their monthly retainer and the roles they play at management team meetings and at company events.

Lest this sound like a peculiar observation, consider that the company pays these people to keep it out of trouble. Will you take their advice, even if they don't tell you what you want to hear? Are you going to search until you find someone to give you the answer you want? Or are you going to ignore the professionals' advice entirely? Second opinions can be useful, but ducking the facts can be risky business. Lawyers and accountants can't defend indefensible actions.

It's appropriate also to mention the negotiation of their professional retainer fees. Define which services will be performed for the retainer and the services that the company will pay for as billable hours. Also, clarify exactly which company personnel are permitted to contact these advisers and for what purposes. Otherwise, the company could exceed the services covered by a retainer and could be very surprised by the amount of the legal and accounting bills.

Another valuable resource arises from relationships the company develops with state licensing authorities and fair housing agencies. Unfortunately, some people see them as adversaries who should be avoided. However, these agencies are very useful for clarifying and interpreting their laws and answering specific questions. Better to ask ahead of time and keep the company out of trouble. These resources willingly help because that lightens their enforcement workload. Everyone on the management team should have the phone numbers of these agencies and the most recent versions of their laws (often available on the Internet).

A final thought is that the object of risk management is to protect the organization, not to bog it down in procedures and paperwork. The virtue of a risk management culture is that as people behave in ways that are attentive to risk, the practice becomes second nature. Then there's less risk, and attending to new threats that come along can be handled rather matter-of-factly.

■ DEFENSE IN RISK MANAGEMENT

A very important point to be made about a risk management culture is that one of the ways to guard the company is with processes, systems, and tools that enable the organization to present a suitable defense should that become necessary.

Regardless of how attentive management is to protecting the institution, a fact of business life is that even the best intentions will not prevent an allegation of misconduct. It may come in the form of a human relations complaint or a court summons.

Dealing with allegations can be as distracting as winding up in a formal legal proceeding. Once an allegation is made, the company has to direct considerable financial and human resources to jumping through the hoops that regulatory agencies and court systems erect. The good news is the matter may be dropped or resolved during that process. Otherwise, the company has a longer journey and expends more resources until a final verdict is reached.

Power of Information

Information empowers the organization to manage risk in two ways. One involves gathering information about its vulnerabilities. Not only about the company's internal systems, processes, and the like but also about laws, regulations, and court proceedings so the company can identify risk and devise appropriate risk management measures. Real estate industry Web sites provide valuable legal references, including analysis of practices and summaries of recent litigation. Complete texts of the laws (selected references are provided in the Bibliography) are also available on the Internet, including government sources that administer the laws. Some of the most significant ones are

- antitrust laws,

- disclosure laws (agency and property conditions),

- environmental laws,

- fair housing laws,

- ADA,

- equal employment laws (including antiharassment),

- RESPA (including pending regulations regarding AfBAs and pending regulations involving referral fees and disclosures),

- Foreign Reinvestment in Real Property Tax Act, and

- intellectual property laws.

The other way is an internal-process issue. This involves assembling the information that the company may need to protect itself in the future. A company will have a much more difficult time resolving an allegation or building a defense for a formal proceeding without the proper ammunition. The most persuasive ammunition is the documentation that resides in the company's transaction files, personnel files, and the policies and procedures manual.

Remember the point earlier about documentation (see discover, disclose, document). Even the seemingly innocuous note in an appointment calendar can be the little treasure that puts the company in a defensible position in a dispute over a commission or the time that a property defect existed. Company's legal counsel is invaluable for recommending defensible documentation procedures.

Insurance

Insurance is the part of a risk management defense that intends to shield the company from financial impacts. It can be viewed as an investment of financial resources to pay for events that the company hopes never occur. The company is often seen as the "deep pockets." While the cost of insurance can be a considerable expense, it will return great benefits if it is ever needed. The company normally insures for a number of events.

The first is workers' compensation. The purpose of workers' compensation is to protect people against loss of income due to injuries sustained on the job. Workers' compensation insurance is a statutory requirement for employees and, depending on state law, may also be required for independent contractors. In addition, the company may consider offering disability insurance to employees to cover loss due to any illness or injury, whether it is job-related or not.

Another is liability insurance. This comes in many forms, but automobile liability is the most common. Insist that each salesperson carry an adequate amount, which in today's economy should be at least $300,000 per person, $500,000 per accident, and $100,000 for property damage. Verify their coverage yearly. In addition, the company can get an umbrella policy to cover its liability over and above that of each salesperson in the event of an accident while on company business.

Other types of insurance include liability insurance to cover injuries to clients or customers on the company's premises, fire, and comprehensive coverage for equipment, replacement of records, and business interruption insurance.

Errors and omissions (E&O) insurance is a must. In fact, some states require that licensees carry this insurance. The company's E&O insurance covers certain claims against *the company* because of the actions of the salespeople. In addition, licensees should have their own coverage, or the company could offer a group policy in which the salespeople can participate. E&O insurance includes the legal defense against a claim as well as damage awards for insurable events. Check your policy to determine what events are insurable. (Violations of the law are normally excluded.)

Dispute Resolution

The legal system in this country is designed to ensure that justice is served, to give everyone his or her day in court and an opportunity to be heard. Nevertheless, the system is stressed to its limits, particularly with civil matters. Often people must cool their heels for years before they are heard. Both the plaintiff and the defendant incur sizable legal bills in the process.

Mediation and arbitration are alternatives for resolving disputes in a speedy, affordable manner, in lieu of going to court. These methods are being used in many types of disputes, and real estate is no exception. Mediation is a forum in which the parties sit with an impartial mediator and negotiate a resolution to their dispute. Arbitration involves an arbitrator, or panel of arbitrators, who takes testimony from both sides of a case (as would be done in court). Then, the arbitrator renders a decision. In most jurisdictions this decision is as binding as any court decision would be.

Recommending these alternatives to buyers and sellers is also desirable for brokers and companies because they are frequently implicated as parties in disputes between consumers. There are services throughout the country that are sanctioned by the legal community to provide mediation and arbitration. Some are sponsored by real estate organizations. The services may provide only mediation, only arbitration, or perhaps both resolution systems. Some sales agreements include language that requires the parties to resolve disputes over specific matters in this manner.

Arbitration Between Brokers

Buyers and sellers are not the only ones who find themselves in disputes. Controversies between brokerage companies arise, particularly over commissions. Professional real estate organizations frequently offer their members an arbitration forum in which these matters can be settled. Again, the advantage is a speedier, less-costly way to resolve these controversies. (Note, too, that these organizations provide forums for ethics complaints as well.)

■ CONCLUSION

The purpose of risk management is to be attentive to threats to the organization. All of management's efforts to monitor activities to keep the organization on course are insufficient to truly insulate the institution from risks that are inherent in doing business. A risk management culture infuses the organization and its systems, processes, and people with vigilance to risk. An organization manages risk not just in the way it attempts to avoid the indiscretions that create vulnerability but also in the ways it prepares to defend itself should the need arise.

■ DISCUSSION EXERCISES

What procedures has your company adopted to manage the risks that are prevalent in your practice?

Discuss the general circumstances of closed legal cases of which you are aware (from personal experience or professional readings), the final rulings, and possible ways that the litigation could have been avoided.

What issues do you anticipate will pose the greatest liability within the next five years?

IN CONCLUSION
OF UNIT FIVE

The control function of management should protect, preserve, and promote the growth of the company. This should empower the organization to pursue its goals and not restrict or burden the operations. Because certain events can inhibit the company's progress, especially risks that could divert the firm's resources into litigation, it's important to be proactive in establishing procedures and monitoring activities to facilitate the way business is conducted. The things you learn about the company in the process are useful as you revisit the management functions and begin planning for the future.

■ THE SCENARIO

Having read this unit, what is your analysis of the following scenario?

The first phone call of the day to the broker brought news from the company's attorney. (Well, from the broker's point of view, these calls were just all part of doing business, so better that than a panicked alert from the chief financial officer. Anything was fixable as long as the company had money.) Several issues were pending on the attorney's desk, some of which could be disposed of relatively easily. Others, however, were more ominous.

The company had completed a business planning session several weeks ago and decided that on January 1 it would implement several new policies. In order to maximize revenue and minimize expenditures, the company would no longer accept listings on properties valued less than $40,000 and would enter into buyer-agency agreements only with prospective purchasers who were qualified to purchase properties valued at $40,000 or more. The company's customary concierge services would be offered only to buyers who purchased properties valued at $500,000 or higher. The company also would require buyers who had houses to sell to enter into listing agreements with the company before their offers could be presented to the company's client-sellers.

By the middle of the next year, the formation of a title abstract and settlement company will be completed. This will enable the company's salespeople to offer buyers and sellers a neat package of services. The fee structure is still under discussion, though the intention is to quote a packaged fee for title and settlement services, which will also include an amount to be paid to the real estate salesperson involved in the transaction.

In the meantime, several company procedures need to be resolved. After the business planning session, the office managers were instructed to go back to their offices and scrutinize several procedures. Their assignment was to make sure that personnel files contain proper documentation and that transaction files contain the required paperwork. They were also instructed to review the company's business policies and procedures manual and go over it with their salespeople and support staffs. It seems that the company has been notified that a former employee is pursuing legal action for wrongful termination. The attorney has also had received a letter, though no formal legal action has been taken yet, from a salesperson alleging sexual harassment.

In addition, the company has had an increasing number of cases in which the attorney has had to unravel disputes over escrow or hand money and property conditions, apparently the result of careless procedures or inappropriate representations by salespeople. Fortunately, formal legal action has been averted. However, because of the increased amount of time devoted to these matters, the attorney is proposing that his compensation and the scope of his retainer be restructured. The company is contemplating assessing each sales office a prorated share of the attorney's retainer and/or charging hourly fees for out-of-the-ordinary services to the offending office.

■ THE ANALYSIS

The scenario in the introduction of this unit says several things about the company. One is that the broker seems to be doing the right thing in keeping legal counsel in the loop, but one would also hope counsel knows about several things that were discussed at the recent business planning meeting.

Although it's likely that financial motives are behind the benchmark of $40,000 for listings and buyer-agency contracts, there is a distinct possibility that this policy could violate the fair housing laws, having the effect of denying persons in the protected classes the company's services. So much for equal opportunity in housing. The benchmark for concierge services, however, would not have fair housing implications.

Presumably, legal counsel is involved in developing the corporate structures that will affiliate the brokerage company with a title abstract and settlement company. Affiliated business associations are a subject of RESPA and pending regulation. Unless disclosure procedures and referral payments are structured appropriately, the companies have some problems.

As a practical matter, a bone of contention among salespeople has been the force or requirement (however it is employed) to recommend the services of an affiliated company to a consumer when the terms are less favorable than can be obtained elsewhere. This is not to say that the company should not embark on such a venture, and in fact, it has appeal to the seamless-service-oriented consumer, but the company should be aware of the consequences, particularly if the consumer is the client.

With respect to files and procedures, the good news is that the company has embarked on a systemwide investigation to ensure that all is in order. The bad news could be that this effort is too late to properly defend a wrongful termination and a sexual harassment case.

It appears that the company needs to take some steps to increase attentiveness to hand money and property condition issues. Fortunately, the issues have been resolved and in fact, most companies can tell of numerous experiences in this same vein. However, it's only a matter of time when resolution won't be enough to avert legal action.

With respect to counsel's fees, the company has several choices. Assessing the offices a share of the expense would be appropriate, especially if the assessment was divided according to the past year's use so as not to overburden offices that have fewer occasions to use the services. The retainer could be restructured to minimize hourly fees, and although this may result in a larger retainer fee, retainers are usually less in the long run than hourly rates. In any event, the company can take steps through training and other risk management oversight activities.

■ THE SUMMARY

Depending on whether you are the broker/owner, a senior manager in a large organization, a sales manager, or a department manager, your involvement in the various activities that are associated with the control function of management may be different. As a guide for understanding your roles, the following summary is provided.

- ■ Monitoring the operations.

  - The broker/owner and senior management are normally involved in evaluating all aspects of the organization's activities.

  - Lower levels of management are most involved in monitoring the activities for which they are directly responsible, though they also may have access to reports of other aspects of the company to see how their areas of responsibility affect the "big picture."

- ■ Managing risk.

  - Although the broker/owner and senior management are normally responsible for establishing policies, a proactive risk management program must involve everyone who works for the company so that risk management permeates the entire organization.

BIBLIOGRAPHY

Adams, Scott. *The Dilbert Principle*. New York: Harper Business, a division of HarperCollins Publisher, 1996.

Americans with Disabilities Act of 1990. Public Law 101-336, U.S. Code, vol. 42, sec. 12101.

Bennis, Warren, and Burt Nanus. *The Strategies for Taking Charge*. New York: Harper Business, 1997.

Bennis, Warren G., and Robert J. Thomas. *Geeks & Geezers: How Era, Values and Defining Moments Shape Leaders*. Boston: Harvard Business School Press, 2002.

Blanchard, Ken [et al]. *High Five!: The Magic of Working Together*. New York: William Morrow, 2001.

Blanchard, Ken, and Jessie Stoner. *Full Steam Ahead!: Unleash the Power of Vision In Your Company and Your Life*. San Francisco: Berrett Koehler, 2003.

Blanchard, Ken, Michael O'Conner, with Jim Ballard. *Managing by Values*. San Fransisco: Berrett-Koehler Publishing, 1997.

Blanchard, Kenneth H., Donald Carew, and Eunice Parisi-Carew. *The One-Minute Manager Builds High Performance Teams*. New York: William Morrow, 2000.

Burley-Allen, Madelyn. *Listening, the Forgotten Skill*. New York: John Wiley & Sons, 1995.

Calvin, Robert J. *Entrepreneurial Management*. New York: McGraw-Hill, 2002.

Frank, Cook, *21 Things I Wish My Broker Had Told Me*. A Dearborn Publication.

Covey, Stephen R. *Principle-Centered Leadership*. New York: Fireside, Simon & Schuster, 1991.

Covey, Stephen R. *The Seven Habits of Highly Effective People*. New York: Fireside, Simon & Schuster, 1990.

de Heer, Robert. *Real Estate Contracts*. Chicago: Real Estate Education Company, 1995.

de Heer, Robert. *Risk Management*. Chicago: Real Estate Education Company, 1998.

Dennison, Mark S. *Environmental Considerations in Real Estate Transactions*. Chicago: Real Estate Education Company, 1994.

Dooley, Tom, Stefan I. Swanepoel, and Michael A. Abelson. *Real Estate Confronts Reality: Consumers, Computers, Confusion*. Chicago: Real Estate Education Company, 1998.

Drucker, Peter E. *Innovation and Entrepreneurship*. New York: Harper & Row, 1985.

Elashmawi, Faird, and Phillip R. Harris. *Multicultural Management 2000: Essential Cultural Insights for Global Business Success*. Houston: Gulf Publishing Company, 1998.

Fair Housing Act. Public Law 90-284, U.S. Code, vol. 42, secs. 3600-20 1989.

Finley, David L. *Agency Plus*. Chicago: Real Estate Education Company, 1994.

Fournies, Ferdinand F. *Coaching for Improved Work Performance*. New York: McGraw-Hill, 2000.

Fourniers, Fernand F. *Why Employees Don't Do What They're Supposed To Do and What To Do About It*. New York: McGraw-Hill, 1999.

Garton-Good, Julie. *Real Estate a la Carte*. Chicago: Dearborn Trade, A Kaplan Professional Company, 2001.

Harlan, Don, Gail Lyons, and John Reilly. *Consensual Dual Agency: A Practical Approach to the In-House Sale*. Chicago: Real Estate Education Company, 1994.

Harris, Philip R., and Robert T. Moran. *Managing Cultural Differences.* Houston: Gulf Publishing Company, 1996.

Harvard Business Review. *Managing Diversity.* Boston: Harvard Business School Publishing Company, 2001.

Johnson, Spencer, MD. *Who Moved My Cheese.* New York: Penguin Putnam Inc., 1998.

Kash, Rick. *The New Laws of Demand and Supply.* New York: Currency/Doubleday, 2002.

Keigher, Patrick J., and Joyce A. Emory. *Professional Real Estate Development.* Chicago: Real Estate Education Company, 1994.

Labovitz, George, and Victor Rosansky. *The Power of Alignment: How Companies Stay Centered and Accomplish Extraordinary Things.* New York: John Wiley & Sons, Inc., 1997.

Lechter, Michael A., Esq. *Protect Your #1 Asset.* New York: Werner Books, 2001.

Levi, Donald R. *How to Teach Adults.* 2nd ed. Chicago: Real Estate Educators Association, 1996.

Lyons, Gail, and Don Harlan. *Buyer Agency.* 3rd ed. Chicago: Real Estate Education Company, 1997.

Lyons, Gail G., Donald D. Harlan, and John Tuccillo. *The Future of Real Estate: Profiting from the Revolution.* Chicago: Real Estate Education Company, 1996.

O'Toole, James. *Leadership A to Z.* San Francisco: Jossey-Bass Publishers, 1999.

O'Toole, James. *Leading Change: The Argument for Values-Based Leadership.* New York: Ballantine Books, 1996.

Peters, Tom, and Robert H. Waterman, Jr. *In Search of Excellence.* New York: Warner Books, 1992.

Pivar, William H., and Donald L. Harlan. *Real Estate Ethics, Good Ethics = Good Business.* Chicago: Real Estate Education Company, 1995.

Reilly, John. *Agency Relationships in Real Estate.* 2nd ed. Chicago: Real Estate Education Company, 1994.

Ritchie, Ingrid, and Stephen J. Martin. *The Healthy Home Kit*. Chicago: Real Estate Education Company, 1995.

Rules and Regulations, "ADA Accessibility Guidelines," *Federal Register* 56, no. 44 (28 July 1991).

Rules and Regulations, "Fair Housing Accessibility Guidelines," *Federal Register* 56, no. 44 (6 March 1991): 9497-9506.

Rules and Regulations, "Fair Housing Act," *Federal Register* 56, no. 13 (23 January 1989): 3232-3317.

Rules and Regulations, "Fair Housing Advertising," *Federal Register* 54, no. 13 (23 January 1989): 3308-3311.

Senge, Peter M. *The Fifth Discipline*. New York: Doubleday/Currency, 1990.

Seraydarian, Patricia E. *Writing for Business Results*. Burr Ridge, Ill.: Business One Irwin/Mirror Press. 1994.

Sewell, Carl, and Paul B. Brown. *Customers for Life, How to Turn That One-Time Buyer into a Lifetime Customer*. New York: Pocket Books/Simon & Schuster, 2002.

Tuccillo, John, Buddy West, and Betsey West. *Targeting the Over 55 Client: Your Guide to Today's Fastest Growing Market*. Chicago: Real Estate Education Company, 1995.

Wheatley, Margaret J. *Leadership and the New Science*. San Francisco: Berrett-Koehler Publishers, 1999.

Whitworth, Laura, Henry Kimsey-House, and Phil Sandall. *Co-Active Coaching*. Palo Alto, Calif.: Davies-Black Publishing, 1998.

Williams, Martha R., and Marcia L. Russell. *ADA Handbook: Employment and Construction Issues Affecting Your Business*. Chicago: Real Estate Education Company, 1993.

This is only a sample of the publications available to inform, inspire, or guide the leaders and managers of real estate brokerage organizations.

APPENDIX

A Citizen's Guide to Radon, 2d ed. (U.S. EPA):
www.epa.gov/iedweb00/radon/pubs/citguide.html

Alabama Legislature: *www.legislature.state.al.us*

Alabama Real Estate Commission: *www.arec.state.al.us*

Alaska Division of Occupational Licensing:
www.dced.state.ak.us/occ/prec.htm

Alaska Legislature: *www.legis.state.ak.us*

Altavista Search Engine: *www.altavista.com*

American Management Association: *www.amanet.org*

American Society of Home Inspectors: *www.ashi.com*

Appraisal Foundation: *www.appraisalfoundation.org*

Appraisal Institute: *www.appraisalinstitute.org*

Arizona Department of Real Estate: *www.re.state.az.us*

Arizona Legislature: *www.azleg.state.az.us*

Arkansas Legislature: *www.arkleg.state.ar.us*

Arkansas Real Estate Commission: *www.state.ar.us/arec/arecweb.html*

Building Owners and Managers Association International: *www.boma.org*

Building Owners and Managers Institute: *www.bomi-edu.org*

California Department of Real Estate: *www.dre.ca.gov*

California Legislative Counsel: *www.leginfo.ca.gov*

CERCLA/Superfund: *www.epa.gov/superfund/action/law/cercla.htm*

Colorado Department of Regulatory Agencies, Division of Real Estate: *www.dora.state.co.us/real-estate*

Colorado (State of): *www.state.co.us*

Commercial Investment Real Estate Institute: *www.ccim.com*

Connecticut Department of Consumer Protection: *www.state.ct.us/dcp*

Connecticut State Library: *www.cslib.org/psaindex.htm*

Counselors of Real Estate: *www.cre.org*

Cyberhomes MLS Listings: *www.cyberhomes.com*

District of Columbia Real Estate Commission: *www.dcra.org*

Fannie Mae: *www.fanniemae.com*

EXCITE Search Engine: *www.excite.com*

Federal Emergency Management Agency: *www.fema.gov*

Federal Housing Administration: *www.hud.gov/fha*

Federal Reserve Board: *www.federalreserve.gov*

Findlaw: Contract Law: *www.findlaw.com/01topics/07contracts*

Florida Division of Real Estate: *www.state.fl.us/dbpr*

Florida Statutes: *www.leg.state.fl.us/statutes*

Freddie Mac: *www.freddiemac.com*

Georgia Code: *www.state.ga.us/services/ocode/ocgsearch.htm*

Georgia Real Estate Commission: *www.state.ga.us/ga.real_estate*

Ginnie Mae: *www.ginniemae.gov*

GOOGLE Search Engine: *www.google.com*

Hawaii State Government: *www.hawaii.gov*

Hawaii State Legislature: *www.capitol.hawaii.gov*

HSH: Fair Housing Act Pamphlet: *www.hsh.com/pamphlets/fair_housing_act.html*

Idaho Real Estate Commission: *www.state.id.us/irec*

Idaho Statutes: *www.state.id.us/idstat*

Illinois Compiled Statutes: *www.legis.state.il.us/ilcs/chapterlist.html*

Illinois Office of Banks and Real Estate: *www.obre.state.il.us*

Indiana Legislative: *www.state.in.us/legislative/ic/code*

Indiana Professional Licensing Agency: *www.ai.org/pla/index.html*

Institute of Real Estate Management: *www.irem.org*

International Real Estate Digest: *www.ired.com*

Iowa Law: *www.legis.state.ia.us/ialaw.html*

Iowa Real Estate Commission:
www.state.ia.us/government/com/prof/realesta/ realesta.htm

Kansas Laws and Legal Services:
www.accesskansas.org/government/ laws-legal.html

Kansas Real Estate Commission: *www.accesskansas.org/krec*

Kentucky Real Estate Commission: *www.krec.net*

Kentucky Revised Statutes: *www.lrc.state.ky.us/krs/titles.htm*

Legal Information Institute: *www.law.cornell.edu/states/index.html*

Legal Information Institute: Landlord-Tenant Law:
www.law.cornell.edu/topics/landlord_tenant.html

Legal Information Institute: State Statutes Topical Index:
www.law.cornell.edu/topics/state_statutes.html#health

Legal Information Institute: Uniform Condominium Act:
www.law.cornell.edu/uniform/vol7.html#condo

Legal Land Descriptions in the USA: *www.outfitters.com/genealogy/land*

Louisiana State Legislature: *www.legis.state.la.us*

Lycos Search Engine: *www.lycos.com*

Maine (State of): *www.state.me.us*

Manufactured Housing Institute: *www.mfghome.org*

Maryland General Assembly: *www.mlis.state.md.us*

Maryland Real Estate Commission:
www.dllr.state.md.us/license/real_est/reintro.html

Massachusetts Division of Registration: *www.state.ma.us/reg*

Massachusetts (General Laws of): *www.state.ma.us/legis/laws/mgl*

Michigan Department of Consumer & Industry Services:
www.cis.state.mi.us

Michigan Legislature: *www.michiganlegislature.org*

Minnesota Department of Commerce: *www.commerce.state.mn.us*

Missouri Real Estate Commission: *www.ecodev.state.mo.us/pr/restate*

Missouri Revised Statutes: *www.moga.state.mo.us/homestat.htm*

Montana Constitution and Laws:
http://leg.state.mt.us/services/legal/laws.htm

Montana Department of Commerce: *www.com.state.mt.us*

National Apartment Association: *www/naahg.org*

National Association of Exclusive Buyer Agents: *www.naeba.org*

National Association of Home Builders: *www.nahb.com*

National Association of Independent Fee Appraisers: *www.naifa.com*

National Association of Real Estate Brokers: *www.nareb.com*

National Association of REALTORS®: *www.realtor.com*

National Association of Residential Property Managers: *www.narpm.org*

National Fair Housing Advocate Online:
www.fairhousing.com/legal_research/index.htm

National Safety Council's Environmental Health Center:
www.nsc.org/ehc/lead.htm

National Safety Council: Radon: *www.nsc.org/ehc/radon.htm*

Nebraska Statutes: *http://statutes.unicam.state.ne.us*

Nevada Law Library: *www.leg.state.nv.us/law1.cfm*

Nevada Real Estate Division: *www.red.state.nv.us*

New Hampshire General Court: *www.gencourt.state.nh.us*

New Hampshire Real Estate Commission: *www.state.nh.us/nhrec*

New Jersey Legislature: *www.njleg.state.nj.us*

New Jersey Real Estate Commission: *www.state.nj.us/dobi/remnu.shtml*

New Mexico Real Estate Commission: *www.state.nm.us/nmrec*

New Mexico Supreme Court Law Library: *www.fscll.org*

New York Assembly: *http://assembly.state.ny.us*

New York Department of State, Division of Licensing Service:
www.dos.state.ny.us/lcns/realest.html

North Carolina General Statutes:
www.ncga.state.nc.us/statutes/statutes.html

North Carolina Real Estate Commission: *www.ncrec.state.nc.us*

Ohio Division of Real Estate and Professional Licensing:
www.com.state.oh.us/real

Ohio Laws, Rules, and Constitution: *www.state.oh.us/ohio/ohiolaws.htm*

Oregon Real Estate Agency: *www.rea.state.or.us*

Oregon Revised Statutes: *www.leg.state.or.us/ors/home.html*

Penn Central Transportation Co. v. City of New York:
www.law.cornell.edu

Pennsylvania Real Estate Commission: *www.dos.state.pa.us/bpoa*

Real Estate Buyer's Agent Council: *www.rebac.net*

Real Estate Buyer's Agent Council: *www.rebac.net/right.htm*

Real Estate Educators Association: *www.reea.org*

South Carolina Code of Laws: *www.lpitr.state.sc.us/code/statmast.htm*

South Carolina Real Estate Commission: *www.llr.state.sc.us*

South Dakota Real Estate Commission: *www.state.sd.us/sdrec*

South Dakota Legislature: *http://legis.state.sd.us/index.cfm*

State of Louisiana Real Estate Commission: *www.lrec.state.la.us*

State of Maine: *www.state.me.us/pfr.olr*

State of Nebraska Real Estate Commission: *www.nrec.state.ne.us*

Texas Real Estate Commission: *www.trec.state.tx.us*

Texas Statutes: *www.capitol.state.tx.us/statutes/statutes.html*

The Inside Story: A Guide to Indoor Air Quality (U.S. EPA): *www.epa.gov/region4/topics/air/indoorair.html*

U.S. Department of Agriculture: Rural Development: *www.rurdev.usda.gov*

U.S. Department of Housing and Urban Development: *www.hud.gov*

U.S. Department of Housing and Urban Development: FAQs About Escrows (RESPA): *www.hud.gov/offices/hsg/sfh/res/reconsu.cfm*

U.S. Department of Housing and Urban Development: Healthy Homes for Healthy Children: *www.hud.gov/consumer.hhhchild.cfm*

U.S. Department of Housing and Urban Development: Office of Housing: *www.hud.gov/fha/fhahome.html*

U.S. Department of Housing and Urban Development: RESPA: *www.hud.gov/fha/sfh/res/respa_hm.html*

U.S. Department of Internal Revenue Service: *www.irs.gov*

U.S. Department of Justice: ADA Home Page: *www.usdoj.gov/crt/ada/adahom1.htm*

U.S. Department of Justice, Antitrust Division: *www.usdoj.gov/atr*

U.S. Department of Veterans Affairs: *www.va.gov*

U. S. Environmental Protection Agency: *www.epa.gov*

U.S. EPA: Asbestos: *www.epa.gov/oppt/asbestos*

U.S. EPA: CERCLA Overview: *www.epa.gov/superfund/action/law/cercla.htm*

U.S. EPA: Indoor Air Quality: Carbon Monoxide: *www.epa.gov/iaq/co.html*

U.S. EPA: Indoor Air Quality: Radon: *www.epa.gov/iaq/radon*

U.S. EPA: Mold Remediation in Schools and Commercial Buildings: *www.epa.gov/iaq/pubs/molds/index.html*

U.S. EPA: Office of Pollution Prevention and Toxics: *www.epa.gov/lead*

U.S. Farm Service Agency: *www.fsa.usda.gov*

U.S. Geological Survey: *www.usgs.gov*

U.S. HUD: Fair Housing: *www.hud.gov/groups/fairhousing.cfm*

U.S. HUD: Fair Housing Act: *www.hud.gov/fhe/fheact.html*

U.S. HUD: Fair Housing Library: *www.hud.gov/library/bookshelf09/index.cfm*

U.S. HUD: Federal Mortgage Programs: *www.hud.gov/mortprog.html*

U.S. HUD: Housing Discrimination Complaints: *www.hud.gov/complaints/housediscrim.cfm*

U.S. HUD: Land Sales Complaints: *www.hud.gov/complaints/landsales.cfm*

U.S. HUD: Office of Healthy Homes and Lead Hazard Control: *www.hud.gov/offices/lead/disclosurerule.cfm*

U.S. HUD: Office of Healthy Homes and Lead Hazard Control Pamphlet: *www.hud.gov/offices/lead/leadhelp.cfm*

U.S. HUD: Office of Housing: *www.hud.gov/offices/hsg/index.cfm*

U.S. Internal Revenue Service: Search for Real Estate Tax Information: *www.irs.ustreas.gov*

U.S. Supreme Court: *www.supremecourtus.gov*

Utah Code: *www.le.state.ut.us/~code/code.htm*

Utah Commerce Department, Real Estate Division: *www.commerce.state.ut.us*

Vermont Real Estate Commission: *www.vtprofessionals.org/opr1/real_estate*

Virginia (Code of): *http://leg1.state.va.us/000/src.htm*

GLOSSARY

Accounts payable Liabilities that represent amounts owed to creditors, usually for goods or services that were purchased.

Accounts receivable Claims against debtors, usually for goods or services that were delivered to the debtors.

Agency A relationship in which one person (the principal or client) delegates authority to another (the agent) to act on behalf of the principal in certain business transactions. This creates a fiduciary relationship, which imposes certain responsibilities on the agent who acts in this capacity.

Agency contracts Written agreements that create an agency relationship between a principal and an agent. These include listing agreements such as an open listing, an exclusive agency and an exclusive-right-to-sell agreement, and buyer agency contracts such as open agreements, exclusive agency buyer agency agreements, and exclusive buyer agency contracts.

Agent A person authorized to act on behalf of the principal and who has fiduciary responsibilities to the principal. In a real estate transaction, the broker is normally considered to be the agent of the principal or client.

Affinity programs Enticements such as coupons, discounts, and points used in marketing programs to attract consumers by giving them increased purchasing power for a wide range of products and services. Also known as cross marketing programs.

Americans with Disabilities Act (ADA) A federal law enacted to eliminate discrimination against people with disabilities in employment, public accommodations, government services, public transportation, and communications.

Andragogy The process by which adults learn, which distinguishes the adult learning process from the child's. It recognizes differences in approaching and processing new information.

Antitrust laws Federal and state laws enacted for the purpose of fostering competition and preventing anticompetitive practices. Antitrust violations include price fixing, certain types of boycotts, allocations of markets, and tying agreements.

Arbitration A nonjudicial proceeding in which a third party determines the resolution of a dispute between parties. The determinations of the arbitrator can be as enforceable as a decision rendered in court.

Autocratic style Management style in which the manager dominates the organization and makes all decisions, but in a more humanistic or benevolent manner than the dictatorial manager. In the autocratic style of management there is greater concern for people, which enables them to feel more secure and comfortable, and the atmosphere is more relaxed. See also Dictatorial style; Laissez-faire style; Participative style.

Balance sheet A financial statement that itemizes assets, liabilities, and net worth.

Blockbusting See Panic selling.

Brainstorming A group discussion held for the purpose of having participants generate a variety of ideas relating to a selected issue or solutions to a specific problem. Management uses brainstorming to encourage people to participate in the organization and utilizes their creativity and talents, rather than making unilateral decisions without the benefit of staff input.

Branch office A secondary office or place of business of a brokerage firm, normally required to be registered, licensed, and supervised according to the real estate licensing laws of the state.

Broker A party, being a person, a corporation or a partnership, that is properly licensed as a broker under the real estate licensing laws within the jurisdiction where the individual or entity serves as a special agent to others in the brokerage of real property.

Brokerage The specialty in the real estate business that is concerned with bringing parties together in the sale, lease, or exchange of real property.

Budget A statement of estimated income and expenses; a forecast to guide the financial operations of a business.

Business plan A long-range blueprint, typically covering three to five years, that includes the mission statement, general objectives, goals, and strategies of the company.

Buyer's broker A broker who represents a buyer in a fiduciary capacity in a real estate transaction.

Caveat emptor The Latin term meaning "let the buyer beware," denoting that a buyer purchases at his or her own risk. This ancient doctrine is replaced today by a more consumer-oriented approach; that is, the seller or the seller's agent has a duty to disclose any factors that might influence a buyer's decision.

Certificate of occupancy A certificate or permit issued by a government authority indicating that the building is fit for use or occupancy according to the laws that the authority enforces.

Chain of command The hierarchy of authority, which normally begins with upper levels of management and filters down to lower levels of management.

Clayton Antitrust Act A federal statute that prohibits price discrimination, exclusive dealing arrangements, and interlocking directives.

Client The person who employs an agent to perform certain activities on his or her behalf, also known as the principal under the law of agency.

Client trust account An account set up by a broker in which clients' monies are segregated from the broker's general business accounts. Individual states' real estate licensing laws prescribe specific requirements for the manner in which these accounts must be administered. Also known as earnest money or escrow accounts in some states.

Closing The consummation of a real estate transaction, in which the seller delivers title to the buyer in exchange for payment of the purchase price by the buyer.

Code of ethics A standard of ethical conduct, normally committed to writing. Any organization can establish a code of conduct for its members, such as the code of ethics of the National Association of REALTORS® and other professional organizations.

Commingling Mixing or mingling monies; for example, depositing client funds in the broker's personal or business account. Licensees who do this are subject to disciplinary action by the regulatory body that enforces a state's real estate license laws. Some states' laws do permit brokers to deposit a small amount of business or personal funds in trust accounts to cover fees or other deposit requirements of a bank or savings institution.

Company dollar Funds remaining from gross income after the cost of sales has been deducted. The cost of sales includes the commissions paid to the salespeople and other brokers cooperating in transactions, overrides to the manager, and sales fees, such as MLS, franchise, and referral or relocation fees.

Comparative market analysis A value analysis of a seller's property compared with other similar properties and their sales prices to arrive at an anticipated sale price for the subject property.

Comprehensive Environmental Response Compensation and Liability Act A federal law that imposes liability on owners, lenders, occupants, and operators for correcting environmental problems on a property. Superfund statutes establish a fund to clean hazardous waste sites and respond to spills and releases on properties.

Computerized loan originations (CLOs) Automated systems that enable a purchaser/borrower to locate a lender, submit a mortgage application, and obtain a conditional loan commitment right in the real estate office. With CLOs, consumers can comparison shop the various mortgage lenders and all of their loan products. CLOs must comply with the requirements of the Real Estate Settlement Procedures Act. See also Real Estate Settlement Procedures Act (RESPA).

Conciliation agreement A settlement or compromise agreement. Under the fair housing laws a respondent in a discrimination complaint can agree to a settlement rather than having the case resolved by judicial proceedings.

Consumer price index A statistical measure prepared by the Bureau of Labor and Statistics that indicates changes in the prices of consumer goods.

Contingency A provision in a contract that requires the completion of certain acts or requires certain events to happen before the contract is binding.

Contingency plans Alternative goals and strategies that a company can implement in case certain events happen. These may be events that could affect a company's operations but have not yet occurred (and may never occur) when the company develops its business plan. Contingency plans provide a course for the organization to follow if these situations arise.

Contract A legally enforceable agreement between competent parties who agree to perform or refrain from performing certain acts for a consideration.

Controlled business arrangements (CBAs) Networks of interrelated companies that offer real estate services associated with a real estate transaction. They offer convenience to consumers and enhance the broker's service because the broker has control over all phases of the transaction.

Cooperating broker A broker who assists another broker to complete a real estate transaction. The cooperating broker may act as a subagent of the other broker's principal, as the agent of his or her own principal, or have no fiduciary obligation to anyone in a transaction.

Corporation A legal entity created under a state's law that is an association of one or more individuals and has the capacity to act as an individual. A corporation is usually governed by a board of directors elected by the shareholders.

Cost of sales Commissions paid to the salespeople, to other brokers cooperating in real estate transactions, overrides to the manager, and sales fees, such as MLS, franchise, and referral or relocation fees. Also included are transaction fees, which are monies brokers are collecting separate from commissions to cover administrative costs associated with processing sales transactions.

Cross-marketing programs Enticements, such as coupons, discounts, and points, used in marketing programs to attract consumers by giving them increased purchasing power for a wide range of products and services. Also known as affinity programs.

Customer service surveys A tool to find out what customers and clients think about the services that the company and its personnel provide. Information gathered from these surveys enables the company to monitor and improve the quality of its services where necessary.

Decentralized organization An organization in which there are fewer levels of management and authority, giving each level greater authority and control over the activities of its departments or divisions.

Demographics The profile of the population in an area, considering such characteristics as age, education, income, employment, and household structure.

Desk cost Reflects the amount of the company's expenses that can be attributed to each salesperson who works for the brokerage firm. It is calculated by dividing the expenses of the firm by the number of salespeople and can be used as a guide to determine the amount of expense each salesperson's production should cover.

Dictatorial style Management style in which the manager has absolute and total control over all decisions. Nothing is delegated, only orders are issued, and there is little interaction with the people being supervised and little concern for them as human beings or for their capabilities. See also Autocratic style; Laissez-faire style; Participative style.

Discrimination Making a distinction against or in favor of a person because of the group or class of people with whom the person is identified. Illegal discrimination is the failure to treat people equally under the fair housing or equal opportunity laws because of the group with which they are identified.

Disparate impact The fact that an action has a significant impact on people in a protected class. This determines that the action is discriminatory, that is, the effect of an action is discriminatory without regard to the intent of the action.

Dispute resolution Mediation and arbitration services for resolving disputes; a speedy and affordable alternative to resolving disputes in civil court.

Dual agency Representing two principals with opposite interests in the same transaction. State law normally specifies whether a real estate licensee is permitted to provide dual agency. In states where it is permitted, the laws require that both principals must provide written consent for the dual representation.

Earnest money A cash deposit made by a prospective buyer as evidence of good faith to perform on a sales contract. It is also known as deposit money, hand money, or a binder.

Earnest money account See Client trust account.

Employee A person who works under the supervision and control of another. For income tax purposes, an independent contractor is distinguished from an employee. See also Independent contractor.

Equal employment opportunity laws Laws that provide for equal employment for all qualified individuals regardless of their race, color, religion, sex, age, disability, marital or family status, or nationality.

Equity with the competition The comparison of a company's compensation or commission program in relation to competitors' programs.

Ethics A system of moral principles or rules and standards of conduct. See also Code of ethics.

Exclusive agency A written listing agreement that gives an agent the sole right to sell or lease a property within a specified time period, with the exception that the owner can sell or lease the property himself or herself without being liable to the agent for compensation.

Exclusive agency buyer agency The buyer contracts with a sole agent for locating a property that meets certain specifications, with the exception that the buyer is relieved of any obligation to the agent if the buyer locates the property without the assistance of the agent or another broker.

Exclusive buyer agency The buyer contracts with a sole agent for locating a property that meets certain specifications. The buyer owes 100 percent loyalty to the agent and is obligated for a commission, whether the buyer, the agent, or another broker locates the property.

Exclusive listing A written listing in which an owner of a property contracts with a sole agent to sell or lease a property. It may be an exclusive agency or an exclusive-right-to-sell agreement.

Exclusive-right-to-sell A written listing giving an agent the sole right to sell or lease a property within a specified time period. The owner is liable to the agent for a commission whether the agent, the owner, or another broker sells or leases the property.

Facilitator A person who assists a buyer or seller to reach an agreement in a real estate transaction. A facilitator does not represent or have fiduciary obligations to either party.

Federal Fair Housing Act Title VIII of the Civil Rights Act of 1964, as amended. It protects people against discrimination in housing because of their race, color, religion, sex, handicap, familial status, or national origin.

Federal Trade Commission (FTC) A federal agency responsible for investigating and eliminating unfair and deceptive trade practices and unfair methods of competition.

Fictitious business name (FBN) A business name, other than the name of a person, under which the business is registered to conduct business.

Foreign Investment in Real Property Tax Act (FIRPTA) A federal law that subjects nonresident aliens and foreign corporations to U.S. income tax on their gains from the disposition of an interest in real property.

Franchise The formal privilege or contractual right to conduct a business using a designated trade name and the operating procedures of the company that owns the franchise.

Fraud An intentional deceptive act or statement with which one person attempts to gain an unfair advantage over another. It may be either a misstatement or silence about a defect.

General objectives Major aspirational objectives an organization intends to accomplish to fulfill its mission.

General partnership A form of business organization in which two or more owners engage in business. All of the general partners share full liability for the debts of the business.

Goals The end results that a company wants to achieve. Goals break down the aspirational or futuristic nature of the general objectives into specific, measurable, short-term accomplishments and show how the organization intends to achieve its general objectives.

Gross income The total income derived from doing business before any costs or expenses are deducted.

Group boycotting An antitrust violation in which two or more competitors band together to exert pressure on another competitor for the purpose of eliminating competition. It may involve withholding goods, services, or patronage that are essential to the competitor's economic survival or dealing only on unfavorable terms with the competitor. Group boycotting is a per se offense if it is done for the express purpose of reducing or eliminating competition.

Hazardous substance Any material that poses a threat to the environment or to public health.

Hazardous waste Materials that are dangerous to handle and dispose of, such as radioactive materials, certain chemicals, explosives, or biological waste.

Home officing A term in business referring to the practice of people working primarily from their homes. This is an increasingly popular trend in business, made possible by technology.

Human resources The people or personnel of an organization.

Income statement See Profit and loss statement.

Independent contractor A person retained to perform certain acts or achieve certain results without control or direction of another regarding the methods or processes used to accomplish the results.

Intellectual property Assets that are original works; the product of an individual's creative efforts, such as manuscripts and art. With the emergence of the Internet intellectual property has gained new meaning as individuals create Web sites and display their wares, including listings.

Internal equity A comparison of compensation plans within a company that prescribes that all people who work in the same class of jobs within an organization be paid at the same rates and that people with greater experience or productivity or specialized jobs be compensated at higher rates.

Job description Precisely defines the responsibilities as well as the activities of a position. This ensures that both the company and the worker know exactly what a person in a specific position is expected to do.

Laissez-faire style A management style in which the manager adopts a hands-off, do-nothing approach, characterized by nonintervention and indifference. This creates a chaotic environment because the manager doesn't exercise any authority. See also Autocratic style; Dictatorial style; Participative style.

Law of agency The common-law doctrine that pertains to the relationship created when one person or entity is authorized to act on legal matters for the benefit of another.

Lead poisoning Illness caused by high concentrations of lead in the body. Common sources are lead that was used in paint prior to 1978 and water contamination from lead pipes and solder containing lead.

License referral company Separate subsidiary of a brokerage company that some companies use as an alternative to accommodate licensees who do not meet their criteria for full-time salespeople, but whom the company wants to capture because of the business that these people may be able to refer to it.

Licensee A person who is issued a valid real estate license by the licensing body in the jurisdiction in which the person provides real estate services as prescribed by law.

Limited liability company (LLC) An alternative business entity with characteristics of a limited partnership and an S corporation. Investors are members rather than partners or shareholders in the business and hold membership interests rather than stock in the company. An LLC has advantages over corporations and partnerships because personal liability and taxes are different.

Limited partnership A partnership in which one person or group, known as the general partner, organizes, operates, and is responsible for the partnership venture. Other individual members are merely investors and are responsible for potential liabilities only to the extent of their original investments.

Line authority The authority given to the people who are responsible for contributing directly to the achievement of the company's objectives, such as the sales office or the property management, leasing, or new construction departments.

Listing agreement A written employment agreement between an owner of real estate and a broker that authorizes the broker to find a suitable buyer or tenant for the property. There are several types of contracts, including an open listing, an exclusive agency, and an exclusive-right-to-sell listing.

Lockbox Small, secure box affixed to a property that enables only certain authorized individuals to access its contents, usually a key to the property.

Management The activity of guiding or directing the financial and human resources of an organization. There are various management philosophies that attempt to define the way in which organizations function and managers use their authority and make decisions. The common theme in current management trends is the participative style, which emphasizes the value of people and their contribution to the organization.

Manager Individuals who are responsible for guiding or directing the financial and human resources of an organization. The prevailing theory in management today is that managers inspire, energize, and support the people they supervise rather than controlling or dominating them.

Market The geographic area in which a company does business or the specific consumers the company seeks to serve with its products or services.

Mediation An alternative to arbitration and judicial proceedings, in which parties can resolve disputes between themselves using an impartial third party to moderate the proceedings and help them find a mutually acceptable resolution. If the parties are unsuccessful in mediation, they may proceed to arbitration or civil court.

Misrepresentation False statements or concealment of a material fact, that is, information deemed to be pertinent to a decision. Misrepresentations may be motivated by an attempt to deceive though, unlike fraud, they are limited to a fact that is material to the transaction.

Mission statement States what a company's purpose is for doing business, specifically what the business does and where the organization intends to be in the future.

Monolithic organization A highly centralized operation that functions as a single (mono) unit, even though it normally consists of a number of work groups, with authority being highly controlled at the top of the organization.

Monthly operating budgets Monthly budgets constructed from the annual operating budget. By dividing the annual gross income and operating expenses by 12, the company has monthly projections to use as benchmarks for monitoring income and expenses during the year.

Multiple listing service (MLS) Information systems that provide their members with a variety of information including mortgage loan information, competitive market analysis data, sample contracts, worksheets for qualifying buyers and estimating ownership and closing costs, investment analysis, and online mapping and tax records, in addition to listing inventory.

Net income The sum arrived at after deducting the expenses of operation from gross income.

Niche marketing Services directed to specialized segments of the consumer population. Niche marketing appeals to consumers because it satisfies their demand for specialized knowledge.

Online services Commercial computer networks providing a wide variety of information that subscribers to the services can access. Commercial online services include CompuServe, Prodigy, GEnie, MCI, and America Online.

Open-ended questions Questions that begin with How, What, Who, When, or Where, and require explanations, as opposed to closed-ended questions that can be answered only "Yes" or "No." Open-ended questions solicit feedback and information in a way not possible with closed-ended questions.

Open listing A listing in which the owner of the property gives the right to sell or lease a property to a number of brokers, who then can work simultaneously to effect a sale or lease. Compensation is owed to the broker who procures a ready, willing, and able buyer or tenant.

Operating expenses Recurring fixed expenses, such as rent, dues, and fees, salaries, taxes, and license fees, insurance and depreciation (funding for depreciation on equipment, buildings, and automobiles the company owns), and variable expenses such as advertising and promotion, utilities, equipment, and supplies and cost of sales.

Operating strategy The methodology employed by an organization to accomplish its goals. A strategy defines how the organization plans to use its financial and human resources.

Organization chart The structure of an organization that identifies the various business units, divisions, or departments within the firm and the line of authority or chain of command for each manager of the units.

Override A method of calculating managerial compensation based on a percentage of the gross commission (before the agents' shares are deducted), a percentage of commission after the sales and listing commissions are deducted, or a percentage of the office's net profits.

Panic selling Efforts to sell real estate in a particular neighborhood by generating fear that real estate values are declining because people in a protected class are moving into or out of a neighborhood, which has nothing to do with the intrinsic value of the real estate itself. Panic selling violates the fair housing laws.

Participative style A humanistic management style in which the manager creates a democratic environment that promotes initiative and recognizes the value of the human resources. Participative management utilizes the talents and insight of people to a greater extent than is common in other styles of management. See also Autocratic style; Dictatorial style; Laissez-faire style.

Performance criteria The basis on which people will be evaluated in a performance review. Criteria include production quotas and other performance-based issues that are considered to be important in the performance of a person's job.

Performance reviews An evaluation of a worker's progress in which the manager and the worker or salesperson can meet one-on-one and discuss a variety of issues about the job and the salesperson's career.

Per se rule Decision by the U.S. Supreme Court that identifies certain antitrust activities that cannot be defended as being reasonable under any circumstances because they are so destructive to competition that their anticompetitive effect is automatically presumed. These include activities such as price fixing, certain kinds of boycotts, territorial assignments, and tying agreements.

Personal success plans A salesperson's business plan that converts the salesperson's aspirations for success into action with specific or measurable goals and strategies to guide him or her along the way. A personal success plan is a holistic approach to defining what a person intends to accomplish as a professional salesperson, in addition to a production quota.

Policy and procedures manual A document that tells people how they are to conduct business for the company. It includes the general business philosophy and business ethics and prescribes procedures for handling a multitude of details of the company's operations.

Polychlorinated biphenyls (PCBs) Used in the manufacture of electrical products (such as transformers, switches, voltage regulators), paints, adhesives, caulking materials, and hydraulic fluids. PCBs can cause birth defects and cancer and other diseases.

POSDC A management model that groups various activities involved in the operation of a business by functions. These functions include planning, organizing, staffing, directing, and controlling.

Profit and loss statement A detailed statement of the income and expenses of a business, commonly known as a P & L, operating statement, or income statement.

Profit center A business unit within a company that is expected to produce enough income to cover its cost of operation plus make a profit for the firm.

Radon A radioactive gas produced by the natural decay of other radioactive substances, which is suspected to be a cause of cancer.

Real Estate Settlement Procedures Act (RESPA) A federal law enacted with the goal of encouraging home ownership. It intends to protect consumers from practices that are considered abusive as well as to see that consumers are provided with more complete information about certain lending practices and closing and settlement procedures.

Referral networks Formally structured organizations that enable a broker to refer buyers and sellers to brokers in other geographic areas or to brokers who specialize in other types of real estate services. There are independent networks as well as those connected with national franchises and corporations.

Relocation networks Formal organizations that may be part of or in addition to referral networks to provide relocation services. There are corporate relocation management companies, otherwise known as third-party equity contractors, who enter into agreements with large corporations to handle their employee transfers. *Residential Lead-Based Paint Hazard Reduction Act* sets forth procedures for disclosing the presence of lead-based paint in the sale of residential properties built before 1978.

Salesperson A licensed individual employed by a licensed broker, either as an employee or independent contractor, to perform certain acts as defined by the real estate license laws of the state.

S corporation A kind of corporation that allows a business to operate as a corporation but not pay corporate tax. Each shareholder is taxed on his or her individual share of the corporation's income, which avoids the double taxation feature of corporations. There are limitations on the number of shareholders and the sources of corporate income.

Sexual harassment According to the federal Equal Employment Opportunity Commission, unwelcome sexual advances, requests for sexual favors, and other verbal or physical conduct of a sexual nature when submission is either explicitly or implicitly a term or condition of a person's employment, used as the basis for employment decisions affecting a person, or has the purpose or effect of unreasonably interfering with a person's work performance or creating an intimidating, hostile, or offensive working environment.

Sherman Act An antitrust law intended to curtail large trusts, cartels, or monopolies that are perceived to threaten healthy competition and the growth of businesses. The theory is that competitive forces must be allowed to function, with the ultimate result being the lowest prices, highest quality, and greatest progress in the marketplace.

Signature The words, graphics and colors that create an identity for the company.

Single agency The practice of representing either the buyer/tenant or the seller/landlord, but never both in the same transaction.

Sole ownership A method of owning a business in which one person owns the entire business and is solely responsible and liable for all activities and debts of its operation. Business may be conducted under the name of the owner or a fictitious name. Also known as a sole proprietorship.

Staff authority The authority given to the people who are responsible for support services, the work groups that provide administrative support. They contribute indirectly to the achievement of the company's objectives by providing such services as accounting, marketing and advertising, training, purchasing (materials for the operation of the business), and maintenance.

Steering The illegal practice of channeling homeseekers to particular areas or neighborhoods. When another person, such as a licensee, does this, the act has the effect of limiting a homeseeker's choices by restricting the person's ability to choose the neighborhood in which she or he will live.

Stigmatized properties Those that individuals consider to be "psychologically impacted" because certain events have occurred that people may find offensive or that provoke emotional reactions. These include events such as a suicide, murder, or other felony, paranormal activities (ghosts), a lingering illness, or death.

Strategies The methodology that will be used to accomplish a specific goal or objective. Long-range planning is otherwise known as strategic planning because it provides not only goals but also the strategic methodology for accomplishing them.

Subagent An agent of a person authorized to act as the agent of the principal under the law of agency.

Target market The specific audience or consumers for the company's products or services.

Team-building The process of mobilizing the collective efforts of people to work toward the goals of the organization and at the same time satisfy themselves.

Telecommuting Using technology to conduct business from any location in which computers can be linked to the base office through the telephone network. See Home officing; Virtual office.

Telephone Consumer Protection Act FCC regulations that govern the use of telephone lines for commercial solicitation and advertisement to protect telephone subscribers who do not wish to receive unsolicited live "cold called," autodialed, prerecorded, or artificial voice messages and fax machine solicitations.

Territorial assignments An antitrust violation in which competitors agree to divide the market geographically or by some other criterion, which destroys competition when the purpose of segregating the market is to establish power in that market.

Text telephone (TT) Typewriterlike unit that displays conversation on a screen that can be read so a person who is deaf or hearing-impaired can communicate via telephone. A TT "talks" with another text telephone or a computer. Formerly known as TDDs.

Transaction expenses See Cost of sales.

Tying agreement An arrangement in which a party agrees to sell one product only on the condition that the buyer also purchases a different or tied product. Frequently the tied product is less unique or desirable than the tying product. The courts have concluded that the only purpose of a tying arrangement is to extend the market power of the tying product and have declared these agreements to be per se illegal.

Urea formaldehyde A chemical used in building materials in the 1970s, particularly in insulation. Urea formaldehyde foam insulation (UFFI) has been targeted because of the formaldehyde gases that leach out of the insulation.

Variable expense budgets Specific budgets prepared to identify individual expenditures within categories of certain general variable expenses, such as advertising and promotion, utilities, equipment and supplies, and cost of sales.

Virtual office A relatively new term used to refer to the fact than an office can exist anywhere people can use technology.

INDEX